CRIMINAL LAW

CRIMINAL LAW

Fifth Edition

Christopher Ryan, LLM

Professor and Head of Department of Law,
City University, London

Series Editor: C.J. Carr, MA, BCL

BLACKSTONE
PRESS LIMITED

This edition published 1998 by Blackstone Press Limited, Aldine Place, London W12 8AA. Telephone: 0181-740 2277

First edition, 1986
Reprinted, 1988
Second edition, 1989
Third edition, 1991
Reprinted, 1993
Fourth edition, 1995
Fifth edition, 1998

ISBN: 1 85431 780 6

Typeset by Montage Studios Limited, Horsmonden, Kent
Printed by Bell & Bain Limited, Glasgow

CONTENTS

PREFACE

Criminal law for law students is compulsory, compelling and complex. This book is one of a series aimed at helping students of law to understand and revise their subjects and to pass their examinations. This book has three aims: firstly, in chapters 1 and 2 to provide some opinions and guidelines on how to study and revise; secondly, in chapters 3 to 10 to highlight and summarise the main areas of criminal law and thirdly, at the end of each chapter to give some examples of examination questions followed by an outline of a possible way of answering the questions.

Note that neither the book nor our suggested outlines are intended to be definitive or comprehensive. This book is like a map for difficult terrain or a guidebook to a foreign city. The aim of the outlines is to suggest to you the sort of content and approach that might be used in answering the type of questions which appear in course work exercises or examinations. Your course of studies and your reading beyond the confines of this book might lead you to think of other points and issues that could be discussed in the outlines which we have given. Remember in law there are few definite answers. Views differ, otherwise there would be no law cases for adjudication. If you have the knowledge and an idea, then argue your point of view. Provided your argument is logical, and especially if supported by cited authorities, you should receive credit for it. You must convince the examiner (or the judge later in life) by the weight of your argument that you know the law and that your application of it is correct.

Questions of degree are often imperative as is the realisation of the role played by social mores, fears and pressure, and the availability of resources (police and penal) on the formation and change that is constantly occurring.

You cannot fully comprehend or explain the decision in *Dadson*; or the controversy of the subjective–objective debate generated by such cases as *DPP* v *Smith* (1961) and *Caldwell* (1982); or the controversy concerning the role of foresight in relation to the *mens rea* of specific-intent offences as shown by *Hyam* (1975) and *Moloney* (1985); or the controversy arising from *Morgan* (1976) as to whether a mistaken belief needs to be both honestly and reasonably held, or the controversy generated by the topic of strict liability, unless you appreciate that there is a tension in society between those who seek to expand the ambit of criminal laws (both in the number of offences and the ease with which they are proved) and those who seek to emphasise traditional values of liberty and justice. The former tend to favour strict liability and objective criteria for liability, the latter tend to seek to eschew, or at least limit, both. This dynamic or tension helps explain some decisions and in particular the expansion and contraction of the scope of criminal law principles.

Criminal law continues to provide controversial and difficult decisions. It is hoped that *mens rea* as regards murder and specific-intent offences generally will now be settled. Lord Bridge's model direction, concerning when intention may be inferred from the foresight of an accused, in *Moloney* as re-defined in *Hancock* v *Shanklin* and *Nedrick*, displaces the concept of *oblique intention* (a matter of law) with 'inferred intention' (a matter for the jury in appropriate cases) but problems still arise (*Scalley, Woollin*): see chapters 4 and 9. The wide-ranging nature of *Caldwell* (failure to think) type recklessness with regard to basic intent offences is being constrained by exceptions which preclude its general application to all offences in that category (see chapter 4). The scope of *Caldwell* though remains problematic in particular whether or not that type of recklessness really is synonymous with gross negligence (see *Seymour, Kong Cheuk Kwan, Shimmen, Reid* and *Merrick* in chapters 4 and 9). The House of Lords has acted positively to make the defence of duress unavailable to a person charged with murder and now, attempted murder (see *Howe* and *Gotts* in chapter 8). The defences of mistake and intoxication still cause difficulty, especially when linked together as in *O'Grady* (see chapter 8). Despite the 'U-turn' by the House of Lords in *Shivpuri*, attempting the impossible remains controversial as does defining when an attempt has occurred, *Gullefer* and *Campbell* and recklessness in relation to attempted rape, *Khan* (see chapter 7), and sexual offences especially indecent assault and marital rape (*R* v *R*) (see chapter 9). In relation to the law of property, *Gomez* (see chapter 10) has significantly settled one aspect, 'appropriation'. *Atakpu* has resurrected uncertainty in relation to jurisdiction, territoriality and the importance of where the elements of the offence occur. Property offences remain volatile especially proprietary rights (s. 5) for purposes of theft, *inter vivos* gifts (*Mazo* and *Hopkins*) and the vexed issue of the offences committed where a money transfer is obtained by deception (*Preddy, Hopkins, Cooke, Graham* and the Theft (Amendment) Act 1996 which also affects the issue of handling) (see chapters 7 and 10).

The revised and updated text includes the recent important House of Lords' and Court of Appeal decisions: on transferred malice (*Attorney-General's Reference (No. 3 of 1994)*); participation (*DPP* v *K and G, Giannetto, Wan and Chan, Powell and Daniels, English, Stewart Scholfield, Hui Chi-Ming, Bainborough, Perman* and *O'Brien*); corporate liability (*ex parte Spooner, OLL Ltd* and *Meridian Global Fund*); inchoate offences (*Geddes, Tosti, Walker, Wai Yu-tsang* and *Yip Chiu-Cheung*); defences (five cases on minority/doli incapax, three on duress); offences against the person on the issue of consent (*Brown, Boyea, Simon Slingsby*); on the issue of 'bodily harm' (*Burstow, Ireland* and *Constanza*); in relation to provocation (*Thorton, Luc, Marshall, Acott, Dryden, Humphries and Baille*); and diminished responsibility (*Campell* and *Mitchell*). Each chapter now concludes with a list of suggested further reading and a bibliography and index are included at the end of the book.

C. L. Ryan
City University
London

TABLE OF CASES

1 STUDY TECHNIQUES

THE LAW STUDENT

This book has practical aims: first to guide persons studying an assessed criminal law course to a successful conclusion; and secondly to help them achieve a standard of understanding and the ability to apply their knowledge in a way that is more than competent and is recognised by results that are at least highly competent, or of commendation or upper-second class standard. Anyone admitted to an assessed law course who is diligent should be able to reach that standard and in fact the accolade of distinction or first-class should not be beyond them.

This book and its aims are relevant no matter what type of assessed criminal law course you are studying. Whether it is a one-year Common Professional Examination or Law Society Diploma in law course, a two-year senior status, law degree for graduates in other disciplines, or a traditional three-year undergraduate degree programme, is immaterial. It does not matter whether you are studying on a course which has the traditional three terms in each academic year or one which is broken into semesters of shorter or longer duration, this book is relevant to all. Similarly, it does not matter if your course permits you to select many different modules — this book is relevant. It is relevant because despite the formal structure of your course, the learning, application, revision and assessment of the principles of criminal law remain the same. On some courses you will have less time to revise, on others there will be more coursework and oral assessment, but, whatever the course structure, the principles of criminal law and their application remain the same. Your first aim or goal as a law student and in some instances the only one is to pass your examinations with the greatest possible merit and economy of effort. In essence this book gives guidance as to how this may be obtained with regard to criminal law. The criminal law student is thrown in at the deep end. It is largely up to the individual to learn how to survive. This book will give you a guide. Recent and continuing structural changes in education, especially the impact of modulatisation and credit-rating of courses, has meant that in many institutions there is increased fragmentation of subjects and traditional courses. Semesterisation has meant that in many institutions end of semester assessments, rather than end of year assessments, have become common. This may mean in such instances shorter periods of revision and correspondingly assessment of shorter duration than the traditional three-hour examination. This may have implications for study during the semester and efforts may need to be more concentrated than over a full year.

Leaving aside the Common Professional Examinaton, Diploma courses, semesterisation, modularisation and credit-rating, the traditional method of assessment is as follows. A student in all three of his undergraduate years is usually required to pass a written examination in each of the subjects studied. The first-year examinations are usually in four subjects (which must be passed in entirety before proceeding to the second year) and are generally marked on a pass/fail basis. The second and third-year examinations, usually of four and five subjects respectively, are marked according to a classification ranging from fail to various classes of adequacy to excellence. Thus a paper may be marked (if it is not a fail) as a first-class honours paper, or an upper-second or lower-second class or a third-class honours paper. The examination results of the final two years of undergraduate study are generally aggregated and are the ultimate arbiter of the student's general degree classification. The common form of virtually all examinations taken during a law student's degree studies is that they are of three hours' duration, they are unseen, written as opposed to oral and involve the answering of a given number of questions (a mixture of problems and essays) from a limited selection.

Some law courses permit additional and alternative methods of assessing academic ability in a subject. One such process, continuous assessment, may involve taking into account course projects, tutorial and seminar perform-ance, or set essays. How such methods of assessment are likely to be implemented will depend on your particular course, no doubt you can obtain constant advice in such matters from your tutors when such methods are used. However, the advice given in this book concerning study and revision remain relevant to all students even those subject to continuous assessment systems. This is particularly so because at present any form of continuous assessment in a subject is not, even when employed, a substitution for the end-of-year written examination, but supplementary to it. Thus when such methods are used they generally contribute no more than 30% towards a student's course assessment, the balance of such assessment is still weighted significantly towards the written examination.

Some people may argue that examinations are inadequate and unfair as a means of assessing a student's academic ability. Even though you are capable and diligent you may for a number of reasons fail to achieve, in the relatively short time allowed in the examinations, the success your academic prowess warrants. This may well have disastrous consequences for your future career. This premise is illustrated in its most inequitable sense in the case of the student who has read extensively, thought deeply about a subject and obtained an impressive and comprehensive understanding of its more involved areas. A three-hour examination would appear to give inadequate scope for such a student to display his or her talents.

Such criticisms are no doubt valid, but they do not portray the entire picture. It has not been established that any of the alternative methods of assessing academic ability are any more accurate or fair to the student. It must be accepted that inaccuracies and inconsistencies are inherent in any system whereby one set of human beings judges another group's capabilities and qualities. In defence of the examination system it may be said that it encourages a student to work towards that particular goal encouraging systematic study and revision if the examination is to be prepared for effectively. It further aids the student who can think under pressure and condense knowledge into a highly accurate précis. It demands a high degree of relevance in answering questions and the ability to think systematically while under stress — qualities essential for a successful legal practitioner (barrister or solicitor) as for any law student. Lawyers should endeavour to be realistic; whatever the merits of the examination system we have to accept that while it remains with us, which it will probably, in some form or other, for the conceivable future, it will have to be faced up to by law students.

Today, innovations in teaching, learning and assessment are commonplace. There are, for example, degree programmes which are centred on a problem-based approach to learning and which reduce dependency on formal lectures, replacing them with group project work and self-directed teaching. It is systems-based and transcends the usual discipline boundaries. Some institutions are developing community-based training. The 'community module' enables students to gain experience of a local community. Community tutors, recruited from community organisations and firms, design the exercises, brief the students on the subject area of their study and subsequently assess the students' work. In addition to providing students with a sound knowledge of the subject, the problem-based approach gives the student an opportunity to acquire a broader range of skills, an awareness of the needs of local communities and of clients, better communication skills and a range of tested clinical skills. Many modern law programmes, while not going this far, try to produce in the theory the same effect in the classroom. For many, rightly or wrongly, skills have become a central component with a dramatic effect on both the curriculum and its assessment. The pursuit of academic excellence has been put at risk by the current vogue to emphasise things like advocacy skills. This means that in many institutions there has been a shift away from the traditional three-hour, closed-book examination to a combination of methods of assessment such as coursework, project work and the assessment of tutorial/seminar contributions or oral presentations.

THE AIM OF SWOT CRIMINAL LAW

The principal aim of this SWOT book on criminal law is to aid you to pass your criminal law assessment or examination with the most economical effort and with a true reflection of your academic ability. Lecturers and teachers of law will invariably be lawyers. They will have law degrees themselves and often a professional qualification as a barrister or a solicitor. They will expect you to learn to think, argue and communicate like a lawyer. What that means exactly is often not made clear. Everybody's perception of what a lawyer does or should be able to do varies but you should gain during the course of your legal studies the following skills and qualities:

(a)   A familiarity with and competent use of legal terminology and legal materials, i.e., law reports, statutes, journals.

(b)   An outline knowledge of the rules and principles of particular areas of the law, e.g., criminal law.

(c)   Familiarity with the mechanisms of formal legal change within each particular subject area, i.e., statute and case law.

(d)   An appreciation of the formal restraint upon legal change by virtue of the doctrine of precedent, together with an understanding of the methods whereby precedent may be circumvented.

(e)   You should also be aware of the underlying motivating factors which induce all forms of legal development and change within the respective subject areas.

(f)   Finally you should have the ability to apply these skills and outline knowledge of a particular subject area to given factual situations and problems. This requires the development of two characteristic qualities which are the hallmark of a good lawyer — the ability to make judgements and the strength of character to do so in a disinterested and independent way.

Criminal law courses are concerned primarily with explaining the techniques and concepts used to specify what is prohibited in our society, disclosing general principles for imposing criminal liability, ascertaining degrees of fault and highlighting the circumstances in which persons, despite doing what is prohibited, are considered justified or excused from criminal liability.

The acquiring of all these tools and characteristics may be regarded as comprising the quality of 'thinking like a lawyer'. 'Thinking like a lawyer' is nothing less than a composite shorthand for a set of skills that must be refined through your undergraduate days and on into your career. The Ormrod Report (i.e., *Report of the Committee on Legal Education*, Cmnd 4595, 1971) stated that the aim of a law degree is to provide the graduate with 'a basic knowledge of the law and where to find it; an understanding of the relationship of law to the social and economic environment in which it operates; and the ability to handle facts and to apply abstract concepts to those facts'. In other words you need to be able to:

(a) find, comprehend, analyse and interpret legal source materials (statutes and reported decisions);

(b) analyse factual situations;

(c) apply legal rules to factual situations and appreciate the difficulties and uncertainties of so doing;

(d) develop reasoned, clear and persuasive arguments to support your conclusions;

(e) think critically about legal principles, rules and institutions.

These are the essential attributes of the legal practitioner. In addition they are the skills that must be fully illustrated and effectively demonstrated in the criminal law assessment or examination in order that you may obtain credible academic success in that subject. The perfecting of these skills may only be obtained with experience and constant practice. Some students (fortunately very few) are not suited to law — they will never learn to 'think like a lawyer'. In brief, to be successful you must distil for yourself the essence of these legal skills and be prepared to demonstrate them within the constraints of a written examination, written assessment or oral presentation.

Assuming by your aptitude, and through your study and reflection, you have acquired the ability to 'think like a lawyer', you must, for the purpose of assessment or examination, combine those skills and your outline knowledge of substantive criminal law into a manageable form suitable for easy reference, study and ultimately practical revision. This is the first step towards assessment success. It boils down to compiling an accurate but concise series of notes reflecting the knowledge and skills you have obtained with regard to criminal law. These notes will be the blueprint for success. They and they alone should be the source relied upon when the time comes for you to do assessed work or to revise. Revision skills (i.e., the effective use of those notes) are the second step to examination success, the final step being a sound technique. These latter matters will be discussed from chapter 2 onwards. The next topic for this chapter is the fundamental requirement: the preparation of a first-class set of notes.

The starting-point is the lecture course.

LECTURES IN CRIMINAL LAW

Many courses involve the teaching of criminal law in the first year of law study. This is a traditional placing because it was once thought that this was a subject that posed few problems for the fledgling lawyer. With recent developments in the subject this is no longer the case and today a student studying criminal law is from the first thrown into the deep end of legal studies. To this extent the lecture course in criminal law has increased its significance for the student. The lecture course forms the first source for the preparation of effective notes upon the subject. A good lecture course on criminal law can give guidance to and stimulate interest in the subject. It can help formulate a structured approach to its study and outline the areas which trial and error have found often cause consternation amongst students. Though this is dependent upon the quality of the lectures given there is much that can be done by you as a new student even when the lecture course is not well presented and even though you are not yet certain what is expected of you.

Today most criminal law lecture courses concentrate upon: (a) general principles of criminal liability; (b) the availability of defences; and (c) a consideration of a representative sample of substantive offences, usually offences against the person and property. A modern course in criminal law may consider all or some of the following matters:

(a)   The external elements of an offence, i.e., acts, omissions, circumstances and/or consequences which constitute the discernable parts of a crime (known generally as the *actus reus* of an offence).

(b)   The accompanying mental state that an accused must in general have in relation to the *actus reus* of an offence before he can be regarded as having committed a crime (this element is traditionally referred to as the *mens rea* of an offence).

(c)   Offences of strict liability, i.e., crimes which do not require *mens rea* in relation to at least one element in their *actus reus*.

(d)   The kinds of individuals and entities who may commit crimes and their mode of participation.

(e)   Inchoate (or preliminary) offences, i.e., incitement, conspiracy and attempt.

(f)   Defences, e.g., insanity, provocation, drunkenness and mistaken belief.

(g) Offences against the person, i.e., homicide, assaults, sexual offences, e.g., rape.

(h) Offences against property, e.g., theft, burglary, offences of deception, criminal damage.

Lecture courses will, of course, differ. Some courses place greater emphasis upon the consideration of particular offences rather than general principles of criminal liability. Thus the lecturer may concentrate upon a very detailed exposition of a limited number of crimes or review a large body of offences which are not limited to crimes against property and persons. Such courses may include consideration of, e.g., public order offences, road traffic and drug offences. Not only are there variations within the contents of a lecture course on criminal law but also in the form and function of such a course. Many lecturers seek to cover their criminal law syllabus in a comprehensive but general sense outlining all the topics within the course and highlighting the areas which experience has shown cause student problems. Their intended function in such cases is to provide a student with a foundation and blueprint for further study of those topics; this is the most common form of lecture course.

Some lecturers take an entirely opposite line, they select a limited number of topics within their syllabus and deal with such issues in enormous detail. You are left to deal with the balance of the course by your own private study and by your own methods. The function of this form of lecture course is to give you a direct insight and detailed knowledge of certain areas of the criminal law as illustrative examples. Other lecturers may in addition place emphasis on the reform of current criminal law. Though different in outlook, these differing kinds of lecture courses require little difference on the part of the student in the technique of note-taking within the lecture. There are certain guidelines in effective note-taking that will help a student deal with the problems of keeping up with the lectures and abstracting only worthwhile information from them.

(a) Never try to take down every word. This is especially the case where the lecturer has a rather conversational style in which ideas and principles cascade from the lips. In such instances you should be concerned with recording the essence and drift of the principal ideas of the lecture. To attempt in such cases to capture every expression delivered will always result in a mishmash of words including the lecturer's asides, his jokes and his errors. Much will be missed or half written down by the student. Avoid the temptation to memorise such notes verbatim and to regurgitate them in the examination. Such notes seldom accurately reflect what a lecturer has actually said and even if accurate in parts are copied 'warts and all' without consideration or reflection. This can have disastrous consequences for a student.

(b)   Use abbreviations (of your own devising) where possible, e.g., 'AR' for *actus reus* 'cons' for 'conspiracy'. No one else need read your notes, it is important only for you to understand them.

(c)   Quotations from academic writings or citations from the law reports, or references to statutory provisions used by the lecturer should only be noted by reference to source and by recording the opening and closing phrases. A space should be left in the notes to complete the quotation or citation following the reading of that quotation, citation or statutory reference in full during private study. Reading through notes and completing them in this way is a valuable technique in clarifying the issues raised in the lecture and also in making sure that quotations are accurately recorded.

(d)   Always keep alert in a lecture, concentrate upon understanding what is being said and not upon becoming a dictating machine; remember that what you are compiling are *'notes'*. A lecture is in reality a comprehension or précis exercise. Practise this technique in many situations, e.g., go to your local county or Crown Court, listen to evidence being given there and imagine rendering what is said in note form in your own words. (Do not, however, actually take any notes while there.) This confidence in one's ability to listen to complicated facts and issues and render them concisely in your own words instead of a mad rush to scribble all that is heard is a skill that will only come with practice. A lecture that is listened to is understood; that which is understood is accurately recorded in note form. That which is initially understood and accurately recorded is more effectively revised and retained for examination, assignment and other purposes.

These techniques are just as suitable in compiling notes from the lecturer who sees his duty as ensuring that you are supplied with a 'perfect' set of notes dictated by him and transcribed by you without omission or imperfection. This bilaterally pointless exercise is a habit which you should not get into. The temptation to sit back and write without thought induces a lazy 'spoon-fed' attitude to legal studies. Such dictated notes encourage a lack of understanding and interest in the subject. They tend to be filed away without further reflection and grow unseen to gigantic proportions. The result is a wholly unmanageable set of notes which do not discriminate between important and background information. That type of student rarely will understand the subject and frequently will fail to obtain any insight into it or to have acquired any legal skills. The mass of poorly understood notes which now must be memorised without reflection or consideration are poor preparation for the examination. Although perhaps the faults of the dictation-style lecture and the kind of approach to legal studies it engenders have been somewhat exaggerated here it is because there are very real dangers for a student who seeks such an apparently easy path. Ultimately, the inability to think, abstract, argue and apply knowledge is detrimental both to your legal development and to your assessment or examination success.

You should appreciate that notes which are clearly set out are easy to follow and help give you confidence in the subject and your understanding of it.

(a) Be generous in the use of paper; leave space between paragraphs. This renders the points, issues, principles and facts recorded therein manageable and easier to digest, understand and revise.

(b) Make frequent use of headings, these help to break the notes into recognisable and manageable units. Frequently the lecturer will expressly make use of such headings in his lecture or they will be apparent from the hand-outs (see below) supplied with the lecture. If the lecturer merely rambles, then supply your own headings, either during the lecture or after when you reread your notes (see below).

Remember, you must develop the confidence to judge what are essential principles and what is dross. You have to realise that you do not need a note on everything you hear or read in any area of the law. Material facts, issues and general principles are the main constituents of notes, not opinions, comments, asides, jokes, digressions or repetitions.

Cases

Criminal law is a case-law subject. Lectures in the subject, irrespective of their content, form or function, or the style of the lecturer, should contain extensive discussion of cases. Your note-taking must deal with this aspect of the subject efficiently. The understanding of the leading cases is one of the keys to a fundamental knowledge of the principles of criminal law. Your notes must facilitate comprehension and revision of those cases. But remember textbooks and lecturers mention hundreds of cases and not all of these warrant note-taking (see 'Private Study' below).

The method suggested in this book is that your notes should be taken using a loose-leaf system. During lectures, the general principles, the view of the lecturer or quotations from academic writings or Law Commission reports should be noted on pages numbered 1, 3, 5 etc. When reference is made to a case it should be noted and underlined within the body of your notes. However, the facts of the case and the principles it determines should be noted on pages numbered 2, 4, 6 etc. This should permit the extension of one's own notes upon the case, without the need to refer to a card-index system (see below) or the untidy insertion of marginal notes. It provides a clear method of study. The notes can be studied in entirety for revision purposes and require only looking from odd to even numbered pages to consider the relevant general principles in conjunction with a full discussion of the leading cases. Setting one's notes in this form permits frequent rereading either for the purpose of gleaning general principles alone *or* using them solely to conduct a quick revision of cases. The advantage of this method will become apparent from the discussion concerning note-taking during private study (see below). Note that such a method of setting out your lecture notes is only a suggestion. What is important is that you devise a method whereby your notes are easy to prepare, to expand where necessary and to revise from and finally that they are manageable. Whatever system is ultimately adopted by you it is important to keep to it — falling behind can be disastrous.

Hand-outs

Apart from tutorial and syllabus sheets which generally are given to you and which will be considered later when tutorials and private study are fully discussed, you may also be given material prepared by the lecturer which is meant to supplement or entirely replace your note-taking during lectures. Obviously such hand-outs differ in both content and quality. Where the hand-out consists of little more than headings and/or a list of the cases to which the lecturer will refer you are at least given an outline of the lecture to come, you can accordingly model and structure your notes using the hand-out as a plan. Some hand-outs may contain a précis of the leading cases and perhaps an outline of the issues and principles that will be discussed during the course of the lecture. In such instances you should regard these as part of your lecture notes and merely record issues, principles or the facts of cases where they are extraneous to the matters referred to in the hand-out. Do not feel compelled to take copious notes in lectures where the accompanying hand-outs are comprehensive and of good quality. Your job of note-taking has been done for you. In such cases take full advantage and concentrate upon what is being said, using the hand-out to address your mind to the issues raised. If questions are raised by others or cross your mind, note them (together with answers if supplied). Hand-outs which are a substitution for written lecture notes permit a student to devote his time in a lecture to a consideration of such issues and to endeavour to obtain a clearer understanding of what is being said.

   Finally, should a student ask questions during a lecture? The simple answer is yes, unless the lecturer makes it obvious that questions are not welcome. Most lecturers will welcome questions, they frequently show which areas of criminal law cause difficulties for students within that particular group. Never be afraid to ask a question in a lecture or to request that something be repeated. It is important for you to understand what is being said. Dispel all feelings of self-consciousness that the question is foolish or the answer obvious; there are almost certainly many others in the lecture who are wishing someone else would raise the issue.

Reading ahead

If you are being 'lectured' in the Socratic (question-and-answer) style you will have to read in advance the cases and chapters of the texts set by the lecturer otherwise your attendance at lectures will be an embarrassing if not a shattering experience for you.

Some lecturers who are presenting the more traditional and more common lecture course, also advise students to read ahead, i.e., to study the topic to be discussed in a forthcoming lecture by prior study of the prescribed textbook and/or the reading of relevant cases which are subsequently to be discussed. Often this is expecting too much from a student who may not have the time for such preliminary work because of the need to flesh out topics already dealt with in lectures while preparing for a tutorial and possibly having an essay deadline to meet. But where possible and particularly if the lecturer requires it, preliminary study of a topic to be considered will prove beneficial, this will be so even when not required by the lecturer. Such study generally need only be limited to a cursory reading and overall view of the topic concerned, detailed knowledge should be sought in private study *after* the lecture.

If the suggestions just discussed are adopted in your note-taking technique you should find some of the usual grumbles and complaints about lectures are no longer pertinent. You should, even if encouraged by a lecturer, avoid the 'spoon-fed' attitude to the gaining of knowledge. The idea that a lecture is a longhand dictation practice is bad. If you gain the confidence to listen to a lecture, précis what you hear and think about it and, if you further make effective use of hand-outs and note-taking techniques (i.e., the use of headings, spacing and abbreviations), you should enjoy and understand the lectures as well as compile an impressive and confidence-building set of study and revision notes.

PRIVATE STUDY

The lecture notes are the foundation of your study and revision programme. For examination success they must be supplemented by notes made during private study. What you study in your own time and how you study will be determined by the syllabus contents and the form and function of your criminal law lecture course. This is discussed in detail below. It is the fashion for lecturers in criminal law to list on their syllabus sheet innumerable cases, Law Commission reports and articles. Usually, this is impractical, especially in view of the level of work required for the other subjects that have to be studied in tandem during the academic year and the similar attitude displayed by the other lecturers to their competing subjects.

In reality the time available to a student is limited. How can this be effectively used? A full-time law student has approximately 38 hours each week, inclusive of lecture and tutorial attendance, for study. It would serve little purpose to lay down stringent work hours to be allocated to each day and which are to be regarded as compulsory and inflexible if success is to be assured. Students tend to work to their own set pattern which in their experience they have found to work for them. However, the following guidelines regarding the allocation of private study hours should prove helpful.

(a)   Try to do a little work at weekends but mainly leave these for rest and recreation. Social, cultural and sporting interests and activities are just as much a part and parcel of a student's life as study and examinations. The free weekend acts as an oasis, a reward following a hard week's work, it prevents a student becoming stale, throughout the long academic year. In short, it is as important to appreciate when not to work as when to do so.

(b)   Although you may be a 'night-owl' who enjoys working at night, try not to make this a regular feature of your study programme. Over a course of a year regular late night study will tend to deprive you of vitality during the day when you will be attending lectures or tutorials, writing assignments or taking examinations.

(c)   Assuming that approximately 10 hours of each week are taken up with attendance at lectures and tutorials consideration should be given to the allocation of the remaining 28 hours of private study. It is best possibly to allocate these hours to a maximum of six per work day and a minimum of four. Try not to work for more than two hours per study session without taking a break.

(d)   Assuming a usual but comparatively heavy working day of spending four or five hours in classes, an accompanying maximum of five hours' private study is not unreasonable. On days when the lecture or tutorial commitment is two hours or less then private study could be extended to a full six hours, with little or no private study in the evening, provided you can do some private study around lecture and tutorial attendance.

Remember — when you do the work is up to you. Putting in the hours is what really counts. The biggest cause of failure and upset on a degree course is the failure to discipline oneself enough to fill up those 28 hours of 'free time' with private study. A regular work pattern will pay dividends.

Note-taking During Private Study

From experience, reading on its own without more is virtually useless. Once you have recognised that a certain case, article or section of a textbook is relevant and important then you must take some notes. The best notes will not be verbatim copying but a précis in your own words. The kind of note-taking that should accompany private study is dependent upon the form and function of the lecture course. Where the lecturer has chosen to consider in detail a limited number of topics within the criminal law syllabus private study should concentrate on researching the topics within the syllabus which have not been considered in the lectures. In such cases the lecture notes taken will give illustrative guidance on the detail of note-taking that should prove sufficient for study and revision purposes. The form of note-taking is different in cases where the lecturer has chosen to be comprehensive in his coverage of the syllabus and has concentrated on outlining and highlighting the principles and issues of all the topics within the course. In such instances the principal function of private study and note-taking is to gain supplementary, detailed knowledge of the topics concerned and to expand the lecture notes where required. Irrespective of the form and function of your private study and note-taking, the sources utilised will be the same.

What to Use for Private Study

Statutes
There are comparatively few key Acts of Parliament (statutes) which affect the criminal law and/or create criminal offences and which are of interest to the student (although there are literally thousands of statutes which create numerous modern offences and cause consternation for the criminal practitioner). However, the ones which are of interest to the student (e.g., the Offences against the Person Act 1861, the Sexual Offences Acts 1956 and 1976, the Criminal Law Act 1977, the Criminal Attempts Act 1981, the Theft Acts 1968 and 1978, the Criminal Justice and Public Order Act 1994) are very important. Many sections of these statutes have been subjected to considerable and complex judicial interpretation, and thus knowledge of these statutes is invariably involved with case law. Although consideration of statutory provisions should begin with a reading of the statutes concerned, their full import can only be realised generally by a review of the interpretative case law. Of course there are still offences in criminal law, such as murder, which exist only at common law, i.e., they are judicial creations. In relation to such offences the only source which can be consulted is the reports of cases. You must therefore master the technique of rapid and effective reading of cases and the ability to render your thoughts and views upon such cases into concise and accurate notes. (See p. 17 for a discussion of how to read a case.) In so far as the major statutes creating criminal offences are concerned, students would find *Blackstone's Statutes on Criminal Law*, edited by Peter Glazebrook, very useful for home study purposes.

Case reports
Virtually all the cases which have formed the criminal law are those decided
in the Court of Appeal or House of Lords. Many of these cases are to be found
in the following reports. The *Appeal Cases,* and *Queen's Bench Division* sections
of the *Law Reports,* the *Weekly Law Reports,* the *All England Law Reports* and the
Criminal Appeal Reports. Those reports, although differing in detail, are in
essence set out in a similar format. The note-taking technique described in
discussing *Morgan's* case (see below) as reported in the *Appeal Cases* reports
will be equally applicable to any case reported in any of the above-mentioned
reports. However, certain cases in criminal law will also be found reported
in *Cox's Criminal Cases,* the *Criminal Law Review, The Times* and the
professional journals (see below). These reports are much more concise,
consisting usually of no more than a page; reading such cases and taking
notes should cause no problems and do not require separate consideration
here.

Casebooks
Casebooks are not a substitute for detailed reading and note-taking from the
leading cases. However, a good casebook can be used for private study when
the facilities of a law library are unavailable. Although a casebook can by its
extraction of the relevant and more important parts of a judgment aid a
student in understanding the principles of criminal law, it suffers from major
disadvantages. It does not teach the student to find the relevant areas of a
judgment by reading a case. In other words, it is an example of 'spoon-
feeding'. Also the casebook by the very fact of its selectivity may exclude not
only cases which your syllabus course has determined as important but may,
even when it outlines a case, fail to consider extracts from the relevant
judgments which, you may be of the opinion on reading such cases in full,
are important. It is for this reason that the question of the purchase of a
casebook is left to the student's discretion. If you have ready access to a law
library then going to the original reports is much more beneficial than relying
on an abbreviated casebook. On the other hand casebooks are portable, save
time (in that the editors have picked out the relevant extracts for you), and
they often contain helpful comments and questions. Examples of casebooks
currently on the market are Clarkson and Keating, *Criminal Law: Text and
Materials, Elliott and Wood's Casebook on Criminal Law,* Smith and Hogan,
Criminal Law: Cases and Materials and Dine and Gobert, *Cases and Materials on
Criminal Law,* London: Blackstone Press.

Journals
The *Criminal Law Review* is a specialist journal devoted entirely to matters of
criminal law and evidence. The *Law Quarterly Review,* the *Modern Law Review,*
and *Cambridge Law Journal* occasionally publish material on the criminal law.

All of the above journals tend to publish learned articles together with case notes. Articles and case notes may help clarify the issues in complicated cases or place them in the context of general legal change and development. Students may also find articles on the criminal law published in the *Solicitors' Journal, New Law Journal* and *Law Society's Gazette* which are generally brief, practically orientated and topical. When you read an article do so in its entirety, making notes of points which appear to be important or to clarify issues. At the end of the reading of the article précis what you have read reviewing the parts of the article which you have noted. Finally, remember, if you make reference to an article in an examination answer, it will invariably be a subsidiary matter although good for gaining extra marks. Voluminous notes on an article are wasteful of time and energy. The details of an article can be left in the pages of the respective journals. Generally this philosophy can be applied to other legal material such as Law Commission reports, Royal Commissions etc. unless it is certain from the lecture course that the lecturer has given unusual prominence to such materials (e.g., if the lecturer emphasises faults in the existing law and suggests or encourages thoughts about possible reform). In that instance the possibility of a reform question in the examination has to be considered and such articles and reports considered in greater detail.

Textbooks
There are many criminal law textbooks on the market. The textbooks seem to be split into three principal kinds. First the practitioners' books like Archbold, *Pleading, Evidence and Practice in Criminal Cases* and *Blackstone's Criminal Practice*. Such books are for occasional student reference only and are far beyond a student's price range or technical need. Secondly, the large textbooks commonly used on degree courses such as Smith and Hogan, *Criminal Law* and Glanville Williams, *Textbook of Criminal Law*. These larger course books, in our opinion, go beyond the requirements of many students and seek to cover a multitude of offences in detail. These books appear to be written as academic treatises and books of reference as well as student texts, and it is frequently the case, in our opinion, that their very comprehensive nature and meticulous detail together with the more limited scope of students' criminal law courses precludes them from reading, digesting and understanding all of such books. The third category of books is more in the line of introductory texts. It includes the writers' own textbook, Scanlan and Ryan, *An Introduction to Criminal Law*, Cross and Jones, *Introduction to Criminal Law*, Allen, *Textbook on Criminal Law* and Seago, *Criminal Law*. These appear to be written specifically with the undergraduate and CPE modular and/or semesterised course student's needs in mind. They outline the main areas of the subject and use a limited number of areas for illustration. To gain a benefit from books of this kind a much greater proportion of such texts must

be read and comprehended but their size and style generally permits any student to do so. Because they are introductory these texts do not include the detail to be found in Smith and Hogan or Glanville Williams which are useful reference texts for you if your course prescribes one of the introductory books as the essential text. Likewise where the set text is one of those two larger books you will find that access to your own introductory text will be very useful. Any tiny summary-type books on criminal law summarising the subject are *not* textbooks for degree, Diploma or CPE courses and should *only* be considered near to an examination as *aide-mémoire*. However, in our opinion, this SWOT book on criminal law may be usefully read early on in a course to obtain guidance on note-taking, study and revision techniques as well as an idea of what is expected of you as a student and in examinations.

Arguments for and against note-taking from textbooks are evenly balanced. You should read textbooks in order initially to get an overview of the subject and then to aid comprehension of specific topics. The taking of notes from a textbook should be limited to two instances. The first situation is where issues have not been made the subject of a lecture. The second situation is where your lecture notes upon a topic are unclear or poor and the reading of other legal materials (such as case reports) has not clarified the issues or aided comprehension. The approach taken by a textbook may help you understand the issues and its treatment of the particular topics when reduced to note form may aid future study and revision.

Law textbooks, because of the volatile nature of the subject-matter, run the risk of suddenly being out of date in some areas. Although your lecturer or tutor should draw your attention to recent changes, it may be to your advantage to check the most recent law reports, *Current Law* and *The Times* law reports to make sure that some recent development has not rendered your lecture notes, or even newly published texts, incorrect. The taking of notes from a textbook should be approached in the same way as in the taking of notes from any written source such as from judgments, articles etc. (See the discussion immediately below about note-taking techniques when reading cases.) Generally speaking any notes taken should be paraphrased or précised in your own words.

Which Cases and How to Read Them

As has been noted above the average syllabus quite simply contains too many cases in its reading lists to expect you realistically to read each one in full. You will save yourself time and aggravation if you realise early on that there are three types of cases:

(a)   Leading cases (from which principles of law of general application can be abstracted).

(b) Subsidiary development cases (which are of less significance but which clarify, refine and sometimes limit these general principles of law).

(c) Factually illustrative cases which do no more than apply and reiterate the general principles of law developed by the leading or subsidiary development cases.

Criminal law is no exception. You will quickly learn more if you distinguish the significant from the merely illustrative. Unless you realise this and make allowances in the number of cases you intend to read in full, you will find that even the most efficient method of reading cases will still not permit you to cover all the cases noted in a syllabus. There are, however, certain leading cases to which you *must* give the fullest consideration. These will become apparent to you either because they are emphasised on the syllabus sheet as such or more frequently they are expressed to be so by the lecturer or by the leading textbooks or casebooks which you are reading. Such cases must be read in full, but this does not mean that every word must always be absorbed or recorded in your notes.

For example, in a decision of the Court of Appeal or House of Lords where there is more than one judgment, there is usually a leading judgment. Generally this is the first reported and is the judgment where the facts of the case are fully recited. In such instances it is wasteful of time and energy to go through the other judgments in so far as they repeat the material facts of the case (i.e., you should skip read). Further where it is apparent that the decision of the court is unanimous a cursory reading of the judgments will indicate if the judges have based their common decision upon the same principles, rules, precedents and policies. Where this is the case, the only fact that needs to be noted is the fact that the court was unanimous both in its decision and in its reasoning. Where, of course, the judges have elected to arrive at their unanimous conclusion by exercising dissimilar legal reasoning, the alternative opinions and reasoning of the respective judges should be noted. This should also be the practice where there are minority dissenting judgments.

The following is an example of how to analyse a leading case report.
You should note the following:

(a) The name and year of the case.

(b) The status of the court. If it is (as it invariably will be) a decision of the Court of Appeal or House of Lords, note whether or not it was a unanimous or only a majority decision.

(c) The material facts (as concisely as possible).

(d) The issue (or issues) to be decided in the case.

(e) The reasoning (a summary of the reasons given by the judge or judges for reaching their conclusion).

(f)   The conclusion or decision (i.e., in whose favour the court decided the issue).

(g)   The *ratio decidendi* (i.e., the rule of law, the principle of general application which you abstract from the decision for future use).

More detailed guidance can be obtained by looking at the leading case, *Director of Public Prosecutions* v *Morgan* [1976] AC 182. The first thing to notice is the headnote (the reporter's own précis at the beginning of the report). This will give the outline facts of the case and the court's decision together with a record of any dissenting judgments. If, for example, the name of the above-mentioned case has been recorded in your lecture notes and you have used the method discussed above to summarise it on the even-numbered pages of your lecture notes, the notes you will take during private study will be a supplement to those already made by you at the lecture and should be recorded on the appropriate even-numbered page of your lecture notes. Where the case has not been discussed in a lecture there is a need, of course, to make a full note of such a leading case, but again it is suggested that the note of the case should be filed in the appropriate part of your lecture notes on the opposite side of the page which records the lecturer's discussion of the corresponding principles and issues. If necessary where your notes of a case (or cases) exceed a page those pages should be indexed by reference to the original even page number with a letter suffix, e.g., page 88a etc. This system of recording cases has all the advantages of a card-index system without the disadvantages.

To return to *Morgan* the 'headnote' at the beginning of the report is not sufficient to give a clear insight into the facts and policies which underlie the reasoning of the judges. Reference must be made to the leading or principal judgment for this purpose. Nevertheless the headnote is a useful guide to your own notes upon the facts of the case and a summary of the court's decision. The headnote in *Morgan* clearly indicates two dissenting judgments (or speeches as they are called in the House of Lords), those of Lord Simon of Glaisdale and Lord Edmund-Davies. The case will therefore require careful reading because the decision was by no means a foregone conclusion: neither is it free from doubt that it will remain settled law. This is why it is insufficient in relation to leading cases such as *Morgan* to read the headnote alone.

Many of the leading cases being landmarks in legal change or development are frequently only majority decisions. The judicial reasoning is frequently tortuous and gives an insight into the processes and techniques used by the judiciary to work judicial change. Moving down the headnote, reference is made to several of the judges' principal and important opinions expressed during their speeches and the page and paragraph where these opinions appear in the report. These extracts when present in the headnote give a useful guideline to key areas of certain judgments. However, like the rest of the headnote they do not excuse a comprehensive review of those judgments, although they are a useful précis of important and possibly (from your viewpoint) highly relevant points. In such instances they may be combined into your notes about the case. *Morgan* in the *Appeal Cases* reports (which report the decisions of the House of Lords) also contains the earlier Court of Appeal decision upon the case. In some instances it may prove useful to read this part of the report. In this instance it is unnecessary because the headnote reported that though the Court of Appeal decision was affirmed by the House of Lords, the House affirmed the decision on its own grounds and for reasons which differed from those adopted by the Court of Appeal. The *Appeal Cases* reports and *Queen's Bench* reports (the former of which note criminal appeals to the House of Lords, and the latter the Court of Appeal Criminal Division and Queen's Bench Divisional Court decisions) also contain a précis of counsel's arguments in each case. Though these should not necessarily be noted, it is sometimes useful to your legal education to read these to develop an idea of how a legal argument may be devised and presented on behalf of the Crown or an accused. It is not uncommon for examiners to set questions requiring a display of such skills.

You should then carefully review the leading judgment first (if there is one); this is either the first judgment in the report or it is apparent from a reading of the opening line of the other judgments. Thus phrases by the judges which refer to a particular judgment as being more comprehensive than their own or with which they are in entire agreement refer you generally to the leading judgment. In *Morgan* this would appear to be the judgment of Lord Hailsham of St Marylebone LC. After carefully reading this judgment and noting by page reference its various parts that are of interest, you should endeavour to précis the leading factors that have shaped the judgment, making reference back to the parts of the judgment noted in the initial reading.

When reading the other majority judgments in *Morgan*, those of Lord Cross of Chelsea and Lord Fraser of Tullybelton (omitting areas of similarity of reasoning with the leading judgment and the repetition of facts), you should refer to your notes made when considering Lord Hailsham's speech. Any legal reasoning in those speeches which differs from that contained in the leading judgment should be noted, as should the fact of agreement.

From a reading of the leading judgment it may be possible to extract what is known as the *ratio decidendi* (*ratio*) of the case. This is the legal ruling based upon the material facts of the case as determined by the judge. Even where it is possible to discern a single *ratio* from the leading judgment the issue may be complicated by the other concurring judges of the court coming to a different legal basis (*ratio*) upon which they justify their respective decisions. A case may thus have multiple *rationes*. Even when the judges of the court are apparently unanimous in their legal reasoning such a single *ratio* can, by subjecting it to various degrees of abstraction of the material facts display a multilayered facet. It can thus be seen that though most cases display a central *ratio*, that *ratio* is capable of being subjected to potentially wider applications. In addition to noting the *ratio* of a case, notes should be made of the factors and policies that may underlie and underpin the *ratio*, i.e., 'the reasoning': the basis or reasons for forming the actual legal ruling.

Finally the minority dissenting judgments, those of Lord Simon of Glaisdale and Lord Edmund-Davies, should be dealt with exactly as the majority speeches have been dealt with above. Such an exhaustive process is not required for all cases noted on the syllabus. Many cases which promote subsidiary developments of leading cases can be analysed and read in a much more cursory manner. Those that are merely illustrative of an already established rule require even less attention.

In so far as subsidiary development cases are concerned, after going through the headnote as described above, it will generally be sufficient to read the leading judgment, or one of the majority or unanimous judgments and possibly, where present, a minority judgment. Notes should be taken following the technique noted above but in even less detail.

Matters to be noted are:

(a)   Does the subsidiary case follow the leading case merely because of the doctrine of precedent?

(b)   Has policy played any part in the decision?

(c)   Does the subsidiary case extend or restrict the ambit of the original principles laid down in the leading authority?

(d)   Is there any attempt to distinguish the authorities?

(e)   Finally, the strength of any dissenting judgments.

There are still too many cases noted in the syllabuses for many criminal law courses merely because they are recent and have a certain novelty value or because they have always been there and have become legal fixtures. Many such cases are no more than factual illustrations of the application of the legal principles developed by the leading or subsidiary development cases. These illustrative cases can be dealt with by merely considering and noting the headnote.

Where a course syllabus in this or any other legal subject cites a long list of cases on any topic, a helpful labour-saving tip is to read the most recent House of Lords (or if there is not one, then the most recent Court of Appeal) decision because in it all the relevant earlier case law will be discussed, applied, distinguished, not followed or overruled. Counsel and the judges will have summarised much of the earlier case law for you.

TUTORIALS AND THEIR PREPARATION

A tutorial or seminar is an opportunity for you to impress the tutor that you are a diligent worker, that you have a competent knowledge of the subject and can demonstrate developing legal skills. Hopefully it is also an opportunity to obtain enlightenment through asking questions of the tutor and your fellow tutees. It is also a chance to consolidate the fruits of your private study; matters raised in outline in lectures or even omitted from a lecture course can be considered in detail. It is important to attend them. A tutorial, usually between a handful of students and a tutor, generally follows a pattern of discussion of issues arising from questions which those present have had an opportunity to consider first during their private study. Tutorial questions often consist of past examination questions or at least questions which are very similar to them. There is, however, one major difference between tutorial and examination questions. The former tend to keep pace with the lecture programme and consequently will require a discussion of one aspect of one topic. The latter often are more wide-ranging, combining issues from various topic areas and requiring a discussion of more than one aspect of more than one area of criminal law.

There is little point in attending tutorials unless you make sure that you are prepared and able to contribute to the general discussion. The purpose of a tutorial is to clarify issues that you may find difficult to grasp notwithstanding your private study. If such difficulties are not raised by you during a tutorial you preclude the possibility of them being considered and possibly clarified by the combined efforts of a group of individuals addressing their minds to such issues. Tutorial preparation involves consideration of the legal materials noted on your syllabus sheet which are connected with the questions raised on the tutorial sheet. It is not necessary for you to make voluminous notes on the tutorial questions in order to prepare for the tutorial, an outline of the issues raised in such questions and of the leading cases will suffice. The technique for analysing such questions follows the pattern for dealing with examination questions, or for that matter set essays which are prepared by you throughout your academic year. This technique will be discussed from chapter 2 onwards in a general context and from chapters 3 to 10 with regard to questions contained in your examination paper by working through specimen questions on various topics within the criminal law.

CONCLUSION

During the course of your studies adopt good work habits. One such habit is to set aside a certain amount of time on a regular basis to review the state of your work and to ensure that you are up to date. No doubt if you follow the method of making notes suggested in this book you will reread them as you complete quotations and citations and possibly expand your notes on the leading cases. No matter what the form of your lectures or note-taking you should always read your lecture notes during the course of the day in which you took them, or at least within the relevant week. This reading should be slow and careful with a priority given to understanding and collating what has been recorded, and placing this in the context of the subject as a whole. However, in addition as noted above you should (e.g., every fortnight) spend two hours of your study time reviewing your notes, tutorial sheets and syllabus, checking that all matters which should be dealt with either have been or are in hand. Never get behind in your work. Experience shows that people who fall behind tend either to panic or to suffer from apathy. Either state, if unchecked, leads to a total loss of confidence. This negative attitude can easily be avoided by a disciplined, methodical approach to your studies.

Finally always try to spend a balanced amount of effort on each of the subjects studied during the academic year, term, module or semester although this should not be extended necessarily to a precisely equal allocation of time to each of the subjects studied. Spending an undue amount of time upon one subject to the detriment of the others being studied usually has a damaging effect upon all those areas of study without an appreciable improvement in the subject concerned. Your first course of action should be to see your subject tutor or lecturer for guidance rather than continuing to give disproportionate private study time to one or two subjects. Remember you must demonstrate a minimum amount of legal skill and outline knowledge in respect of all the subjects you study; each deserves an adequate and equitable allocation of your time, effort and concentration.

2 LEARNING, REVISION AND EXAMINATION TECHNIQUES

It is now the practice for lecture and tutorial courses at most universities, particularly those that have modular and/or semesterised courses, to allow only a short period of clear time for revision before the beginning of the examinations. It is certain therefore that your revision must start even though your criminal law course has not ended. From very early on in your course you should plan to revise; it will help to construct a realistic revision programme corresponding with and supplementing your private study programme. You may never feel you have satisfactorily completed an adequate programme of revision even when you have worked constantly and to your utmost capacity. You must be content with having completed a realistic and effective revision programme, accepting that certain topics will not necessarily be fully comprehended causing you some uneasiness. Given the choice generally available, however, on a criminal law examination paper you hopefully will be able to avoid the few topics with which you are not entirely comfortable.

REVISION PROGRAMME

The following points should assist you to construct a realistic revision programme.

(a) Assuming that you are given a week or more of free time for revision, you should allocate at least the same 38-hour week used in your study programme for your revision course.

(b)   Revision should be conducted in no more than two-hour blocks. You should try to limit your working day to no more than eight hours.

(c)   Some of the guidelines suggested in chapter 1 on the approach to be taken with regard to private study could be adopted when you undertake a revision programme.

(d)   This programme should commence following a short break from work altogether, if possible, to refresh you physically and mentally.

(e)   The course of revision should only be interrupted by any coverage through lectures and tutorials of additional topics. The consolation for a student in such cases is that these last topics should not themselves require much, if any, revision because they should be fresh in your mind.

(f)   You must allocate roughly equal time between the subjects to be revised. As in the case of private study a disproportionate interest and effort in trying to revise one subject to the detriment of other subjects studied during the year is ultimately counter-productive to your overall prospects of examination success.

In addition you should conduct revision not on a subject basis but rather by looking at various topics selected from each subject area. This avoids the paralysing boredom which can arise if your revision is built upon the exclusive coverage of an entire subject with each subject being considered on a strict rota and given an inflexible order of priority. More important, however, is that this inflexible revision method produces the unfortunate consequence that the subject first studied will not have been in the forefront of your mind for some time when the examination looms. Topic coverage by moving from subject area to subject area avoids these disadvantages, but does not seriously disrupt the ultimate aim of achieving an overall knowledge and understanding of any given subject area. In this way the subjects studied during the course should be classified and broken down into topics. You should seek to allocate a realistic amount of time to each topic considered to warrant revision.

The sorts of topics that may be considered as part of the detailed revision programme for the subject of criminal law have already been considered in chapter 1 when a typical criminal law syllabus was discussed. For the purposes of revision such a syllabus could be further subdivided into a number of topics which can be studied in comparative isolation and in conjunction with topics from other subject areas. The topics may be listed as follows:

(a)   *Topics which cover the fundamental structure of any given criminal offence and the modes of participation of parties to a crime:*

(1)   *Actus reus.*
(2)   *Mens rea.*

    (3)   Strict liability.
    (4)   Participation in criminal offences.
    (5)   Vicarious liability.
    (6)   Corporate liability.

(b) *Conduct which, although falling short of the commission of a full substantive offence, will still be regarded by the law as criminal:*

    (7)   Inchoate offences, i.e., conspiracy, attempt, incitement, and so-called preparatory offences.

(c) *Various defences to criminal offences.* These will include:

    (8)   Insanity and automatism.
    (9)   Intoxication.
    (10) Mistake.
    (11) Self-defence and the lawful application of reasonable force.
    (12) Duress.
    (13) Superior orders, and necessity.

(d) *Various crimes will also have been examined.* These may include:

    (i)   The major offences against the person:

    (14) Murder.
    (15) Voluntary manslaughter including consideration of the special defences of provocation, diminished responsibility and suicide pact.
    (16) Involuntary manslaughter.
    (17) Assault and battery and the statutory 'assault'-based offences within the Offences against the Person Act 1861.
    (18) Sexual offences including rape.

    (ii)   The major offences against property:

    (19) Theft.
    (20) Burglary.
    (21) Robbery.
    (22) Offences involving deception.
    (23) Handling.
    (24) Blackmail.
    (25) Criminal damage.

(e)   *Various optional or miscellaneous matters.* There may also be consideration of other offences such as:

(26)   Offences relating to drugs, road traffic and public order.

In addition certain themes may predominate, for example, reform of the criminal law or comparative criminal law.

Obviously with unlimited time all the above topics, if they comprised your criminal law course, could be revised. In view of the practical realities of life this is not possible. The standard criminal law examination paper today will vary in size and style depending on the nature and structure of the course. The traditional three-hour law examination will consist on average of 10 questions from which the candidate must select and answer four or five in the specified period. Therefore in preparation you must generally be selective and from the full revision programme exclude certain topics which formed part of your criminal law syllabus. In short the average student cannot hope to master every topic in each of the subjects which must be studied in each academic year or semester. In failing to cover every topic in your criminal law syllabus you run the risk of not being able to answer the required number of questions on the examination paper and especially so if you are too selective. If you are sensible and discriminating in making your selection the risk run is small. There is a great deal of difference between reckless gambling and careful, calculated and acceptable risk-taking in one's examination preparation. Clearly you must be a master of some criminal law topics in order not only to pass but also to rise above the mediocre in the examination. If you are to obtain proficiency in certain topics it must be (because of the constraints upon revision time) at the cost of mastery of other areas of the subject, hence the tendency to be selective with care. Despite being selective you should at least read the topics excluded from your detailed revision programme though this may involve no more than a cursory review of your study or lecture notes. This may have advantages if your examiner is the sort who delights in setting questions which involve a number of issues, e.g., a problem question involving apparent murder with *mens rea* as the central issue but with possibly incitement or participation and possibly the defence of duress or superior orders included as subsidiary issues (the problem of multiple issues in examination questions will be considered below).

SELECTING YOUR TOPICS

Looking at the breakdown of a typical criminal law syllabus above into 26 or so topics the obvious question that arises is how you can select a safe number to revise in detail. Selection should take account of a number of points. First, you must be fully conversant with the concepts of *actus reus* and *mens rea*. These topics permeate the criminal law and they should always be included in your revision programme especially the issue of causation in relation to *actus reus* and of the various states of mind that may constitute *mens rea* and the difference between crimes of basic intent and the so-called crimes of specific or ulterior intent.

Secondly, the topics numbered 3 to 6 in the model syllabus above (with the possible exception of participation which might appear as part of more than one question) will generally, if they are in the examination, form the subject-matter (in whole or in part) of one question only. They are unlikely to appear in various guises throughout the paper. Consequently you might consider revising in detail two out of those four topics.

Thirdly, in relation to the inchoate offences it is unlikely that incitement, conspiracy or attempt will each merit an independent question on the same examination paper. It may be wise, however, to revise fully at least one of these inchoate offences, usually either conspiracy or attempt. If incitement appears on the examination paper it is likely to be as part only of a problem question although the apparent difference in law between it and the two other inchoate offences on the issue of impossibility currently may form the basis of an essay question.

Fourthly, the general defences, topics 8 to 13, may in various guises be found in more than one question in the examination; however, insanity, automatism and duress tend to get a prominent place in examination questions, and frequently merit a central place in a problem question or may be the exclusive issue in an essay question. You may elect as a tactic to revise in detail these defences or as an alternative seek an overall view of the other defences listed above (with perhaps detailed knowledge of two of them, e.g., intoxication and mistake) to prepare for the eventuality of one or more of these topics being present as subsidiary matters in an examination question.

Fifthly, in relation to the substantive offences that may be covered in your syllabus, obviously they may appear as the centre-piece of a given question or as an element in a question which involves several offences (although generally these will be related). You should endeavour to cover a good percentage of these offences. In particular the various forms of homicide receive considerable attention in both lecture and tutorial courses and in examination questions because they permit the examiner to test the niceties of your knowledge especially relating to *mens rea*, causation and the availability of certain defences as well as your ability to argue by analogy and from general principles.

Of the other offences against the person that may have been included in your course, it is unlikely that the various statutory 'assaults' would be combined with any sexual offences. You could at the cost of perhaps one question exclude detailed revision of one of these areas, with perhaps only a review of a couple of self-contained offences within that area of the syllabus. In relation to the statutory assaults examiners often seek to test your appreciation of the difference between s. 18 and s. 20 of the Offences Against the Person Act 1861 and the availability of certain defences (e.g., intoxication) for each of these offences. Alternatively a question involving a discussion of the law of rape is not uncommon, particularly as the concepts of consent, mistake and recklessness can usually be made issues in such a question.

The offences relating to property, topics 19 to 25 on the above list, also require careful consideration. It would be foolish to exclude either the offence of theft or the offences involving deception. Those two topics generally are central to any course of study concerning offences against property. In addition, you could select one or possibly two subsidiary offences, e.g., burglary or criminal damage. This process is equally applicable to any group of substantive offences that form an element in your criminal law syllabus. You should not find on your examination paper questions relating to unusual offences, reform or comparisons between the criminal law in this and other countries unless the course lecturer has either dealt with those topics in lectures or emphasised that you should study them yourselves despite the fact that he will not lecture on such topics.

Unless you are desperately unlucky you should find that despite being selective for revision purposes you are able to answer the required number of questions in the examination with some spare capacity. You should aim to cover nearly 70% of the course in anticipation of being able to answer the required number of questions. This precautionary measure should make provision for the situation where some of the revised topics do not appear in the examination paper. This may also include the situation where a particular topic though revised arises in such a way that you do not feel able to answer the question to your advantage. This may occur either because the topic is combined with several others with which you are unfamiliar or it is presented in a rather arcane fashion. Of course, not every topic you revise is guaranteed to appear on your examination paper. Apart from topic selection in relation to your revision programme and discriminating between the various parts of the course how else do you decide what to revise? Other common-sense factors may help ensure that the selection process is pertinent to the prospective examination questions. For example, undoubtedly most lecturers in criminal law are fair and sensible in their approach to examinations and seek to ensure that the examination they set is an equitable reflection of their course. Clearly the emphasis placed upon topics during your lecture and tutorial courses may indicate the topics which are likely to appear in the examination. Also it is wise to give careful consideration to areas of the law which have been the subject of a new case especially a Court of Appeal or

House of Lords' decision. Such topicality, especially if it arises in the early part of the course before the examination paper is set (which in many universities occurs months prior to the examination) almost always provides an examiner with an irresistible urge to give the area of law dealt with in that case a place in the examination paper.

Furthermore you should always consider the idiosyncrasies of the lecturer and his private obsessions within his subject. If a lecturer bores you with his repeated views on a topic of the criminal law there is a good chance that it will appear in some form either as part of or as a full examination question. More likely than not such a question will be slanted towards the possible reforms within that area.

Areas of particular interest to the lecturer should also be given careful consideration by a student in determining which topics to select for revision. This may be indicated by ascertaining what are the recent publications of the lecturer. These may, because of their prominence in his or her mind, often form the subject-matter of a question in the examination.

Another useful guide to possible examination questions arises from a review of tutorial questions and especially past examination papers. Sometimes these give an invaluable indication of the style of examination paper to come and a possible insight into the topics likely to arise. The value of this guide, however, turns largely on whether or not the same person who set those previous questions will also set your forthcoming examination paper. Do not put too great a store upon the past papers if a different lecturer sets the paper from year to year.

Finally, if you follow the above advice, you should be able to answer the required number of examination questions and if you are forced to answer a question which includes a topic which you did not include in your detailed revision programme you should not despair. In so far as such a question contains topics which you did revise you should pick up an acceptable set of marks from answering those parts of the question. If you have followed the suggestion of reading over all your criminal law notes you should have sufficient outline knowledge of those other aspects of the question which you did not fully revise at least to make a reasonably relevant response (e.g., being able to identify the issue and any leading case at least). Remember that such aspects of any topic will only amount to a fraction of the totality of marks for the question concerned. This is a small risk and a small price to pay to give yourself an opportunity (through following the revision programme and topic selection practice noted above) to revise a considerable part of all the subjects you have studied during the course not just your criminal law. This should enhance your chance of achieving success in all your examinations. Remember too that a first-class paper in criminal law cannot compensate for poor performances in the other examinations.

THE MECHANICS OF REVISION

The final issue to consider in relation to revision is the manner in which it can be conducted effectively.

What Materials Should You Use?

Your prime and almost exclusive revision source should be your own notes. Exceptions should be a review of journals and the law reports for any significant recent developments in any areas on your criminal law syllabus. Such practices are not only good legal technique but a reference to a new case or recent article always impresses an examiner. At the revision stage textbooks should be used only to clarify issues which remain confused or difficult for you to grasp even after rereading your notes.

Where Should you Begin to Revise?

Should you start revising the topics which you find interesting and/or easy or those which you find tedious and difficult? It is not easy to give advice but you could commence with the topics with which you feel you are most confident. This approach enables you to cover rapidly the topics with which you are at ease. This ensures you keep pace with your revision timetable and helps to build your confidence in your ability to master the bulk of each subject. Should your later revision of certain topics prove difficult you have the satisfaction of knowing that you have already mastered much of the essential revision programme and should have enough knowledge and understanding to pass. The contrary view is that topics which you find difficult should be revised first. The rationale of this approach is that you will master those areas of the subject while you are fresh, your mind uncluttered and while the lecturer and/or tutors in the subject are available for consultation. This is a matter of differing approaches to revision which is the student's choice. Note, however, that the difficult-topics-first approach does present difficulties. The temptation to commence a revision programme by expending a great deal of time upon a few topics with which you have difficulties definitely does not help build confidence, and can generate panic as time runs out. There is also an unfortunate tendency for some students to become obsessed with such topics and to spend an undue amount of time on them, leaving little time to revise the topics with which they are more familiar or which are more easily comprehended. Lecturers should be present at your place of study and available early on in your revision programme enabling you to seek their advice upon difficult topics. However, their presence cannot be guaranteed after formal teaching has concluded and before the date of the examination. Most lecturers even if not present at the exact moment when their help is needed are generally amenable to being contacted to arrange a mutually convenient appointment to see you. Do not be reluctant in making such a request, the lecturer is only doing his job, and should do it willingly and with pleasure. Do not be shy, therefore; plan your revision around your own needs and not the actual or rumoured availability of your tutor. Politeness and persistence on your part should obtain the desired guidance.

What and How Should You Revise?

How much knowledge or learning should you retain? You are not a parrot, do not try to learn like one. Just as learning is not a passive process with the acquiring of adequate knowledge being assured by attendance at lectures and tutorials so too you must quickly realise that the effective communication of your knowledge and intellect in an examination is not achieved simply by regurgitation. You should read your notes in paragraphs and small blocks (say, no more than a page), then without looking at what you have read recall the relevant issues, facts and arguments in your mind or preferably by verbal recall in your own words. Aim at understanding clearly what you have just read, remember that an examination question requires more from you than the reproduction of your notes. Consider the issues you have just read from various angles, reflect whether the area of the law you are recalling could be subject to change and under what circumstances. When reading a case consider its possible extension to new factual situations or its possible future restriction. Being able to argue or reason by analogy is a hallmark of an able lawyer. The point in revision is not merely to recall the area or topic you are reading in all its technical detail but to comprehend it. This can only be achieved if the issues and concepts you are studying and revising are your tools or your servants and not some dogma which you blindly recite. They must be understood fully and capable of being applied in any given set of situations or circumstances because that is how the examination will seek to test your comprehension and knowledge of the criminal law. Being able to analyse, illustrate and argue are vital skills. Learning and recall are stimulated by:

    (a)   setting yourself specific targets;

    (b)   establishing your own system of organisation with regard to the material studied; and

    (c)   rehearsal. (Musicians need to rehearse, so do law examination candidates.)

It is for this reason that a good form of revision is to use questions on past examination papers for mock tests. They can be used to test your ability to spot the issues contained in questions and the purposes behind them and to apply the relevant areas of law. In short to test your skill in constructing an answer to questions. This can be done either by the sketching of outline answers with or without using notes and legal sources or by writing out full answers, in the latter case under mock examination conditions. This skill will be considered in detail in relation to particular types of question covering the various topics that may be studied in your criminal law course and forms the basis of chapters 3 to 10. To have conditions as nearly similar as possible for learning as for recall creates the optimum rehearsal conditions. Remember, however, that you will generally learn more effectively if longer periods of intensive revision are broken up by brief periods of rest and that a complete reading of a whole section before learning aspects of it will be helpful.

THE CRIMINAL LAW ASSESSMENT AND EXAMINATION

First some preliminary matters which are largely common sense:

(a)   As the day of the criminal law examination draws near check when it is to take place, its starting time and its location. At virtually every examination at least one student gets the time or date of the examination wrong. When you are sure of the place in time and space record this in a diary, or on a paper pinned to your wall.

(b)   Have a good night's sleep before the examination after a relaxed evening *without work* or with only a little last-minute reviewing, such as a brief look at your revision notes or the names of leading cases listed under subject headings. Any work the night before an examination has little if any practical value. The risk is that a prolonged bout of heavy learning will make you overtired, slowing the ability to recognise issues and recall facts. Worse, it will often confuse facts in your mind causing panic and a corresponding loss of confidence which can be fatal to success. Many students swear by such night-before 'crams', but they tend to have only an illusory, pyschological benefit and should be avoided.

(c)   Arrive at the examination location in good time. In other words make sure that you have planned your travel to the examination hall with a good margin of error, taking into account bus delays, heavy traffic and break-downs.

(d)   Take absolutely no notice whatsoever of anything said to you by your fellow students concerning how much preparation they have or have not done. You are in competition and for a number of reasons, but often in an attempt to gain a psychological advantage your fellow students, even good friends, will exaggerate or denigrate the amount of their own revision. The better prepared you are the less effect anything they say will have on your confidence.

(e) Once you are in the examination hall check you have the correct examination paper in front of you then carefully check the rubric on the paper. Confirm by the heading the required number of questions that must be attempted. Further ensure whether you are required to answer a minimum or a maximum number of questions from particular sections on the examination paper. A paper which requires the answering of four questions may be divided, for example, into section A and section B. The first section may consist of essays, the second of problems. The rubric may require that at least one question is attempted from each section. If this requirement is ignored and the student answers his four questions from one section only his last question will be ignored. From a simple inability to obey instructions you will have deprived yourself of 25% of the marks you may have obtained. Attempting to answer the required number of questions as demanded by the rubric is essential. This is frequently ignored by students and in our opinion is the most common cause of examination failure and virtually all cases of underachievement.

(f) Divide the time available in the examination after deducting the time spent on reading the paper (unless reading time is permitted, see below) by the number of questions that must be answered. It is certain that your first question will generally take a little longer to answer than the others, nevertheless ensure that you do not exceed the allocated time. After this time you must have the discipline to leave the first question, even if incomplete, and move to the next. The remaining questions should be answered strictly within their allotted time. This should ensure an adequate period for answering the last question. If the final question is answered with time to spare you can return to the other questions and add any additional matters and issues you care to mention. A disciplined methodical treatment is necessary to ensure that you answer the required number of questions. This is important because of the working of the examination system. Each question is given an equal number of marks (unless the contrary is indicated on the examination paper); irrespective of the brilliance of an answer or the time lavished upon it, it can earn no more than the maximum marks allocated to it. Failure to answer the required number of questions automatically excludes you from obtaining a percentage of marks that would otherwise be available. For example, if you answer four questions when five should have been completed you are automatically restricted to a possible 80%. In the case of failure to answer one question when the required number is four the loss of marks is correspondingly greater.

Assuming that 40% is the required pass mark this is more easily obtained by answering (depending on the rubric) the required four or five questions adequately rather than by trying to answer three or four questions brilliantly. This is because it is generally easy to obtain the first 40% of the marks in a question by following a competent examination technique combined with an adequate knowledge of the relevant areas of the subject. Marks above the pass mark get increasingly more difficult to obtain. Towards the end of a question you are spending valuable time in a scramble for increasingly elusive marks — a prime example of diminishing returns. This is the strongest reason to allocate adequate time to ensure that you attempt the required number of questions in any law examination.

(g)   Once the invigilator had announced the beginning of the examination read the entire examination paper carefully. Select the questions you will answer but before you begin writing you should re-examine the questions you have rejected, only then after their second rejection should you begin to answer your first question. Although this may take a period of time which you consider could be better spent writing, it does have advantages. In the initial panic after a preliminary reading of the examination paper you frequently select the required number of questions and in doing so see in those questions what you want to see rather than what their true purpose is or what they actually require from you in terms of content. You must ensure that the questions you finally select are those in which you are certain you can fully demonstrate your knowledge and legal skills and in which the purpose and requirements of the questions are clear to you. Questions initially rejected may on a second reading be clear and more appropriate to demonstrate your capabilities than those initially selected. A few extra minutes of reflection to ensure that you have made the most appropriate selection of questions from the examination paper which will display your talents must be considered a worthwhile exercise. This is irrespective of the presence of reading time (i.e., a period when you may read the examination paper although you are not permitted to start writing any answers to questions). This reading time does not form any part of the examination proper. If you are given this luxury be sure to make proper and effective use of it.

General Examination Points

Although you are under pressure during an examination you should endeavour to present your examination paper in a coherent and readable form. This means structured, well planned essays which are easy to read. Leave a space between your paragraphs and write as neatly as possible. Even when a student's script is marked by a lecturer who is tolerant of handwriting deficiencies you must recall that your script is one of many that may be marked by him. If a lecturer finds your script difficult to decipher he will not give you the benefit of the doubt, he may merely assume the worst. Needless to say that will be bad for you.

With each question attempted the student should follow a set and methodical pattern. The question should be read carefully as a whole. Take note of any particular instructions as to how the question is to be answered. Examples would include 'Discuss' which will require the question to be examined in a general sense. Sometimes a question (always a problem question) will require you to consider the facts from the viewpoint of *one* of the fictional parties only. Most essays require more than a mere factual discussion of issues and frequently imply a critical response. Remember, if you write essay answers, always conclude with a brief final paragraph which sums up your views, theme or conclusion.

It is frequently advisable to sketch out a plan of your answer before commencing to write, whether it is a problem question or an essay. But, be brief and quick. If time becomes short do not panic; remember that many of the best papers and individual examination answers have been concise but highly relevant. An examination is not a competition to find who can write the most; marks are not awarded simply because you spent a long time on a question. Among other things an examination tests your answers for relevance. You must answer the precise question and only that question. Assuming facts to suit yourself and putting down copious legal facts (i.e., 'throwing in the kitchen sink' or using what is called the 'shotgun' technique) even when perfectly correct in law, will not gain you any marks if such material is irrelevant to the question asked. Much can be written in the abstract about good examination technique, but the finer points of such matters are dealt with in the context of examples of examination questions in the chapters that follow. These questions will display a leading single theme (i.e., a given aspect of the criminal law, e.g., the *actus reus* of an offence, defences or a substantive crime). Each question will then be analysed to indicate what the issues for discussion are and how to recognise them. An outline plan of an answer will then be provided for each question with general guidelines on the examination technique that is appropriate and which could be followed in such situations.

These guidelines on examination technique will sometimes be pertinent to that particular type and form of question and/or its actual subject-matter. Other points on examination technique, though made within the discussion of a particular question, will be points of general application to all examination questions. In the latter instance this fact will be made apparent in the text. At the beginning of each chapter an outline will be given of the salient parts of the substantive law which will form the theme of the relevant questions.

3 ACTUS REUS

In general, before an accused can be convicted of an important or serious offence the prosecution must establish beyond reasonable doubt that he has brought about the relevant prohibited circumstances and/or consequences and that he has done so voluntarily, with a particular state of mind and that there has been no break in the chain of causation. The conduct of an accused, either by way of positive act or in some instances an omission to act (see later), together with the relevant consequences and/or circumstances of an offence are known collectively by the Latin term 'actus reus'. These are the external elements of a crime that must be proved. The required state of mind that an accused must have in relation to the external elements of an offence is known as the 'mens rea' of an accused. In addition, a third element often has to be proved and that is the absence of a defence. Although, generally, all three of these elements need to be present for an accused to be held criminally responsible for any crime (see R v Taaffe [1984] AC 539) it is frequently the case that separate questions in a criminal law examination will concentrate upon one or other of these elements alone. This chapter will address the kinds of questions chosen by examiners to test acquaintance with the concept of *actus reus* but first it will consider in outline some basic principles, followed by the constituents of the *actus reus* of a crime and the kinds of issues this subject raises for a student.

GENERAL PRINCIPLES

As a general rule, in order to be convicted of a crime the jury must be convinced of three main requirements. These requirements are:

(a) *actus reus*, i.e., the act, the conduct, the omission (see below) the condition of illegality, the verifiable physical or external elements of an offence (see below);

(b) *mens rea*, i.e., the condition or state of mind, moral blameworthiness or fault, the condition of culpable intentionality, the mental or internal element of an offence (see chapter 4);

(c) the absence of a defence (see chapter 8).

The other requirements which are not lacking in importance in determining criminal liability are:

(d) Voluntariness: this is a pre-requisite which has nothing to do with either *actus reus* or *mens rea*. In effect voluntariness on the part of the accused is presumed unless some doubt is thrown on that matter, or the contrary is alleged.

(e) Causation: the accused must be proved to have been the cause of the *actus reus*, and that nothing has allegedly intervened to break that chain of causation.

(f) Coincidence of *actus reus* and *mens rea* must be proved.

(g) The burden of proof is on the prosecution (i.e., 'he who alleges as a general rule must prove'), although on occasions the accused must satisfy the evidential burden of proving enough to raise an inference which the prosecution must then disprove.

(h) The standard of proof as a general rule in criminal cases requires the prosecution to prove what it alleges beyond reasonable doubt (see *Woolmington* v *DPP* [1935] AC 462 (Viscount Sankey's famous 'gold thread' speech)).

(Points (a) and (d) to (f) are discussed further in this chapter, and points (b), (g) and (h) in chapter 4.)

The elements that make up the *actus reus* on an offence vary from offence to offence. An *actus reus* can consist of any one or more of the following elements:

(a) conduct (and sometimes omission, or failures to act);
(b) circumstances (and sometimes events in being or states of affairs);
(c) consequences.

The analysis of the common law definition of murder illustrates this: Murder requires:

(a) the killing of, or causing grievous bodily harm to, the victim (conduct element);
(b) the death of the victim (consequence element);

(c)   that the victim was a human being (circumstance element);

(d)   that the killing or harm was unlawful (circumstance element).

Other offences, depending on their definitions, may only require proof of conduct or an omission, or of conduct and one circumstance, or conduct and a consequence, or a circumstance alone.

Depending on the definition of any offence, if any element of its *actus reus* cannot be proved then the prosecution cannot make out its case and the accused must be acquitted without considering whether or not the *mens rea* or mental elements of the offence could be proved. The converse is equally true, i.e., if *mens rea* cannot be proved there is no point in proving that the accused caused the *actus reus*.

Voluntariness

The criminal law has always recognised an individual's positive conduct as capable of constituting an element in the *actus reus* of an offence but did not, generally, penalise an individual's failure to act. A positive act on the part of an individual means that it is voluntarily and consciously executed. Although this element constitutes a mental state, it in no way forms a constituent of the *mens rea*. Furthermore, it does not form any part of the *actus reus* of a crime. Its nature is best explained when an accused claims a defence known to the law as automatism (see chapter 8). Where the accused brings about the *actus reus* of an offence consciously but involuntarily, e.g., through an accident or through an involuntary reflex, he cannot be held responsible for that conduct, see *Hill* v *Baxter* [1958] 1 QB 277 where the example was given of a person who was attacked by a swarm of bees while driving and consequently lost control of the vehicle; that loss of control or any purely reflex action in response to such an attack would be considered involuntary. See also *Blayney* v *Knight* (1975) 60 Cr App R 269 concerning what might be considered 'accidental' conduct. Note too the 'states of affairs' or 'situations offences' mentioned under 'circumstances', below.

Mental Aspects of Actus Reus

Certain forms of positive conduct require a mental element (independent of *mens rea*) to constitute that conduct criminal. For example, in relation to theft the conduct required of a potential thief is the appropriation of property. This is the assumption of the rights of an owner (see Theft Act 1968, s. 3(1)). The outward physical manifestation of such an act may be the physical seizure of an object, but unless an individual makes a mental resolution to treat the object as his own his conduct cannot be regarded by the law as an appropriation, strange as it may seem. This mental element makes or converts conduct that otherwise may be innocuous into a constituent of the *actus reus* of the offence of theft.

POSITIVE ACTS

If an individual is to bring about the *actus reus* (or external elements of an offence) he must consciously or voluntarily undertake an act or course of conduct or, in certain cases, omit to act, and thereby bring about the prohibited consequences (and/or circumstances) which constitute the external elements of an offence (see above for a consideration of conscious or voluntary conduct). There is also the issue of causation to consider in offences which require the accused's conduct to result in certain consequences. In *R v White* [1910] 2 KB 124 and *R v Hensler* (1870) 22 LT 691 it was determined that where an accused's conduct failed to bring about the prohibited consequences of an offence even though the external elements of what could be the *actus reus* of such a crime have occurred simultaneously, fortuitously or independently, the accused cannot be said to have caused such an occurrence and cannot be held criminally responsible for the commission of that *actus reus*. For example, where the accused, intending to kill, puts poison in the victim's drink but the victim dies of a heart attack and not as a result of the drink. The accused may have wanted that *actus reus* to occur and taken some action towards bringing about that *actus reus* but unless his conduct does produce that prohibited event, he cannot be liable, at least not for the full offence. The accused, however, may be held liable, if he has the prescribed *mens rea*, for an offence of attempt (see chapter 7).

CHAIN OF CAUSATION

Causation raises its head in a more prominent way once an accused's conduct (in conjunction with any relevant circumstances) has set in course a train of events which if uninterrupted would bring about the *actus reus* of an offence. An accused in such cases may only escape potential criminal responsibility, for the prohibited consequences, if he can establish that there has been a subsequent overwhelming or supervening event which is now the ultimate cause of the consequences that form part of the *actus reus* of the offence, and not his initial conduct. In such a case the accused may not be held criminally responsible for the commission of the *actus reus* of the full offence. (Whether or not in those circumstances the accused would be liable for an attempt is discussed in chapter 7.)

The issue of causation raises considerable problems but it is in essence simply a matter of fact. In *R v Smith* [1959] 2 QB 35 the court considered whether the chain of causation had been broken in a case involving the death of a soldier. The accused, himself a soldier, had stabbed the deceased in a barrack-room brawl. The deceased had subsequently received medical treatment which was in the words of the court 'thoroughly bad' and affected his chances of ultimate recovery by as much as 75%. The court had considered the earlier but similar case of *R v Jordan* (1956) 40 Cr App R 152 in which it had been determined that the medical treatment administered to the deceased had been the cause of death and not the accused's act of stabbing the deceased. The chain of causation had been broken in that instance and the accused was held not responsible for the deceased's death. This latter authority did not lay down any general principle with regard to causation, it was a case determined on its own peculiar facts, in particular the grossly negligent medical treatment inflicted on the victim. The general rule as to causation was finally formulated in *Smith*. This authority has determined that if an accused's conduct is a substantial or operative cause of the prohibited consequences of an offence an accused will remain criminally responsible for their occurrence notwithstanding that other external factors are operating to bring about the proscribed consequences of the offence. Today it will be sufficient if the accused's conduct remains an effective or operative and significant cause. In *R v Mellor* [1996] Crim LR 743 the Court of Appeal endorsed 'significant cause' as the test but it confusingly stated that the relevant question is whether the accused's act 'contributed substantially'! However, in a death by dangerous driving case the Court of Appeal has held it acceptable for the jury to be told that they did not have to be sure that the accused's driving was the principal or a substantial cause of the death, as long as they were sure that it was a cause and that there was something more than a slight or a trifling link, i.e., that the contribution of the dangerous driving to the death was more than minute (see *R v Kimsey* [1996] Crim LR 35).

It has been determined, no doubt as a matter of policy, that an individual's death is still to be regarded as caused by an accused's conduct, notwithstanding the deceased's refusal to undergo reasonable and safe medical treatment, see *R v Blaue* [1975] 3 All ER 446, i.e., the accused has to 'take the victim as he finds him or her'. According to *Blaue* the accused cannot say that the victim's religious views which prevented her accepting a blood transfusion, were not reasonable. If the victim of an assault by you happens to have an 'egg-shell skull', you have to accept the consequences of that, likewise if the victim happens to be a Jehovah's Witness.

But do you have to accept the consequences if your victim does something 'daft' or unforeseen? The courts have yet to reconcile the *Blaue* principle with the indirect causation cases discussed below, which seem to imply that you do not have to take a 'daft' victim as you find him. In other words if the victim's conduct is unforeseeable, i.e., not within the range of responses that might have been expected in the circumstances, then the conduct of the victim will break the chain of causation (see *R v Dear* [1996] Crim LR 595). In *Dear* the appellant had repeatedly slashed the deceased who died two days later.

The appellant maintained, however, that the chain of causation was broken because the deceased had committed suicide either by re-opening the wounds or, if they had re-opened themselves, by failing to take steps to staunch the fatal flow of blood. The Court of Appeal held that whether or not the renewed bleeding was deliberately caused by the deceased the jury were entitled to find that the appellant's conduct made an operative and significant contribution to the death.

Since *Jordan* (see above) it has been accepted that normal medical treatment for injuries sustained by the conduct of an accused, even though it may contribute to the death of an individual, will not be regarded as providing a break in the chain of causation and that includes even the proper switching off of a life support machine by doctors (*R v Malcherek; R v Steel* [1981] 2 All ER 422). In *R v McKechnie* (1992) 94 Cr App R 51 the accused attacked the victim rendering him unconscious. In hospital the doctors took the decision not to operate on the victim's duodenal ulcer because he might die from anaesthesia. He died, instead, from a ruptured ulcer. The Court of Appeal held that whether or not the doctor's decision was correct was immaterial provided it was a reasonable decision. The doctors' failure to intervene was like their positive intervention in *R v Malcherek* above in switching off the life support machine and did not constitute a *novus actus interveniens*.

A break in the chain of causation is only provided (according to *Smith*) where the accused's conduct has ceased to be an operating or effective and substantial (but see above) cause of the prohibited consequences, i.e., the accused's actions are no more than a setting in which a latter cause operates to bring about the proscribed consequences. This can be reformulated and expressed in terms of first and second cause: if the accused's conduct is the first cause, then the second cause must be so overwhelming as to relegate the accused's conduct to a matter of history (e.g., the proper switching off by doctors of a life-support machine, while it may be seen as a second cause for the death of a person violently attacked by the accused, will not be considered as negating the first cause). The accused's conduct need not be the sole or even the main cause of the victim's death. It is sufficient that his acts contribute significantly to that result (see *R v Mellor* [1996] Crim LR 743). Even if negligence in treating the victim is the immediate cause of death, that should not exonerate the accused, 'unless the negligent treatment was so independent of his acts and in itself so potent in causing death that the contribution made by the accused's acts can be regarded as insignificant' (*R v Cheshire* [1991] 1 WLR 844). Where there is alleged intervening negligence or incompetence there is no burden on the defence to prove medical negligence nor on the Crown to disprove it but if the jury concluded it did exist they must take it into account when deciding whether the injuries inflicted by the accused were a significant cause of death. That is the really relevant question (see *R v Mellor* [1996] Crim LR 743). But see also the case of *R v Dyos* [1979]

Crim LR 660 in which there were two possible causes of death and the accused was responsible for only one of them. It was held that there could be no criminal liability unless it could be established that the accused's conduct was either the primary or a continuing (and presumably 'significant') cause of death.

For a good example of the issue of causation in relation to manslaughter arising from the supply of heroin and whether or not that chain was broken by the deceased's injecting himself, see *R* v *Armstrong* [1989] Crim LR 149, and also *R* v *Watson* [1989] Crim LR 733, where the issue arose of whether or not a burglary could have been the operative cause of death by triggering the home owner's fatal heart attack. If it was the operative cause then causation was established. Likewise, it would still be considered a cause of death if the predictable arrival of the police or other emergency services triggered off the fatal heart attack. They are not intervening events that break the chain of causation. Arguably, if the victim dies of fright as a result of the accused's illegal act that should be causation enough. Perhaps the real key to causation is the application of the simple 'but for' test. That is: ask the question 'but for what the accused did would the victim have been killed or would he be in his current condition?'. Usually that test confirms the accused's liability. Remember too that the accused's act need not be the sole or even the main cause of the victim's death (or injury) for his act to be held to have caused the death (or injury) of the victim provided it played a significant part, that is enough (*R* v *Mellor* above).

INDIRECT CAUSATION

Where the accused has done something which causes the victim to react, e.g., try to escape, and in so doing is injured or killed (see *R* v *Pitts* (1842) C & M 284 where the victim jumped into a river to escape further violent assaults by the accused and drowned). Two modern examples involve the victims jumping from moving motor vehicles. In *R* v *Roberts* (1971) 56 Cr App R 95 a girl was injured when she jumped from a moving car to escape sexual molestation by the driver, and in *R* v *Williams* [1992] Crim LR 198, the deceased jumped to escape robbery or theft of his wallet by other passengers in the vehicle. In *Roberts* Stephenson LJ said:

> The test is: was it the natural result of what the alleged assailant said and did, in the sense that it was something that could reasonably have been foreseen as the consequence of what he was saying or doing? As it was put in one of the old cases, it had got to be shown to be his act, and if of course the victim does something so 'daft', in the words of the appellant in this case, or so unexpected, not that this particular assailant did not actually

foresee it but that no reasonable man could be expected to foresee it, then it is only in a very remote and unreal sense a consequence of his assault, it is really occasioned by a voluntary act on the part of the victim which could not reasonably be foreseen and which breaks the chain of causation between the assault and the harm or injury.

In *Williams* the Court of Appeal took the view that in escape cases if there is any doubt as to whether the victim's flight broke the chain of causation (i.e., was a *novus actus interveniens*), then the jury must be asked to consider whether the victim's response was within the range to be expected from somebody in his situation, bearing in mind that much deliberation was not expected of a person being threatened.

COINCIDENCE OF ACTUS REUS AND MENS REA

The *actus reus* of an offence must be carried out with the prescribed *mens rea*. This has sometimes been called the doctrine of coincidence of *actus reus* and *mens rea*. The reality is that for criminal liability to attach it is only necessary for both elements to be present and coincide for an instant and not for a joint and equal amount of time. Thus where the *actus reus* of an offence is constituted by a continuing state of affairs, it is only necessary for an accused to have *mens rea* for part of the time during which the *actus reus* subsists (see *Fagan v Metropolitan Police Commissioner* [1969] 1 QB 439). This case concerned the continuous application of force, in that the accused unintentionally parked a motor vehicle on a policeman's foot (the *actus reus*) and subsequently refused to move the vehicle on realising the situation (the *mens rea*) (for a discussion of 'assault'-based offences see chapter 9). The court held that the *actus reus* was continuing and eventually coincided with the accused's *mens rea* when he realised the policeman's predicament but refused to alleviate it. James J stated: 'It is not necessary that *mens rea* should be present at the inception of the *actus reus*, it can be imposed on an existing act. On the other hand, the subsequent inception of *mens rea* cannot convert an act which has been completed without *mens rea* into an assault'.

Alternatively it has also been decided that where an individual by his conduct (which may be totally innocuous) puts a person or property belonging to another in danger of injury or damage, and he subsequently realises that actual or further injury or damage could arise from his initial conduct, his intentional or reckless failure to rectify the situation of actual or potential danger (which he has caused) is the *mens rea* which combines with the *actus reus* of failing to correct the consequence of his initial conduct. This is one of the situations where the law recognises an omission to act as constituting the *actus reus* of an offence (see later). It was first clearly established in the case of *R v Miller* [1983] 2 AC 161, a decision of House of Lords.

The converse to the *Fagan*-type situation is one where an accused sets out to commit the *actus reus* of an offence with the prescribed *mens rea* (see chapter 4) and abandons his action believing it to be completed, but in fact the *actus reus* is at the moment of abandonment in an inchoate state (e.g., where he deliberately hits the victim on the head with a hammer and then throws the victim over a cliff presuming him to be dead whereas in fact the victim dies hours later from a combination of the injuries and exposure). The courts have determined in such cases that if the *actus reus* is then brought about by external circumstances (e.g., exposure to cold) the law may regard the entire incident as one 'transaction' and marry the conduct and *mens rea* of the accused with the eventual fruition of the *actus reus*. This is apparently dependent upon the accused having *mens rea* during the continuance of the 'transaction' whatever form it may take. This is the principle of law developed by the case of *Thabo-Meli v R* [1954] 1 WLR 228 which concerned the offence of murder. Lord Reid said: 'It appears ... impossible to divide up what was really one series of acts ... the accused set out to do all these acts in order to advance their plans'. He went on to say that they should not escape liability simply because at one point they mistakenly thought that their guilty purpose was achieved before it actually was achieved (see also *R v Church* [1966] 1 QB 59 which is discussed in chapter 9 under manslaughter). See also *R v Lebrun* [1992] 1 QB 61 where a man struck his wife not intending really serious harm. Later, in trying to conceal her unconscious body, he dropped her causing a fatal injury. He appealed against his conviction for manslaughter. Lord Lane in dismissing it said:

> the unlawful application of force and the eventual act causing death are parts of the same sequence of events, the same transaction, the fact that there is an appreciable interval of time between the two does not serve to exonerate (the appellant). That is certainly so where the appellant's subsequent actions which caused death, after the initial unlawful blow, are designed to conceal his commission of the original unlawful assault.

OMISSIONS

Generations of law students have been thrilled by the spine-chilling tale of individuals watching a small child drown in an inch of water or being swept away to its doom having fallen into a river. Generally none of those individuals can be held criminally responsible for the death of that child by virtue of their omission to act. The criminal law generally only punishes an accused for his positive conduct.

Nevertheless the law has provided numerous exceptions to the above principle based on status, relationship, undertaking or some other justifying ground. The law has in such situations imposed a duty to act upon an individual and failure to act in such cases amounts to an omission which is punishable by penal sanction.

The exceptional circumstances recognised by law are where a duty to act arises or is imposed by virtue of:

(a) A contract, usually of employment, see *R v Pittwood* (1902) 19 TLR 37 where the accused, a railway gatekeeper, omitted to close the gates when he went off to lunch, with fatal consequences. The duty to act may be an implied term of the contract (see *R v Instan* [1893] 1 QB 450 where the accused who was the niece of the deceased had lived with and off the deceased's beneficence and yet had failed in her express or implied undertaking to care for the deceased in providing the necessities of life for her).

(b) A statute may impose a duty upon an individual to act, see Road Traffic Act 1988, s. 170, which provides that in cases of certain road accidents an individual must provide any one reasonably requiring it certain information, e.g., his name and address. Failure to comply with such a request will not constitute an offence unless an accused also fails in such instances to report the road accident to the police as soon as practicably possible or in any event within 24 hours. Sections 171 and 172 of that Act also create duties for motorists. Similarly, s. 1(1) of the Children and Young Persons Act 1933 places a duty on parents to take care of their dependent children. Whether a statute imposes such a duty is a question of statutory construction (see *R v Ahmed* (1986) 84 Cr App R 64).

(c) A duty to act may be imposed upon an individual by virtue of relationship. Parents or persons *in loco parentis* by virtue of their relationship to a child are under a duty to care for such a minor (see *R v Friend* (1820) Russ & Ry 20 and *R v Gibbins & Proctor* (1918) 13 Cr App R 134). Furthermore where an individual voluntarily takes upon himself the obligation to care for another who is in a position of dependence upon others then that situation of dependence creates a relationship between those parties. Failure to fulfil this obligation once voluntarily undertaken can constitute an omission which is punishable by the criminal law (relationship here is not dependent on ties of blood or family but rather on the fact of having voluntarily undertaken to care for someone who is dependent on you, *R v Stone and Dobinson* [1977] QB 354). It is uncertain whether a person who is in such a dependent state can consent to release another from the obligation to care for him or her (see *R v Smith* [1979] Crim LR 251). Even if accepted as possible as a matter of law, it will be a matter of fact depending on the circumstances of the case whether an individual has been released from such an obligation.

(d)   A person may by virtue of holding an office be under an obligation to act. In *R v Dytham* [1979] QB 722 it was determined that a police officer by virtue of his office was liable for his omission to prevent a violent assault upon an individual who died as a result. (Dytham was convicted of 'misconduct as an officer'.) The accused was also held responsible for failing to arrest the individuals who had violently assaulted the deceased. (Although referring to a police officer there is no reason that by analogy the same should not be true for the holder of any public office who wilfully neglects to perform any duty.) The court determined in that case, however, that if the duty to act would be attended with 'greater danger than a man of ordinary firmness and activity may be expected to encounter' an individual may not be held criminally responsible for his failure to act. The failure to act must be wilful and without reasonable excuse or justification for an 'officer' to be held in breach of duty.

(e)   A duty to act may arise from the accused's conduct. In *R v Miller* [1983] 2 AC 161 the accused, a squatter, started a fire in a room, though at that time he did not appreciate the fact. On realising the fact he did nothing but left the room in order to go to sleep in another room. The House of Lords determined that where an accused was unaware he had set in motion a chain of events which could cause or which was causing damage to property but, at a time when further or any damage could be avoided he became aware of his responsibility for that state of affairs, his failure to correct that situation would constitute an omission punishable by the criminal law. This principle, it is suggested, is not limited to the situation of damage to property but to circumstances of injury to persons (see Lord Diplock at p. 176). Unlike the duty to act imposed upon persons who hold an office, their lordships did not consider when or if an accused could escape liability for such an omission where performance of the duty to act may involve undue danger or burden. There is no need to have recourse to the principle in *Miller's* case to affix responsibility for bringing about the prohibited consequence of an offence where liability for that consequence is strict (see *Wings Ltd* v *Ellis* [1984] 1 WLR 731). For a discussion of strict liability, see chapter 5.

In all the situations where an accused can be held criminally liable for an omission to act remember that the offence with which the accused is charged as a result of his failure to act will depend on the consequences (e.g., the death or damage caused) and his *mens rea* at the time. Proof of his omission to act will satisfy the conduct element of whatever the offence with which he is charged. Note that while we are all under a general common law duty not to kill (and therefore euthanasia is not lawful), in rare instances the withholding or withdrawal of medical treatment leading to death may not amount to a criminal offence: see *Airedale NHS Trust* v *Bland* [1993] 1 All ER 821 (this was a civil appeal, but see Lord Goff's judgment which is significant for criminal law purposes).

CIRCUMSTANCES

States of Affairs

The external elements of an offence may be constituted in part by a positive act or in certain cases an omission which may or may not require attendant consequences. Virtually all offences, however, require that an individual's conduct takes place within a set of circumstances. Thus a potential thief may not commit the offence of theft except with regard to property which *belongs to another* (see Theft Act 1968, s. 1). A man may only rape a woman who *does not consent* to the act of intercourse. These are circumstances which must be present in the *actus reus* of such offences. Some offences, however, are constituted entirely by circumstances and do not appear to require that an accused actually brings himself by his conduct within the *actus reus* of such an offence. Such crimes are known as state-of-affairs offences. A modern statutory example is the offence of being in charge of a motor vehicle upon a road or in a public place while being unfit to drive through drink or drugs. This type of 'being' offence is generally restricted to minor offences such as being found drunk in a public place (see the Licensing Act 1872, s. 12, and *Winzar* v *Chief Constable of Kent, The Times,* 28 March 1983) although this form of offence was first recognised with regard to the serious offence of being an alien to whom leave to land in the United Kingdom had been refused and who was *found* in the United Kingdom (see *R* v *Larsonneur* (1933) 24 Cr App R 74). This offence was committed by the accused even though she had been brought to the United Kingdom against her will under police escort and following deportation from the Irish Free State to which she had gone on first leaving the United Kingdom. It may well be that she had deliberately gone to Ireland knowing that she would be deported back to England and, in a sense, had voluntarily brought about her presence in England. Alternatively, it may be that the judge and counsel were at fault in failing to assert the fundamental principle of criminal liability that the accused must have acted voluntarily, or voluntarily been in the forbidden state or place. That basic principle has been appreciated and asserted in similar situations in the United States, even in the State of Alabama (see *Martin* v *State of Alabama* (1944) 31 Ala App 334 where it was held that in such state-of-affairs offences an accused must be responsible for bringing himself within the terms of the offence). The accused must have acted consciously and voluntarily. This is correct and much more fair to the accused even where the penalty is minor or the purpose of the provision creating the offence is paternal or protective, see *Winzar* v *Chief Constable of Kent*. Usually the few existing state-of-affairs offences, because of their nature, are crimes of absolute or strict liability (see chapter 5).

Unlawfulness

The normal form of an offence, however, comprises an act or omission on the part of an accused together with attendant circumstances (sometimes known as conduct crimes) and offences which require in addition that an accused's conduct not only takes place within the prescribed circumstances but also produces certain consequences (sometimes known as result crimes).

Theft is a classic example of a conduct crime and murder is the classic example of a result crime. Certain result crimes including murder and many assault offences have within their definition the requirement that an accused shall not act unlawfully in killing or assaulting or battering the victim. It was once thought to be the law that such a requirement did not form an element in the *actus reus* (see the Divisional Court decision of *Albert* v *Lavin* [1981] 1 All ER 628 at p. 639 per Hodgson J). The basis for this view was that in offences such as murder or the assault-based crimes the requirement that an individual shall not act unlawfully was no more than a recognition that no offence is committed where an accused has acted lawfully. This covers, e.g., the situations where his use of force or his killing of another was in self-defence. The element of unlawfulness in such offences was thus negated by the establishing of certain generally applicable defences. These defences however, would be applicable irrespective of whether the definitions of those offences contained the requirement that an accused acted 'unlawfully' or not. Now it is clear that the element of 'unlawfulness' within such offences does amount to an element in their *actus reus* (see *R* v *Kimber* [1983] 3 All ER 316 at p. 320, *R* v *Gladstone Williams* (1984) 78 Cr App R 276 and *Beckford* v *R* [1987] 3 WLR 611). This is more than a question of semantics or academic classification, it has significant effects, *inter alia*, upon the application of the defence of mistaken belief (see chapter 8). Notwithstanding, however, the assimilation of the element of 'unlawfulness' into the *actus reus* of the offence in cases of crimes involving the application of force, differences remain between this element and the other forms of circumstances that may be found in the *actus reus* of offences. This is illustrated by the contrasting cases of *R* v *Deller* (1952) 36 Cr App R 184 and *R* v *Dadson* (1850) 4 Cox CC 358. In *Deller* the accused believed he had obtained property from another by making false pretences (see now obtaining property by deception contrary to the Theft Act 1968, s. 15). In fact through *ignorance* of the actual facts the representations that he believed to be false were actually true. An element of the *actus reus*, that his representations be false (a circumstance), was thus absent. The accused was found not guilty. *Deller* is simply authority for the proposition that unless every single element of the *actus reus* is proved the accused must be acquitted no matter how criminal his state of mind. In Dadson the accused shot at an escaping thief wounding him. This was, on the facts as believed by the accused, an unreasonable and unlawful application of force. *Unknown* to the accused there were facts concerning the victim's criminal status which (as the law then stood) constituted the accused's assault upon the victim lawful. Nevertheless the appellate court affirmed his conviction, notwithstanding that on an objective assessment of the facts the accused's conduct was a 'lawful' application of force. Some would say that because *Dadson* did not act unlawfully (he was entitled to shoot a fleeing felon) consequently he was wrongfully convicted of causing the victim grievous bodily harm. This decision is not, it is suggested, in conflict with *Deller*, it merely determines that certain elements of the *actus reus* of offences (in this instance, as the law now stands, the circumstance of unlawfulness) require the accused to be aware of the grounds which negate the circumstance in fact before he may claim that he can escape criminal responsibility for his conduct. In such cases the law will not permit such circumstances to be negated unless they are accompanied by a corresponding mental element on the part of an accused (i.e., unless he knew of them at the time). Furthermore there would seem to be a strong policy element in *Dadson*, in that it does not seem unreasonable to require that individuals in cases like *Dadson* should be aware of the grounds which justify their use of violence before they can claim their conduct is justified, particularly where the use of weapons or dangerous things is concerned. Alternatively, lawfulness in this instance related not to the *actus reus* of grievous bodily harm but to the separate issue of entitlement to, or reliance on, a defence (i.e., in this case the claim that he was justified in shooting that particular victim who was discovered subsequently to be a felon). What the case decides (arguably) is simply that in order to rely on a defence of justification you must have been aware of it (i.e., aware of the circumstances that entitled you to claim the defence) at the time you acted. In *Dadson*, this was at the time he fired the bullet and at the time he did not know that the fleeing person was a felon. Therefore, when he discovered that fact later, he could not claim the defence that he was justified in shooting the victim, and was rightly convicted.

PLANNING YOUR REVISION

This area of the criminal law is of crucial importance. Not only do problems involving the issue of *actus reus* arise frequently in particular examination questions, but this part of the criminal law permeates many criminal law examination questions which have other topics as their central theme. It is important to appreciate the nature of the *actus reus* of a crime: the elements which can or may form its constituents.

Remember that an offence may be constituted by all or some of the following elements:

(a) A positive act. (Understand the various mental elements that may be required to constitute an accused's conduct a positive act which nevertheless do not form an element in the *mens rea*.)

(b) Omissions. (You must be prepared to explain fully the various situations in which the law determines that an accused's failure to act may incur criminal responsibility.)

(c)   Circumstances. (Understand the various forms of circumstance which may constitute the elements within the *actus reus* of an offence. Consider the special position of state-of-affairs offences.)

(d)   Consequences. (Note that some crimes such as murder require a consequence or result as well as circumstances and/or conduct.)

(e)   The final issue to master is that of causation. Be aware that for criminal responsibility to attach to an accused's conduct, his acts or omissions must not only take place within the context of given circumstances but must, in cases of result crimes, bring about the consequences or result prohibited by the offence. Be fully conversant with the intricate case law upon this aspect of the *actus reus*.

EXAMPLES OF QUESTIONS

Question 1

Frequently an examiner will seek to test a student's understanding of the doctrine of causation. For example:

Dr Death has been treating his wife for an incurable but long-lasting disease. From time to time she suffers terribly but never complains. In order to spare her the pain and depression he (of his own initiative) has been injecting her with drugs which are poisoning her. He now plans to administer a final fatal overdose. He approaches her bedside with the fatal injection but before he can administer it he is called away to the telephone. He leaves the syringe by her bedside. He returns 10 minutes later to find his wife apparently dead (evidently she had thought it was an ordinary dosage and had injected herself). In order to avoid detection by an autopsy he sets fire to the bed and dilutes the remaining contents of the syringe. In fact Mrs Death was only in a very deep coma when the bed was set alight and she died from the inhalation of experimental foam which the fire brigade had obtained to fight large chemical blazes and which was used by mistake on this occasion.

Discuss.

There are several principal issues that should be raised by you in answering a question of this kind. The major issue is: has Dr Death, in law, brought about the death of his wife by his course of conduct, i.e., has he brought about an *actus reus* which, depending upon his *mens rea*, may constitute the offence of murder (see chapters 4 and 9)?

Another matter to consider is the question of attempt (see chapter 7 for a discussion of this issue of criminal law). If an accused intends to bring about an offence but fails in his endeavours he may commit the statutory offence of attempting that offence, see the Criminal Attempts Act 1981, s. 1(1). By virtue of this provision the only issue with regard to *actus reus* in relation to an attempt is whether the accused has done an act which is more than merely preparatory to the commission of an offence (see later).

Although it must be accepted that all questions contain a central core of issues which should be tackled by a student, there are always subsidiary issues that can be considered if examination time permits. You should plan your answer to a question to ensure the principal matters contained in the question are discussed first.

We can now turn to a consideration of an outline answer to the above question, discriminating as to which of the above issues should be included in an answer.

The factors that should be discussed may be outlined as follows.

The first conduct to consider on the part of Dr Death which could constitute the *actus reus* of the offence of murder are the injections of poison which he has been giving his wife prior to the final fatal injection. A student could make reference to the Criminal Attempts Act 1981, s. 1(1), and the relevant authorities which determine whether Dr Death's conduct in giving his wife poisonous injections amounts to the *actus reus* of attempted murder. This may also be a relevant consideration with regard to Dr Death's conduct in preparing the last injection with which he intended to inject his wife and to his conduct following that incident. (See *R v White* [1910] 2 KB 124.)

The second principal issue is the fact that the *actus reus* in the case of murder requires, *inter alia*, the death of a human being and this must be caused by the accused's conduct. The accused's injections and the mistaken self-injection by the deceased (which has nevertheless been made possible by Dr Death's actions) have contributed to the deceased's ultimate death. It can be argued that the deceased's self-injection and Dr Death's attempts to cover up what he believes to be the successful conclusion of his nefarious plans were causative factors in bringing about the ultimate death of his wife. The actual cause of death is Mrs Death's inhalation of experimental foam which was used by the fire brigade in error in attempting to put out the fire started by Dr Death. Whether this ultimate cause of death should be regarded as being such an overwhelming cause as to constitute a new second cause relegating all of Dr Death's actions to a matter of history or whether they are all considered to be causative, is a question of fact that would have to be determined by the jury. It is important for a student to cite the authorities and principles relevant to this issue, in particular *R v Smith* [1959] 2 QB 35 and *R v Dear* [1996] Crim LR 595. The essential question is whether or not Dr Death's conduct remained a significant cause throughout. Assuming that Dr Death's conduct could be determined as the operative and effective cause of his wife's death he may nevertheless claim that at the time of his spouse's demise he lacked the prescribed *mens rea*. Nevertheless, following *Thabo-Meli v R* [1954]

1 WLR 228 as applied in *R v Church* [1966] 1 QB 59, it can be argued that Dr Death's conduct can be regarded as relating to and being part of one transaction starting with the first injection given to his wife and ending with his efforts to cover up his activities which resulted ultimately in her death. This course of conduct and subsequent events if regarded as one transaction in which Dr Death is the principal protagonist and combined with a continuing *mens rea* on his part can be amalgamated to render him responsible for the death of his wife. Whether this is the case is a matter of fact.

Question 2

An examiner may seek to test your knowledge of the circumstances which may constitute the elements in the *actus reus* of an offence, in particular, the legal consequences that may follow where a circumstance is absent or negated. An example of a problem question on such issues is as follows:

> Sam, a soldier, is on a tour of guard duty at a Government defence establishment. For some time protestors have been outside the boundary fence keeping a 24-hour vigil. One evening he sees someone breaking through the wire boundary fence. Believing he recognises (correctly) that the person concerned is one of the more troublesome protestors who have made his tour of duty a misery, he decides to shoot her, wounding her seriously. He is charged with the offence of unlawfully and maliciously wounding another with intent to cause grievous bodily harm contrary to the Offences against the Person Act 1861, s. 18. It later transpires that the woman was a member of a proscribed organisation and was entering the establishment to plant an explosive device in the guardroom. Sam is under orders to shoot anyone entering the establishment who is armed or who is engaged upon terrorist or other criminal activities. Discuss Sam's criminal responsibility.

This question is principally concerned with a consideration of the issue that Sam believes he has committed a criminal offence and has in fact intended to do so, yet it would appear that what he has done may be within his orders, it may be an act of necessity, or it may be the use of reasonable and lawful force in the prevention of a serious arrestable offence (see chapter 8 for a consideration of these matters as possible defences). For our present purposes the relevance of these matters to the *actus reus* is that the establishing of any of these defences would not only provide a justification for Sam's conduct, but any of them would negate the element of 'unlawfulness' within s. 18 of the Offences against the Person Act 1861. The question demands a discussion of the authorities which consider the fact that the element of 'unlawfulness' forms an element in the *actus reus* of any offence involving the use of violence.

Further consideration should be given to the principles considered by the courts in the leading cases of *R* v *Deller* (1952) 36 Cr App R 184 and *R* v *Dadson* (1850) 4 Cox CC 358 and in *R* v *Kimber* (1983) and *R* v *Gladstone Williams* (1984) and *Beckford* v *R* (1987).

The element of unlawfulness is a part of the *actus reus* of the offence under the Offences against the Person Act 1861, s. 18, and it is absent on the facts in the question. Does *Deller* thus apply with the consequential acquittal of Sam, or does the principle in *Dadson* apply? In other words will Sam need to be aware of the facts which justify his conduct before he can claim that the circumstance of unlawfulness which is part of the *actus reus* of the offence with which he has been charged is to be regarded as being negated?

Some 'Do's and Don'ts'

The first universal rule is do not repeat any part of the question in your answer unless it is essential to illustrate the points you raise. An examiner can see if you are repeating the facts to no good purpose or effect except to fill out the answer book. Avoid the temptation. Go straight to the main issue or else first identify the various issues requiring discussion and then deal with each of them in turn.

Secondly, when you have identified an issue how do you deal with it? For example, having recognised the issue of causation in the problem involving Dr Death you need to deal with it directly and in some detail. At the same time you must show to its best advantage your knowledge of and skill in the use of authority. One illustration of how to go about doing that is as follows:

Dr Death's conduct must be the operative and effective cause in bringing about his wife's death otherwise he may not be held responsible for that consequence. In the case of *R* v *Smith* (above) the Courts-Martial Appeal Court determined that an accused who set in course a train of events by his conduct could only escape responsibility for the consequences of that conduct if the conduct of another and/or the occurrence of a supervening event were such that these latter matters could be considered to have become the operative and effective causes of the prohibited consequences (i.e., an element in the *actus reus* of an offence) and overwhelmed and supervened all prior causes. These secondary effects must relegate the accused's conduct as a causative factor in bringing about the prescribed consequences to a matter of history. The issue of causation is clearly a matter of fact for the jury's consideration and in the circumstances it would be a permissible inference for that tribunal to conclude that Dr Death's conduct was still an operative cause in his wife's death. To this extent policy may play a part.

Only one principal authority upon the issue of causation has been referred to in answering this part of the question. Students are frequently exhorted to use authorities in abundance but you should be aware of when not to use an excess of cases. The question demands the discussion of the principles of law enunciated in *Smith*. The issue of causation being in essence a question of fact little is gained by including further cases such as *Jordan* and *Blaue*, unless the facts of the question so dictate or such cases are necessary in coming to a conclusion about the fact of causation in your answer.

As a further illustration the consideration of the more complicated issue of coincidence of *actus reus* and *mens rea* within the question concerning Dr Death could be dealt with as follows:

An accused's conduct in serious offences must not only bring about the external elements of the crime (i.e., the *actus reus* of the offence) but the accused must generally have an accompanying mental state (known as the *mens rea*). The law, however, does not demand that both these elements be present from precisely the same point in time or for the same period of time. In the case of *Thabo-Meli* (above), a decision of the Privy Council, the accused had violently assaulted the deceased as part of a prearranged plan to murder him. Wrongly believing this evil plan had been executed, the accused had then disposed of the deceased's body, by rolling it over a cliff. The exposure to the elements then brought about the deceased's actual death. The accused claimed that at the time of the deceased's death (the *actus reus* of the murder with which he was charged) he no longer had the prescribed *mens rea* (intention to kill or to cause grievous bodily harm) and therefore he should not be criminally liable for the death. This argument was rejected by the court. The accused's conduct (similar to that of Dr Death in the question) was to be regarded as one transaction, for which the accused was to be held criminally responsible. This principle was later refined in the case of *R v Church* in the Court of Appeal, so that it would appear to be the law today that any conduct (at least with regard to the offences of murder or manslaughter) which is intended to bring about the *actus reus* of any such offences or to cover up what is believed to be the completed offences, if accompanied throughout by the prescribed *mens rea*, will be regarded as part and parcel of one transaction for which an accused will be liable. The *actus reus* and *mens rea* must be contemporaneous at a point in time but not necessarily for all the time that either the *actus reus* or the *mens rea* are in existence. An instance where an earlier *actus reus* sufficiently coincides with a later *mens rea* is shown in *Fagan v Metropolitan Police Commissioner* [1969] 1 QB 439.

A deceased's death brought about in such circumstances can thus be regarded as murder on the part of the perpetrator. This is the situation found in Dr Death's case.

This extract has discussed the facts of the relevant cases in sufficient outline to illustrate to the examiner that you are aware of the close correlation between the facts of the question and those of the leading cases of *Thabo-Meli* and *Church*. Further, the issue raised in the question would be difficult to discuss without some reference to the actual reasoning in those leading cases. Thirdly, be sure that the law which you put down on any issue is applied then to the facts of your problem. Too many students either forget to do this or are too lacking in confidence to reason, to argue or to draw a conclusion.

Summary

In answering a problem question a statement of principle (whether accurate or not) without reference to case law will not score well; at most it will constitute a bare pass. A reference to legal principle without accompanying case law or authority is a very common fault in assessment exercises and examination papers and is a prime reason for examination failure. The addition, however, of case names in an answer to a question (whether in abundance or not) without more, generally will not raise an answer to above a mediocre pass. What is needed is an effective and economical use of case law when constructing an answer. Nevertheless, in certain parts of an answer to a question, the citation of a relevant authority alone may well suffice. Even when reference to the facts of a case is necessary it can be limited to sufficient key facts and reference to the judge's reasoning to explain the relevant principles of law. The facts of a case should also be used to compare and contrast the case law with the facts in the question, perhaps for the purpose of distinguishing where material facts differ sufficiently to permit such an argument.

The advantage of a problem question is that you are provided with clear guidelines on what is required of you if you can recognise the issues. If the question is understood and the issues it raises are recognised and further-more, if they are issues with which you are conversant, then a problem question should cause few difficulties. As a normal practice, taking the issues in the order in which they appear in the problem and answering each as it arises will constitute in most instances the most effective way of presenting your answer (some exceptions to this general principle will be seen later). The main keys to success are: (a) identifying the major issues that should be discussed and (b) having the discipline to restrict your answer to those issues.

Essay Questions

Essay questions pose different problems for a student. Generally you are faced with a two-stage task. First you must identify the relevant areas of law which are the subject-matter of the question and then identify the point of the question. In essence this means divining the approach or perspective that is required by the person who set the question to its subject-matter. Generally essays require a stand to be taken, a thesis expounded, a theme explained, a criticism made. Some essay questions are comparatively straightforward, for example:

> At common law a man should not be made criminally liable for failure to act but only for his positive conduct.
> To what extent is this attitude reflected in the principles of liability in the criminal law today?

This question seeks a general discussion of the exceptions to the general rule of criminal law that only positive conduct on the part of an individual will merit penal sanction.

As essay questions go this is a comparatively easy one. The first part of the question is a comment, an expression of opinion with which an individual is free to agree or disagree but in this instance you are not required to express an opinion. The second part directly questions whether the statement reflects the law in its present and actual state, and that is all you are asked to assess and state your opinion about. This question does not demand that you say whether you agree or disagree with what was stated in the first part of the question. You are only being asked on this occasion to assess what the law actually is.

An outline of your answer may go something along these lines:

(a)   Positive acts are the principal form of conduct which form the conduct elements of the *actus reus* of an offence. This is the general rule governing criminal liability for conduct.

(b)   The law has provided exceptional situations where omissions may merit penal sanction.

(c)   Outline these exceptions (see above: arising from contract, statute, relationship, office or conduct).

(d)   You should come to a conclusion as to whether the view in the quotation is tenable in light of the exceptions. A consideration of whether or not omissions should be punishable by the criminal law is not relevant. Save such opinions, theories and arguments for an essay question which specifically asks you to judge the law or argue for its reform.

Some General Do's and Don'ts when Answering Essay Questions

As an invariable rule with all essay questions you must read the question thoroughly. Read the last part of the question very carefully for this usually contains the key to answering it. The question noted above was straightforward. Later examples in this book considering other areas of the law will be more complex and require you to balance competing cases, theories or opinions and then express a clear conclusion of your own. The technique of dealing with such essay questions will be discussed in greater detail later in this book.

CONCLUSION

Remember that without an *actus reus* traditionally there could *never* be a criminal conviction. This basic rule still holds true today subject only to the inroad made by the House of Lords' decision in *R v Shivpuri* [1987] AC 1 which, *inter alia*, has held that a person may now be convicted of attempting to commit a substantive offence which it is legally impossible to commit. Proof of a guilty mind together with preparatory conduct may now be sufficient to obtain a conviction (see chapter 7).

The *actus reus* may consist of the voluntary doing of a prohibited act or the voluntary omission to do what the law requires to be done. Sometimes a mere act or omission in itself is sufficient to constitute an *actus reus* but for some offences an attendant consequence is also required and sometimes certain circumstances or circumstances together with a consequence. Always you must establish the causal link, the chain of causation stretching from or linking the accused to the prohibited conduct, circumstance or consequence. In rare instances an intervening event may break that connecting chain. In most instances the accused must take his victims as he finds them and generally the accused is responsible for all the consequences of his criminal conduct towards them. Should the accused seek to rely on a justification for his conduct as a defence the preponderance of opinion is to the effect that he must be aware of the facts justifying his conduct before he will be permitted to avail himself of its protection. These are the key issues, together with coincidence of *actus reus* and *mens rea*, that you must be prepared to identify and discuss.

FURTHER READING

Actus Reus

Ashworth, A., 'The Scope of Liability for Omissions' (1989) 105 LQR 424.
Glazebrook, P., 'Criminal Omissions: The Duty Requirement ...' (1960) 96 LQR 386.
Hart and Honore, *Causation In The Law*, 2nd ed. (Oxford: Oxford University Press, 1985).
Hogan, B., 'The *Dadson* Principle' [1989] Crim LR 679.
Law Commission Report No. 177.

MacDonald, E., 'The Twice-Killed Corpse — A Causation Issue' (1995) 59(2) JCL 207.

Norrie, A., 'A Critique of Criminal Causation' (1991) 54 MLR 685.

Padfield, N., 'Clean Water and Muddy Causation: Is Causation a Question of Law or Fact, or Just a Way of Allocating Blame?' [1995] Crim LR 683.

Smith, J.C., 'The Element of Chance in Criminal Liability' [1971] Crim LR 63.

Stannard, J. E., 'Medical Treatment and the Chain of Causation' (1993) 57 JCL 88.

Weinrib, E.J., 'The Case for a Duty to Rescue' (1980) Yale LJ 247.

Williams, G., 'Finis for Novus Actus' [1989] CLJ 391.

Williams, G., 'Criminal Omissions — The Conventional View' (1991) 107 LQR 86.

Yeo, S., 'An Australian Evaluation of Causation in Fright Cases' (1993) 57(4) JCL 390.

4 MENS REA OR STATE OF MIND

One of the cornerstones of liberty in English law is the prevailing tradition that a person who is accused of having committed a criminal offence must be conclusively proved (i.e., beyond reasonable doubt) not only to have committed the *actus reus* of the offence but also to have had the requisite *mens rea* at the same time. The *actus reus* (or external element of any crime) is the doing of a prohibited act or it can be failure to do what the criminal law requires or it can be sufficient for the accused to be responsible for a prohibited event or statement, or being in possession of prohibited things or even being in a prohibited state or place (see chapter 3). The *mens rea* (or internal element of any crime) is the blameworthy, guilty or criminal state of mind of the accused at the time that person caused the *actus reus* to occur. These traditional principles are summed up in the Latin maxim: *'actus non facit reum nisi mens sit rea'*: 'an act does not make a man guilty of a crime unless his mind be also guilty'. Generally, both the external or factual elements of an offence and the internal or mental elements together with the absence of a defence must be proved beyond reasonable doubt by the prosecution if a conviction is to be obtained. That is the general rule but there are exceptions today:

(a)   There are instances where failure to give any thought or consideration to what is being done, in circumstances where the law says a prudent person would have thought about or considered it, now may result in criminal liability (see the discussion of *Metropolitan Police Commissioner v Caldwell* [1982] AC 341 and *R v Lawrence* [1982] AC 510 below).

(b)   There are many offences created by statute which apparently impose an absolute or strict liability rendering the accused's state of mind irrelevant in regard to all or at least one of the elements of the *actus reus* of the offence created by that statute (see chapter 3 and in particular *R* v *Larsonneur* (1933) 24 Cr App R 74 and chapter 5). For common law offences (e.g., murder, manslaughter, assault, battery, conspiracy to corrupt public morals, etc.) there is a presumption that *mens rea* must be proved (together with the *actus reus*).

For offences created by statute the use of certain words in the statute generally indicates that *mens rea* must be proved: words such as 'malice', 'intention', 'reckless', or 'knowingly', 'maliciously', 'wilfully', 'dishonestly', 'heedlessly', 'fraudulently', etc. How the court decides what is required where no such words are used in a statute is discussed in chapter 5.

Mens rea is not simply any state of mind (of which human beings are capable of having innumerable varieties) but that state which the law considers blameworthy. In some instances that can result from proof that the accused simply was negligent (which strictly is not a state of mind at all). Remember that proof of what the law considers a blameworthy state of mind (i.e., *mens rea*) for one offence may not be sufficient to satisfy the *mens rea* requirement for another offence. For example, the *mens rea* of manslaughter may be satisfied by proof of a certain degree of negligence whereas the *mens rea* of murder will only be satisfied by proof of intention to kill or seriously injure on the part of the accused.

Proof of the actual state of mind of the accused at the time of the *actus reus* is vital. You must be able to show the examiner that you appreciate the fact, that you can categorise the possible states of mind and distinguish between them. Awareness, belief, consciousness, desire, deliberateness, foresight, heedlessness, carelessness, knowledge, malice, wickedness, wilfulness are all states of mind but for purposes of criminal law they generally must be inserted into one of three categories to have criminal consequences:

(a) Intention.
(b) Recklessness.
(c) Negligence.

Depending on the particular offence (because what may constitute *mens rea* for one offence may not for another) proof of any one of these three blameworthy states of mind may make the accused liable in conjunction with proof of an *actus reus*.

Offences can be categorised according to the degree of difficulty with which *mens rea* may be proved. At one end of the scale lie offences the *mens rea* of which can be satisfied only by proof of intention on the part of the accused to commit the *actus reus*. These are called specific or ulterior intent offences.

Intention is the most difficult state of mind to prove because it requires ascertaining the actual, subjective state of the accused's mind. At the opposite end of the scale lie absolute and strict liability offences. These are the easiest offences to prove because either no *mens rea* at all, or no *mens rea* as to one aspect at least of the *actus reus*, needs to be proved. In effect the prosecution is relieved in part or in whole of the burden of proving that the accused had any state of mind at the time of the offence. Between these two extremes lie offences the *mens rea* of which can be satisfied by proof of the state of mind called recklessness (these are called basic or general intent offences) and offences the *mens rea* of which can be satisfied by proof of negligence or a negligent 'state of mind'.

This may be summed up as follows: every offence is in one of four categories depending on the degree of *mens rea* (or blameworthy state of mind) that must be proved for a conviction. In descending order of significance insofar as seriousness of offences and difficulty of proof (but not number of offences) are concerned, offences may be categorised as follows:

(a)   Crimes of specific or ulterior intent.
(b)   Crimes of basic or general intent.
(c)   Crimes of negligence.
(d)   Crimes of absolute and strict liability.

Category (d) is dealt with in detail in chapter 5. For crimes in category (d) no question of *mens rea* usually arises: criminal liability will turn on proof of an *actus reus* alone or proof of an *actus reus* and of *mens rea* in relation to part only of that *actus reus*. In relation to crimes in the other categories (crimes requiring proof of full *mens rea*) you must know what state or states of mind will constitute *mens rea* in each instance and you must be able to distinguish between them, particularly between crimes of specific and basic intent and between crimes of basic intent and crimes of negligence.

It is common for examination questions to seek to discover whether or not you understand the differences. They are important because specific intent is more difficult to prove than basic intent and negligence, and because the defence of intoxication, for example, is not applicable generally in the case of basic intent and negligence offences (see chapter 8). Also remember that the way in which each category is defined determines the width of the offence and hence whether more or fewer people are likely to be prosecuted and convicted.

A summary of the two central areas of evolution and controversy is provided before the discussion of problem and essay questions at the end of this chapter.

NEGLIGENCE OFFENCES

Negligence is a failure to take care: a breach of a duty of care owed to another as a result of which, damage or injury occurs. According to the Law Commission Report No. 89: The Mental Element in Crime (1978), 'a person is negligent if he fails to exercise such care, skill or foresight as a reasonable man in his situation would exercise'; (i.e., it is the failure to do what a reasonable man in the circumstances would have done or doing in the circumstances what a reasonable, prudent man would not have done).

You must be able to show that negligence, while not strictly a 'state of mind', is treated as such in law and is the most objective and the easiest to prove category of *mens rea*. Even if it is proved, however, it will only constitute sufficient *mens rea* for one common law offence, i.e., manslaughter (and then only if the degree of negligence is exceptional or 'gross'), and some statutory offences which make clear that proof of a simply negligent 'state of mind' will suffice such as s. 2 (dangerous driving) or s. 3 (careless and inconsiderate driving) of the Road Traffic Act 1988. Although not a major topic an examiner might seek to ascertain whether or not you appreciate that the degree of negligence sufficient to constitute *mens rea* for the common law offence of manslaughter is different from those statutory offences. In relation to the former, *R v Bateman* (1925) 94 LJ KB 791 at p. 794 stated the prosecution must prove (as would be required for the tort of negligence in the civil courts) the breach of a duty of care which injured the victim and further that that negligence 'went beyond a mere matter of compensation and showed such disregard for the life and safety of others as to amount to a crime ... deserving punishment'. In other words what was referred to in *R v Finney* (1874) 12 Cox CC 625 as 'gross negligence' as opposed to 'inadvertence' or 'an accident' must be proved.

The *mens rea* requirement of the statutory offences of negligence, however, may be satisfied by proof of simple negligence, carelessness, inadvertence or lack of attention; proof of gross negligence is not necessary. You should be able to show that you appreciate that the difference between these two requirements is a matter of degree dependent on the experience and skill of the accused in the circumstances. Such factors will dictate whether or not his failure to act prudently or reasonably was, on the one hand, merely negligence or on the other, grossly negligent. If it was the former then even if death resulted the accused could not be liable for manslaughter although he or she may be liable for some lesser statutory offence if one is applicable, e.g., careless and inconsiderate driving if a motor vehicle was involved.

Clearly where an accused is charged with manslaughter (gross negligence), proof of a reckless or intentional state of mind will also produce a conviction. Where a person is accused of a statutory offence of negligence then proof of simple negligence will be sufficient but if produced, proof of gross negligence or recklessness or intention will also satisfy the *mens rea* requirement and produce a conviction. In that instance the law says simple negligence is the minimum that must be satisfied, consequently proof of greater or higher degrees of blameworthiness must constitute *mens rea* as well. Remember that the converse is not true. If the law requires proof of intention (as in the case of a charge of murder) to constitute *mens rea* for that offence then proof of intention and only intention will be sufficient. That is then the minimum, and proof of any lesser state of mind (recklessness or either type of negligence), will *not* produce a conviction.

Everything stated in the previous paragraph has been confirmed. *R v Sulman; R v Prentice; R v Adomako* [1994] 3 WLR 288; *R v Holloway* [1993] 3 WLR 927 reiterate that gross negligence is still a separate and distinct ground for a manslaughter conviction (see chapter 9 for more detail).

CRIMES OF SPECIFIC/ULTERIOR INTENT

For these offences the *mens rea* requirement will be satisfied only by proof of intention. In each case an extra, special intention must be proved.

A specific intent offence will require proof that the accused intentionally or recklessly committed the *actus reus* but in addition it must be proved that the accused had the special, specific intention required by the definition of such offences. For example, in the case of murder the accused must do the act (intentionally or recklessly) which killed or seriously injured the victim (and, of course, he must act voluntarily and not as an automaton) and in addition the accused must have *intended* either to kill or cause serious injury.

An ulterior intent offence is similar except that the special intention that has to be proved goes beyond the *actus reus*, i.e., there must be proof that the accused intended to do some further prohibited act in addition, or ulterior, to his intentional or reckless commission of the *actus reus* of the offence charged. An example is burglary with intent as defined in s. 9(1)(a) of the Theft Act 1968. That section requires proof that the accused entered a building or part thereof as a trespasser (intentionally or recklessly) but also it requires proof of an additional or ulterior intention that the accused did so enter *intending to* rape any woman therein, or to inflict grievous bodily harm upon a person or to steal or to damage any property therein.

The best examples of specific/ulterior intent offences are statutory and a knowledge of the precise words of the provisions most commonly dealt with in a law course will indicate whether any offence falls into the category of either basic or specific/ulterior intent. Useful examples of the latter category in addition to murder and burglary (mentioned above) are theft contrary to s. 1 of the Theft Act 1968, wounding with intent, which is s. 18 of the Offences against the Person Act 1861, and another example, like murder, from the common law, is any attempt at a substantive offence. The *actus reus* of attempting may be committed intentionally or recklessly *but* the law requires that in addition the prosecution prove an intent to commit the full, substantive offence attempted. Similar requirements exist in relation to the other inchoate offences, namely conspiracy and incitement, see chapter 7.

Intention

Direct intention

To commit a criminal offence deliberately and intentionally is the most blameworthy state of mind for an accused to possess and attracts harsher punishment than if that person acted recklessly or negligently. Examiners like to formulate questions to ascertain whether or not you know what is intention primarily for purposes of crimes of specific/ulterior intent (although intention may also be used to prove basic intent or negligence offences if the prosecution have sufficient evidence and so choose).

If the prosecution seek to prove, or have to prove, intention they may be able to do so in one of two ways. First by showing that the accused deliberately wanted, sought after or aimed at the forbidden act, omission or consequence. This conscious, deliberate aim is 'intention' irrespective of the accused's motive which, as stated below, may be good or bad but which is irrelevant to the accused's criminal liability (although it may be relevant to sentencing once the accused has been convicted). Acting deliberately, knowing what the result will be and wanting it to happen, is 'intention' and is often referred to as 'direct intention' in order to distinguish it from another method of defining and showing intention called 'oblique' or 'inferred' intention which is discussed below.

Motive

In many cases, especially those involving a direct attack on a victim, the accused's desire or motive would be clear and his intent the same. The two converge. It is best, however, to consider and treat them separately. Motive may be evidence of intention and it may, after someone has been convicted, be relevant to sentencing. But an accused's motive may be good or bad and is irrelevant to his criminal liability. This point can be usefully illustrated by either of the cases *R v Steane* [1947] KB 997 and *Chandler v DPP* [1964] AC 763. In the former the judges clearly (and wrongly) confused motive with intention. There a British subject allegedly, after being beaten and threats having been made to his wife and children, made propaganda broadcasts in Germany during the Second World War. He was charged with 'doing acts likely to assist the enemy with intent to assist the enemy'. His conviction was set aside by the Court of Appeal on the basis of a failure to prove intent (i.e., he had acted out of a desire to protect himself and his family, not because he intended to assist the enemy). However, he did intend what he said to be broadcast when he spoke into the microphone (he knew what he said would be broadcast and wanted that) although his motive for so doing was to protect his family. The verdict is not necessarily wrong but the right decision was reached arguably for the wrong reason, in the sense that he could more properly have been found not guilty on the basis of the defence of duress (see chapter 8). The confusion of motive and intention should be avoided.

In *Chandler* the accused was charged with conspiracy to enter a prohibited place 'for a purpose prejudicial to the safety of the state' contrary to s. 1 of the Official Secrets Act 1911. He and others had entered an airforce base to protest against nuclear weapons and had prevented planes using the runway for about six hours. In Lord Devlin's view 'purpose' in this context did not mean motive or else 'a spy who gathered information for money would not be guilty; that interpretation could not be right'. The majority of their lordships thought the accused's immediate purpose was to block the airfield and that was prejudicial to the safety of the state. The *mens rea* here was the purpose or intention to block. The accused's motive in so doing was in his view to save the world from the risk of nuclear war, but that, in the court's view, was irrelevant to whether or not he had intentionally committed the *actus reus*.

A good attempt to distinguish intention and motive is given by Lord Hailsham LC in *Hyam v DPP* [1975] AC 55 where he says:

> motive means an emotion promoting an act ... the motive for murder in this sense may be jealousy, fear, hatred ... in this sense motive is entirely distinct from intention or purpose. It is the emotion which gives rise to the intention and it is the latter and not the former which converts an *actus reus* into a criminal act.

Oblique/inferred intent

In most instances where intention has to be proved, proof of something less than acting deliberately, which used to be called *oblique intention*, will also suffice. In other words proof that the accused was aware that he was acting in a prohibited way or that a prohibited consequence would follow inevitably from his behaviour will amount to evidence from which a jury may infer intention. However, there is some debate about whether anyone can ever know that a consequence is inevitable, hence the tendency in both courts and textbooks to substitute the terms 'virtually certain', 'morally certain' or 'almost certain' for 'inevitable'. Although direct intention may be necessary for some offences (see *R v Steane*), 'oblique intention' or foresight of inevitability has been recognised in relation to wounding with intent (*R v Belfon* [1976] 3 All ER 46), possibly in relation to attempts (*R v Mohan* [1976] QB 1) and in relation to murder (*R v Moloney* [1985] AC 905). Generally the issue of foresight will not be raised. For example, in relation to a charge of murder, if you stab someone else 20 times in the chest then you intended to kill or cause serious harm. There is absolutely no need to query whether or not you foresaw death or serious harm as an inevitable consequence of your conduct. (The only other issue will be whether or not you are insane or have some other defence.) On the other hand if you dangle someone by their fingers from the top of a three-storey building in order to frighten them into telling you where their jewels are hidden then your foresight of that person's death or serious injury may be in issue and proof that you foresaw either consequence as inevitable may result in your being deemed to have the degree of foresight from which the jury may infer that you had intention if you foresaw that, should the person fall, death or serious injury was a virtual or moral certainty. Law Commission Report No. 122 (1992) sums up the issue concisely:

> A person acts 'intentionally' with respect to a result when it is his purpose to cause it; or although it is not his purpose to cause that result, he is aware that it would occur in the ordinary course of events if he were to succeed in his purpose of causing some other result.

In the past one of the favourite vehicles for testing your understanding of intention was a question involving the *mens rea* of murder. The reason for this was that *Hyam* v *DPP* [1975] AC 55 had appeared to create a further category of intention beyond direct and oblique intention. The case actually held that foresight of a high probability (i.e., something less than inevitable) could constitute the *mens rea* of murder. Arguably an accused acted intentionally, at least insofar as murder was concerned, when he or she directly or obliquely intended death or grievous bodily harm to the victim or when the accused foresaw that it was highly probable that his or her conduct would result in death or grievous bodily harm. This could have been taken to imply that in relation to all specific/ulterior intent offences, intention (in addition to direct and oblique intention) could also be foresight on the part of the accused if it was highly probable that a prohibited object or consequence would result from his or her behaviour.

However, that aspect of *Hyam* v *DPP* concerning foresight of less than inevitability has been negated by the House of Lords in *R* v *Moloney* [1985] AC 905 (as explained by the House in *R* v *Hancock* [1986] AC 455 and by the Court of Appeal in *R* v *Nedrick* [1986] 1 WLR 1025) so that in relation to murder or any other specific/ulterior intent offence, foresight of consequence is not now to be equated with intention unless that consequence was foreseen as inevitable. Today intention is either proof that the accused's aim, object, purpose or goal was prohibited *or* proof from which the jury may infer intention because the accused knew or was aware (or foresaw) that his or her conduct would inevitably or certainly, or as a matter of 'virtual' or 'moral' certainty would, have prohibited consequences. Any other lesser degree of foresight does not constitute intention but will be recklessness, which is sufficient *mens rea* for crimes of basic intent but *not* for crimes of specific/ulterior intent such as murder.

You must have a detailed knowledge, however, of *Moloney's* case and of *R v Hancock* and *R v Nedrick*. Their lordships have stated that in a murder trial (and by analogy for any specific/ulterior offence) the trial judge may direct the jury, as a point of *evidence* only, that in the *unusual* circumstances of the particular case they might decide that the accused's foresight of prohibited consequences leads them to conclude that he or she did intend that consequence.

You must appreciate the degree of foresight which now permits the jury to infer intention. In *R v Moloney*, Lord Bridge of Harwich referred to foresight of a prohibited consequence as a 'natural consequence' as synonymous with foresight of inevitable or virtually certain consequences. In *R v Hancock*, the House of Lords considered that a direction to a jury based on the *Moloney* model and referring to foresight of natural consequences was inadequate and too wide and could encompass any direct consequence whereas the rest of Lord Bridge's judgment had made it clear that the foresight had to be that the consequence was morally certain or an overwhelming probability. This view was confirmed by the Court of Appeal in *R v Nedrick* with the emphatic statement that the jury should be directed that they are not entitled to infer the necessary intention unless they feel sure that the prohibited consequence (death or serious bodily harm in that case) was a virtually certain result of the accused's action and he appreciated that fact. In *Nedrick*, Lord Lane posed two questions: how probable was the consequence which resulted from the accused's voluntary act and did he foresee the consequences? Lord Scarman's words in *R v Hancock* provide the jury with a little further assistance: '[The jury] require an explanation that the greater the probability of a consequence the more likely it is that the consequence was foreseen and that if that consequence was foreseen the greater the probability is that the consequence was also intended'. Their lordships, in *Moloney*, were careful to indicate that in such rare circumstances where foresight is appropriately in issue the jury 'may' draw (i.e., are not bound to draw) that conclusion. This is in line with the provision contained in s. 8 of the Criminal Justice Act 1967 which in effect abrogated that aspect of the House of Lords' decision in *DPP v Smith* [1961] AC 290 (see below). Today, since *Moloney, Hancock* and *Nedrick*, in the rare instances where it is proper for a judge to direct a jury by reference to foresight of consequences it will be necessary for him to tell them that they should ask whether or not the relevant prohibited consequence is a virtually certain consequence of the accused's voluntary act and whether or not he foresaw or knew that it was a virtually certain consequence of his act. If they believe he did the inference that he intended that consequence may properly be drawn by the jury. Trial judges must, however, be very careful to give an unequivocal and clear direction that foresight is no more than an evidential guide, i.e., foresight must not be equated with intent: *R* v *Scalley* [1995] Crim LR 504.

Students tend to panic about two issues:

(a)   the significance of *Hancock* and *Nedrick*; and
(b)   the circumstances in which the amended '*Moloney*' direction will be appropriate.

First, remember that *Hancock* and *Nedrick* are of relevance only on the issue of what degree of foresight entitles the jury to infer 'intention'. Otherwise, Lord Bridge's '*Moloney*' direction applies subject to the requirement that the accused must have foreseen the prohibited consequence or circumstance as 'virtually certain'.

Secondly, normally a person's conduct (or omission) 'speaks for itself' about their state of mind. To stab someone 13 times indicates that you 'intended' to kill or seriously harm the victim (or that you are mad). No *Moloney* direction need be given. The *Moloney* direction should only be given where the facts are ambivalent or equivocal (i.e., where there are a number of explanations apart from the recognised defences) and the accused is denying that he intended to do that for which he is now on trial.

Two further points to reiterate are:

(a)   Indirect, oblique or inferred intent, i.e., the permissible inferring of intention from foresight is *not* confined to murder. It can be used, where appropriate, in relation to any offence where the prosecution must either prove or choose to prove intention.
(b)   J. C. Smith states (Smith & Hogan, *Criminal Law*, 7th edn, at p. 55) that Lord Lane has acknowledged the unsatisfactory nature of the *Moloney/ Nedrick* direction to a jury. Some further judicial adjustment or reform seems likely: see the Law Commission's draft Criminal Law Bill on offences against the person and general principles (Law Com. No. 218, Cm 2370 (1993)).

The point in (b) above is confirmed by cases like *R* v *Woollin* [1997] 1 Cr App R 97 where the Court of Appeal looked at the issue of the evidence from which intention may be inferred and invented a wholly artificial and unsatisfactory distinction between cases where the only evidence of the accused's intention are his actions and their consequences on the victim, and cases where there is evidence in addition to that of his action and their effects. In the latter cases a judge's direction to the jury does not need to refer to 'overall' or 'virtual' certainty or 'overwhelming probability' (the reason being that s. 8 of the Criminal Justice Act 1967 requires the jury to refer to all the evidence before drawing any inferences). This ruling will confuse trial judges and juries and provides no enlightenment on what 'intention' means anyway.

CRIMES OF BASIC INTENT

Recklessness

The third type of *mens rea*, apart from intention and negligence, is recklessness. Any offence which requires (a) proof of *mens rea* but (b) which does not specifically require that *mens rea* be 'intention' and (c) which cannot be satisfied by proof of negligence, is a crime of basic intent. The *mens rea* requirement may be satisfied by proof of either or both 'intention' or 'recklessness' (see below), proof of recklessness being the minimum that will be sufficient. Proof of a reckless state of mind will never constitute sufficient *mens rea* for a crime of specific/ulterior intent but it will for crimes of basic intent (and any crime which has negligence as the minimum *mens rea* for a conviction).

This aspect of *mens rea* (i.e., recklessness) has undergone substantial and dramatic judicial development in recent times so that today it constitutes a veritable minefield for the unprepared student. You cannot hope to answer well or even satisfactorily an essay or problem question involving recklessness unless you have a good knowledge of two leading cases (*R v Cunningham* [1957] 2 QB 396 and *Metropolitan Police Commissioner v Caldwell* [1982] AC 341) and several subsidiary development and ancillary cases (such as *R v Lawrence* [1982] AC 510, *R v R (SM)* (1984) 79 Cr App R 334, *Elliott v C* [1983] 1 WLR 939, *R v Miller* [1983] 2 AC 161, *R v Mohammed Bashir* (1982) 77 Cr App R 59, *R v Satnam S and Kewal S* (1984) 78 Cr App R 149, *R v Breckenridge* (1984) 79 Cr App R 244, *W v Dolbey* [1983] Crim LR 681, *R v Kimber* [1983] 1 WLR 1118, *R v Seymour* [1983] 2 AC 493, *R v Stephen Malcolm R* (1984) 79 Cr App R 334, *R v Grimshaw* [1984] Crim LR 109, *R v Crossman* [1986] Crim LR 406, *Chief Constable of Avon & Somerset Constabulary v Shimmen* (1986) 84 Cr App R 7, *R v Sangha* [1988] 2 All ER 385, *R v Farrell* [1989] Crim LR 376, *R v Rainbird* [1989] Crim LR 505 and *R v Reid* [1992] 1 WLR 793; *R v Sulman*; *R v Prentice*; *R v Adomako*; *R v Holloway* [1993] 3 WLR 927; and *R v Merrick* [1996] 1 Cr App R 130).

Two Heads of Recklessness

N.B. The House of Lords in *Metropolitan Police Commissioner v Caldwell* did not overrule the decision in *R v Cunningham*. *Cunningham* was endorsed as embodying one definition of recklessness and another was added to it.

First, in *R v Cunningham* [1957] 2 QB 396 the accused was charged with a crime of basic intent (maliciously administering poison etc. so as to endanger life . . . contrary to s. 23 of the Offences Against the Person Act 1861) and the judge said that the prosecution must prove either:

(a)   an actual intention to do the particular kind of harm that was done (i.e., a direct intention to do that harm), or

(b)   recklessness as to whether or not such harm should occur (i.e., foresight that such harm might result and going ahead, taking the risk, despite that awareness).

In effect this case defines advertent or subjective recklessness as conscious risk-taking or foresight of consequences that are less than inevitable. If you know the risk and are willing to take it then you must suffer the legal consequences. (The facts of some cases indicate that an accused's state of mind could be intentional but at least was reckless in the *Cunningham* sense, see, for example, *Yugotours* v *Wadsley* [1988] Crim LR 623, in which it was held that since the statement made in a holiday brochure and accompanying letter were known to be false by the advertising company and nothing was done by it to correct them, this amounted to sufficient evidence from which recklessness could be inferred on the part of the makers of the statement.) The words 'knowledge', 'conscious' and 'foresight' indicate that a degree of awareness is essential for you to be held reckless under the *Cunningham* definition. *Cunningham* laid down the rule that offences involving 'malice' require foresight of consequences i.e., a subjective test. This meant that persons responsible for injury or damage who were blissfully unaware that their acts or omissions might have such consequences should not be criminally liable. But what if any reasonable person would have been aware that such acts or omissions would be likely to produce the injurious and prohibited consequence?

The Court of Appeal in *R* v *Stephenson* [1979] QB 695 considered the point and concluded that the test was subjective, the accused must be proved to have foreseen the risk and harm that might occur and yet to have gone on to take the risk. Knowledge of, or an appreciation of, the risk to others must be proved to have entered the accused's mind even though he may have disregarded, suppressed or dismissed it. Furthermore that risk must be one which it is, in the circumstances, unreasonable to take. In other words it must amount to conscious, unjustifiable risk-taking. In *Stephenson* it was held that the accused, who claimed he was a schizophrenic, may have been suffering from a mental condition which might have prevented him from being aware of or appreciating a risk which would have been evident to normal people. Therefore the jury should have been given the opportunity, if they believed the evidence of schizophrenia, to acquit him. In effect this decision reaffirmed the *Cunningham* definition of recklessness but approximately two years later in *Metropolitan Police Commissioner* v *Caldwell* [1982] AC 341 the House of

Lords created a second definition of reckless (confirmed in *R v Lawrence* [1982] AC 510) and made it clear that proof of either form or type of recklessness would satisfy the *mens rea* requirement of basic-intent offences. (However, several exceptions were soon recognised limiting the scope of the new limb of recklessness: see below.)

The new, second limb of recklessness recognised in *Caldwell* is often referred to as inadvertent or objective recklessness and is definable as a failure to give any thought to whether there was any risk in circumstances where, if any thought had been given, the risk would have been obvious. This appears to mean that an obvious, unreasonable risk arises when an ordinary, prudent person would have appreciated the risk of harm which was not trivial or negligible. Failure to think about the risk or consequence now will result in criminal liability (for further comments on the significance of that see the outline to the essay question concerning recklessness below).

You must note that a difference exists in relation to the essential content of a direction to a jury in a criminal damage case as opposed to other basic intent offences defined in terms of reckless conduct. In the former the risk only has to be 'obvious' but on a charge of reckless driving (although no such charge now exists under the revised Road Traffic Act 1988) it would have been a misdirection if the judge omits either the word 'obvious' or the word 'serious' i.e., it was for the jury to decide whether the risk created was 'both obvious and serious' (*Lawrence* per Lord Diplock) despite the fact that it is not clear what if anything the word 'serious' means or adds in the context: *R v Lamb* [1991] Crim LR 522. This, however, may still be important because the significance of *Lawrence* (heard by the House of Lords on the same day as *Caldwell*) is that it shows Lord Diplock intended the new objective definition of recklessness to apply to other recklessness (or basic intent) offences apart from offences under the Criminal Damage Act 1971, which had been in issue in *Caldwell* and in relation to those offences the unjustified risk in question must have been both an obvious and a serious one.

To sum up if you do or omit to do something which creates a serious risk of danger to others or to property which is obvious to reasonable people (and which is both obvious and serious in the case of reckless driving), you will have one of these states of mind: either:

(a) you will be aware of the risk, or
(b) you will not have considered the risk, or
(c) you will believe there is no risk.

If (a) is true you are reckless in terms of the *Cunningham* definition of recklessness. If (b) is true you are deemed to be reckless in terms of the *Caldwell* definition. If, however, (c) is true (i.e., you did something after having thought about it and wrongly concluded there was no risk), you will not in theory be held to be reckless. That situation, however, will be uncommon unless possibly the rejection of that risk was itself reasonable (see *Shimmen* below) although the implication of *dicta* in the Court of Appeal in *R v Reid* [1992] 1 WLR 793 is that even the person who considers the risk and decides wrongly and unreasonably that there is no risk is not reckless. (In that case the accused was convicted of causing death by reckless driving brought about by his decision while driving on a dual carriage-way to overtake another vehicle on its near-side and in so doing his car struck a taxi drivers' rest hut.)

However, if the risk would have been obvious (serious and obvious in relation to reckless driving) to the ordinary, prudent man, you are deemed reckless if you were not aware of it. The conclusion that category (b) above is very wide is deducible from an analysis of a line of subsidiary-development cases since *Caldwell* such as the cases *Elliott* v *C* [1983] 1 WLR 939 and *R* v *R (SM)* (1984) 79 Cr App R 334. In the former the Divisional Court on appeal held that a risk is obvious if it is one which must have been obvious to a reasonable, prudent person not necessarily to the particular accused and therefore it is not a defence for an accused alleged to have had *Caldwell*-type recklessness in relation to an offence to claim that he did not see the risk and would not have appreciated it even having given the matter some thought because of limited intelligence or because he was suffering from exhaustion (or for that matter from inexperience, drink, drugs, anger or tiredness). Although Lord Goff in *Reid* though it might possibly be an exception to the *Caldwell* test 'where a driver, who, while driving is afflicted by illness or shock which impairs his capacity to address his mind to the possibility of risk' ... 'it may well not be right to describe him as "driving recklessly" in such circumstances'. This, however, seems totally at variance with *Elliott*; *R* v *R (SM)* and *R* v *Coles* [1994] Crim LR 820, CA.

In *R* v *R (SM)*, the Court of Appeal held that the reckless man is not to be defined by reference to a particular defendant's sex, age and other characteristics.

The inescapable conclusion to be drawn from these decisions (together with *Caldwell*, *R* v *Lawrence* [1982] AC 510 and *R* v *Miller* [1983] 2 AC 161) is that *Caldwell* recklessness is to be ascertained by an application of purely objective criteria. This means that the subjective interpretation (i.e., the view that the risk must have been obvious to the actual accused as stated, for example, in *R* v *Mohammed Bashir* (1982) 77 Cr App R 59, a rape case) is incorrect except in so far as the offence of rape is concerned. On the issue of reckless rape, see also *R* v *Satnam S and Kewal S* (1984) 78 Cr App R 149 in which it was decided that *Caldwell*-type recklessness is inapplicable (see below and chapter 9) but in doing so that decision impliedly accepted that the objective interpretation of the *Caldwell* definition of recklessness is now the law for other basic-intent offences (unless, of course, there are other exceptions) (see below).

The objective nature of *Caldwell*-type recklessness is confirmed by *R v Sangha* [1988] 2 All ER 385 in which the accused set fire to furniture in a flat and was charged with criminal damage 'being reckless whether the life of another would be thereby endangered'. It was accepted by the court that at the time of the fire there was no one in the flat and, because of its construction, there was no danger of the fire spreading to adjacent properties. The accused argued that if he knew no one was in the flat or if in fact no one was there, his conduct could not be said to have created a risk of danger to the life of another and he could not have been reckless whether life was endangered. The Court of Appeal rejected that argument and held that the test whether an obvious risk had been created was whether an ordinary and prudent bystander would, at the time, have perceived an obvious risk that property would be damaged and that life would thereby be endangered, and the fact that the risk in the circumstances could not materialise was irrelevant. This means that even though no one was actually endangered, the fact that a prudent bystander thought someone might be endangered is sufficient to make the accused liable. The Court of Appeal has confirmed in *R v Parker* [1993] Crim LR 856 that the Crown does not have to prove that a life was in fact endangered. All that was required was a risk that life might be endangered. (In other words the Crown must prove the accused was reckless in this regard and may do so by proving that when the accused started the blaze he created an obvious risk that life would be endangered.)

Scope of Recklessness

The wide scope of the new definition of recklessness is shown by the House of Lords' decision in *R v Seymour* [1983] 2 AC 493 and *Kong Cheuk Kwan v The Queen* (1985) 82 Cr App R 18 which wrongly state that *Caldwell* recklessness (as objectively interpreted) is deemed to be synonymous with gross negligence. Proof of either will be sufficient *mens rea* for manslaughter (that has always been the case) but it would seem, according to those cases, that the proof of gross negligence (being likened to *Caldwell* recklessness) will be sufficient *mens rea* for crimes of basic intent and that was a controversial innovation. Negligence, albeit gross, has never before been sufficient *mens rea* generally for basic-intent offences, but those cases purported to make it so under the title of recklessness. Whether or not the two concepts were synonymous still remained uncertain, see *Shimmen* and *Reid* below, until the House of Lords' decision in *R v Sulman, R v Prentice* and *R v Adomako* [1994] 3 WLR 288. Arguably, the recognition in *Reid* of the so-called 'lacuna', i.e., that the person who concludes that there is no risk is not *Caldwell* reckless, also confirms that they are not synonymous. Such people may not be deemed to be reckless but in the main they will be negligent and while that is not enough to make them liable for basic intent offences (like reckless/dangerous driving) if it is gross negligence it will be enough to make them liable for manslaughter.

In instances of recklessness and of gross negligence the central issue is whether or not the risk taken by the accused or his or her inaction was justifiable, i.e., whether or not the social utility of the act or inaction outweighs the risk and the injury or damage likely to result. Largely what distinguishes *Caldwell* recklessness, gross negligence and simple negligence is a question of degree. Was the risk of injury or damage to another or to property high or remote? Was it highly probable, probable, possible, unlikely, very remote or virtually impossible? By an objective criterion the jury will decide what standard to expect of the reasonable man of the same calling, profession or experience in the circumstances.

An examiner might expect you to explain or show that you know at least the current limits of the *Caldwell* (objective) definition of recklessness. In summary form that requires knowledge of the following facts:

(a) First, as stated above, the *Caldwell* definition does not apply to a person who has given thought to the possibility of risk but decided wrongly that none exists even if the rejection of that risk was itself unreasonable: *R v Reid* [1992] 1 WLR 793. However, that argument is not available to someone who has not thought about the risk at all: *Chief Constable of Avon & Somerset Constabulary v Shimmen* (1986) 84 Cr App R 7. Also, a person who recognises an obvious risk but believes he has eliminated it will be deemed reckless if that risk subsequently materialises; such a person is reckless in miscalculating. It would appear therefore that the first limitation on the *Caldwell* principle in effect will apply only where the so-called 'lacuna' in Lord Diplock's test in *Metropolitan Police Commissioner v Caldwell* operates as explained by Taylor J in *Chief Constable of Avon & Somerset Constabulary v Shimmen* (1986) 84 Cr App R 7 at p. 11, namely, where an accused had given consideration to the possibility of the risk and concluded, albeit mistakenly, that there was no risk. But, according to *Shimmen* if a person has recognised that there was some risk involved he is outside the lacuna established by Lord Diplock in *Caldwell* and is either *Caldwell* or *Cunningham*-reckless. If, like Shimmen, an accused is aware of the kind of risk which would result from his act if he did not take adequate precautions and he seeks to rely on the fact that he did take precautions that were intended, and by him expected, to eliminate the risk and he was wrong so that the risk materialised, then he is reckless. The fact that he was conscientious in trying to minimise the risk does not take him outside the dual definition of a reckless state of mind proposed in *Caldwell* (but it may well be considered in mitigation of sentence). See also *R v Merrick* [1996] 1 Cr App R 130 which concerned an appeal against conviction for damaging property being reckless as to whether life was endangered. The electric cable which the accused damaged had been dangerous for a period of about six minutes. The accused did not believe that there was any risk to life and felt competent to deal with the cable in question. On appeal, which was dismissed, he had argued that he was not *Caldwell* reckless because he had considered the risk and, unlike Shimmen, he had not acted recognising the existence of a risk, rather he had genuinely decided there was no risk, i.e., he was within the lacuna. The Court of Appeal disagreed on the basis that there is an obvious distinction between avoiding a risk and taking steps to remedy a risk which has already arisen. In the Court's view the only steps taken that would have precluded a finding of recklessness would have been steps directed towards preventing the risk at all and not steps to remedy it once it had arisen. Once he had admitted creating a risk by exposing the wire or cable then any steps he took fell into the latter category.

(b) Both *Caldwell* recklessness and the old *Cunningham* type are only applicable to crimes of basic intent (*R v Belfon* [1976] 3 All ER 46, *R v Mohan* [1976] QB 1, *R v Pearson* [1985] RTR 39), and not to crimes of specific/ulterior intent such as burglary and the offence of obtaining by deception under ss. 9 and 15(1) respectively of the Theft Act 1968, or the common law offences of murder or attempt. But see *R v Khan and Others* [1990] Crim LR 519 which imports recklessness into the offence of attempted rape. It states, arguably wrongly, that the *mens rea* for this offence is the same as for the full offence. The latter is a basic intent offence, the former (the attempt), a specific intent offence (see chapter 7).

(c) However, even though they are crimes of basic intent, *Caldwell* (inadvertent) recklessness is also *not* applicable to the following:

(i)　　Rape: *R v Satnam S and Kewal S* (1984) 78 Cr App R 149.

(ii)　　Any statutory offence which is expressed in terms of 'maliciously' doing a prohibited act: *W v Dolbey* [1983] Crim LR 681 confirmed in *R v Grimshaw* [1984] Crim LR 109 and *R v Morrison* [1989] 89 Cr App R 17.

(iii)　　In addition, *R v Parmenter* [1992] 1 AC 699 and *R v Spratt* [1990] Crim LR 709 make it clear in relation to s. 47, s. 20 of the Offences against the Person Act 1861 and common assault and common battery that the necessary *mens rea* is *Cunningham*-type recklessness only. *Caldwell* has no part to play. Now it is clear that the *Cunningham* subjective test only, must be applied to any offence the definition of which contains the word 'malicious' (or a variation of that word). This overrules the decision in the acid in the hand drier case, *DPP v K* [1990] 1 WLR 1067, which was wrongly decided.

(iv)　　Even though the offence contains in its definition the term 'reckless' the court in *Large v Mainprize* [1989] Crim LR 213, limited its meaning to subjective, *Cunningham*-type recklessness only. (This interpretation or ruling may, of course, be confined to the offences in question but it could also be a persuasive precedent at least in relation to any offence which may be committed by making false statements recklessly.)

RELATIONSHIP OF ACTUS REUS AND MENS REA

As a general rule *actus reus* and *mens rea* must be related and must coincide, e.g., forming the intention (*mens rea*) to kill someone one week generally cannot be married up with a fortuitous killing (*actus reus*) of that person which occurs a week later. Having said that, however, there are instances where the *mens rea* or the *actus reus* have been held to continue for a period of time and in this way eventually to coincide with a sufficiently related *actus reus* or *mens rea*. Cases of a prolonged *actus reus* eventually coinciding with a *mens rea* formed later are *Fagan* v *Metropolitan Police Commissioner* [1969] 1 QB 439 and *R* v *Miller* [1983] 2 AC 161, and a case illustrative of a continuing *mens rea* which eventually coincides with a related *actus reus* is *Thabo-Meli* v *R* [1954] 1 WLR 228.

Where the *mens rea* comes first in time then *actus reus* and *mens rea* will be regarded as coincident if the prosecution can show:

    (a)　in the case of murder that death (*actus reus* consequence) occurs within a year and a day of the act of causing grievous bodily harm (*actus reus* conduct); or

    (b)　alternatively in the case of murder and in all cases other than murder that the separated *mens rea* and *actus reus* are part of 'one transaction' or event.

Where the *actus reus* occurs first and the *mens rea* comes later then:

    (a)　for any crime involving assault or battery, the *actus reus* can be continuing so that a later *mens rea* may coincide while the *actus reus* continues (*Fagan*), and

    (b)　in the case of any basic-intent offence, failure to prevent, or warn others of, harm from an unintentionally caused danger (*Miller*), e.g., the *actus reus* of criminal damage may be joined with the later *mens rea* of intentionally or recklessly omitting to do anything about the now realised danger.

Transferred Malice

Another general principle of English law is that the *mens rea* of an accused may be deemed to have been transferred to coincide with the *actus reus* which has occurred but not quite in accordance with what was actually intended by the accused. The best example being where an accused fires a gun intending to kill A but by chance kills B of whose presence the accused was oblivious. *R* v *Salisbury* (1553) 1 Plow 100, and *R* v *Latimer* (1886) 17 QBD 359 have long established that the *mens rea* (so-called 'malice') toward A can be deemed transferred to B so that the consequential death of B (albeit accidental in fact) can result in the accused being convicted of murder. However, as stated above the *mens rea* and *actus reus* must be related. *R* v *Pembliton* (1874) 12 Cox

CC 607 makes it clear that the *mens rea* of one offence relating to injuring persons could not be joined with the *actus reus* of an offence relating to damaging property and vice versa. They must relate to the same offence and they generally must coincide. It does not follow, however, that where they do not match up, e.g., where the accused throws a rock at a person intending seriously to injure that person but misses and smashes an expensive glass window, that the accused will escape liability. In such an instance it is open to you to display your knowledge of attempts and of recklessness in offering an opinion to an examiner as to the likely, possible charges.

To display up-to-date knowledge of the application of transferred malice you should refer to the difficult, complex but interesting issues posed by *Attorney-General's Reference (No. 3 of 1994)* [1996] 2 All ER 10. The accused had stabbed a mother-to-be who was carrying a child in *utero*. The wound penetrated the foetus and the child died 120 days after its premature birth. In relation to the *mens rea* of murder of the child the Court of Appeal held that it could be satisfied if there was an intention to cause really serious harm to the mother, by the doctrine of transferred malice, and it was not necessary that the person to whom the malice was transferred was in existence at the time of the act causing death. Subsequently the House of Lords on a further reference at the request of the accused, overturned the Court of Appeal's decision on this point. The House ruled, it is submitted wrongly, that murder could not be committed where unlawful injury was deliberately inflicted on a pregnant woman and the child is eventually born alive but later dies. There had to be evidence of intention to injure either the foetus or the child. The doctrine of transferred malice was inapplicable but the accused could be guilty of manslaughter. For a scathing attack on the leading judgment of the House, given by Lord Mustill, which rules out murder and transferred malice in the circumstances, see the commentary of Sir John Smith ([1997] Crim LR 829 at 830–31).

PROOF OF MENS REA

Sometimes you will need to show that you understand how *mens rea* may be proved from the evidentiary point of view. Generally the burden is on the prosecution to prove beyond reasonable doubt that the accused was responsible for the *actus reus* and the coincidental *mens rea* (see Viscount Sankey's famous 'golden thread of English law' speech in *Woolmington v DPP* [1935] AC 462). Also it must negate every defence which might be raised by the accused. But in almost every instance there will be at least a tactical burden on the accused to introduce the prospect of a defence and in some instances he must go further and satisfy the evidential burden by at least producing sufficient evidence of the defence relied upon to make it a fit and proper issue for the prosecution to negate in the eyes of the jury.

Whereas it is easy to appreciate that *actus reus* can be proved by witnesses testifying to perceived events it is not so easy to understand how *mens rea* (a state of mind) can be proved. The law, however, allows the jury to infer the accused's state of mind from attested evidence of factual events. The jury may draw its own conclusion about the accused's state of mind from what he or she said or did in the circumstances together with any apparent motive and any explanation offered by the accused. This is summed up by the presumption that a man intends the natural consequences of his conscious acts or omissions. You must be clear, however, that this is only a presumption and not a conclusive rule. In the notorious case of *DPP v Smith* [1961] AC 290 the House of Lords purported to state that it was proper for a trial judge to direct mandatorily a jury that once the act or omission of the accused was proved the jury must find that he intended the natural consequences of that act or omission. In effect that decision was saying that a jury was bound to infer that the accused foresaw what a reasonable man would have foreseen in the circumstances. In other words the intention, knowledge or foresight of a hypothetical reasonable man was to be attributed to the accused; what the accused actually contemplated or whether he contemplated anything at all was to be irrelevant.

This judgment was so criticised that Parliament attempted to negate it by s. 8 of the Criminal Justice Act 1967 which purports to specify how intention may be proved in relation to those offences where proof of intention is required for a conviction. In effect the provision states that a jury is not prevented from inferring an accused's intention from evidence that he appreciated what the natural and probable consequences of his acts would be but it does prevent trial judges directing juries that they must draw that conclusion. If the jury accepts his honest mistake about the consequences of his acts then it should not convict him regardless of what any reasonable person would have thought or foreseen. Remember that today it is only in relation to allegations of either *Caldwell*-type recklessness, gross negligence or negligence *simpliciter* that, as a matter of substantive law, an objective assessment of what the ordinary, reasonable man would have thought or foreseen may become conclusive in establishing criminal liability.

In the majority of cases the prosecution must prove the guilty mind of the actual accused (not some hypothetical bystander). This is a subjective test. Most often it is successfully concluded by asking the jury the simple question: 'members of the jury, what other explanation is there on the facts but that the accused intended the prohibited outcome to happen?'. If you stab someone 18 times and at your trial for murder you offer no explanation, the jury will be entitled to conclude that you did intend the victim's death or grievous bodily harm. On those bare facts there is no other explanation possible (unless, of course, you are too mad to plead insanity!). Alternatively, if the facts or your explanation are ambivalent then that might be an appropriate case for the judge to invite the jury to infer the necessary *mens rea*. A typical direction on a charge of murder for example might be: 'members of the jury if you believe that the accused foresaw that death or grievous bodily harm were virtually certain to occur from what he was doing then you may, if you wish, infer that by going ahead he did intend the death or grievous bodily harm that resulted and therefore you may conclude that he is guilty of murder'.

EXAMPLES OF QUESTIONS

Examination questions confined purely to a discussion of *mens rea* or an aspect of it will generally be in the form of an essay question. *Mens rea*, however, will form one of the constituents of a large number of problem questions although it may not be immediately obvious because it is mixed in with other issues often relating to defences.

Essay questions concerning *mens rea* may be very wide-ranging such as the question which simply says:

(1) Define *mens rea* and its purpose.

Other essay questions may be more specific in that they concentrate on only an aspect of *mens rea* and require discussion of only that aspect, such as the following:

(2) 'The present law relating to the concept of recklessness has become incomprehensible and dangerous.'
Discuss.

Or:

(3) Consider critically the impact of the courts on the criminal law in the context of recklessness.

Or:

(4) 'The term reckless plays an important role in the definition of criminal liability yet its meaning still appears uncertain.'
Discuss.

Or:

(5) 'The decision of the House of Lords in *Metropolitan Police Commissioner* v *Caldwell* [1982] is contrary to the true spirit of traditional English criminal law and should be reversed immediately by statute.'

Discuss with particular reference to *Caldwell's* case and the case law prior to and subsequent to it.

Or even:

(6) 'The fundamental basis of the debate between the subjective and objective view of criminal law is very clearly illustrated by the way the courts have treated *mens rea.*'
Discuss.

Apart from the first and the last of these sample questions all the rest require you to deal directly and specifically with one aspect of *mens rea,* i.e., with recklessness. Recklessness, however, will also have to come into your awareness as regards the first and last of these sample questions.
To answer the first question you could:

(a) Sketch the change that has taken place in the meaning of *mens rea* generally from a wicked or evil mind through the concept of guilty mind to prescribed states of mind and to the position today where negligence and *Caldwell* recklessness can constitute *mens rea* although they are not truly 'states of mind'.
(b) Outline the states of mind which will constitute *mens rea* in the eye of the law (i.e., intention, recklessness, negligence).
(c) Indicate that the state of mind which may constitute *mens rea* for one offence may not amount to *mens rea* for another or any other offence.
(d) Explain point (c) by outlining the types of offences and the states of mind, proof of which will constitute *mens rea.* You would compare and contrast:

(i) Specific/ulterior-intent offences, which require proof of intention which may be proved by showing direct intention, although a jury (properly directed) may infer intention if they believe the accused foresaw the result or consequence as a virtual certainty or overwhelming probability (sometimes referred to in the past as oblique intention).
(ii) Basic-intent offences, which may be proved by showing either intention (of either the direct or the inferred type) or recklessness. Recklessness may be proved by showing either *Cunningham*-type recklessness or, in most but not all cases involving basic intent offences, *Caldwell*-type recklessness.
(iii) Negligence, which may be proved by showing either gross negligence in the case of manslaughter at common law or simple negligence in the case of some statutory offences of negligence.

(e)   You could close your essay with a brief conclusion summing up, as best you can, your perception of *mens rea*.

Sample questions (2) to (5) above all require a sound knowledge of:

(a)   *Cunningham* [1957] 2 QB 396.
(b)   *Caldwell* [1982] AC 341 and *Lawrence* [1982] AC 510.
(c)   The reason why *Caldwell* is considered contrary to the traditional ethos of English criminal law and therefore dangerous to society.
(d)   The cases which have confirmed the fears of many that an objective test for the new concept of recklessness was intended by the House of Lords: cases such as *Elliott* v *C* [1983] 1 WLR 939, *R* v *R* (1984) 79 Cr App R 334 and *R* v *Sangha* [1988] 2 All ER 385.
(e)   The cases which have defined the parameters of the new recklessness, in particular *R* v *Seymour* [1983] 2 AC 493, *Shimmen* (1986) 84 Cr App R 7, *R* v *Reid* [1992] 1 WLR 793, *Parker* [1993] Crim LR 856 and *R* v *Merrick* [1996] 1 Cr App R 130.

In all of the sample questions you could also usefully discuss the recent cases which have apparently cut down the broad ambit of *Caldwell*-type reckless-ness. You would need to mention such cases as:

(a)   *R* v *Satnam S and Kewal S* (1984) 78 Cr App R 149, which says that *Caldwell* recklessness has no application to rape and consequently overrules *R* v *Pigg* (1982) 74 Cr App R 352.
(b)   *W* v *Dolbey* [1983] Crim LR 681, *R* v *Grimshaw* [1984] Crim LR 109 and *R* v *Morrison* (1989) 89 Cr App R 17, which support the view that recklessness in relation to statutory offences containing the word 'maliciously', is limited to *Cunningham*-type (conscious risk-taking) recklessness.
(c)   For the purposes of the offence of recklessly furnishing false informa-tion as to the size of a fishing catch the meaning of reckless has been limited to *Cunningham* only type recklessness and will be persuasive authority for the many other offences which may be committed by making false statements recklessly (*Large* v *Mainprize* [1989] Crim LR 213).

An answer to sample question (6) (above) need not be limited to a discussion of the developments to have taken place in relation to recklessness. However, those developments do provide a useful foundation. On the one hand there are those who support the traditional view that in so far as serious criminal charges are concerned liberty is so precious that any accused must be proved conclusively guilty and given the benefit of any doubt. In support it would be useful to cite from the leading judgment in a case like *Woolmington* v *Director of Public Prosecutions* [1935] AC 462. On the other hand there are those (presumably the majority of the judges in *Caldwell*, *Lawrence*, *Elliott* v *C*, *Seymour*, *Shimmen* and *Sangha*, for example) who consider that some acts or omissions are so irresponsible and have such dangerous consequences for others in society or their property that even though the accused was blissfully unaware of the risk or consequences, or miscalculated the likelihood of the risk occurring, he should be made liable to a criminal penalty. The former protagonists are supporters of a subjective view of criminal law, the latter are willing to take an objective approach to ascertaining criminal liability. This means that it is necessary to ascertain what a reasonable person would have foreseen the obvious risks of his conduct to be and then to judge the accused by that criterion. The argument then runs that if he did not foresee the risk, he should have and therefore he should be liable, and likewise if he thought about it but miscalculated the possibility of the risk materialising.

Another area of *mens rea* where the tension between the proponents of subjective and objective criteria was evident arose from the controversial decision of the House of Lords in *DPP* v *Smith* [1961] AC 290 in relation to murder. There the majority implied *mens rea* (intention to kill or cause grievous bodily harm), on the basis of an objective test, to the accused who drove in such a way as to shake off the police officer who had clung to the accused's car. In effect the jury had been directed that it was not necessary for the prosecution to prove that the accused intended death or foresaw it as certain or even as a possibility. If a reasonable man would have foreseen death or grievous bodily harm as a natural consequence then the accused must have intended that consequence.

Having discussed that case critically you would have to go on and mention s. 8 of the Criminal Justice Act 1967 which at least prevents judges giving a mandatory direction to juries that an accused must have intended what were the natural and probable consequences of his actions. The jury may come to that conclusion of their own volition having heard all the evidence but now they cannot be told that they must reach that conclusion.

An objective test applies in relation to both the defence of provocation and the defence of duress. In the former the characteristic to be viewed objectively is self-restraint. In the latter it is firmness of purpose (i.e., the ability to resist threats of physical harm) (see *R* v *Hegarty* [1944] Crim LR 353). However, even in relation to provocation the trend has not been all one way. Cases such as *DPP* v *Camplin* [1978] AC 705 show the judiciary at pains to get the members of the jury to think of themselves as being the same age, sex and colour as the accused with all his or her characteristics in order to try to ascertain precisely what that accused actually felt, i.e., what the actual subjective state of his or her mind was in fact when the accused claims he or she was provoked to kill.

In answering this sort of question you can either display your wide knowledge of criminal law by illustrating your thesis with diverse examples or alternatively you may make it clear to the examiner that (while aware of other possible examples) you are opting to discuss only one example (e.g., recklessness) in detail.

Hasty Decisions and Red Herrings

The examples of typical questions set out above indicate that generally an essay question concerning *mens rea* or some aspect of it (such as recklessness or intention) will be easy to recognise. The rubrics may differ in that some of those questions require you to be purely descriptive whereas others of them require you to analyse, argue a point of view and come to a conclusion. Be careful, however, in reading a question because the fact that *'mens rea'*, 'intention', 'guilty mind' or 'mental state', for example, are mentioned in a question does not always mean that a discussion of *mens rea* and its elements or constituents is required. It is best not to be hasty: reread the question and also beware of red herrings. The following two example questions illustrate this point:

(1) 'The difficulty in determing whether a statutory crime requires *mens rea* is because of a failure both by the legislature and the courts to do what is both simple and necessary.'
Discuss.

(2) Once it is clear that a particular mental state is required in relation to an offence what then should be sufficient to establish that a defendant has the particular mental state in question?

Neither of these questions requires a discussion of the nature of or constituents of *mens rea* and yet the writers have seen students' scripts which indicate that in the rush and panic of the examination those candidates have thought the contrary because they latched on to the words *'mens rea'* and 'mental state' respectively.

The first of these questions is really concerned with strict liability and how the judges decide whether an offence is a strict liability offence or one requiring proof of *mens rea* as to all the elements of its *actus reus*. It does *not* require any discussion of *mens rea* as such. The second question is concerned not with *what* has to be proved to satisfy the *mens rea* requirement but with *how mens rea* is to be proved. It is true that in answering this question your knowledge of the constituents of *mens rea* (the types of mental state which will constitute *mens rea* in relation to various offences) will have to be displayed but that is not the essential point of the question. What the question really wants is a discussion of the subjective and objective tests or criteria used in the courts. In particular in answering such a question an examiner would expect to see some discussion of at least the following:

(a)   In relation to intention (a subjective test or criterion is to be applied):

  (i)   *DPP* v *Smith* [1961] AC 290.
  (ii)   Section 8 of the Criminal Justice Act 1967.
  (iii)   *Hyam* v *DPP* [1975] AC 55.
  (iv)   *R* v *Moloney* [1985] AC 905.
  (v)   *R* v *Hancock* [1986] AC 455.
  (vi)   *R* v *Nedrick* [1986] 1 WLR 1025.
  (vii)   *R* v *Woollin* [1997] 1 Cr App R 97.

(b)   In relation to advertent recklessness (a subjective test or criterion is to be applied):

  (i)   *R* v *Cunningham* [1957] 2 QB 396.

(c)   In relation to inadvertent recklessness (a partly subjective and partly objective test or criterion is to be applied).

  (i)   *Metropolitan Police Commissioner* v *Caldwell* [1982] AC 341.
  (ii)   *R* v *Lawrence* [1982] AC 510.
  (iii)   *Elliott* v *C* [1983] 1 WLR 939 and *R* v *R* (1984) 79 Cr App R 334.
  (vi)   *Chief Constable of Avon & Somerset Constabulary* v *Shimmen* (1986) 84 Cr App R 7.
  (v)   *R* v *Sangha* [1988] 2 All ER 385.
  (vi)   *R* v *Reid* [1991] Crim LR 269.
  (vii)   *R* v *Merrick* [1996] 1 Cr App R 130.

(d)   In relation to negligence (a purely objective test or criterion is to be applied):

  (i)   *R* v *Bateman* (1925) 19 Cr App R 8.
  (ii)   *R* v *Seymour* [1983] 2 AC 493.
  (iii)   *R* v *Sulman, R* v *Prentice* and *R* v *Adomako* [1994] 3 WLR 288.

(e)   General principles of who must prove what and to what degree:

  (i)   Prosecution must prove: *Woolmington* v *DPP* [1935] AC 462.
  (ii)   Prosecution must negate defences: *R* v *Bone* [1968] 1 WLR 983.
  (iii)   'Beyond doubt': *Miller* v *Minister of Pensions* [1947] 2 All ER 372.

Mens Rea of Specified Offences

Another example of an essay question concerning *mens rea* but confined to a particular crime rather than to a particular aspect of *mens rea* would read as follows:

'The difficulties of definition of the *mens rea* required to establish murder were increased rather than lessened by the Homicide Act 1957.'

How far have subsequent developments in the law added to, or decreased, the difficulties?

Or:

'[B]ut it appears to the court that the passage of years has achieved a transformation in this branch of the law and, even in relation to manslaughter, a degree of *mens rea* has become recognised as essential. To define it is a difficult task.'

How has that task been approached by the courts in relation to involuntary manslaughter?

These questions require a detailed analysis of the *mens rea* of murder and involuntary manslaughter respectively. A discussion of both topics and an outline of the essentials which an examiner would expect to see in answer to questions such as these will be found in chapter 9 of this book.

Problem Questions and Mens Rea

In many problem questions, *mens rea*, if not the main issue, will be a subsidiary issue. Because of the nature of problem questions you will be required to discuss the *mens rea* of one or more offences. Your ability to recognise whether they are specific/ulterior-intent, basic-intent or negligence offences will be evident to the examiner without the degree of description that might be expected in an essay-type discussion.

Below are two samples of problem-type questions which, among other things, require a high degree of discussion of *mens rea*.

(1) Jack breaks into Anthea's flat, where she is asleep, intending to steal from the gas meter. In breaking open the gas meter Jack damages a gas pipe causing gas to escape. He is uncertain whether or not North Sea Gas is toxic if inhaled but, on hearing a noise, he panics and runs away. Unbeknown to Jack, Anthea has a habit of lighting up her first cigarette each morning before getting out of bed. Her attempt to do so that morning results in an explosion which kills her.

Discuss the possible criminal charges confronting Jack.

In so far as *mens rea* is concerned an examiner would expect you to have considered Jack's state of mind in relation to the requirements of various possible offences. It would make sense to start by considering the most serious offence that might be charged, i.e., murder.

The facts bear a marked similarity to those of the case of *R* v *Cunningham* [1957] 2 QB 396. However, there are differences and whether or not these are material differences is something about which you would be expected to argue and express your opinion.

The central issue in deciding whether or not there is sufficient *mens rea* for murder is whether Jack can be proved to have intended either in the sense that he aimed to bring about (direct intent) or knew it was inevitable that death or serious harm would result to Anthea or whether he foresaw to some degree that either was possible or likely. The leading authority, *R* v *Moloney* [1985] AC 905 as explained in *R* v *Hancock* [1986] AC 455 and *R* v *Nedrick* [1986] 1 WLR 1025, must of course, be cited and *R* v *Woollin* [1997] 1 Cr App R 97 if there is evidence to be considered by the jury in addition to the accused's actions and their effects.

In passing, reference could be made to *Hyam* v *DPP* [1975] AC 55 to show that foresight of any other degree of probability less than the inevitable while once thought to be sufficient to constitute intention in relation to the offence of murder, is no longer so in light of *Moloney* as amended by *Nedrick* and reiterated by the Court of Appeal in *R* v *Scalley* [1995] Crim LR 504.

On the facts you might conclude that the requisite intention for murder cannot be proved but that Jack is reckless in the *Cunningham* sense (cite *R* v *Miller* [1983] 2 AC 161) and therefore has sufficient *mens rea* for any appropriate basic-intent offence and in particular manslaughter. Even if you conclude that he was not reckless but negligent, provided his negligence is considered 'gross' (cite *R* v *Bateman* (1925) 19 Cr App R 8, *R* v *Finney* (1874) 12 Cox CC 625 and especially *R* v *Sulman*, *R* v *Prentice* and *R* v *Adomako* [1994] 3 WLR 288) he will have sufficient *mens rea* to be convicted of manslaughter.

The opening sentence of the question, by mentioning Jack's intention to steal, permits you to discuss briefly the general irrelevance of motive and the distinction between it and intention (citing, e.g., *R* v *Steane* [1947] KB 997 and/or *Chandler* v *DPP* [1964] AC 763). You would gain marks, however, by indicating that a possible charge (apart from murder or manslaughter) is burglary contrary to s. 9 of the Theft Act 1968 and in that instance proof of Jack's intention to steal from inside the building would be vital to gain a conviction because that particular form of burglary (see chapter 10) requires that the accused enters a building as a trespasser with the (ulterior intent) to damage, rape or steal or to inflict grievous bodily harm upon someone.

Finally the perceptive candidate would recognise in the facts the scope for a mention of *R* v *Miller* [1983] 2 AC 161. Jack's running away, his omission to warn of, or rectify, the consequences of his conduct once he is aware of the possible danger he has created, since *Miller*, will constitute both the *actus reus* and *mens rea* of an offence, in this instance either manslaughter or criminal damage.

Also there may be scope to mention defences. Remember to sum up in a brief final paragraph what, in your opinion, will be the likely prospects for Jack.

(2)   Luke taught a small group of extremists, which included Mark and John, how to make small bombs which were to be used in any way necessary to further their cause. Some time later, Mark planted a bomb in a large department store while John waited outside with a get-away car. Mark warned the people in the store that the bomb would explode in five minutes, and everyone left the store in good time except for one unfortunate shopper, who was stone deaf, and did not hear or notice what was going on, and who was killed in the explosion. Mark and John are appalled by what has happened as they only meant to air their grievances and did not intend to harm anyone, but Luke, who has been in prison for some months as a result of his activities, is delighted and says it is time the group developed 'teeth'.

Discuss the criminal liability of Luke, Mark and John for the shopper's death.

In your answer to this problem note that you must limit your discussion to liability for the shopper's death. That still permits you to play 'spot the offences' or in other words to identify the potential offences with which Luke, Mark and John might be charged in relation to the shopper's death. An examiner would expect to see a recognition of incitement, conspiracy, murder, manslaughter and/or being a party to murder or manslaughter. In so far as the first two offences are concerned the only *mens rea* that could be proved would be in relation to inciting or conspiring to cause damage or the possession or use of explosives and not the death or serious injury of the shopper. There is no evidence that Luke incited or that all three of them conspired with the intention to kill (s. 1 of the Criminal Law Act 1977 and cases like *Churchill* v *Walton* [1967] 2 AC 224 could be mentioned).

In relation to murder the only prescribed *mens rea* will be proof of intention (having death or serious injury as your deliberate aim) or in some instances foresight or knowledge that the inevitable consequence of your conduct will be death or serious injury. The House of Lords' decisions in *R* v *Moloney* [1985] AC 905 and *R* v *Hancock* [1986] AC 445 and the Court of Appeal's opinion in *R* v *Nedrick* [1986] 1 WLR 1025 (which has amended the *ratio* or model direction to the jury in *Moloney*), must be cited and some comment could be made on the wider but discredited view of foresight of a high probability of death or grievous bodily harm as *mens rea* for murder as expressed in *Hyam* v *DPP* [1975] AC 55. You must express an opinion on whether or not in light of these cases any of the accused would have sufficient *mens rea* for a murder conviction.

Luke may have been reckless in the *Cunningham* sense; that is not sufficient *mens rea* for murder but it would make him liable for manslaughter. You would need to discuss whether or not Mark and John have been reckless in the *Cunningham* sense or in the *Caldwell* sense or grossly negligent in light of the definition in *R* v *Bateman* (1925) 19 Cr App R 8, *R* v *Finney* (1874) 12 Cox CC 625, *R* v *Seymour* [1983] 2 AC 493 and especially considering *R* v *Sulman*; *R* v *Prentice*; *R* v *Adomako*; *R* v *Holloway* [1993] 3 WLR 927 and [1995] AC 171, in which case they too will be guilty of manslaughter. You would need to consider whether or not Mark and John would be liable for the death if they were simply negligent or if they were not negligent at all, the death being pure accident or misadventure.

Other Issues

Other *mens rea* issues that are likely to arise in problem questions may involve the questions whether or not:

(a)   The accused's *mens rea* coincides with the *actus reus* (i.e., the issue in *Thabo-Meli* v *R* [1954] 1 WLR 228 and *Fagan* v *Metropolitan Police Commissioner* [1969] 1 QB 439).

(b)   The *mens rea* which does coincide with an *actus reus* relates to the same offence (i.e., the issue in *R* v *Pembliton* (1874) 12 Cox CC 607 and *R* v *Latimer* (1886) 17 QBD 359).

(c)   The accused's *mens rea* can be transferred so as to make him liable (e.g., where he intends to kill Y, but by mistake or by chance he kills X).

You should look out for each or all of these, not as the main issue or issues but rather as issues subsidiary to the main question of the accused's state of mind.

CONCLUSION

To sum up:

(a)   Serious crimes requiring proof of specific/ulterior intent can be satisfied by proof of intention and in very rare instances a properly directed jury may infer intention from proof of foresight that the consequence was a virtually certain (or overwhelmingly probable) consequence of the accused's conduct (see *R* v *Moloney* [1985] AC 905, *R* v *Hancock* [1986] AC 455, *R* v *Nedrick* [1986] 1 WLR 1025 and *R* v *Woollin* [1997] 1 Cr App R 97).

(b)   Crimes of basic intent require proof of intention or recklessness.

(c)   The crime of manslaughter at common law requires proof at least of gross negligence but proof of recklessness or intention clearly will suffice.

(d)   Some statutory offences require proof of simple negligence; obviously proof of any of the above states of mind (gross negligence, recklessness or intention) would also suffice.

(e)   Finally crimes of strict or absolute liability require proof of *actus reus* only or *mens rea* (intention, recklessness or possibly negligence) in relation to only part of the *actus reus*. See chapter 5.

It can be said without exaggeration that *mens rea* is an absolutely vital topic which must be mastered by you. This necessitates a clear understanding of the distinction between:

(a)   mere voluntariness and those 'mental' states (intention, recklessness and negligence) which the law recognises as constituting *mens rea* or blameworthiness,

(b)   motive and those mental states of awareness recognised as constituting *mens rea*, and

(c)   what the law requires to be proved to constitute sufficient *mens rea* first for crimes of specific intent, secondly for crimes of basic intent and thirdly for crimes of negligence.

In addition you must be able to discuss how the *mens rea* of each type is to be proved (i.e., whether by a subjective or an objective means).

FURTHER READING

Mens Rea

Ashworth, A., 'Belief, Intent and Criminal Liability' in Ecklar and Bell, *Oxford Essays in Jurisprudence* (1987).
Buxton, R., 'Some Simple Thoughts on Intention' [1988] Crim LR 484.
Buzzard, J. H., 'Intent' [1978] Crim LR 5.
Duff, R., 'The Politics of Intention: A Response to Norrie' [1990] Crim LR 637.
Horder, J., 'Intention in the Criminal Law — A Rejoinder' (1995) 58 MLR 678.
Horder, J., 'Two Histories and Four Hidden Principles of *Mens Rea*' (1997) 113 LQR 95.
Lacey, N., 'In(de)terminable Intentions' (1995) 58 MLR 692.
Law Commission Working Paper No. 31: Codification of the Criminal Law: General Principles, The Mental Element in Crime (1970).
Law Commission, 'The Mental Element in Crime' (Law Comm No. 89).
Norrie, A., 'Oblique Intention and Legal Politics' [1989] Crim LR 793.
Simester, A. P., and Chan, W., 'Intention Thus Far' [1997] Crim LR 704.
Smith, J. C., 'Intent — A Reply' [1978] Crim LR 14.
Smith, J.C., 'A Note on Intention' [1990] Crim LR 85.
Williams, G., 'Oblique Intention' (1987) 46 CLJ 417.

Motive

Sullivan, G., 'Bad Thoughts and Bad Acts' [1990] Crim LR 559.

Coincidence

Horder, J., 'A Critique of the Correspondence Principle in Criminal Law' [1995] Crim LR 759.
Marston, G., 'Contemporaneity of Act and Intention in Crimes' (1970) 86 LQR 208.
White, A. R., 'The Identity and Time of the *Actus Reus*' [1977] Crim LR 148.

Recklessness

Brownlee, I. D., and Seneviratne, M., 'Killing with Cars after *Adomako*: Time for Some Alternatives' [1995] Crim LR 389.
Elliott, D. W., 'Endangering Life by Destroying or Damaging Property' [1997] Crim LR 382.
Leigh, L. H., 'Liability for Inadvertence' (1995) 58 MLR 459.
Pain, J., 'The New Recklessness' (1983) 2 CLLR 89.
Syrota, G., 'A Radical Change in the Law of Recklessness' [1982] Crim LR 497.
Williams, G., 'Divergent Interpretations of Recklessness' (1982) 132 NLJ 289.
Williams, G., 'The Problem of Reckless Attempt' [1983] Crim LR 365.

Transferred Malice

Seneviratne, M., 'Pre-natal Injury and Transferred Malice: The Invented Other' (1996) 59 MLR 884.

5 STRICT LIABILITY

NATURE OF STRICT LIABILITY

Definition of Strict Liability Offences

The nature of strict liability offences is that they are crimes which do not require any *mens rea* (see chapter 4) with regard to at least one element of their *actus reus*, i.e., the conduct, consequences and/or circumstances of the offence (see chapter 3).

Types of Strict Liability Offence

The clearest and most extreme examples of strict liability offences are those constituted entirely by a 'state of affairs' and sometimes known as absolute liability offences (see *R* v *Larsonneur* (1933) 24 Cr App R 74; *Winzar* v *Chief Constable of Kent, The Times*, 28 March 1983. In such offences it is sufficient that an accused is found to be within the terms of the crime, it is no defence that he is within the terms of the offence involuntarily or as a result of an inevitable accident, because no mental element is required on the part of the accused. Such crimes are by no means the prime example or norm of strict liability offences, which generally require a considerable mental element. A good example is the case of *R* v *Prince* (1875) LR 2 CCR 154 where the accused was charged with having unlawfully taken an unmarried girl under the age of 16 out of the possession of her father and against the latter's will (contrary to Offences against the Person Act 1861, s. 55; see now Sexual Offences Act 1956, s. 20). The court in effect determined that this offence was one of strict liability, for the circumstance of the age of the girl did not require any mental element on the part of the accused. It was irrelevant that the accused honestly and reasonably believed that the girl was over 16 years of age. However, the other elements of the offence, e.g., that the girl had a father and the intention to take the girl out of her father's possession did require *mens rea* (see *R* v *Tegerdine* (1982) 75 Cr App R 298). *Prince* illustrates the usual form of strict liability offence.

It is frequently stated that liability is strict not absolute. Apart from the fact that usually *mens rea* as to only one element of the offence is not required to be proved, this means no more than the fact that certain generally available defences are usually applicable to offences of strict liability. Thus the fact that an accused is an involuntary agent, or an automaton, is suffering from insanity or is subjected to duress should generally provide defences even to offences of strict liability (see chapter 8 for a consideration of these defences), but not necessarily if the offence is deemed one of absolute liability. The confusing use of the terms 'strict' and 'absolute' could be controlled if the approach of Dickson J in the Canadian case *R* v *City of Sault Ste Marie* (1978) 85 DLR (3d) 161 (referred to below) was accepted. The learned judge said that offences should fall into one of three categories. The first category would contain offences in which *mens rea* must be proved. The second would contain strict liability offences in which there is no need for the prosecution to prove the existence of *mens rea* — once his responsibility for the prohibited act has been proved the accused is presumed liable unless he proves either that he reasonably believed in a mistake of fact which, if true, would render the act or omission innocent, or that he took all reasonable steps to avoid its occurrence or that some other defence is available to him. The third category would contain offences of absolute liability where once it is proved that he did the prohibited act nothing the accused says or does will free him from liability (i.e., no defence whatsoever would be available to him).

Strict Liability, Possession and Awareness

An accused's state of mind can constitute a defence even in relation to offences which do not require *mens rea* because certain elements of the *actus reus* of those offences may require a mental element to constitute them. The clearest example is to be found in the offence of unlawful possession of a controlled drug contrary to Misuse of Drugs Act 1971, s. 5(2). An accused may not 'possess' a controlled drug unless he is aware of its existence. Thus a controlled drug is not 'possessed' by an individual, e.g., where it has been slipped unknown into his pocket by another, see *Lockyer* v *Gibb* [1967] 2 QB 243 per Lord Parker CJ and Lord Pearce in *Warner* v *Metropolitan Police Commissioner* [1969] 2 AC 256 at p. 305. However, if an accused is aware of the existence of a substance (which is in his control), although he is mistaken about its quality, he will be regarded as being in possession of it for the purposes of s. 5(2). In *Warner* it was accepted that though a mistake about the quality of a substance would not preclude a person from being found to possess it even though it was a controlled drug if he was aware of its existence, a mistake about its nature would. In *R v McNamara* (1988) 87 Cr App R 246, the Court of Appeal determined that where an accused was found in possession of a box containing unlawful drugs, though believing the box contained pornographic videos, it was for the prosecution to show: (a) that the accused had the box in his control; (b) that the accused knew it contained something; (c) that the box contained unlawful drugs. Once these three matters had been established the accused bore the burden of establishing the defence afforded by Misuse of Drugs Act 1971, s. 28(3). The accused needed to show that he had no right or opportunity to open and inspect the contents of the box, or reason to doubt the legitimacy of its contents, and that he believed the contents were different in kind and not merely in quality from what they were. There is a limitation to this line of authority. In relation to the offence of possessing a firearm or carrying a firearm in a public place (Firearms Act 1968, ss. 1 and 19) the Court of Appeal in *R v Vann and Davis* [1996] Crim LR 52 confirmed that they are 'absolute' offences and knowledge or lack of knowledge, as to whether the article possessed or carried was a gun was irrelevant provided the accused knew that he or she was carrying or had in their possession something. Apart from enquiring into the accused's state of knowledge as to whether anything was possessed, no *mens rea* is required. In relation to firearms, *R v Walter* [1991] Crim LR 381 makes it clear that the *Warner/McNamara* 'halfway house' (i.e., that the accused was unaware of the *nature* of the article held, or of the contents of the container, and had no reasonable opportunity to discover what it was) does not apply. See also *R v Steele* [1993] Crim LR 298 and *R v Harrison* [1996] 1 Cr App R 138. In the former case the accused was given a holdall not knowing it contained a gun and in the latter the accused took a gun from a co-accused in the course of a robbery. The fact that the bag contained the gun in *Steele* and the gun contained a bullet in *Harrison*, unbeknown to each recipient, made them each automatically liable under ss. 1 and 19 respectively. Similarly, in the case of *R v Bradish* [1990] 2 WLR 223, which concerned possession by the accused of a prohibited weapon (a CS gas canister), the court determined that the canister itself was a prohibited weapon under the Firearms Act 1968, s. 5(1)(b), and was not to be regarded as merely the container of such a weapon. In this circumstance the reasoning in *Warner* and *R v McNamara* was inappropriate. The court therefore rejected suggestions that a rifle is, for example, a simple container for a bullet.

However, given that Lord Pearce in *Warner* considered that a belief that one 'possessed' sweets which were in fact controlled drugs would not constitute a mistake about the nature of the objects but only about their quality it cannot be said the defence is particularly wide. Since *R* v *Marriott* [1971] 1 All ER 595; *Searle* v *Randolph* [1972] Crim LR 779 and *R* v *Boyesen* [1982] AC 768 (as applied in *R* v *Lewis* (1988) 87 Cr App R 270) it has been accepted that a person may 'possess' a controlled drug even though the quantity concerned is not capable of being used if it amounts to something and an accused is aware of its existence. The charge under the Misuse of Drugs Act 1971, s. 5, is 'possessing' not 'using'. According to *Bocking* v *Roberts* [1973] 3 All ER 932 the quantity is immaterial (the maxim *de minimis non curat lex* does not apply to being in possession of a dangerous drug without authority) and so in *R* v *Boyesen* it was held that a person is guilty if he has in his possession any quantity of a controlled drug, however minute, that is visible, tangible or measurable, provided it amounts to something and the accused is aware of its existence. Both *R* v *Boyesen* and *R* v *Colyer* [1974] Crim LR 243 confirm that if the quantity of a controlled drug is so minute that the accused's knowledge of its existence could not be proved then he could not be proved to be in possession. In short, the more minute the quantity the more difficult it is for the prosecution to prove that the accused knew he had it. However, the fact that an accused may have forgotten about the presence of a controlled drug (e.g., where he put it in his wallet and forgot about it) is no defence. Possession does not, according to *R* v *Martindale* [1986] 1 WLR 1042, depend on the alleged possessor's powers of memory: if he put an article into his wallet and then into his pocket knowing what it was then he remained in possession of it even though his memory of its presence faded or disappeared altogether. See also *R* v *McCalla* (1988) 87 Cr App R 372.

It is possible that an examiner might test your knowledge of leading cases in this area, in particular the curious anomaly which arose in *Warner's* case with regard to drugs in a container. To reiterate, the effect of that case and of *R* v *McNamara* is that, prima facie, if an accused has physical possession of a container and is aware of the fact that it has contents then he 'possesses' those contents. This remains so even when the accused has not examined the contents but he has reason to suspect the container contains controlled drugs and/or he has a legal right and opportunity to examine the contents. If either or both situations can be established then an accused will be regarded as possessing those contents, irrespective of whether he has examined the contents or not. Furthermore where an accused is aware of the contents of a container but is merely mistaken about their or its quality he will possess those contents but if he is mistaken about the nature of the contents and has no legal right or opportunity to examine them he will (in the absence of any suspicious circumstances) be deemed not to be in 'possession' of the contents if they are found to be controlled drugs. Remember, however, that this argument does not apply to the offences of possession of a firearm, or the carrying in a public place of a loaded firearm as discussed above.

Strict Liability Offences at Common Law

The topic of strict liability can also be a vehicle for discussing the role of the judiciary. Although strict liability offences are almost exclusively creatures of statute, they do exist at common law. Thus, contempt of court (as modified by the Contempt of Court Act 1981), public nuisance and criminal libel (as modified by the Libel Act 1843) are examples of common law (judge-created) strict liability offences, though it has been argued that the latter two offences are more realistically to be considered as offences of vicarious liability (see chapter 6). But clearly the courts have not given up the power to create strict liability offences at common law. In the case of *Whitehouse* v *Lemon* [1979] AC 617 the House of Lords (notwithstanding the protestations of the majority of their lordships to the contrary) created to all intents and purposes an offence of strict liability with regard to the crime of blasphemous libel by maintaining that *Lemon* only had to be shown to have known that he was publishing something and not that he knew it to be blasphemous. This view was unanimously adopted by three judges sitting on the Queen's Bench Divisional Court in maintaining that Salman Rushdie's *Satanic Verses* could not be charged as blasphemous libel because that offence was confined to Christianity (see *R* v *Bow Street Magistrates' Court, ex parte Choudhury* [1990] Crim LR 711).

Yet another example of judicial creation of strict liability at common law is shown in *R* v *Gibson* [1990] 2 QB 619 where, in relation to the offence of conspiracy to outrage public decency (by displaying 'foetus earnings'), it was held that the prosecution did not have to prove any intention to outrage or recklessness as to whether or not outrage might occur.

The Rationale of Strict Liability

Sometimes an essay question in an examination may seek to test your opinion about the basis or the rationale of strict liability. This was succinctly expressed in the Canadian case of *R* v *City of Sault Ste Marie* (1978) 85 DLR (3d) 161 at p. 171 per Dickson J where he maintained that the justification for the imposition of strict liability is that individuals are thereby exhorted to exercise constantly higher standards of care to ensure that such offences are not committed. In this way individuals who undertake activities which are dangerous to the public are encouraged to regulate their affairs for they know that ignorance or mistake or accident will not excuse them.

The second principal justification is evidential and administrative. Many strict liability offences are part of an integrated system that helps regulate the many commercial, social and leisure activities of a modern, complex society. Many prosecutions for such offences are carried out by The Crown Prosecution Service and local authority officials. The number of such prosecutions is such that the administrative burden would be impossible if *mens rea* needed to be established in every case in respect of every element of the *actus reus*. The third justification is substantive. Lord Diplock in *Lemon* said: 'the usual justification ... is the threat that the *actus reus* of the offence poses to public health, public safety, public morals or public order'.

These arguments fail to impress many academics who maintain the first proposition remains unproven and the second is contradicted by practice. Indeed many would maintain that making people strictly liable despite the care they have taken to comply with the law is counterproductive. It leads to the attitude 'Why should we bother to take care if we are to be equally liable with others who have taken no care at all?' Nevertheless they are believed, by those who administer the law, to be valid.

The existence of strict liability cannot be denied. You must be prepared to discuss in an examination when it might be held to apply as well as being able to argue whether or not it should apply in a given situation or in any situation at all.

MATTERS USED TO DETERMINE WHETHER OFFENCES ARE ONES OF STRICT LIABILITY

It is crucial to be able to determine whether a statutory offence is one of strict liability. The courts have determined the issue by reference to both the wording of the statutory provision and factors external to the statute.

The Statutory Interpretation Approach

Certain words when contained in a statute are thought apt to indicate that *mens rea* must be proved as to all the elements of the *actus reus*. The following are examples:

(a)   'Knowingly': this generally imports *mens rea* (see *Sherras* v *De Rutzen* [1895] 1 QB 918).

(b)   'Wilfully': there is considerable judicial disagreement with regard to this term. When used in the Children and Young Persons Act 1933, s. 1, the term imports *mens rea* as to all the external elements of the offence (see *R* v *Sheppard* (1981) 72 Cr App R 82). However, in the case of the offence of wilful obstruction of a police officer contrary to the Police Act 1964, s. 51(3), the authorities, though divided, appear to be in favour of construing the offence as one of strict liability. 'Wilful' in this statute would appear to be no more than a requirement for an accused to act positively, i.e., consciously. If that conduct then gives rise objectively to a factual obstruction of a police officer the offence is committed (see *Rice* v *Connolly* [1966] 2 QB 414 and *Lewis* v *Cox* [1985] QB 509).

(c) 'Malicious': this will almost always indicate an offence as one requiring *mens rea* (see *R* v *Vickers* [1957] 2 QB 664).

(d) 'Permitting': this word generally imports *mens rea* as to all the elements of the *actus reus* (see *James & Son Ltd* v *Smee* [1955] 1 QB 78).

(e) 'Using': this has been interpreted as creating an offence of strict liability (see *Green* v *Burnett* [1955] 1 QB 78), whereas the words 'knowingly using' require proof that the accused had actual knowledge that the premises in question were being used in the prohibited manner (see *Westminster County Council* v *Croyalgrange* [1986] 1 WLR 674).

Nevertheless the exclusion of such words from a penal section of a statute will not necessarily lead to a conclusion that the offence does not require *mens rea* as to all its external elements. In *Roper* v *Taylor's Central Garages (Exeter) Ltd* [1951] 2 TLR 284 at p. 288 Devlin J expressed the opinion that using the word 'knowingly' was only saying expressly what should normally be implied. In his lordship's view the general need for *mens rea* in a statutory offence was normally to be implied, irrespective of the presence or absence of words such as 'knowingly'. This view is apparently supported by the earlier case of *Sherras* v *De Rutzen* [1895] 1 QB 918. Nevertheless the judiciary have accepted that a statutory offence may be interpreted as imposing strict liability where there is an absence of words which generally import *mens rea* (see *Cundy* v *Le Cocq* (1884) 13 QBD 207). It can be said that there is no clear principle of statutory interpretation which will indicate whether a given statutory offence is or is not one of strict liability.

Clearly, as with any other problem of construing or interpreting a piece of legislation, counsel will try to convince the court of Parliament's intention by argument based on the legislative history, wording of similar statutes, title to the Act etc. Since the decision in *Pepper* v *Hart* [1992] 3 WLR 1003 reference may now be made to *Hansard* (the record of speeches in Parliament) to try to ascertain that intent or purpose.

External Factors

The lives of law students, lecturers and lawyers would be easier if, when Parliament absolutely forbids something to be done, it also made it absolutely clear that if it is done the offender will be liable to a penalty whether or not he has any *mens rea*. No less an authority than Lord Devlin stated in his book *Samples of Lawmaking* (1971):

> The fact is that Parliament has no intention of troubling itself about *mens rea* ... All that Parliament would have to do would be to use express words that left no room for inclination. One is driven to the conclusion that the reason why Parliament has never done that is that it prefers to leave the point to the judges and does not want to legislate about it.

A common form of assessment or examination question will seek to ascertain whether or not you are aware of the ways in which the judiciary generally seek to justify the imposition of strict liability by reference to matters external to the words of a statute or *Hansard* and the lack of any clear principles on which this process takes place. The following examples though were mentioned by Wright J in *Sherras* v *De Rutzen* [1895] 1 QB 918:

(a)   *Quasi-criminal offences.* The fact that the offence seeks to prohibit conduct which is not 'criminal in any real sense' (i.e., quasi-criminal), but seeks to regulate an activity through penal sanction, has been thought a sufficient ground to impose strict liability (see *Sherras* v *De Rutzen* [1895] 1 QB 918). Examples include the sale of food containing extraneous matter, see Food Act 1984, s. 2 (*Smedleys Ltd* v *Breed* [1974] AC 839), and the unsupervised sale of drugs (*Pharmaceutical Society of Great Britain* v *Logan* [1982] Crim LR 443 and *Pharmaceutical Society of Great Britain* v *Storkwain Ltd* [1986] 1 WLR 903).

(b)   *Public nuisance.* Offences which seek to regulate conduct which may give rise to a public nuisance (e.g., pollution) are frequently interpreted as being offences of strict liability (see the Rivers (Prevention of Pollution) Act 1955, s. 2(1); the Control of Pollution Act 1974, ss. 32 and 33 (repealed by the Water Act 1989, sch. 27); *Alphacell Ltd* v *Woodward* [1972] AC 824 and *F.J.H. Wrothwell Ltd* v *Yorkshire Water Authority* [1984] Crim LR 43).

Other factors have been highlighted in more recent judgments, for example:

(a)   *Grave social danger.* Today wherever a statute seeks to prohibit by penal sanction an activity which if uncontrolled may give rise to a grave social danger the courts may be willing to declare such an offence to be one of strict liability (see *Gammon (Hong Kong) Ltd* v *Attorney-General for Hong Kong* [1985] AC 1). Examples of such offences have been noted above and include the use of defective and dangerous motor vehicles, the possession of firearms (see *R* v *Bradish* [1990] 2 WLR 223, *R* v *Waller* [1991] Crim LR 381, *R* v *Vann and Davis* [1996] Crim LR 52 and *R* v *Harrison* [1996] 1 Cr App R 138), possession of controlled drugs (see *Warner* v *Metropolitan Police Commissioner* [1969] 2 AC 256) and the pollution of the environment.

Against the argument of grave social danger must be balanced the fundamental liberties, ideals and traditions of English common law.

(b)   *Presumption against the imposition of strict liability.* In *Sweet* v *Parsley* [1970] AC 132 a case concerning the offence of being involved in the management of premises which are used for the purpose of smoking cannabis (contrary to the Dangerous Drugs Act 1965, s. 5(b) which has now been superseded by Misuse of Drugs Act 1971, s. 8) the House of Lords determined that this offence was one requiring *mens rea* as to all its external elements. Their lordships were of the opinion that Parliament did not generally intend to create offences of strict liability in relation to crimes which were serious and which had grave social and penal consequences for an accused on conviction. This principle has been applied in later cases such as *R v Pheeko* [1981] 3 All ER 84 but may be displaced if the offence is concerned with an issue of public concern which warrants the imposition of strict liability (see *Gammon (Hong Kong) Ltd v Attorney-General for Hong Kong* [1985] AC 1). *Sweet v Parsley* lays down a presumption against construing a penal statute as being one of strict liability where the offence may have grave social or penal consequences for an accused if convicted, nevertheless it is only a presumption and apparently a court may paradoxically use the fact of the gravity of the offence, insofar as the safety of the general public is concerned, to impose strict liability. *Warner v Metropolitan Police Commissioner* [1969] 2 AC 256 is not therefore necessarily in conflict with *Sweet v Parsley*. What the judges perceive to be the graver social consequence will be the deciding factor.

(c) *Imposition of an impossible duty.* The courts will sometimes ask themselves whether construing an offence as one of strict liability will enhance or assist the enforcement of that particular offence. This means that if strict liability cannot exhort or encourage an accused in a particular instance to act to a higher standard of care or to avoid the bringing about of the *actus reus* of an offence, this may indicate that the offence was not intended to be one of strict liability. In support of this see *Lim Chin Aik v R* [1963] 1 All ER 223. In *Harding v Price* [1948] 1 KB 695, the accused was charged with failing to report an accident involving his motor vehicle. The definition of the offence did not require any *mens rea* to be proved. His argument that this should not be treated as a strict liability offence turned on the fact that he was driving a traction engine and did not realise that a collision had occurred because of the noise made by his vehicle. Lord Goddard said: 'If the duty be to report, he cannot report something of which he has no knowledge ... any other view could lead to calling on a man to do the impossible'. Note, particularly, Lord Evershed's words in *Lim Chin Aik*: 'It is not enough ... merely to label the statute as one dealing with a grave social danger [in that case, illegal entry into Singapore] and from that to infer that strict liability was intended. It is pertinent also to inquire whether putting defendants under strict liability will assist in the enforcement of the regulations ...' [which it would not, in this instance, because the banning or prohibition order excluding the accused from Singapore has not been notified to him or published]. Of course, if it is thought that strict liability would encourage vigilance and care on the part of an accused and thus enhance the enforcement of an offence this may be a cogent reason for construing it as such an offence (see *Gammon (Hong Kong) Ltd v Attorney-General for Hong Kong* [1985] AC 1).

Summary

The above factors are used by the judiciary in their interpretation of penal statutes. They show no consistency or coherence and are applied by the judges as they see fit, balancing the freedom of the individual with what they conceive to be the dangers to society from the commission by individuals of various offences. Whichever of these latter issues predominate may determine which factors are used by the judges to aid their interpretation of a given penal statute directing it towards or away from strict liability. It is precisely in this situation that the forensic skill of and the cogency and potency of counsel's argument to the court may tip the decision of the judges one way or the other. The same skills can earn a good assessment or examination mark.

Mitigation of Statutory Strict Liability Offences

Often a statute in creating a strict liability offence will also provide that an honest and reasonable belief in facts which if true would negate the external elements of the offence (even those elements for which strict liability is imposed) will provide a defence. Such defences amount to a negation of the fact of *mens rea* and establish that the accused was not negligent. These defences collectively are sometimes called 'no-negligence' defences. An example is the Misuse of Drugs Act 1971, s. 28(2), which provides that it is a defence for an accused to establish that, notwithstanding his possession of a controlled drug (itself an offence contrary to s. 5(2) of that Act), he neither knew of, nor suspected nor had reason to supect the existence of some fact alleged by the prosecution which it is necessary for the prosecution to prove if he is to be convicted of the offence charged.

Other strict liability offences provide for particular types of defences tailored for that particular crime. A discussion of numerous examples would serve little purpose; however, such a defence is provided by the Food Safety Act 1990, ss. 20 and 21, which determine that the accused may escape strict liability if he can establish that the contravention resulted from the act or default of a third party and that the accused acted with all due diligence in complying with the Act. There are similar examples of this type of defence in the Trades Description Act 1968, s. 24(1) (discussed in *Tesco Supermarkets Ltd v Nattrass* [1972] AC 153 and *Texas Homecare v Stockport BC* [1987] Crim LR 54) and in the Consumer Credit Act 1987, s. 39. Where the accused is a company charged with a strict offence difficult issues arise as to whether or not it will be deprived of the defence of having taken all reasonable precautions (e.g., under the Health and Safety at Work etc. Act 1974, s. 2) if its most junior employee is at fault or failed to take reasonable precautions in the course of his employment. See *Austin Rover Group Ltd v H.M. Inspectorate*

[1990] 1 AC 619, *R* v *British Steel plc* [1995] 1 WLR 1356, *R* v *Associated Octel Ltd* [1997] Crim LR 355 and *R* v *Gateway Foodmarkets Ltd* [1997] Crim LR 512.

It is a moot point what effect the provision of 'no-negligence' or due diligence defences has on such offences. The current view is that those defences do not deprive such offences of their strict liability tag but merely mitigate their rigour in application, i.e., they are strict unless the 'proviso' is satisfied.

Possible Mitigation of Strict Liability at Common Law

In the case of *Sweet* v *Parsley* [1970] AC 132 the House of Lords suggested a set of common law alternatives to the simple imposition of strict liability. These have been viewed as being of the following nature:

(a) Lord Reid (at p. 150) was of the opinion that in appropriate cases the prosecution would have the burden of establishing that the accused had been grossly negligent with regard to the *actus reus* of an offence. This would be necessary in order to affix criminal responsibility to the accused in relation to offences which would otherwise be ones of strict liability.

(b) That the burden of disproving *mens rea* should be upon the accused, i.e., he must show that he lacked intention, awareness or recklessness with regard to the consequences or circumstances of an offence (per Lord Reid at p. 150). This suggestion has found earlier judicial favour in the case of *Harding* v *Price* [1948] 1 KB 695 at p. 704 per Singleton J, and Day J in *Sherras* v *De Rutzen* [1895] 1 QB 918 at p. 921 (see also *Kirkland* v *Robinson* [1987] Crim LR 643).

(c) Lord Diplock in *Sweet* v *Parsley*, following his interpretation of the Australian case of *Proudman* v *Dayman* (1941) 67 CLR 536, considered that it would be sufficient, assuming the prosecution had established the fact of the *actus reus* of an offence, for the accused to leave as a fit and proper issue for the jury to consider that he lacked *mens rea* and that he was not negligent. This was formulated in terms of an accused possessing 'an honest and reasonable belief in a state of facts which if they existed would make the accused's act innocent'. The accused would thus bear an evidential burden (see Murphy, *A Practical Approach to Evidence*) in establishing this defence which would only be negated by the prosecution by contrary evidence which satisfied the jury beyond reasonable doubt. This was similar to the suggestion which Lord Pearce and Lord Reid proposed. The difference being that in their lordships' view the accused bore not only the evidential but the legal burden in establishing the fact that he lacked *mens rea* and that he was not negligent. This would have to be established by the accused on a balance of probabilities (see Murphy, *A Practical Approach to Evidence*). These latter suggestions would, if applied generally, introduce by way of the common law the various no-negligence defences which are recognised in certain statutory offences of strict liability, although it is the suggestion proposed by Lord Pearce and Lord Reid which most nearly accords with usual statutory practice. None of these suggestions has been generally implemented largely because of the traditional view strongly cherished in English law and embodied in cases like *Woolmington* v *DPP* [1935] AC 462, that in general the prosecution *must prove* beyond reasonable doubt the essential elements of an offence.

PLANNING YOUR REVISION

Strict liability tends to be treated as a self-contained subject by examiners. Because of that and because of the element of policy in it you could elect not to include it in your revision programme. If that is the case you risk not being able to answer a question on your examination paper, but generally no more than that. If you do decide to revise this topic you should seek to clarify the following matters in your mind:

(a) The full nature and consequences of an offence being held to be one of strict liability.

(b) The effect and nature of the statutory defences available to certain statutory strict liability offences.

(c) An outline knowledge of a sample of the leading authorities which have interpreted the effect of certain words (e.g., knowingly, wilfully) in statutory offences as either negating or endorsing strict liability.

You should be able to explain the inconsistencies of statutory interpretation in this area of the criminal law illustrated by the authorities which reflect shifting judicial policy. Always be aware of the mechanisms of judicial interpretation either by the differing interpretations that may be given to a word in different statutory offences or the judicial policy of interpreting such words as not applying to all the external elements of an offence.

(d) The central core for you to master in the consideration of strict liability in statutory offences are the factors, external to the words of a statute, which are used by the courts in interpreting the statute as one of strict liability or as requiring *mens rea* as to all its external elements.

The factors in favour of imposing strict liability are:

(i)   that the offence is quasi-criminal;

(ii)   that the offence relates to the prevention of a public nuisance;

(iii) that the offence is one which seeks to prevent the occurrence of a grave social danger;

(iv)   that the imposition of strict liability will encourage the enforcement of the offence.

Those factors should be contrasted with the matters which the courts have construed as militating against construing an offence as one of strict liability. These factors are:

(a) That the offence is of such a nature that it will have very serious social and penal consequences for an accused if convicted.
(b) That the imposition of strict liability will not encourage or enhance the enforcement of the offence.

You should be aware of the potential relationship and apparent conflict between all these factors and know how they have been utilised by the courts in the construction of statutory offences.

You should be able to make reference to a number of important strict liability offences and to understand their particular and peculiar incidents. Examples from your syllabus may well suggest to you the offences of which you should gain a working knowledge. It generally pays to have a good understanding of the offence of unlawful possession of a controlled drug (see above), in particular a familiarity with the concept of possession and the problems associated with controlled drugs in containers. Remember also the possible common law alternatives to strict liability suggested by the House of Lords in *Sweet* v *Parsley* [1970] AC 132.

Finally, remember that strict liability offences also exist at common law, though they are a very rare legal animal; be fully conversant with the leading authority of *Lemon* v *Whitehouse* [1979] AC 617.

EXAMPLES OF QUESTIONS

Generally an examination question on strict liability takes the form of an essay and usually justifies a whole question. A classic, almost perennial, example will take the following (or similar) form:

(1) 'The presence of strict liability is the very acme of injustice,'
Discuss.

This essay question requires a critical approach. You must first define accurately with examples the nature of strict liability offences. A short survey (no more than a paragraph) of their ambit will set the scene. It is now that the kernel of the question arises. The question seeks to elicit your view of whether or not strict liability is unjust. You must be prepared to back your view with authority and reasoned argument. Can it be justified in any of the situations in which it is presently used and for the purposes and reasons expressed by the judiciary in such cases? Should it be abolished, restricted to certain situations or extended? If it is to be abolished or restricted how may it be replaced if at all so that injustice does not occur?

Such an essay gives an opportunity not only for you to discuss case law but to review legal materials outside the law reports and the statute book, e.g., the Law Commission Report No. 89 and its suggested statutory restatement of the mode of creation and existence of strict liability offences, and the presumption that *mens rea* should be required to be proved by the prosecution as to all the external elements of an offence. This latter presumption is only displaced by an expressed and unambiguous contrary intention in a particular statute. You should make it clear, however, that this presumption would only have prospective effect.

The basic theme of the above question may be given other slants such as:

(2) 'The imposition of liability for gross negligence in offences of strict liability would satisfy those who would advocate the requirement of fault for all criminal offences, yet preserve the advantages that strict liability has for the prosecution.'
Discuss.

This question seeks a response from you concerning the function and purpose of strict liability. It demands a consideration of whether in the words of Roscoe Pound:

The good sense of the courts has introduced a doctrine of acting at one's peril with respect to statutory crimes which expresses the needs of society. Such statutes are not meant to punish the vicious will but to put pressure upon the thoughtless and inefficient to do their whole duty in the interest of public health or safety or morals.

This passage has been utilised by many as a justification for the existence of strict liability. Nevertheless it would appear that the principles stated in it which are said to justify the existence of strict liability would be equally well served by a general requirement that the prosecution establish that an accused has been grossly negligent in the commission of an offence.

The issue to consider is whether the substitution of gross negligence for strict liability would satisfy the advocates of strict liability and in addition preserve the advantages presently enjoyed by the prosecution when prosecuting a strict liability offence. Ultimately this is a matter of opinion, though factors to consider are:

(a) If the prosecution are required to establish an accused's gross negligence in respect of the commission of an offence would it in practical terms increase their administrative burden? (This should be considered in conjunction with the fact that in many strict liability offences the prosecution need in any event to establish the fact of the *mens rea* of an accused in respect of certain parts of the *actus reus* of the offence.) The substitution of gross negligence on the part of an accused in respect of the external elements of an offence which may presently be satisfied by strict liability may not therefore prove too onerous a burden for the prosecuting authorities to bear.

(b)   Because gross negligence is more a state of fact which is concerned with the 'mind' and conduct of how the ordinary reasonable man should behave and how an accused has failed to comply with that standard, it should not place an unduly heavy burden on the prosecution to establish this factor. It is after all an objective not a subjective test.

(c)   The fact should be noted that many strict liability offences in any event generally provide defences that an accused lacks *mens rea* and that he was not negligent.

It is the very fact that gross negligence is concerned with 'objective' states of mind and conduct that proves objectionable, however, to many of those who find strict liability equally contrary to the normal principles of criminal justice. Such a school of thought would only be satisfied by the establishing by the prosecution of an accused's intentional or reckless state of mind with regard to the *actus reus* of an offence. It is to these matters that you should address your mind in considering the type of question noted above.

A favourite variation of the strict liability essay is something along the following lines:

(3)   'The House of Lords' decision in *Sweet* v *Parsley* was a victory for those advocating the need for *mens rea* in offences.'
Discuss.

It is important to outline the basic facts of the case before coming to a conclusion in such a question. Remember that the House of Lords in *Sweet* v *Parsley* determined that there was a rebuttable presumption favouring the imposition of *mens rea* as to all the external elements of an offence, where that offence was of a serious nature having grave consequences, social and penal, for an accused who may be convicted.

This presumption does not affect nor necessarily apply to the cases of quasi-criminal offences and the other situations envisaged by Wright J in *Sherras* v *De Rutzen* [1895] 1 QB 918 which may give rise to a presumption of strict liability. Neither is the case of *Warner* v *Metropolitan Police Commissioner* [1969] 2 AC 256 overruled. In other words the presumption may be rebutted by evidence that the offence in question is gravely dangerous to society generally. See also *R* v *McNamara* (1988) 87 Cr App R 246. You must discuss the law relating to strict liability prior to *Sweet* v *Parsley*, consider the implication of this decision in some detail and finally discuss the development of the law after this decision as in, for example, *Alphacell Ltd* v *Woodward* [1972] AC 824. You should come to a conclusion about what effect the presumption as to *mens rea* in offences established by *Sweet* v *Parsley* has had on this area of the criminal law and the ways, if any, and the situations in which the courts have seen fit, notwithstanding *Sweet* v *Parsley*, to declare offences to be ones of strict liability.

Half Questions

Strict liability may frequently justify only a half question in an examination. A classic of its kind is:

    (4)   'Liability is strict not absolute.'
    Discuss.

Such a question demands a discussion that a strict liability offence (the nature of which should be explained) does not necessarily preclude the applicability of general defences (see chapter 8), even possibly in offences which are constituted by 'states of affairs' (see chapter 3) although those offences are apparently absolute rather than strict in that no *mens rea* at all is required. Strict liability offences do not require proof by the prosecution of *mens rea* as to one or more but not all of the elements of the *actus reus*. The first group of defences which may be applicable to strict liability offences are those of involuntary conduct, automatism, either insane or non-insane: i.e., that the accused was not acting consciously, or the fact that he was mistaken about the nature of goods in his control or their existence in cases where the offence requires him to possess them. Apart from the mistaken belief noted above, and statutory exceptions aside, a mistaken belief generally will not provide a defence to offences of strict liability, neither should voluntary intoxication (see *R* v *Young* [1984] 1 WLR 654). Apart from these, all the other generally applicable defences should be available, e.g., duress. Such a question needs little critical analysis, just a thorough understanding of the incidents of strict liability and of the available defences to such criminal charges.

Problem Questions

There are few examples of problem questions involving issues of strict liability; they frequently form only part of a question in an examination. They usually require a consideration on your part of the incidents of a particular strict liability offence or group of such offences.
    An example would be:

(5)   Rex, an ageing 'swinger' and college lecturer intends to hold a party for his students at his home (which is owned by the college by whom he is employed). In the local public house prior to the party and while he is intoxicated he is given a parcel by one of the students which contains 'something to make the party go' which Rex is to take to the house. The parcel contains controlled drugs. Rex and some of the students arrive at the house and later while Rex lies in a stupor the police arrive and find some of the students smoking cannabis.

Discuss Rex's criminal liability.

Ostensibly this question requires a consideration of two offences. The first is Rex's possession of the controlled drug contrary to the Misuse of Drugs Act 1971, s. 5 (a strict liability offence). You should consider whether Rex possesses the drug and if, having analysed the leading cases such as *Warner* v *Metropolitan Police Commissioner* [1969] 2 AC 256 and *R* v *Marriott* [1971] 1 All ER 595 and especially *R* v *McNamara* (1988) 87 Cr App R 246, you are of the opinion that he has committed the offence, the next stage, notwithstanding his intoxication (which you should indicate will not provide him with a defence, saying why that is the case; see *R* v *Young* [1984] 1 WLR 654), is to review the possible applicability of the statutory defence contained in s. 28 of the Act. This section states that an accused charged with an offence under s. 5 may establish as a defence that he did not know or suspect or have reason to suspect that he had in his possession a controlled drug. The incidents of this statutory defence should be considered in full.

The above offence should be contrasted with the second offence relevant to the facts, that of being concerned in the management of premises which are used for the purposes of smoking cannabis contrary to the Misuse of Drugs Act 1971, s. 8. Apart from this being an offence requiring *mens rea* as to all the external elements (see *Sweet* v *Parsley* [1970] AC 132 concerning the precursor of s. 8, namely the Dangerous Drugs Act 1965, s. 5(b)), the only issue is whether Rex can be brought within the terms of the offence. Is he, for example, the person who is concerned in the management of the premises and of whom knowledge of the circumstances of the offence is required or is the college to be regarded as that person? You must argue your opinion from your knowledge of the established cases using the legal skills of analogy and distinguishing to support your view.

CONCLUSION

Strict liability is a technical area of the law. Its apparent simplicity is complicated by many inconsistencies and anomalies within many of the statutory offences that form the bulk of its manifestations. Its advantage for a student is that once understood, it forms an independent area of study that frequently takes the form of an assessment or examination question devoted entirely to this topic. Finally the nature of strict liability is such that the areas of the topic that may form the subject-matter of an examination question are rather limited, and the approaches that may be taken by an examiner more readily predictable by you.

FURTHER READING

Strict Liability

Budd, M. and Lynch, A., 'Voluntariness, Causation and Strict Liability' [1978] Crim LR 74.

Carson, W. G., 'Some Sociological Aspects of Strict Liability' (1970) MLR 225.

Hogan, B., 'The Mental Element in Crime; Strict Liability' [1978] Crim LR 74.

Jackson, B. S., '*Storkwain*: A Case Study of Strict Liability and Self-Regulation' [1991] Crim LR 892.

Law Commission Working Paper No. 30: Codification of Criminal Law: Strict Liability and the Enforcement of the Factories Act 1961 (1970).

Richardson, G., 'Strict Liability for Regulatory Crime: the Empirical Research' [1987] Crim LR 295.

Smith, M. and Pearson, A., 'The Value of Strict Liability' [1969] Crim LR 5.

Spencer [1979] CLJ 2.

Wells, C., 'Swatting and Subjectivist Bug' [1982] Crim LR 209.

Wootton, B., 'Crime and the Criminal Law', The Hamlyn Lecture Series, 2nd ed. (London: Stevens, 1981) see particularly pp. 40–57.

6 PARTICIPATION

In our society the persons who may be held criminally responsible for the commission of an offence, and the various ways criminal responsibility may arise, are important topics which come under the heading of participation. The law recognises several ways in which an individual may be a participator in a criminal offence.

TYPES OF PARTICIPATOR

Principal Offender

An individual who is directly responsible for bringing about the commission of the *actus reus* of an offence is (provided he has the prescribed *mens rea*) regarded by the law as *a principal offender*. For example, the person who dishonestly appropriates property belonging to another with the intention permanently to deprive the owner is a principal offender with regard to the offence of theft. There may, of course, be more than one principal offender with regard to an offence. Thus if several individuals each with the common purpose of killing another stab the latter with knives, all are principal offenders to the resulting offence of murder for each has contributed to the death of the deceased. In that instance any one of the participators by their conduct could have brought about the death of the deceased without the active contribution of the others. The fact that the prosecution cannot identify any other attacker does not mean that none exists nor does it mean that the accused must be acquitted if there was. The jury may find the accused guilty whether or not he was assisted provided they were sure it was the accused who participated in causing the victim's injury or death (*R* v *Labbie* [1995] Crim LR 317).

Furthermore the law recognises that a number of individuals may each be regarded as joint principal offenders to a crime, though each individual's conduct when examined in isolation could not have brought about the *actus reus* of an offence, in short, generally anyone who joins in the commission of the crime is equally liable (see *Tyler* v *Whatmore* [1976] RTR 83 and *R* v *Grundy* [1989] Crim LR 502). In such instances, however, the individuals concerned must act in concert and as part of a joint enterprise (see *Smith* v *Mellors* (1987) 84 Cr App R 279). Short of such a joint concord each individual who has contributed to the commission of the *actus reus* will generally stand as joint principal to *an attempt* to commit the offence. This will be a very rare occurrence. In the case of a joint enterprise it may be put to the jury that the accused is either a principal or an aider or abettor and if the jury believe he was either they may convict him of the full offence (*R* v *Gaughan* [1990] Crim LR 880 and *R* v *Labbie* [1995] Crim LR 317).

Where there is insufficent evidence of persons having acted together then a problem arises which some students find difficult to comprehend. The rule is that if two people are jointly indicted and the evidence does not point to one rather than the other, the jury should return a verdict of not guilty in the case of both. It is not enough usually if the prosecution can prove only that the crime must have been committed by one or other of them (*R* v *Abbott* (1955) 39 Cr App R 141). (See Law Commission Consultation Paper No. 131, 'Assisting and Encouraging Crime' London: HMSO 1994 and 'Secondary participation in Crime — can we do without it?' (1994) 144 NLJ 679.) One solution approved by the Court of Appeal in *R* v *S and M* [1995] 2 Cr App R 347 where it was not possible to prove which of two people (the mother or her boyfriend) had assaulted her child, was to convict both of them of criminal neglect under the Children and Young Persons Act 1933 on the basis that one must have assaulted the injured child and the other (or both of them) had refrained from seeking medical treatment for the child which amounted to neglect.

The Principal Offender and the Innocent Agent

An accused may still be regarded as a principal offender though the *actus reus* of an offence has actually been brought about by the conduct of another. This is restricted to cases where the accused has used the actual perpetrator of the *actus reus* as the innocent instrument of his (i.e., the accused's) criminal intentions. That is to say the actual perpetrator of the *actus reus* must be an innocent agent otherwise it would be that person and that person alone (see *R* v *Butt* (1884) 15 Cox CC 564 and *R* v *Michael* (1840) 9 C & P 356) who would constitute the principal offender (see *R* v *Wheelhouse* [1994] Crim LR 756 and

R v Loukes [1996] Crim LR 341). Any other person who had put the idea in the perpetrator's mind or joined with the perpetrator in the commission of the offence would be liable then either as a party (secondary participation, see below and *DPP v K and G* [1997] 1 Cr App R 36) or for some other offence (such as incitement, see chapter 7).

The actual perpetrator of the *actus reus* of an offence is an innocent agent wherever he commits the *actus reus* and one of the following situations is established:

(a)   he lacks *mens rea*, or
(b)   he is of insufficient age to form a criminal intent, or
(c)   he is insane or suffering from non-insane automatism, or
(d)   he is under a reasonable and/or honest mistake of fact which if true would have justified his actions, or
(e)   he has been forced to commit the *actus reus* while under duress (see *R v Manley* (1844) 1 Cox CC 104).

The doctrine of innocent agency is inapplicable to cases like bigamy which may only be committed by the actual perpetrator except perhaps when the marriage takes place by proxy which is a possible but unlikely occurrence. The commission of offences involving assault or any direct personal link between the *actus reus* and the principal offender is possible through the medium of an innocent agent except rape despite the *dicta* of Lawton LJ to the contrary in *R v Cogan and Leak* [1975] 2 All ER 1059. In that case Leak encouraged Cogan to rape Leak's wife and was held guilty of aiding and abetting the rape (knowing that the wife did not consent to intercourse) even though Cogan was found not guilty of rape on the ground that he honestly believed Mrs Leak was consenting but the suggestion was made in the case that the husband might be held liable as principal offender through the innocent agency of the weak-minded Cogan. The difficulty with that notion at that time was that a husband could not rape his wife (but the law has changed, see chapter 9) hence the Court of Appeal confirmed the husband's conviction as a secondary party to rape and not as a principal offender. Further support for the view that rape cannot be committed via an innocent agent is provided by *DPP v K and G* [1997] 1 Cr App R 36 where the accused were both female. Both, however, were guilty of procuring the *actus reus* of rape, i.e., they were secondary parties and not principals. In other instances of offences against the person the doctrine of innocent agency should apply.

Secondary Participation

An individual may be indirectly involved in the commission of an offence. This is sometimes referred to as being an accomplice, an accessory or a party to the offence! Such an individual may nevertheless be regarded by the law *as if* he were a principal offender. By s. 8 of the Accessories and Abettors Act 1861 (as amended) a person who aids, abets, counsels or procures any indictable offence (an offence triable in the Crown Court) shall be liable to be tried, indicted and punished as a principal offender. There is a similar provision covering summary offences (offences triable in a magistrate's court) — see s. 44 of the Magistrates' Courts Act 1980. (You should become familiar with the forms of secondary participation noted in the statutory provisions.)

A person may thus be regarded by the law as a principal offender though his involvement in an offence may be of the following kinds: aiding, abetting, counselling or procuring. In *R* v *Giannetto* [1997] 1 Cr App R 1, the accused was convicted of murder. The Crown's case was that he either killed his wife or hired a killer. The Court of Appeal confirmed his conviction stating that because of the Accessories and Abettors Act 1861 if he did no more than encourage another to kill his wife he was liable to be tried, indicted and punished as a principal offender. The jury must find that he either killed his wife himself or at least encouraged another to do so and it did not matter which. It did not matter that the Crown could not positively show which, provided the jury agreed that the accused had the *mens rea* and caused the *actus reus*, i.e., the death of his wife in this case. The Crown does not have to specify the means. The jury need only be certain that if he was not the principal, he was the accessory or party. This is the principle embodied in *R* v *Swindall and Osborne* (1864) 2 Car & K 230. The fact that in reality participation is considered less reprehensible than acting as a principal offender is shown by the lighter sentence that a party may receive on conviction.

Aiding

A secondary party may aid another in the commission of an offence. This has been defined as giving help, support or assistance to the principal offender in the carrying out of the principal offence. Examples of such conduct are:

(a)   Driving the principal offender to the scene of the crime (*DPP for Northern Ireland* v *Lynch* [1975] AC 653).
(b)   Acting as a look-out (*R* v *Betts and Ridley* (1930) 22 Cr App R 148).
(c)   Restraining the victim of an assault (*R* v *Clarkson* [1971] 3 All ER 344).
(d)   Supplying the principal offender with the materials or tools to carry out the principal offence (*R* v *Lomas* (1913) 9 Cr App R 220).

In *R* v *Bullock* [1955] 1 All ER 15 and *National Coal Board* v *Gamble* [1959] 1 QB 11 the courts accepted that returning to a person his own property which he then used in committing an offence could not amount to aiding him. Though criticised, this principle still seems to be law, see *Garrett v Arthur Churchill (Glass) Ltd* [1969] 2 All ER 1141 at p. 1145. A person can only aid another by conduct which takes place before or at the time of the commission of the principal offence, see *Thambiah v R* [1966] AC 37. It is not necessary for an aider to be present at the scene of the crime when he renders his assistance, see *DPP for Northern Ireland v Lynch* [1975] AC 653. An aider, however, needs to provide some active or at least passive assistance to a principal offender, see *R v Bland* [1988] Crim LR 41.

Abetting

This was once thought to be a synonym for aiding, or to describe the *mens rea* which accompanied such conduct (see *National Coal Board v Gamble* [1959] 1 QB 11 and *DPP for Northern Ireland v Lynch* [1975] AC 653 at p. 698 per Lord Simon of Glaisdale). This view seems to have been rejected by Lord Widgery CJ in *Attorney-General's Reference (No. 1 of 1975)* [1975] 2 All ER 684 at p. 686 who was of the opinion that to aid, abet, counsel or procure were each independent forms of activity. Upon this view it can be said that abetting is constituted by any conduct which amounts to encouraging, instigating, inciting, countenancing or exhorting a principal offender to commit an offence. It is generally thought that such conduct should take place at the time of the commission of the principal offence, which means that generally abetting may only take place at the scene of the crime. Participation aside, such conduct prior to or simultaneous with the commission of the principal offence would constitute the inchoate offence of incitement (see chapter 7).

Counselling

This encompasses the same form of activity as abetting, but is generally to be limited to such conduct which takes place *before* the commission of the principal offence and therefore usually some distance from the vicinity. Both counselling and abetting require that the conduct impinge upon the mind of the principal offender, i.e., there must be a consensus between the parties. There is no requirement, however, that the secondary party's conduct helps bring about the principal offence, see *R v Calhaem* [1985] 2 WLR 826, i.e., there is no need for there to be a causal connection between the secondary party's conduct and the commission of the principal offence. This latter element is relevant to the final form of secondary activity, procuring.

Procuring

The nature of this form of secondary participation was considered in *Attorney-General's Reference (No. 1 of 1975)* [1975] 2 All ER 684. In this case, knowing that a friend would shortly drive a car the accused surreptitiously laced the friend's drink with double measures of spirits. The friend was subsequently convicted of driving under the influence of alcohol. The accused could be liable for procuring that offence because unknown to the driver and without his collaboration he has been put in a position in which he has committed an offence which he otherwise would not have committed. In the words of Lord Widgery CJ at p. 686:

> To procure means to produce by endeavour. You procure a thing by setting out to see that it happens and taking the appropriate steps to produce that happening.

His lordship considered that such activity did not require any conspiracy between the principal offender and the procurer, i.e., there is no need for a consensus between the parties. The question of causation was crucial, however. In the words of his lordship at p. 687: 'You cannot procure an offence unless there is a causal link between what you do and the commission of the offence.' The secondary party's help must be linked (causative) to the bringing about of the offence.

Presence at the Scene of the Crime and the Inactivity of the Secondary Party

Secondary parties present at the scene of the crime (generally aiders and abettors) do not usually render assistance to the principal offender merely by being a passive spectator (see *R* v *Clarkson* [1971] 3 All ER 344), or by merely being with the principal offender and knowing of and doing nothing to prevent the commission of an offence (see *R* v *Bland* [1988] Crim LR 41). There is a need for the prosecution to establish beyond reasonable doubt that there is encouragement of some active or passive assistance or some element of control exercised by the secondary party. However, it may be argued that mere presence at the scene of a crime *may* encourage (and thus abet) the principal offender to commit the principal offence (see *R* v *Coney* (1882) 8 QBD 534). In relation to participation in a crime by way of a joint enterprise, proof of presence is not enough but proof of deliberate presence and non-interference and lack of dissent might be cogent evidence of wilful encouragement, aiding or abetting (*R* v *Mason Lidgard and Herrington* [1996] Crim LR 325). The following situations may constitute a secondary party an abettor though he is a passive spectator at the scene of a crime:

(a)   Where an abettor shows by his conduct either prior to or even after the commission of the principal offence that he sought, by his presence at the scene of the crime, to encourage the principal offender (see *Wilcox* v *Jeffrey* [1951] 1 All ER 464).

(b)   Where a secondary party is present at the scene of a crime pursuant to an antecedent agreement then his passivity may nevertheless amount to abetting a principal offender.

(c)   Where the secondary party stands in a position of authority to the principal offender, the presence of the former at the scene of the crime may amount to a tacit abetting of the principal offence (see *Du Cross* v *Lambourne* [1907] 1 KB 40, *Tuck* v *Robson* [1970] 1 All ER 1171 and *R* v *J. F. Alford Transport Ltd and others*, *The Times*, 28 March 1997).

(d)   Where a person is under a duty or has a right to intervene to prevent the commission of a crime, his failure to intervene may be a positive encouragement to the person committing the illegal act and if the inactive person knows his inertia will have that effect, then his inactivity amounts to aiding and abetting (see *R* v *Forman and Ford* [1988] Crim LR 677).

Such situations may render a person who is passive at the scene of the offence an aider of a principal offender though it will be more difficult to establish such a fact than in an equivalent case of abetting.

THE MENS REA OF A SECONDARY PARTY

A secondary party must intend to aid, abet, counsel or procure a principal offender in his commission of an offence. It is clear that intent will incur responsibility (see *National Coal Board* v *Gamble* [1959] 1 QB 11). Be careful, even the Court of Appeal in some joint enterprise cases made the mistake of requiring the *mens rea* of a principal when considering the guilt of a secondary party. The secondary party must be proved to have intended not to commit the substantive offence, but to aid, abet, counsel or procure the commission of that offence which is committed by someone else. In *R* v *Slack* [1989] Crim LR 903 where during the course of a robbery one participant killed the victim it was made clear that the other participant may not have been present, may not have known of the killing or may have hoped that the other would not kill, but if it was part of their joint plan, i.e., it was understood by them expressly or impliedly that if necessary one of them would kill or do serious harm as part of the joint enterprise, they are both guilty of murder. The one who did not kill is guilty because he lent himself to such a criminal enterprise. As long as he is aware that the other party may act with the fault required by the offence he will be equally guilty. His guilt depends on his intentional participation in the other's crime and it is not necessary to prove that he intended the actual outcome caused or committed by the other person, the primary party (*R* v *Hyde, Sussex, Collins* [1991] Crim LR 133; cf. the case of *R* v *Wakely* [1990] Crim LR 119 where foresight of a real possibility of serious violence being used was said to be sufficient *mens rea* to be a party to murder and not, as one would have thought, whether the parties have agreed expressly or tacitly to kill or cause grievous bodily harm, see *R* v *Hyde* below).

An issue for you to consider is whether an individual may by his conduct recklessly aid, abet, counsel or procure the commission of a principal offence. The balance of authority appears to be against this notion but it is a matter to which you should give some consideration.

An individual must have some knowledge of the material circumstances which will constitute the *actus reus* of the principal offence, which is to be committed by the principal offender (*Johnson* v *Youden* [1950] 1 KB 544). It is not necessary that the secondary party is aware that the principal offender's conduct constitutes a criminal offence. It is certain that awareness of, or wilful blindness to, the material circumstances of the principal offence will affix a secondary party with criminal responsibility as will subjective *Cunningham*-type recklessness (see *Carter* v *Richardson* [1974] RTR 314 and *Smith* v *Mellors* (1987) 84 Cr App R 279). Knowledge includes what ought to be known at least in the case of strict or absolute offences (*R* v *Roberts and George* [1997] Crim LR 209). However, *R* v *Alford Transport Ltd and others, The Times*, 28 March 1997 held that 'knowledge' (or 'contemplation') does not include constructive knowledge, which is a form of negligence, i.e., failure to make such enquiries as a reasonable person would have made is not equivalent to knowledge. This may mean, in the case of a strict liability offence, that the perpetrator may be convicted without knowledge but the alleged party cannot be. That being the case, it is arguable that *Caldwell*-type recklessness would also fail to suffice to constitute the required knowledge with regard to such matters.

An area of considerable difficulty for a student is the problem of how far a secondary party needs to be aware of the peculiar characteristics of the principal offence. In *R* v *Bainbridge* [1959] 3 All ER 200 the Court of Criminal Appeal determined that it is sufficient if a secondary party is aware of the material circumstances which indicate the 'type' of offence which the principal offender is about to commit, e.g., a robbery, a theft or burglary, but not its unique, peculiar characteristics, i.e., the vicinity, the subject-matter or, where appropriate, the victim. This test has been extended in the case of *DPP for Northern Ireland* v *Maxwell* [1978] 3 All ER 1140, a decision of the House of Lords. Where an individual aids, abets, counsels or procures the commission of the principal offence with the prescribed *mens rea* it is sufficient that he be aware of or wilfully blind to the fact that the principal offender may commit any one of a limited number of offences within a given 'group' or 'type'. The width and nature of the 'groups' or 'types' of offences that must be within a secondary party's contemplation remains unclear.

For the *mens rea* needed to be liable as a participator in an inchoate offence, see below.

Secondary Participation in Strict Liability Offences

A secondary party needs *full mens rea* irrespective of the kind of offence which is committed by the principal offender. Thus even in cases of offences of strict liability, for which the principal offender can be held criminally responsible without *mens rea* as to all the elements of the offence on his part a secondary party needs *mens rea* with respect to all the elements of the offence, see *Callow* v *Tillstone* (1900) 83 LT 411.

Principal Offender must Commit an Actus Reus

Secondary participation cannot hang in the air. The principal offender who is the subject-matter of the aiding, abetting, counselling or procuring must bring about the *actus reus* of an offence. This factor is crucial to the secondary party's criminal responsibility. Whether the principal offender is found guilty of the principal offence is, however, of no legal significance to the secondary party. It matters not that because of procedural or evidential restrictions the principal offender may not be prosecuted (see *R* v *Humphreys and Turner* [1965] 3 All ER 689). It is also irrelevant that the principal offender has a defence, e.g., lack of *mens rea* (see *R* v *Cogan and Leak* [1975] 2 All ER 1059) or duress (*R* v *Bourne* (1952) 36 Cr App R 125). These latter cases establish that a secondary party's liability is dependent upon his aiding, abetting, counselling or procuring (with the prescribed *mens rea*) another's commission of the *actus reus* of an offence. Thus where an individual (i.e., a potential principal offender) fails (irrespective of his particular *mens rea*) to bring about an *actus reus* there is nothing contrary to the criminal law which a secondary party can help or assist in bringing about. In such cases the secondary party is innocent of any criminal complicity (see *Thornton* v *Mitchell* [1940] 1 All ER 399, *Morris* v *Tolman* [1923] 1 KB 166, *R* v *Millward* [1994] Crim LR 527 and *R* v *Loukes* [1996] Crim LR 341). But see below where the principal offender brings about an attempted offence.

Conviction of Secondary Party of an Offence Different from that of the Principal Offender

The *actus reus* of participation is aiding, abetting, counselling or procuring, the external elements of a principal offence. It stands to reason that the secondary party's full criminal responsibility for these external elements is ultimately dependent upon his own *mens rea* (see *DPP* v *Merriman* [1973] AC 584). Once this fact is fully understood it is easy for you to grasp the fact that a secondary party's criminal responsibility with regard to his involvement in the *actus reus* of a principal offence may be different from that of the principal offender, who may have a different *mens rea* from the secondary party. In addition either party may have a defence which is available only to him. To this general principle there was one anomalous exception. In *R* v *Richards* [1973] 3 All ER 1088 it was determined that a secondary party who was *not* present at the scene of the commission of an offence could not be convicted of a greater offence than the principal offender, apparently *irrespective* of the reasons for that person's lack of *mens rea*, or the availability to him of defences. Fortunately, *R v Richards* was overruled in *R v Howe* [1987] AC 417. It is now clear that in all cases the criminal responsibility of a secondary party with regard to his involvement in the *actus reus* of an offence is governed exclusively by his *mens rea* or the availability of defences to him. Thus, where an individual aids another in killing a person, the secondary party will, if he intended to help the principal party kill or inflict grievous bodily harm, be convicted of aiding murder (see *R v Slack* [1989] 3 WLR 513) and this remains so even if the principal offender, though he may have intended to kill or inflict grievous bodily harm, has the defence of provocation available to him and may only be convicted of voluntary manslaughter. Conversely, if two people have agreed a joint enterprise to inflict minor injuries on the victim and one of them then intentionally kills the victim, the fact that the killer went beyond the common design and did something not contemplated by his fellow conspirator should absolve the latter from liability for manslaughter or as a party to murder (see *R v Wan Chan* [1995] Crim LR 297).

Unforeseen Consequences and Joint Enterprise

An area of difficulty for students is that of a secondary party's liability for *unforeseen* consequences. Generally, once a person renders secondary assistance in whatever form to a principal offender he is equally liable with all the other parties for all the consequences that flow from the principal offender's conduct, be they contemplated or unforeseen (provided that person also has the required *mens rea*) (see *R v Anderson and Morris* (1966) 50 Cr App R 216; *Chan Wing-Siu v R* [1985] AC 168; *Davies v DPP* [1954] AC 378; *R v Ward* (1987) 85 Cr App R 71; *Hui Chi-Ming v R* [1992] 1 AC 34; *R v Roberts* [1993] 1 All ER 583; and *R v Mahmood* [1994] Crim LR 368).

This was confirmed in *R v Hyde* [1990] 3 All ER 892 where three appellants kicked and punched a man outside a public house. He died from a kick to the head. All three were charged with murder for their joint attack even though it was not possible to say which one had inflicted the fatal blow but each either had the intention to cause serious injury or knew that such was the intention of the others when he took part. They denied both propositions. The trial judge's direction was if all three intended serious harm then all three were guilty of murder; if they did not so intend but one of them decided to do it, then if either of the others could be shown to have the same intention, inasmuch as he foresaw the real possibility that that might be the result which he was putting in train, then he too shared the responsibility. The Court of Appeal agreed and stated that if a secondary party realised, without agreeing to such conduct being used but still participated with the assailant in the fight, then that amounted to sufficient mental element for the secondary party to be guilty of murder, if the assailant, with the requisite intent, killed the victim during the fight. In those circumstances the secondary party has lent himself to the enterprise and thus given assistance and encouragement to the assailant to carry out an enterprise which the secondary party realised might involve murder.

In relation to a joint unlawful enterprise in order to convict the accused of being a party to murder he will possess the appropriate *mens rea* if he contemplated that the principal might kill or might intentionally cause some serious injuries and it is not necessary to show that the principal contemplated that he himself might act in that way (see *Hui Chi-ming* v *R* [1992] 1 AC 34). The contemplation, realisation or awareness by the accused that death or serious injury might occur (even though he stops short of agreeing to such conduct) and his continued participation, will make the accused liable whether or not weapons were carried and whether or not the object of the enterprise was to cause physical injury or to engage in some other unlawful act such as robbery, theft or burglary (see *R* v *Roberts* [1993] 1 All ER 583). As Lord Taylor CJ said in *Roberts*: 'The nub of the case was therefore not whether the appellant realised that force might be used but whether he realised only that some physical harm might be done or that really serious harm might be inflicted'. Serious bodily harm does not have to be in the contemplation of both parties at the outset of the venture for a person to be convicted as an accomplice. According to *R* v *Stewart and Scholfield* [1995] 1 Cr App R 441, *R* v *Hui Chi-Ming* is also authority for the proposition that a person might be a party to a joint venture or enterprise which led to death and be guilty of manslaughter even though the actual killer might be guilty of murder because the former lacked the *mens rea* for murder. *Stewart and Scholfield* indicated that in such cases the central issue is whether the act in question was within the scope of the joint enterprise or not. If it was not then where a specific intent crime is charged the state of mind of each determines their individual liability. On the other hand if there was a tacit agreement and two parties realised, without agreeing to such conduct, that another party might intentionally kill or cause serious injury in pursuance of the agreement, and they nevertheless continue to participate, that is a sufficient mental element for all three of them to be guilty of murder on the basis of their joint enterprise (*R* v *Powell and Daniels* [1996] 1 Cr App R 14 and *R* v *Powell* and *R* v *English* [1997] 4 All ER 545).

A useful illustration of the principles is the case of *R* v *Mahmood* [1994] Crim LR 368, where the driver and passenger of a stolen car abandoned it while in motion, leaving it to mount the pavement and smash into a pram killing the baby inside it. Clearly, a secondary party in a joint enterprise is liable for the unforeseen consequences of that enterprise. In the case of the passenger (the secondary party to the enterprise) it must be proved that the act which caused the death was done in pursuance of the joint enterprise. If the driver has gone beyond anything which the passenger had foreseen he might do when setting out on the enterprise then the passenger is not liable for the consequence of that unforeseen act. If death had been caused, for example, by any ordinary (foreseeable) act of reckless driving, then the secondary party would be liable. In light of the unusual facts, therefore, only if the passenger had foreseen that there was a real risk of abandoning the car while it was in motion, when he set out on the enterprise of taking the car without authority, would he be properly convicted.

However, where the principal offender executes an *unauthorised* act which is outside that agreed and contemplated by the parties, none of the other participants, be they joint principals or secondary parties, can be held responsible for the consequences that flow from that unauthorised act (see *R v Saunders and Archer* (1576) 2 Plow 473, *R v Creamer* [1966] 1 QB 72 and *R v Dunbar* [1988] Crim LR 693).

This defence of unauthorised act appears inapplicable to individuals who contemplate the murder of or the infliction of serious bodily harm upon another and who contemplate the use of weapons (see *R v Kelly* (unreported, 5 April 1984) and *R v Williams and Blackwood* (1973) 21 WIR 329). The fact that different weapons or methods are used from those originally contemplated is, and should rightly be, legally irrelevant. This approach was followed in *R v Bamborough* [1996] Crim LR 744. Bamborough and another carried out a robbery. Bamborough knew the other assailant carried a gun. The victim was pistol-whipped but then the other assailant shot and killed him. Both assailants were convicted of murder. Bamborough claimed that he should have been a party to the use of the gun only to cause grievous bodily harm (the pistol whipping) which did not cause death, because he had no idea that the gun was loaded until his colleague fired it. Therefore Bamborough claimed he should be convicted only of manslaughter. The Court of Appeal said it made no difference what form of really serious harm was contemplated. If he knew that really serious harm, of whatever type, was likely to be inflicted with the gun then he was rightly convicted of murder. But is this necessarily always correct (the facts aside)? What if the participants had agreed to use a cosh to frighten and inflict non-life threatening injuries and unknown to 'Bamborough' and not contemplated by 'Bamborough' his colleague pulls out a gun and intentionally kills the victim?

Repentance

A secondary party may avoid criminal responsibility for his complicity in a criminal offence (at least as regards his status as a secondary party) by withdrawing from the enterprise. The withdrawal must be made *before* the principal offender has completed the commission of the principal offence (see *R v Becerra* (1975) 62 Cr App R 212 and *R v Saunders and Archer* (1576) 2 Plow

473). A secondary party must give a clear, effective and timely warning of such an intention of withdrawal to the other parties in order to avoid responsibility for their criminal activities. According to *Becerra* such conduct will provide a defence to a secondary party only where he has counselled the principal offender in the preparatory stages of a criminal offence. The more the secondary party has become involved in an offence the greater needs to be the counteracting activity he undertakes to avoid the charge of complicity. Whether a secondary party has by his conduct repented of his involvement in an offence is a matter of fact (see *R v Grundy* [1977] Crim LR 543 and *R v Whitefield* [1984] Crim LR 97). There must be timely and unequivocal communication of a change of mind, or intention to withdraw, to the other participants (see *R v Rook* [1993] 1 WLR 1005) although in *R v Perman* [1996] 1 Cr App R 24 the Court of Appeal seemed willing to accept that leaving the shop during the course of a robbery by a co-accused could amount to withdrawal from the joint enterprise so that what followed afterwards (the killing of a shop assistant) was outside the scope of the original enterprise.

Victims of Crimes as Secondary Parties

This area is principally involved with offences involving physical assault or a sexual element. Since many of these offences are designed to protect the victim little point would be served by making the victim a secondary party to the principal offender, although the victim may be a consenting party. But see for example Sexual Offences Act 1956, s. 6 (having intercourse with a girl below the age of consent), and s. 11 of the same act regarding the offence of incest. In both offences it is irrelevant that the 'victim' consents to the act — she will not be held to be a secondary party (see *R v Tyrell* [1894] 1 QB 710 and *R v Whitehouse* [1977] 3 All ER 737) although it has been held that a woman may aid and abet her own illegal abortion (*R v Sockett* (1908) 1 Cr App R 101).

Assisting Offenders

There are two offences created by statute (Criminal Law Act 1967, ss. 4 and 5) which involve impeding the apprehension or prosecution of, or accepting a consideration in return for failing to disclose information relating to the commission of, an arrestable offence committed by another. These offences should be fully understood by you as they may form an integral part of a question.

Secondary Participation and Inchoate Offences

There can be no offence of attempting to aid, abet, counsel or procure an offence, see Criminal Attempts Act 1981, s. 1(4)(b).

However, a secondary party clearly may aid, abet, counsel or procure an attempted substantive offence by the principal offender (see *R v Dunnington* [1984] QB 472 and table 7.1).

In *R v O'Brien* [1995] 2 Cr App R 649 the Court of Appeal upheld the trial judge's view that the jury could convict the accused of attempted murder if they were sure that when he assisted or encouraged he knew his co-accused might shoot to kill (which is what the latter had done). Knowledge that the co-accused might kill or cause serious injury was sufficient for murder and there was no reason why liability for attempted murder should be any different.

Corporate Liability

It is not uncommon for you to be confronted, in an examination, with the concept of corporate crime. The law deems that certain entities which have no physical existence may nevertheless be deemed in law legal persons which are recognised as having an existence independent from the human beings who are their members or who form their management structures or who are their employees. In English law, apart from the human being, the only other 'person' with legal rights and duties is the corporation. The commonest example of such an entity is the limited liability company registered under the Companies Act 1985 (see *Mayson, French and Ryan on Company Law* for a discussion of this form of corporate entity). Such a company may be held criminally responsible in two situations:

(a) *Statutory construction.* A penal statute may provide expressly or by implication that a company can be held criminally responsible for a breach of its provisions (see *R v Birmingham & Gloucester Railway Co.* (1842) 3 QB 223).

These are usually strict liability offences and require conduct such as selling, conducting businesses or being of a certain status, e.g., a landlord, which a company can, in law, undertake.

(b) *The doctrine of identification.* Where on the face of it a common law offence or a penal statute could not be applied to a company, e.g., because it requires *mens rea*, judges have developed a device for attributing a mind to this artificial corporate person in order to justify holding that entity criminally liable in such cases. They have done so by the doctrine of identification. Because the company is an artificial entity it can only act through its 'agents'. This doctrine is that certain 'agents' of a company are deemed to be its directing mind or *'alter ego'*. The conduct and *mens rea* of such individuals are then ascribed to the company. When such individuals are authorised to act on behalf of and in the course of the company's business, the *mens rea* of those individuals is deemed to be the *mens rea* of the company.

You should be aware of the leading authorities upon this area which determine who may be the directing mind of a company for the purposes of the doctrine of identification (see, e.g., *H. L. Bolton Engineering Co. Ltd v T. J. Graham & Sons Ltd* [1957] 1 QB 159; *Tesco Supermarkets Ltd v Nattrass* [1972] AC 153; and *R v Andrews-Weatherfoil Ltd* [1972] 1 WLR 118). All the cases show that the company will only be liable for the acts of persons whose status, authority, independent discretion and necessary knowledge makes their acts the acts of the company. Note also *R v Coroner for East Kent, ex parte Spooner* (1989) 88 Cr App R 10 and *R v P & O European Ferries Ltd* (1991) 93 Cr App R 72 in which it was held that a company can be guilty of manslaughter but only where the *actus reus* and *mens rea* can be proved against those persons collectively who are identified as the company itself. There the company, two directors and two senior managers, were tried for manslaughter in relation to the Zeebrugge ferry disaster. The issue was withdrawn from the jury because there was no evidence that anyone constituting the mind of the company had the necessary *mens rea* and the judge would not permit the knowledge or acts of each of the four accused officials to be aggregated for the purpose of determining corporate liability.

In 1994 a small company, OLL Ltd, was convicted of manslaughter on 8 December 1994 at Winchester Crown Court, together with its managing director because he was aware of the dangers of permitting 'adventure holiday' students to canoe across Lyme Bay with inadequate training and safety precautions. Clearly, for a crime committed in the course of a company's business, conviction of the company will be easier the smaller it is. A large company will be better able to claim that blame should be shared amongst several senior managers none of whom is individually guilty of the crime.

A move away from the 'directing mind and will' principle is seen in the Privy Council decision in *Meridian Global Fund Management Ltd v Securities Commission* [1995] 2 AC 500. Lord Hoffmann said that whose state of mind would be the company's state of mind depended on the rule, its interpretation, taking account of its policy and content. The statutory rule in question said that the company must give notice as soon as it knew or ought to have known that it was a substantial shareholder. In this instance it was held that the knowledge to be attributed to the company was that of the individuals who had authority to acquire the shares for the company whether or not they were part of its directing mind and will.

Vicarious Liability

Vicarious liability for a criminal offence frequently forms an element in a question. Though not a general rule of criminal liability (see *R v Huggins* (1730) 2 Ld Raym 1574), the law provides exceptions and in some instances

imposes criminal responsibility vicariously. These should be fully understood by you.

The exceptions where vicarious liability for a crime may be imposed are:

(a) *Statutory construction (extensive construction).* As with the statutory
construction principle applied to corporations, a penal statute may by its
express or implied meaning determine that an individual or company may
be held criminally responsible vicariously for the conduct of others.

Examples of the express imposition of statutory vicarious liability are cases
where penal statutes state that an individual will be held liable for his own
conduct *or* that of his employee or agent. *Coppen* v *Moore (No. 2)* [1898] 2 QB
306 is an example of implied vicarious liability. This case concerned a statute
which governed the sale of goods to which a false trade description had been
applied. Conduct such as 'selling' or 'using' can be carried out by persons
other than by an individual, but for or on his behalf. Vicarious liability is thus
imposed in such cases but only where the employee or agent so constituted
is acting within the scope or course of his employment (i.e., where he is doing
either an authorised act or an authorised act in an unauthorised way: the
employer generally will not be liable for his employee's or agent's
unauthorised acts). This principle has only been applied to penal statutes
which impose strict liability. Where a statute requires *mens rea* as to all the
relevant elements of the offence the courts have imposed vicarious liability
through the doctrine of delegation.

(b) *Delegation.* In such cases the person actually responsible for bringing
about the offence with the prescribed *mens rea* must be an employee or agent
of the person held vicariously responsible and must be acting within the
scope and course of his employment (see above). The person held vicariously
responsible must be under an obligation or have a right to perform a function
by virtue of office, statute or the possession of a licence and he must be under
a duty to see that such a function is properly performed. The law determines
that he shall not escape criminal responsibility for the commission of an
offence by an employee merely because of the fact that he has delegated the
execution of that function (although quite properly within the terms of
employment or agency) to an employee (see *Allen* v *Whitehead* [1930] 1 KB
211). Although the propriety of this doctrine was doubted in *Vane* v
Yiannopoullos [1965] AC 486 it seems to have survived. What constitutes
delegation in a given case (notwithstanding *Vane* v *Yiannopoullos*) remains
uncertain, but is probably a matter of fact (see *Howker* v *Robinson* [1973] QB
178). The judges in *Vane* v *Yiannopoullos* considered it could only possibly
apply where all of a person's authority to perform a function had been
entrusted to his subordinate, whereas in *Howker* v *Robinson* the licensee was
still on the premises but held liable for his employee's breach of the law which
occurred in another room. Remember, in the circumstances noted above

without the fact of delegation the individual who may otherwise be vicariously liable for an offence must be held criminally responsible personally or else acquitted.

Liability of Employee or Agent

You may also have to consider the personal criminal responsibility of the employee or agent who has actually brought about the commission of the offence.

Where a person has been convicted as a principal offender through the medium of delegation the actual perpetrator of the offence may only be convicted as a secondary party. This is because in cases of delegation, the person held responsible as a principal offender must be an individual of a particular status, e.g., a licence holder. In cases where vicarious liability is imposed by express or implied statutory construction there is no objection to holding the actual perpetrator a co-principal with any other individual who is held liable vicariously.

Defences

In many statutory offences there are examples of specific defences which may apply to those who may otherwise be liable vicariously. Little would be gained from reviewing all such examples but it may be useful to cite one as an illustration, e.g., s. 24 of the Trade Descriptions Act 1968 which provides a defence if an accused, who would otherwise be held liable vicariously for an offence under the Act, can establish that the commission of an offence under the Act occurred *but* that he 'took all reasonable precautions and exercised all due diligence to avoid the commission of such an offence' by himself or any person under his control. An individual cannot be held vicariously responsible for the criminal activity of another when that activity consists of no more than abetting an offence or an attempt (see *Ferguson* v *Weaving* [1951] 1 KB 814 and *Gardner* v *Akeroyd* [1952] 2 QB 743).

PLANNING YOUR REVISION

Corporate liability and vicarious liability, although technical and complex, cause few problems to students. Secondary participation, however, seems to be an area of general difficulty to the average student. Confusion may be dispelled by a careful consideration of the following matters.

Much of the case law governing criminal liability for secondary participation was developed prior to the abolition of the classification of crimes as either felonies or misdemeanours. The terminology used to describe secondary participation in cases of felonies differed from that used in cases of misdemeanours. These classifications of criminal offences were abolished by the Criminal Law Act 1967 and the law of secondary participation rendered uniform for all kinds of crimes.

It is not possible to ignore all the pre-1967 case law which considered secondary participation.

You need to be familiar with the terminology that was used to describe secondary participation in cases of felony in order to make such cases intelligible. In brief, in cases of felony a principal offender was described as a principal in the first degree. Individuals who rendered assistance *at the time* of the commission of the principal offence *irrespective* of their *presence* were called principals in the second degree. The modern equivalent will generally be aiders, abettors or possibly procurers. Individuals who rendered assistance to a principal offender *prior* to the commission of the offence were known as accessories before the fact. The modern equivalent may be either a counsellor (the most common) or an aider or procurer. It was recognised with regard to felonies that a secondary party could render assistance *after* the commission of an offence, such a person being known as an accessory after the fact. Since the abolition of felonies there is no such offence. It is, however, partially preserved in a more limited form in the statutory offence contained in the Criminal Law Act 1967, s. 4 (assisting offenders), with which you should be conversant together with s. 5 of that Act (concealing arrestable offences or giving false information).

It is suggested that the need to make reference to pre-1967 case law and the unfortunate continuing need to translate the old felony terms and classifications into their modern equivalents is the prime cause of confusion in this area of the law. Nevertheless you should bear in mind that although the modern law on secondary participation seeks to produce a uniform body of rules common to all individuals who participate in a criminal offence, irrespective of the nature of their involvement, there are still differences between such individuals because of their degree of participation. It is hoped the following examination question will raise and illustrate these differences. If you fully understand these differences and to a lesser extent, if you have mastered the terminology, old and new, then you possess the key to success in this area of the law.

EXAMPLES OF QUESTIONS

Problem Involving Participation

(1)   Albert, Carl, Maurice and Graham, four evil brothers, plan to steal valuable antiques from their uncle Rodney's large mansion. To this end they agree that Carl, Maurice and Graham will attend Rodney's private birthday dinner (they are the only guests); Albert, feigning illness, is to be absent.

In accordance with their plan, Maurice and Graham distract Rodney at the dinner table while Carl puts a dangerous and potentially poisonous drug into his uncle's wine. Unknown to Maurice and Graham, but known to Albert and Carl, the drug used will and does kill Rodney. The three brothers then begin to carry out their prearranged plan. Maurice, going upstairs, sees that Rodney has a clandestine house guest, one Letitia, a nubile young lady. He rapes her; Carl and Graham stand by watching.

Discuss the criminal liability of the parties.

This is the kind of problem of which tutors and examiners are enamoured. It involves a multitude of parties and issues. A method of dealing with such a question is to construct a plan divided into a consideration of the criminal liability of each party. This can be done by a review of each individual's situation within the problem but it is best done by reference to the possible criminal offences that are committed within the problem. To each of these offences can be attached the names of the individuals who have participated and in what capacity. Reduce the names of the parties to their initial letters.

Plan

(a)   Conspiracy to commit burglary (see Theft Act 1968, s. 9, and chapter 10). A, C, M and G (all principal offenders).

(b)   Conspiracy to administer a noxious substance (contrary to Offences against the Person Act 1861, s. 24; see chapter 9). A, C, M and G (all principal offenders).

(c)   The administering of the noxious substance. C (principal offender), A, M and G (secondary parties).

(d)   Manslaughter of R. M and G (secondary parties).

(e)   Murder of R. C (principal offender), A (secondary party). Conspiracy to murder. A and C (principal offenders).

(f)   Burglary. C, M and G (principal offenders), A (secondary party).

(g)   Rape of L. M (principal offender), C and G (secondary parties).

A bare analysis of the question in this fashion will help you to construct your answer but such an answer alone is insufficient to constitute more than an outline which might achieve only a bare pass. It is in the consideration of the relationship between the various offences that have been committed and the detailed review of the differing degrees of complicity each of the parties enjoys in relation to each offence together with the understanding of how and where their degree of participation differs that the meat of the question is to be found.

Thus in relation to the conspiracy to burgle, all (A, C, M and G) are principal offenders, as they are in relation to the offence of conspiracy to administer a noxious thing. However, the one conspiracy offence for which only two of the parties, A and C, are liable is the conspiracy to murder R.

In relation to the administering of the noxious substance, only C can constitute himself a principal offender; A is a counsellor and M and G are aiders. It is when you come to review the consequence of R's death that the true difficulties in the question begin to arise.

M and G have the *mens rea* sufficient to mark them as aiders of the manslaughter of R. They intend to and help C cause R to suffer actual bodily harm. They intend to help the administration of the substance which has proved fatal to R. They are aware of the fact that manslaughter is one of a number of offences which could be said to come within the 'type' or group of offences within their contemplation (see *DPP for Northern Ireland* v *Maxwell* [1978] 3 All ER 1140). Furthermore it has been the law for some considerable time that parties are liable for all the consequences that flow from an authorised, jointly contemplated act, whether those consequences are seen or unforeseen (see *R* v *Anderson and Morris* (1966) 50 Cr App R 216). However, the administering of the poison by C with the intent to kill amounts to the offence of murder (see *R* v *Moloney* [1985] AC 905) for which C stands as a principal offender. A is a clear counsellor of the offence of murder.

The interesting point for you to consider is that two of the parties, M and G, are secondary parties to the manslaughter of R, one party, A, is a secondary party to his murder and C is his actual murderer. This requires a discussion of the fact that the *actus reus* of the death of R is merely the external factor which is the consequence of the joint action of all the parties. Their actual criminal responsibility is governed by their conduct and *crucially* by their *mens rea* with regard to the death of R, see (*DPP* v *Merriman* [1973] AC 584).

You could give final consideration to the issue of authorised and unauthorised acts and how the latter affect the criminal responsibility of the various parties to a joint enterprise. In the question, C, M and G are joint principals to the theft of the antiques (i.e., burglary) and A is a counsellor of this offence.

When M rapes L the issue is complicated. You first have to consider the case law on whether C and G can be regarded as either aiders or abettors to this offence notwithstanding their passive presence (see *R* v *Coney* (1882) 8 QBD 534, *Wilcox* v *Jeffrey* [1951] 1 All ER 464 and *R* v *Clarkson* [1971] 3 All ER 344). Secondly, could C, G and A be constituted secondary parties to the rape of L in their respective capacities because M's act was within their common enterprise or contemplation? According to *DPP for Northern Ireland* v *Maxwell* [1978] 3 All ER 1140 the issue is determined by whether or not the rape of L is within the 'type' of offence contemplated by the parties. This is a matter of fact and in the absence of clear guidance it would be a permissible inference to conclude that this latter offence is the result of an unauthorised act on M's part uncontemplated by the other parties. If this is the inference that can be drawn from the facts the conclusion must be that M stands alone as principal offender in respect of the rape and neither A, nor C and G (subject to the issue considered above) can be held responsible as secondary parties.

This question could have raised a number of other issues by addition to or modification of the principal facts. For example, the question of innocent agency could have arisen had C put the poison into R's glass at A's behest believing it to be a medicine, A knowing it to be a poison. Further matters that could be raised are the questions of a secondary party being convicted of a greater offence than that of the principal offender. This would be the case where A was the only party who knew the drug would kill R, the others believing it would merely render the uncle unconscious. Remember that it is possible for a secondary party to be convicted of a greater offence than the principal offender (see *R* v *Howe* [1987] AC 417 and *DPP* v *Merriman* [1973] AC 584).

Vicarious Liability

A fairly common assessment or examination topic is the issue of vicarious liability. Questions on this topic may read as follows:

(2)   Compare and contrast strict and vicarious liability. (This may be a half question.)

(3)   'Vicarious liability is by no means the same thing as strict liability. The point requires emphasis for there is an unhappy judicial tendency to confuse the two concepts.' (Smith and Hogan.)

Compare the two concepts and consider how far either concept can be justified.

Both questions require similar treatment.

You should be prepared to discuss fully the nature of strict liability (see chapter 5). The confusion between strict liability and vicarious liability lies in the fact that many offences which are of strict liability may be committed vicariously. Be prepared to consider the principal ground for imposing vicarious liability where the offence is also one of strict liability, i.e., the principle of statutory construction (sometimes known as extensive construction). Remember delegation as a principle for imposing vicarious liability is only applicable to statutory offences which require *mens rea* as to all their external elements. Reference can be made to the few offences at common law which can be committed vicariously and which are also offences of strict liability, e.g., public nuisance. The above issues are common to both questions.

The second question in addition requires you to consider the justifications (if any) for the existence of strict and vicarious liability. Remember the leading case which sets out the prime reasons for the imposition of strict liability *R v City of Sault Ste Marie* (1978) 85 DLR (3d) 161. The justification for vicarious liability lies in dicta of the judiciary in cases such as *Coppen v Moore (No. 2)* [1898] 2 QB 306. When it is imposed in cases where the offence is also one of strict liability, its justification in such cases is that not to impose vicarious liability would render the statutory offence a nullity. The rationale of imposing vicarious liability in cases of delegation of duties or rights imposed or created in statutory offences was clearly expressed in *R v Winson* [1969] 1 QB 371 per Lord Widgery CJ and is based upon the premise that where the law permits the exercise of a power or imposes a duty to act, failure to act on the part of the accused cannot be excused by claiming the fact of delegation.

It is rare for the topic of vicarious liability to be raised other than as a half question and usually it takes the form of an essay. It will occasionally raise its head as a half question in problem form. Usually this involves considering the potential liability of the actual perpetrator of the *actus reus* of an offence and a person who may be held vicariously liable for that conduct, the classic situations envisage various licensing or road traffic offences. The person who actually causes the prohibited consequences or event concerned must have done so within the scope and course of his or her employment (as in all cases of vicarious liability). The facts of such a question, however, usually disclose the possible commission of two offences either by the same individual or different persons who nevertheless may both be employees or agents of the person who may ultimately be held vicariously liable for their conduct. The purpose of such a stratagem on the part of the tutor or examiner is to see that you fully understand the two principal methods of imposing vicarious liability. One offence will usually be a strict liability offence where vicarious liability is implied by the courts into the statute. In such cases the actual perpetrator may logically be convicted as a co-principal of the person held responsible vicariously. This should be contrasted with any offence that requires *mens rea* as to all its external elements. In such cases vicarious liability is imposed through the medium and principle of delegation. In such cases the actual perpetrator of the *actus reus* may only be convicted as a secondary party to the person held vicariously responsible (see above).

Nevertheless an example of a problem question which involves issues of vicarious liability may be as follows:

(4)   The Firearms Act 1968, s. 1(1), provides: 'Subject to any exemption under this Act, it is an offence for a person — (a) to have in his possession, or to purchase or acquire, a firearm to which this section applies without holding a firearm certificate in force at the time'. Section 58(2) of the Act reads: 'Nothing in this Act relating to firearms shall apply to an antique firearm which is sold, transferred, purchased, acquired or possessed as a curiosity or ornament'.

Alan owns a chain of public houses and employs Bert to be responsible for maintaining them in repair and arranging for the provision of furniture and fittings. Bert decides to buy some pistols for the lounge of the 'Smugglers Inn' but, knowing about the Firearms Act, first takes advice from Colin, a firearms expert, who assures him that the pistols he is proposing to buy are antiques. Acting on this advice, Bert purchases the pistols and has them mounted on the wall of the inn. The pistols are not antiques.

Consider the criminal liability of Alan and Bert.

Apart from the question of the incorrect advice that Bert received, the offence committed is one of strict liability (see *R v Howells* [1977] 3 All ER 417). The question is difficult but the issues you should consider are as follows: Was Bert acting in the course of his employment? Is this a statute for which vicarious liability can be imposed through the doctrine of extensive construction, i.e., implied into the statute? Can Alan thus be held vicariously liable for Bert's act? These are difficult issues, but this is a situation where spotting the issues is as significant, if not more so, than your attempt to answer them.

This brings us to the final topic, that of corporate liability. This topic, like vicarious liability, frequently forms a half question in examinations, but almost always takes the form of an essay question, and the following are typical examples:

(5) 'The imposition of corporate liability is plagued with inconsistency and uncertainty and cannot be justified by policy or logic.'

Discuss.

(6) 'In general a corporation is in the same position in relation to criminal liability as a natural person and may be convicted of common law and statutory offences including those requiring *mens rea*' (*Halsbury's Laws of England*, 4th ed.).

Consider the extent to which a corporation's liability for the acts of its servants is similar to and how far it differs from the liability of a natural person.

Where such questions occur they tend to seek out and test the student's knowledge of the underlying theories and mechanisms by which a corporation can be held criminally liable. You should start answering questions such as those noted above by describing the nature of the corporation and the difficulties of ascribing to such a body responsibility for the commission of the *actus reus* of an offence. You should then perhaps consider the two methods chosen by the law for imposing criminal liability upon a corporation. It may well be suggested that the principal objection to imposing criminal liability upon a corporation is that such organisations or entities have no actual, physical presence or personality, only an artificial personality attributed by the law, and therefore they are incapable of forming and cannot have *mens rea* in the traditional sense. If this is your view you may go on to consider that in offences of strict or absolute liability where the *actus reus* of an offence may be committed without any *mens rea* on the part of the perpetrator and which can therefore realistically be ascribed to a corporation there can be no objection to holding a corporation criminally responsible by the doctrine of statutory construction. Such a principle offends neither policy nor logic. Strict liability offences frequently seek to regulate social and economic activities in which corporations play a leading part. It may be argued that to be entirely consistent with the enforcement of the policies which lie behind such strict liability offences corporations should be held responsible under the same situations as when the law penalises individuals.

It is perhaps in the doctrine of identification that the law reaches in the fullest degree a situation of inconsistency and uncertainty. After explaining the doctrine of identification which imposes liability upon corporations for offences which require *mens rea*, you may come to a conclusion as to whether it is inconsistent with imposing corporate liability in cases of strict liability offences through the principle of statutory construction. Whatever your conclusion the other matter to consider is the lack of certainty in determining who shall be regarded as the *alter ago* or persona of a company for the purposes of identification (see *Tesco Supermarkets Ltd* v *Nattrass* [1972] AC 153 and *R* v *Andrews-Weatherfoil Ltd* [1972] 1 All ER 65). You may feel, however, that this is both a matter of common sense and of fact which should not and cannot be rendered into a definitive test. You may consider Lord Denning's analogy with the human body (distinguishing the brain from the limbs) in *H. L. Bolton Engineering Co. Ltd* v *T. J. Graham & Sons Ltd* [1957] 1 QB 159 to be a useful starting-point but ultimately the determination in differing organisations and cases of who may be regarded as the persona of a company (and therefore acting as the company) cannot be made otherwise than on a case-by-case basis using very general tests of authority and control. Mention must be made of *P & O European Ferries (Dover) Ltd* (1991) 93 Cr App R 72, *OLL Ltd*, convicted of manslaughter on 8 December 1994 at Winchester Crown Court and *Meridian Global Fund Management* [1995] 2 AC 500.

The final matter to consider is the policy and logical basis of corporate liability. A corporation's existence is in the world of commerce and public life; the offences which corporations are likely to commit are almost exclusively concerned with the regulation of the very activities in which corporations are major agents. Although the methods used by the courts to rationalise the imposition of liability on corporations may not convince a philosopher or logician they work within a practical context. The underlying justification for it is public policy. Commercial crime, frauds and misrepresentations and the infringements of protective social policies (for example, laws relating to conserving the environment, health and safety of workers and public health) are frequently perpetrated through the medium of corporations (see *R* v *Rozeik* [1996] 1 WLR 159, *Moore* v *Bresler Ltd* [1944] 2 All ER 515 and *Belmont Finance* v *Williams Ltd* [1979] Ch 250). To hold individuals in a company responsible for their perpetration of certain criminal activities may prove difficult or impossible or of little value in helping to enforce the policies which are backed up by those criminal offences, but holding corporations themselves responsible and imposing heavy fines against their assets has proved a more realistic sanction in controlling such antisocial activities. The courts have found a way to do precisely that. Most assessment or examination questions concerning corporate liability will consider all or some of the matters considered above.

A final question to consider is as follows:

(7) To what extent is an employer criminally responsible for his employee's acts?

What difficulties are there in determining such liability if the employer is a corporation?

This question is purely descriptive. It requires a full consideration of the ways in which the law imposes vicarious liability upon individuals. It then requires a review of corporate liability and a consideration of how a corporation can be held vicariously responsible.

CONCLUSION

Keep the following in mind as an aid to comprehension and successful revision of these topics.

Secondary Participation

The principal difficulty here is terminology. If you remember, however, that an individual is either a principal offender or is regarded as being such even if he is a secondary participator (i.e., a party, accomplice, accessory). Although he may be regarded as a principal offender by the law, he or she is *factually* involved either as an aider, abettor, counsellor or procurer of the *actus reus* of an offence committed by another. Once this is grasped the other principal difficulties relating to the conviction of a secondary party where the principal offender is acquitted and the possibility of parties to a crime being convicted of different offences in relation to the same *actus reus* should appear logical to you. Each individual's involvement in a crime should be examined independently and their liability for their involvement in the *actus reus* of the principal offence determined by their conduct and *mens rea* or the availability of defences.

Corporate Liability

This topic is governed by policy. The criminal law requires that corporations should be held criminally responsible in certain circumstances. If you understand the two principal methods utilised by the law to achieve these ends, namely statutory construction (strict liability) and the doctrine of identification (where *mens rea* has to be proved), this area of the law should pose no real problems for you.

Vicarious Liability

Remember the ways in which an individual or a corporation may generally be held criminally liable vicariously. This principle for imposing criminal liability is mainly concerned with statutory offences. A statute may expressly or impliedly by its terms recognise the possibility of vicarious criminal responsibility. This construction is only given to statutes which are offences of strict or absolute liability.

Nevertheless a statutory offence which requires *mens rea* may be interpreted as imposing liability vicariously through the doctrine of delegation. Be fully conversant with the authorities which consider the issue of delegation. Finally, remember the anomalous rule that in cases where vicarious liability has been imposed through the medium of delegation that the actual perpetrator of the *actus reus* of the offence may only be convicted if at all as a secondary party.

FURTHER READING

Participation

Buxton, R., 'Complicity and the Law Commission' [1973] Crim LR 223.

Buxton, R., 'The Extent of Criminal Complicity' (1979) 42 MLR 315.

Clarkson, C., 'Kicking Corporate Bodies and Damning Their Souls' (1996) 59 MLR 557.

Dennis, I., 'Intention and Complicity: A Reply' [1988] Crim LR 649.

Giles, M., 'Complicity — the Problem of Joint Enterprise' [1990] Crim LR 383.

Gobert, J., 'Corporate Criminality: New Crimes for the Times' [1994] Crim LR 722.

Griew, E., 'It Must Have Been One of Them' [1989] Crim LR 129.

Harvard Law Review Editorial Board, 'Development in the Law — Corporate Crime: Regulating Corporate Behaviour through Criminal Sanctions' (1979) 92 Harv LR 1227–1369.

Law Commission Consultation Paper No. 131: Assisting and Envouraging Crime (1993).

Law Commission Working Paper No. 44: Codification of the Criminal Law: General Principles: Criminal Liability of Corporations (1972).

Padfield, N., 'Assisting and Encouraging Crime' (1994) 58(3) JCL 297.

Payne, J., 'Who's Minding the Company?' (1996) 146 NLJ 1365.

Reed, A., 'Duress of Circumstances and Joint Enterprise' (1995) 139 SJ 1052.

Reed, A., 'Joint Participation in Criminal Activity' (1996) 60(3) JCL 310.

Smith, J. C., 'Secondary Participation in Crime — can we do without it? (1994) 144 NLJ 679.

Smith, J. C., Commentary to *R v Wan Chan* [1995] Crim LR 297.

Smith, J. C., 'Criminal Liability of Accessories' (1997) 113 LQR 453.

Sullivan, G. R., 'Intent, Purpose and Complicity' [1988] Crim LR 641.

Sullivan, G. R., 'Aiding and Abetting the Commission of a Non-Existent Offence' (1976) 39 MLR 350.

Sullivan, G. R., 'The Attribution of Culpability to Limited Companies' [1996] 55 CLJ 515.

Toczek, I. R., 'Homicide and Accomplices' (1995) 145 NLJ 956.

Toczek, I. R., 'Accomplices Revisited' (1996) 146 NLJ 1625.

Wells, C., 'Corporations and Criminal Responsibility' (Oxford: Clarendon Press, 1993).

Wells, C., 'Corporations: Culture, Risk and Criminal Liability' [1993] Crim LR 551.

Williams, G., 'The Extension of Complicity' (1975) 34 CLJ 182.

Williams, G., 'Which of you did it?' (1989) 52 MLR 179.

Williams, G., 'Complicity, Purpose and the Draft Code' [1990] Crim LR 4 and 48.

7 INCHOATE OFFENCES

Society would not be adequately protected if persons could be made criminally liable only when they completed substantive offences. Incitements, conspiracies and attempts (all of which are activities preliminary to the completion of a substantive offence) would not produce criminal consequences. Our law, however, considers these activities so dangerous that it has declared them to be crimes and refers to them as inchoate or preliminary offences. They are designed to punish persons who fully intend to commit a substantive offence (or to see others commit an offence) and who have taken some overt steps towards the commission of their criminal ambitions but who, for some reason, have not fully realised that intention. The potential liability for any inchoate offence arises as soon as the person does something which is sufficient evidence of the intention to put criminal thoughts or plans into effect even though the intended offence has not yet been completed and may never be completed. What amounts to sufficient evidence depends on the circumstances. For incitement, words or gestures are enough in themselves. An attempt requires the taking of some step that is more than merely preparatory. Conspiracy generally falls somewhere between incitement and attempt. It is not as instantaneous as incitement because it requires an agreement but it does not require going as far as is required for attempt.

You must appreciate the basic principle that each and every inchoate offence must be charged in relation to an intended substantive offence. They are not themselves criminal offences in their own right. They are only criminal in relation to a substantive criminal offence. For this reason the three recognised inchoate offences fall into the category of specific intent offences.

The accused is only liable, in other words, if he engages in overt conduct (intentionally or recklessly) aimed at the commission of a specified substantive offence *and* in addition he intended to commit, or to see another commit, that specified, substantive offence, such as rape, robbery, murder, blackmail, theft etc. Inchoate offences require that the specific intent to commit, or to see another commit, an identifiable, substantive offence be proved. Therefore recklessness as to whether or not the accused (or another) will commit a substantive offence will not constitute *mens rea* if either of them is charged with an inchoate offence (*Millard* [1987] Crim LR 393).

THREE OFFENCES

The three inchoate offences are: incitement, conspiracy and attempt. Of these only the first still, in the main, remains a common law offence (although there are now specific statutory instances providing for offences of incitement, see Criminal Law Act 1977, s. 54, inciting a girl under 16 to have incestuous sexual intercourse). Conspiracy is largely governed now by the Criminal Law Act 1977 but that enactment is not a code, it leaves certain common law offences still in existence namely (a) conspiracy to defraud, (b) conspiracy to corrupt public morals and (c) conspiracy to outrage public decency. Attempts are now completely governed by the Criminal Attempts Act 1981.

CRIMINAL ATTEMPTS

Criminal conduct in relation to the offence of attempt has three stages to it:

(a)   The formation of the *mens rea* (evil thoughts).
(b)   The preparation.
(c)   The attempt (falling short of completion).

The fourth and final stage is completion of the intended substantive offence. If the accused has gone that far then he will generally be charged with the final offence and not with an attempt at it.

Evil Thoughts

The whole tenor of chapter 4 was to the effect that as a general rule (in relation to more serious crimes) unless some prohibited act or omission, together with attendant circumstances and consequences, is proved to *coincide* with the *related* criminal state of mind no liability will arise. In short there can be no liability for criminal thoughts without criminal deeds. Remember that chapter 5, however, showed that in many instances today (mainly relating to less serious, regulatory offences) you may be criminally liable for prohibited acts, omissions, conduct, events or language (generally in certain prescribed circumstances) either *without* proof of any thought, any *mens rea* or any guilty mind (in the case of absolute offences) or *without* proof of *mens rea* or guilty mind as to some element of the *actus reus* (in the case of strict liability offences). So far, however, English law does not permit the converse. Currently it is not possible to be made criminally liable for criminal thoughts, *mens rea* or guilty mind alone. While, thankfully for the principle of freedom, that as a general rule is true, the common law with society's acquiescence introduced into our legal system the concept of inchoate offences. These mean that while thoughts alone (no matter how evil) are not as a general rule punishable, the moment these thoughts are transmitted into or reflected in some ascertainable, external conduct then the prospect of prosecution becomes a serious possibility. The inchoate offence of conspiracy provides an excellent example. Conspiracy may appear to be simply a state of mind which may be punished in English law even if there is no positive, external conduct taken to achieve the aim or object of the conspiracy. But those convicted of conspiracy are not in such instances being convicted for their thoughts alone, there necessarily will have been some communication between the parties to the conspiracy and it is that intentional overt, external conduct which is prohibited and gives rise to potential liability, not the evil thought alone. What, however, is more worrying is the decision of the House of Lords in *R v Shivpuri* [1987] AC 1 because its broadest implication is that thinking that you are stealing something, for example, will make you liable for the offence of attempt even though what you thought you were stealing was already your own property and therefore incapable of being stolen by you. According to *Shivpuri* you are liable for an attempt even though arguably there is no *actus reus* because no substantive offence was possible. For more detail see the discussion of *Shivpuri* and impossibility, below.

Preparation

Secondly there is a degree of controversy concerning the dividing line between acts of preparation and acts of perpetration which may provide examiners with a useful question. Even today, despite s. 1(1) of the Criminal Attempts Act 1981 it is not easy to say where precisely the line is to be drawn and even the broadest and most liberal interpretation of that section or the definitions of conspiracy or incitement, will not bring within the net of the inchoate offences every act of preparing to commit a substantive offence. Those who wish to widen the ambit of criminal law are not adverse to maintaining that acts of preparation for the commission of a crime are themselves crimes at common law as evidenced by the decision in *R v Gurmit Singh* [1966] 2 QB 53. Of course, if this is correct there is at common law an inchoate offence prior to attempt and possibly prior to incitement or conspiracy.

The Criminal Attempts Act 1981, s. 6, abolished the offences of attempt at common law and any offence at common law of procuring materials for crime. This provision may abrogate the decision in *Singh's* case but by its use of the limited words 'procuring materials', s. 6 leaves open whether other acts of preparation may still be criminal at common law in their own right. *Singh's* case stands alone and has little, if any, precedent value and the preponderance of opinion is against the recognition of a general common law offence of preparation. Parliament, however, has created specific statutory offences of preparation. Two good examples are s. 3 of the Criminal Damage Act 1971 and s. 25(1) and (2) of the Theft Act 1968. Each makes it an offence (in specified circumstances) to have anything capable of being used to cause criminal damage or in connection with any burglary, theft or cheat respectively. For such offences liability turns on the dangerousness and abnormality or incongruity of the thing possessed in light of the surrounding circumstances. To establish the *mens rea* for such offences it is necessary to prove that the accused knew he possessed the object and secondly to prove that he intended to use it (or permit it to be used in the case of s. 3 of the 1971 Act) in the course of or in connection with any of the specified offences. The serious anomaly brought to light by *R v Geddes* [1996] Crim LR 894 is that no corresponding statutory provision exists for offences against the person. There was clear evidence that Geddes was going equipped for kidnapping (of children). He was seen in the lavatory block of a school and ultimately when his rucksack was searched it contained a large kitchen knife, lengths of rope and a roll of masking tape. The Court of Appeal held that while there was evidence of preparation he had not taken a step that was more than preparatory and therefore was not guilty of attempted false imprisonment and in the absence of an appropriate statutory 'preparation' or 'going equipped' offence he must escape liability.

In *R v Tosti* [1997] Crim LR 746 the two accused had taken oxyacetylene cutting equipment to the scene of the planned burglary of a barn. They concealed the equipment in a hedge and approached the door of the barn to examine the padlock on it. They then realised they were being watched and ran away. They were convicted of attempted burglary presumably because they had made contact with their target (unlike Geddes who had not made contact with a child to imprison) and when Tosti and the other accused began examining the padlock they had moved from planning to perpetration, i.e., in the jury's view taken a step that is more than merely preparatory.

Completion and Attempt

Liability for attempting to commit an offence is significant only if, having been commenced, the course of events leading to the intended, complete offence is not completed. Although it is possible for a person who has committed an offence to be charged with attempting to commit it (*Webley* v *Buxton* [1977] QB 481), this ought to happen very rarely. Possible reasons for not completing a substantive offence are:

(a)   The accused may change his or her mind. If this occurs before a step has been taken that is 'more than merely preparatory', as prescribed in s. 1(1) of the Criminal Attempts Act 1981, then the accused will not be liable even for an attempt. If the accused changed his or her mind after doing things that go beyond mere preparation, he or she will have committed the inchoate offence (i.e., attempted to commit the substantive offence which he or she set out originally intending to complete).

(b)   The accused may have been prevented from doing some act necessary to complete the intended substantive offence. Often the intervention of the police or a citizen is primarily aimed at preventing the accused achieving his or her intended criminal goal. As with the voluntary change of mind situation (above), if the intervention of a third party is too early the accused may not have done enough to amount to an attempt within s. 1(1) of the 1981 Act.

(c)   The accused may have failed to complete the intended crime because of his or her own incompetence, often through trying to achieve it by the use of inadequate means.

(d)   It may be impossible, but unbeknown to the accused, to commit the intended offence because it is absolutely, physically impossible (generally because of some unexpected intervening event, e.g., the prior removal by someone else of valuables from the pocket, purse or safe from which the accused intended to steal).

(e)   The accused may have completed what he or she intended, thinking it to be a crime, but contrary to that belief what he or she has done is not in fact a crime. In other words it was not legally possible for what was thought of as a crime to be a crime in fact.

Definition of Attempt

Under the old common law what amounted to an attempt was set out in *R* v *Eagleton* (1855) Dears CC 515: 'Acts remotely leading towards the commission of the offence are not to be considered as attempts to commit it, but acts immediately connected with it are.' What acts were sufficiently connected with the intended offence so as to amount to an attempt were judged by a choice from a variety of criteria consisting of (1) proximity, (2) equivocality, (3) *locus paenitentiae*, (4) impossibility and (5) social danger. Today, however, attempt is no longer a common law offence but is governed by the definition in s. 1 of the Criminal Attempts Act 1981:

If, with intent to commit an offence to which this section applies, a person does an act which is more than merely preparatory to the commission of the offence, he is guilty of attempting to commit the offence.

It should be obvious that this definition does not assist the judge, the lawyer or the student to know where the line is to be drawn between mere acts of preparation, which are not attempts, and acts of perpetration which are punishable attempts. For this reason, as suggested in *R v Ilyas* (1984) 78 Cr App R 17 and confirmed in *R v Boyle* (1987) 84 Cr App R 270, reference may still be made back to the old common law tests and criteria. Consequently this topic with its attendant uncertainty and the scope it allows to display extensive case knowledge and legal skills of argument is ideal for examinations. A knowledge, therefore, of the old common law criteria for attempt should be useful. But there has been a move away from the old case law; in *R v Jones* [1990] Crim LR 800 the Court of Appeal stated that an invitation to construe the 1981 Act by reference to previous conflicting case law was misconceived (see also *R v Campbell* [1991] Crim LR 268 to that effect). The Act was a codifying statute. The correct approach is first to look at the natural meaning of the statutory words, and not to turn back to earlier cases seeking to fit some previous test to the words in the sections. The court added that s. 1(1) does not embody the 'last act' test of *Eagleton*. By implication the associated 'Rubicon test' is also rejected by the court (see the proximity test at common law, below). In *R v Gullefer* [1990] 3 All ER 885 the Court of Appeal said the Act seeks to steer a course midway between the 'last act' and the unequivocality or 'first act in a series leading to' tests. The line is reached when preparatory acts end and the accused 'embarks on the crime proper'. 'When that is will depend on the facts in any particular case'. The court in *Campbell*, having said that it is unnecessary to direct the jury on pre-Act law, stated that the jury may convict of attempt if satisfied 'so as to feel sure that the (accused) intended to commit the offence and that, with that intent, he did an act which was more than an act of preparation to commit the offence'. It is a question of fact and the jury decides whether an act was more than merely preparatory but as with any question of fact the judge may withdraw the matter if he thinks there is no evidence of it. That is a matter of law and so the law may declare what is not an attempt but it does not and cannot dictate what amounts to an attempt which is a matter for the jury in each instance. For example in *Attorney-General's Reference (No. 1 of 1992)* [1993] 2 All ER 190 the accused and a girl were both walking home at night having been drinking. The accused dragged her off the path and behind a hedge. He forced her to the ground and lay fully on top of her. He told her that he would kill her if she did not stop screaming. Police arrived and found her lying on her back with her skirt pulled around her waist. The accused was found kneeling nearby with his trousers down. He accepted that she was in no fit state to consent to sexual intercourse and that he did not ask her (whether she would consent to intercourse). He was unable to have sexual intercourse due to his drunkenness.

The Court of Appeal was asked to quash his conviction for attempted rape because the *actus reus* of rape requires penetration. There was no evidence of any such attempt here. Sexual intercourse was therefore still a few steps away.

The Court, dismissing the appeal, said it was not necessary to establish that he had attempted to penetrate her vagina. It was sufficient if there was evidence that he had the necessary intent and from the evidence the jury could infer that he had gone beyond mere acts of preparation. In *R v Jones* shortening a shotgun barrel and brandishing the gun at a woman, although the safety catch was still on, was held to be sufficiently 'beyond mere acts of preparation' to allow conviction for attempted murder; in *R v Campbell* [1991] Crim LR 268 approaching a post office with an imitation firearm, having spent time on reconnaissance and planning a robbery, was *not* sufficient for attempted robbery according to the Court of Appeal, as 'the accused was still engaged in acts of preparation'. See also *R v Griffin* [1993] Crim LR 515. In *R v Geddes* [1996] Crim LR 894 the test was said to be whether or not the accused's conduct 'showed that he had actually tried to commit the offence in question, or whether he had only got ready or put himself in a position or equipped himself to do so'. There, despite Geddes having kidnapping equipment with him and having entered a school, the court (reluctantly) felt that because he had not made contact with or confronted any pupil at the time he was apprehended, he could not be said to have done an act that was more than merely preparatory.

The Common Law Tests

At common law (a) there were a number of criteria or methods used indiscriminately to decide what was or was not an attempt, (b) some of these methods produced unsatisfactory results and (c), satisfactory or not, they all tended to indicate that there was (and still is) a very narrow dividing line between preparation and attempt. At the end of a case review the conclusion that it is a question of fact and degree is irresistible. The old law still provides some useful insights.

Proximity

At common law the most prominent test of attempt was proximity. In *R v Robinson* [1915] 2 KB 342 it was stated that acts remotely leading to the commission of the offence are not, but acts immediately connected are, an attempt. Penultimate acts would be proximate and likely to be an attempt and possibly even pre-penultimate acts would fall into that category. *R v Robinson* concerned attempt to defraud, as did the earlier case of *R* v *Button* [1900] 2 QB 597. In *Robinson* the accused was not convicted but in *Button* he was and the difference between the cases lies in the fact that the accused in *Button* had done all he could towards the commission of the defrauding whereas the accused in *Robinson* had not. *Comer* v *Bloomfield* (1970) 55 Cr App R 305 supported the view in *Robinson* that it was not an attempt to intend to make a fraudulent insurance claim or even to write enquiring whether or not a claim could be made because the steps taken in fabricating a robbery and/or writing to the insurance company were not sufficiently proximate to obtaining compensation. In *Button* and in *DPP* v *Stonehouse* [1978] AC 55, on the other hand, the accused was convicted of attempt to defraud because the concealing of his pre-race form and the faked drowning respectively were sufficiently proximate to the fraudulent claiming of the prize in *Button* or the insurance money in *Stonehouse*. This apparent conflict of results is explainable on the basis that in *Button* and *Stonehouse* both accused had done everything they could to commit the complete offence whereas in *Robinson* and *Comer* the two accuseds still intended to make an insurance claim but had not yet done so. From these cases it would appear that an act was sufficiently proximate if it was the 'last act' needed by the accused to commit the full offence even though something remained to be done by someone else (such as in *Stonehouse* where his unsuspecting wife still had to make the actual insurance claim).

The 'last act' as the test is now discredited (*R* v *Jones* [1990] Crim LR 801) and especially Lord Diplock's notion concerning proximity, expressed in *Stonehouse* and applied in cases like *R* v *Widdowson* (1985) 52 Cr App R 314, that the accused must have 'crossed the Rubicon and burnt his boats' (i.e., that he had gone so far that he could not change his mind and retreat). That notion has been overruled by the Court of Appeal in *Gullefer* which makes it clear that an attempt may be committed before the accused reaches a point beyond which it would be impossible for him to go back.

Even so, Gullefer successfully appealed on the basis that his actions (in jumping onto the track in an attempt to distract the greyhounds during a race) were not sufficiently proximate to the complete offence of theft to be capable of comprising an attempt to commit theft of his stake money from the bookmaker. His appeal was allowed because it could not properly be said at that stage he was in the process of committing theft and there was insufficient evidence that when he jumped onto the track, he had gone beyond mere preparation (*R* v *Gullefer* [1990] 3 All ER 882).

Equivocality

Because of the uncertainty created by those proximity cases another test developed at common law. This was known as the equivocality test. In effect it meant that an accused's intention could be deduced from his conduct if that indicated beyond reasonable doubt the criminal goal towards which it was directed. In *Davey* v *Lee* [1968] 1 QB 366 the cutting of the fence wire near to a store of valuable copper was held to be attempted theft because that conduct could not reasonably be thought of as having any other purpose than the theft from that stock of copper. The court took the view that no other explanation was possible and the accused's act of climbing through the cut wire (at which point he was apprehended) was therefore an attempt.

The unsatisfactory nature of this so-called equivocality test is shown by the decision in *Jones* v *Brooks* (1968) 52 Cr App R 614 where the accused was convicted of attempting to take a motor vehicle having been apprehended trying door handles. (This problem has been resolved and probably would not arise today because the Criminal Attempts Act 1981, s. 9, created a new offence of 'interference with vehicles'.) The case, however, illustrated the unsatisfactory nature of this test because although the equivocality principle purportedly was relied upon, the trying of the car door handles arguably was equivocal. There were a number of explanations for trying the handles other than theft of the car itself. The court, however, combined the equivocal conduct and the accused's express intention (i.e., his admission that he intended to drive home in one of the cars) to conclude that he was guilty of an attempt.

'Change of heart'
Locus paenitentiae applied where an accused voluntarily changed his mind in which case his or her conduct up to that point more likely than not would be preparation and not perpetration provided it was completely harmless. If the conduct either came close to completing the full offence (see the comment on Lord Diplock's 'Rubicon test', above) or if any harm, injury or damage was caused then that conduct would be an attempt despite the accused's change of heart and remorse.

Social danger
The courts at common law sometimes overtly and sometimes more covertly were swayed by the degree of social danger involved. The seriousness of the intended, substantive crime and the danger apprehended from it were factors that caused judges to consider that certain conduct amounted to an attempt whereas it might otherwise have been considered as mere preparation: see *R* v *Brown* (1889) 24 QBD 357 where the perceived social danger to health from quackery might well have been instrumental in the decision that supplying an innocuous substance to try to induce an abortion was an attempt to procure an abortion.

Impossibility
Finally at common law the test of impossibility was devised to deal with a particular issue. A person may commence to do things which he thinks will

lead to the successful commission of a crime but unbeknown to that person it will be physically or legally impossible for the full substantive offence to be completed. The law on this topic has changed over the years. *R v McPherson* (1857) Dears & B 197 and *R v Collins* (1864) 9 Cox CC 497 held a person could not be convicted of attempt in such circumstances. Later in *R v Brown* (1889) 24 QBD 357 and *R v Ring* (1892) 17 Cox CC 491 the opposite outcome resulted, so, for example, it became an attempt to steal even though the other person's pocket, into which you surreptitiously inserted your hand, was empty. Years later in *Haughton v Smith* [1975] AC 476 the law changed again reverting to the view taken in cases like *McPherson* and *Collins*. This 'toing and froing' and uncertainty in the law concerning attempting the impossible led ultimately to the Criminal Attempts Act 1981. That legislation was designed to cancel out the common law, in particular the view in *Haughton's* case, that no liability for attempt arose if it was physically or legally impossible for the complete offence to be committed. You should keep in mind, however, that impossibility is very wide ranging and it could be said that it is impossible to commit the full offence if you are prevented from reaching your intended goal because (a) you start but change your mind about proceeding, or (b) you start but are prevented from proceeding by the intervention of a third party (e.g., a policeman) or an event (e.g., you fall off the ladder which you are climbing with intent to burgle) or (c) you start but you are incompetent (e.g., taking inadequate implements to break open a hardened steel safe).

In *Haughton v Smith* these three situations (even though they involve an element of impossibility) were considered as being capable of resulting in a conviction for attempt because in each the intended goal could have been achieved but for the accused's change of mind or incompetence. Those situations were distinguished from others where it was absolutely, physically impossible or else legally impossible to commit the intended offence. The classic examples respectively being the act of trying to steal from another's empty pocket and the taking of something (e.g., an umbrella or a coat) with the intent to steal it but subsequently discovering it belonged to you all along and therefore could not in law be stolen by you. In regard to both such instances their lordships, in *Haughton*, had declared you could not be liable for attempt.

It is suggested that in *Haughton* the judges decided that the dividing line between what is and what is not an attempt lay in between incompetence (or inadequate means) and physical impossibility (e.g., the empty pocket situation). If you were apprehended or incompetent you could be liable for attempt whereas if what you 'attempted' was physically or legally impossible, you could *not* be liable. The Criminal Attempts Act 1981, s. 1, moved the dividing line. Whether it was shifted to the extent that you could be liable for attempting to do what was physically *and* legally impossible was open to debate. Professor Glanville Williams, in 'The Lords achieve the logically impossible' (1985) 135 NLJ 502 maintained you could be liable in both instances after the 1981 Act. You might also look at Professor Williams's three articles, 'The Government's proposals on criminal attempts' (1981) 131 NLJ 80, 104, 128, which highlight the background to the Criminal Attempts Act 1981, although they should be read critically and with an eye to subsequent events. In *An Introduction to Criminal Law*, para. 5.6.10 (see also Hogan [1984] Crim LR 584), it was conceded that attempting the physically impossible is an offence but maintained that, whatever the statute was intended to say, on its current wording it could not make persons liable for attempt where the intended substantive offence was legally impossible. In other words the dividing line should be drawn between physical and legal impossibility. On this view the result of s. 1(2) of the 1981 Act would be to make you liable for the former today in the same way as you are if apprehended before completion of the intended offence, incompetence or using inadequate means whereas you would not be liable for situations of legal impossibility.

For examination purposes you *must* know the wording of the Criminal Attempts Act 1981, s. 1(1) to (3), and be able to express an opinion on how those paragraphs have been interpreted. Despite the decision in *R v Shivpuri* [1987] AC 1, discussed below, the section should be read as a whole. Arguably subsection (3) deals only with *mens rea* and not *actus reus*. This is significant because subsection (1) requires that a person must intend and act towards the commission of an offence. If a person intends to carry out an act which if completed would not be a crime because there is no *actus reus* there must be no offence and if that is the case that person should not be liable for an attempt because there was no substantive offence to attempt. It is true the person may have believed and intended to commit an offence (e.g., he may intend to steal an umbrella) but if there is no offence (because the umbrella already belongs to him) there can be no *actus reus* and no amount of inferring of intention by s. 1(3) will create one. It is true s. 1(2) states:

> A person may be guilty of attempting to commit an offence to which this section applies even though the facts are such that the commission of the offence is impossible.

However, the 'offence to which this section applies' (i.e., attempt) is defined in s. 1(1) as follows (emphasis added):

> If, with intent to commit *an offence* to which this section applies, a person does an act which is more than merely preparatory to the commission of *the offence*, he is guilty of attempting to commit *the offence*.

To reiterate, if there is no substantive offence to attempt, the accused should not be liable for attempt. If you cannot be liable for theft because the thing taken (with intent to steal) turns out to be your own, surely there is no *actus reus* for a complete offence and on the words of the section surely no liability for attempted theft otherwise that person would be punished simply for his criminal thoughts. If that was what Parliament intended it was not clearly stated: it did not unambiguously declare that trying to do what is legal can amount to the offence of attempt.

This view that legal impossibility remains a defence despite the 1981 Act appears to have been accepted and endorsed by the House of Lords in *Anderton v Ryan* [1985] AC 560 where Mrs Ryan was charged with dishonestly attempting to handle a stolen video recorder. She admitted she believed it was stolen but the prosecution on appeal conceded that it was not stolen or at least that there was no evidence that it had been stolen. The House of Lords quashed her conviction for attempt on the basis that the Act was more concerned with *mens rea* than *actus reus* but both elements still must be proved. As the recorder was not stolen there was no *actus reus* and no crime despite the accused's guilty state of mind. Their lordships at that time were not willing to concede, as Lord Roskill put it, that 'erroneous belief in the existence of facts which, if true, would have made [the accused's] completed act a crime makes [the accused] guilty of an attempt to commit that crime'. (For criticism of that decision, see Professor Glanville Williams (1985) 135 NLJ 502 and more importantly his views in [1986] CLJ 33 and for comments on the criticism, see Scanlan and Ryan, *An Introduction to Criminal Law*, para. 5.6.11.)

However, within 12 months and probably influenced by Professor Glanville Williams's article ([1986] CLJ 33) the House of Lords completely changed its opinion and overruled its recent decision in *Anderton v Ryan*. The opportunity for this volte-face came about when *R v Shivpuri* [1987] AC 1 reached the House on appeal. Shivpuri had been apprehended by customs officers entering Britain with a suitcase which he admitted he believed to contain prohibited drugs. On analysis, however, the substance in question was found to be a harmless powdered vegetable extract. Shivpuri was convicted of attempting to be knowingly concerned in dealing with a prohibited drug. His appeal was dismissed by the Court of Appeal and the House of Lords. Now, according to their lordships, all that needs to be proved to obtain a conviction for attempt (or conspiracy, given the similarity of the offences) is that the accused had the intention to commit a substantive offence and then whether in furtherance of that intention he has taken a step that is more than merely preparatory towards the completion of that substantive offence. The fact that the completion of the offence is impossible is now of no consequence since *Shivpuri*. Their lordships have interpreted s. 1 of the 1981 Act in such a way that it is the offence which the accused believes he is committing that is relevant and whether, if the facts had been as he believed them to be, he has taken a more than merely preparatory step towards the completion of that intended offence irrespective of its impossibility.

In *DPP v Nock* [1978] AC 979 (a case involving conspiracy, the law relating to which is analogous to that of attempt) the accused tried to extract a controlled drug out of chemicals which could not produce it. It was declared to be a case of physical impossibility and under the prevailing laws *at that time* (i.e., *Haughton v Smith*) they were not guilty of any inchoate offence. Today, of course, they would be guilty under the 1981 Act of attempt or under the 1977 Act (as amended) of conspiracy and, from the beginning of 1982 until the decision in *Shivpuri*, had they argued that what they set out to do was legally impossible then they may well have had a good defence to either charge. *Shivpuri* has put an end to that possibility.

Paradoxically if, for example, today an accused (intending to produce a prohibited drug) produced a substance which is not a proscribed drug then he has not committed a substantive offence yet he would be liable for an attempt (or conspiracy if others are involved). Whether or not he or they *should* be so liable is open to debate but since *Shivpuri* they will be liable. Why? The answer must lie in public policy, i.e., the fact that the judiciary has decided that persons who attempt or conspire to commit offences (even those which it is impossible to complete) are as dangerous to society as those who successfully complete their intended offences. In reality prosecution efforts are likely to be concentrated on those who, like Shivpuri, are potential drug dealers than on the Mrs Ryans of this world. Nevertheless she and others in situations like hers will now be liable. Such persons would be well advised to remain silent rather than admit that they thought the goods they were receiving were stolen.

Finally there is still one situation distinguishable from *Shivpuri* that falls outside the wide scope of the decision in that case. This is where the accused believes that he is committing or attempting to commit an offence but unbeknown to him there is no such offence known to English law. Shivpuri thought he was committing an offence but it was impossible for him to do so in the circumstances. Had the circumstances been different he could have committed his intended offence. The former situation can be illustrated by the case of *R v Taaffe* [1984] AC 539. There the accused imported into Britain packages which he believed contained foreign currency thinking that he was committing an offence in so doing. Exchange control had ended. There was no such offence in existence. Therefore he had neither committed any substantive offence nor any inchoate offence despite the morally bad state of his mind.

What distinguishes Mr Taaffe (who was not found guilty) from Mr Shivpuri (who was)? Both are morally reprehensible, both think they are engaged in committing a crime. For one it is impossible ever to commit what he intends because no such crime exists; for the other it is impossible because one of the circumstances pertaining to the *actus reus* is absent (namely that the goods he receives are not stolen or the goods he receives are already his own) but had the circumstances been as he believed them to be he would have been able to complete the intended crime. If social danger is to be the governing factor then surely each of these men has evidenced that he is a danger, that he is prepared to break laws (or what he perceives to be laws) although it is impossible for either actually to do so. Currently one of them will be liable for inchoate offences but the other will not.

Mens Rea of Attempt

It is vital you remember that there can be no conviction for attempt if the prosecution does not prove the accused's intention to commit a specified substantive offence. You could cite in support of this proposition Edmund-Davies LJ in *R v Easom* [1971] 2 QB 315 to the effect that 'it is implicit in the concept of an attempt that the person acting intends to do the act attempted' (see also the discussion on *R v Taaffe* above).

Attempt involves intention as to consequences (i.e., to commit the complete offence) so there must be proof that the accused did intend that consequence even though a lesser degree of *mens rea* (e.g., recklessness) might result in his conviction *had he been charged with the complete offence* instead of with attempt. A useful reference on this point is *R v Whybrow* (1951) 35 Cr App R 141 where the Court of Appeal held in relation to a charge of attempted murder that only proof of intent to kill will be sufficient, 'intent becomes the principal ingredient of the crime'. If the charge were murder then proof of intent to kill *or* to cause grievous bodily harm would suffice, (see also the useful discussion discounting any concept of reckless attempts in *R v Millard* [1987] Crim LR 393).

Moreover the intent referred to for attempt would appear to be limited to 'direct intent'. This proposition was supported by the case *R v Mohan* [1976] QB 1 (where the accused drove at a police officer who avoided being injured) in which it was stated that, for the *mens rea* of attempt, intention means 'specific intent' and can be defined as 'a decision to bring about a certain consequence' or as the 'aim'. The implication of these words in the judgment of James LJ would seem to have been that the offence of attempt requires proof of direct intent. Later in his judgment James LJ said in effect that the *mens rea* of attempt could not be satisfied by proof that the accused 'knew or correctly foresaw that the consequences of his act unless interrupted would "as a high degree of probability", or would be "likely to", . . . [bring about] the commission of the complete offence'. Such knowledge or inference is only evidence from which intent may be established, it is not in itself intent. It would seem that James LJ thought that proof of such a state of mind, i.e., (knowledge of a probable but undesired consequence) should not as a matter of law be sufficient *mens rea* for an attempt. If only proof of direct (*Steane*-type) intent will be sufficient then an attempt is an exceptional, specific-intent offence for which even foresight of *Moloney* type virtually certain consequences may play no part in the determination of *mens rea* (but see *Pearman*, below).

Remember, however, that the Criminal Attempts Act 1981, by s. 6(1), abolished the offence of attempt at common law 'for all purposes'. It could be argued that the Act made a fresh start in so far as the offence of attempt is concerned so that the 'intent' referred to in s. 1(2) could be construed free of the views expressed in *Mohan*. But there are now two cases which are contrary to the argument. First *R v Boyle* (1987) 84 Cr App R 270 permits reference back to the old common law cases to help interpret the provisions of the new Act.

Secondly in *R v Pearman* [1984] Crim LR 675 the Court of Appeal has stated that in relation to the specific-intent offence of attempting to cause grievous bodily harm, foresight of probable consequences must not be equated with intent to do the act. This reiterates, in relation to the new Act, the views expressed in *Mohan* in relation to the *mens rea* of attempt at common law. This leaves open the issue of whether or not foresight of inevitable consequences may, as a matter of evidence in appropriate cases, permit the jury to infer intention to attempt an offence. This is reinforced by the opening words of the Criminal Attempts Act 1981, s. 1(1), which reads: 'If, *with intent* to commit an offence' making it clear lesser states of mind such as recklessness or negligence are not relevant despite the fact that proof of lesser states of mind might have obtained a conviction had the accused been charged with a complete, substantive offence (even one of strict liability), instead of an attempt at such an offence.

One significant aspect of the Criminal Attempts Act 1981, s. 1, relates to *mens rea* as to circumstances in attempts. The accused must intend to produce the prohibited consequences (i.e., the full offence) but knowledge is also required of the factual circumstances of the full, substantive offence. The new Act, by s. 1(3), provides for situations where the accused would not have intended to commit the full offence because of a lack of knowledge of necessary circumstances. For example, the accused may be charged with attempt to have sexual intercourse with a girl under age (see Sexual Offences Act 1956, ss. 5 and 6) and he believes her to be under age *but he does not know* whether or not that is so. Attempt in this instance requires intent to have intercourse with a girl under the legal age and as the accused does not know her age he would not have the necessary intent under the old common law (even though, had he gone on to have intercourse and be charged with the full offence, recklessness as to this aspect would be sufficient *mens rea*). Under s. 1(3) of the Act his *belief* that the girl is under the legal age is deemed to constitute knowledge that she is and in this way the intent together with the necessary knowledge for the offence of attempt is satisfied. In short the person who believes but who does not know for certain is deemed to have the intention to commit the offence and therefore can be liable for an attempt to commit it.

Proof of intention as to consequences and mere recklessness as to circumstances should not be sufficient, but see Professor Glanville Williams's article [1983] Crim LR 365, in which he maintains that recklessness as to a necessary circumstance is sufficient and his views have found some favour in the Court of Appeal in *R v Khan and others* [1990] Crim LR 519. Against this are Parker J's words in *Gardner v Akeroyd* [1952] 2 QB 743 that 'So far as an attempt is concerned ... knowledge and intent are clearly necessary'. (Professor Williams maintains that is inconclusive because the learned judge was not asked to consider whether or not recklessness might be an alternative to knowledge for an attempt.) Professor Williams relies on cases such as *R v Pigg* [1982] 2 All ER 591 to show that attempted rape could be committed by a person who was reckless as to a circumstance, i.e., as to the female's consent, but persuasive as that argument may be two arguments to the contrary suggest that this is not the correct view of the law as it stands. First, Parliament did not take the opportunity provided by the enactment of the Criminal Attempts Act 1981 to make that view clearly the law and more importantly subsequent cases such as *R v Satnam S and Kewal S* (1984) 78 Cr App R 149 have stated that recklessness of the *Caldwell* type which was under discussion and which formed the basis for the decision in *R v Pigg* had no application to the law of rape. This would suggest that *Pigg's* case is not a strong authority to rely on in this matter. Professor Williams's view that proof of actual knowledge of necessary circumstances is not necessary to commit an attempt may now become the law where circumstances are a relevant part of the substantive offence which has been attempted because the Court of Appeal appears to have adopted that view in *Khan*. The decision in *R v Millard* [1987] Crim LR 393 confirms that recklessness as to whether or not a substantive offence will be committed generally is not sufficient *mens rea* for an inchoate offence. In *Khan*, however, the Court of Appeal has held that the offence of rape requires an intention to have sexual intercourse, plus a knowledge of, or recklessness as to, the absence of consent and that same analysis would be properly applied to the *mens rea* for attempted rape as the *mens rea* was identical. The attempt relates only to the physical activity. The recklessness is of course subjective recklessness only in the case of rape: *R v Satnam S and Kewal S* (1984) 78 Cr App R 149 and that should also be so in the case of attempted rape. *Caldwell* recklessness is incompatible with a claim that the accused thought the victim was consenting (see chapter 9).

For an excellent discussion by J. C. Smith of the *mens rea* of attempted murder see the commentary on *R v Walker and Hayles* [1990] Crim LR 44 at p. 46 and *R v Fallon* [1994] Crim LR 519: the *Moloney* or *Nedrick* direction is only necessary where the accused claims, or there is evidence, that he had something in mind other than what he is alleged to have attempted.

CONSPIRACY

Conspiracy is governed partly by the Criminal Law Act 1977 and partly by the common law. The central requirement is an agreement (*R v Bolton* (1992) 94 Cr App R 74). This means that no one can be a conspirator if he lacks *mens rea*. However, on a charge of conspiracy to traffic drugs a conspirator may be convicted even where his co-conspirator is an undercover agent acting with his superiors' authority or under orders. This is because the executive does not have the power under our constitution to authorise a breach of the criminal law. The fact that the officer would not be prosecuted did not mean that he did not intend to commit a criminal offence. Consequently, the agreement between him and the accused was a conspiracy to traffic in drugs (*Yip Chiu-Cheng* v *The Queen* [1994] 2 All ER 924 PC).

Prior to the 1977 Act the common law definition of a criminal conspiracy was very wide, so wide in fact that it encompassed any genuine *agreement* to do an unlawful act *or* a lawful act in an unlawful way (see *Mulcahy* v *R* (1868) LR 3 HL 306). It was wide enough to catch agreements to commit both serious and summary offences but in addition torts and acts tending to corrupt public morals or to outrage public decency. Its width was displayed in *Kamara* v *DPP* [1974] AC 104 which held that an agreement to trespass on another's land (a civil wrong), if accompanied by an intent to inflict more than nominal damage, was a criminal conspiracy. See also the decision in *Scott* v *Metropolitan Police Commissioner* [1975] AC 819 which held that there could be a conspiracy to defraud even though there was no agreement to commit a crime. In *Kamara* an agreement to do a civil wrong was made into an offence; in *Scott* an agreement to do something which was not criminal was made into an offence (likewise in *Shaw* v *DPP* [1962] AC 220 where the publishing of a *Ladies' Directory* was held to be the, hitherto unheard-of, offence of conspiracy to corrupt public morals). These decisions caused such criticism that eventually Parliament enacted the Criminal Law Act 1977.

Section 5(1) abolishes conspiracy at common law subject to the retention in s. 5(2) of conspiracy to defraud and in s. 5(3) the conspiracies to corrupt public morals and to outrage public decency. These three remain operative common law offences although *R* v *Ayres* [1984] AC 447 and *R* v *Tonner and Evans* [1984] Crim LR 618 state that if there is evidence of conspiracy to commit a substantive offence then the accused should be charged under s. 1(1) of the Act and not with one of these remaining common law conspiracies but where appropriate those old conspiracies may still be charged. For the problems caused by these decisions in relation to fraud cases see *R* v *Cooke* [1986] AC 909 and more importantly see the Criminal Justice Act 1987, s. 12, which was passed by Parliament to resolve those problems. That section makes it clear that the prosecution is now free, subject to the Code for Crown Prosecutors, in any case involving fraud to choose whether to charge with statutory conspiracy under the 1977 Act or conspiracy to defraud at common law.

Conspiracy to Defraud Defined

First, in *Scott* v *Metropolitan Police Commissioner* [1975] AC 819 Viscount Dilhorne defined conspiracy to defraud as:

> an agreement by two or more by dishonesty to deprive a person of something which is his or to which he is or would be or might be entitled and an agreement by two or more by dishonesty to injure some proprietary right of his.

In that instance the accused, who intended to make a profit by showing copies of films for a fee without paying the copyright holders anything, were held to have conspired to defraud although there was no theft or deception on their part.

Secondly, economic loss is not essential. In *R* v *Moses* [1991] Crim LR 617 the two accused were convicted of conspiracy to defraud by facilitating applications for immigration work permits which involved them withholding important information from their National Insurance departmental supervisors. Their appeal on the grounds that the Department (i.e., The Crown) had not suffered economic loss, was dismissed.

Thirdly, conspiracy to defraud can also be committed where the aim of the agreement is to deceive the victim into taking an economic risk (*R* v *Allsop* (1976) 64 Cr App R 29). In such cases the prosecution must prove that the victim had a right or interest which was capable of being prejudiced either by actual loss or by being put at risk and that an accused who dishonestly concealed from another person information which he was under a duty to disclose, to that person, or which the person was entitled to require him to disclose, could be guilty of fraud (*Grant Adams* v *The Queen* [1995] 1 WLR 52, (PC), where it was held that a company is entitled to recover secret profits made by its directors; for the directors to impede that recovery by hiding information or money in overseas companies was a conspiracy to defraud the company).

Fourthly, 'defraud' was interpreted widely in *Moses* and in *Welham* v *DPP* [1961] AC 103, to include inducing the supervisors into acting in a way contrary to their public duty. In the words of Lord Denning in *Welham* 'if anyone may be prejudiced in any way by the fraud, that is enough'.

Fifthly, in relation to the *mens rea* of conspiracy to defraud, despite Lord Diplock's view in *Scott*, it is not necessary to prove that the accused intended any economic loss to the victim(s) (*Wai Mu-Tsang* v R [1992] 1 AC 269. The chief accountant of a bank dishonestly concealed the fact that the bank would suffer a big loss through the purchase of dishonoured cheques. His defences to a charge of conspiracy to defraud were that he acted on instructions and secondly that he acted in the best interests of the bank to maintain confidence and stop panic withdrawals by customers. The fact he did not intend any economic loss and the assertion that his underlying motive was 'sound' or 'good', were held irrelevant). What the *mens rea* for this offence should be, has been controversial. It is intention to defraud and dishonesty. Intention to defraud cannot be limited to proof of intent to cause economic loss because the (direct intent) aim or purpose of most conspirators is to make a profit for themselves. The main cases indicate that it is sufficient to prove an intention to practise a fraud on another or an intention to prejudice some other person's rights. Clearly proof of intention to cause economic loss or to deceive someone into taking an economic risk or acting contrary to public duty would equally suffice (*Welham, R* v *Allsop* and *R* v *Cooke* [1986] AC 909 and *Wai Yu-tsang* v R [1991] 4 All ER 664).

Conspiracies Relating to Public Morals and Decency

In *Shaw* v *DPP* [1962] AC 220 the accused was convicted of conspiracy to corrupt public morals by publishing a directory of prostitutes. Such an offence was unknown but the House of Lords claimed it to be part of the common law and that they had the power to preserve the moral welfare of the State.

In *Knuller (Publishing, Printing & Promotions) Ltd* v *DPP* [1973] AC 435 the accused was convicted of conspiracy to outrage public decency by publishing advertisements relating to homosexual practices. Here even though the conduct referred to in the advertisement was not illegal it was held to be the offence of conspiracy because such conduct might be likely to result in corruption of that kind. Because of the criticism heaped on the decision in *Shaw* the judges in *Knuller* (while stating that *Shaw* was correct and creating the conspiracy to outrage decency) conceded that they had no general power to create any further new offences of this type.

The latter offence continues to be used (see *R* v *May* (1989) 91 Cr App R 157, *R* v *Gibson* [1990] 2 QB 619, *R* v *Lunderbech* [1991] Crim LR 784 and *R* v *Rowley* [1991] 4 All ER 649). It seems, however, that such an act must be committed in public at least in a place where there exists a real possibility that members of the general public might witness what happens although the actual spot where the act occurs need not be a place of public resort (*R* v *Walker* [1996] 1 Cr App R 111).

Conspiracies under the 1977 Act

The *actus reus* of a conspiracy under s. 1(1) is proof of entering into an agreement with another or others (who need not be identified: *R* v *Phillips* (1987) 86 Cr App R 18) to commit a substantive criminal offence. The alleged conspirators must have agreed on a course of conduct which will undoubtedly result in the crime they conspired to commit if their agreement is carried out as they intended.

The *mens rea* of conspiracy is proof of an intention to carry out the agreement and knowledge of those facts which make the agreement unlawful. As with other inchoate offences, conspiracy is an intentional crime, a specific intent offence. Its *mens rea* can be satisfied by proof of an intention to commit an agreed substantive offence but full intention and knowledge of this sort may not now be essential since the decision in *R* v *Anderson* [1986] AC 27 although the views expressed by Lord Bridge of Harwich are open to criticism but obviously warrant consideration. For example, he maintained that a person is guilty of a statutory conspiracy if, *irrespective of his intention*, that person had been a party to an agreement which, if pursued, would necessarily result in a crime. In *R* v *Siracusa* (1990) 90 Cr App R 30 the Court of Appeal interpreted Lord Bridge to mean that the *mens rea* of statutory conspiracy will be satisfied 'if, and only if, it is shown that the accused, when he entered into the agreement, intended to play some part in the agreed course of conduct in furtherance of the criminal purpose which the agreed course of conduct was intended to achieve'. Neither of these notions were the law prior to *Anderson*. Now, however, a very strong Privy Council decision (*Yip Chiu-Cheung* v *R* [1994] 3 WLR 514) has reiterated persuasively what should be the true position, namely 'the crime of conspiracy requires an agreement between two or more persons to commit an unlawful act with the intention to carry it out'. Intention to carry it out constitutes the necessary *mens rea* for the offence.

Section 1(2) of the Criminal Law Act 1977 states that if the intended substantive offence is a strict liability offence (in so far as the circumstance elements of the *actus reus* are concerned) there can be no conviction for conspiracy (a lesser offence) unless that circumstance is known to the persons charged with conspiring.

Other Factors

Impossibility

Remember that s. 1(1)(b) of the Criminal Law Act 1977, like s. 1(2) of the Criminal Attempts Act 1981, states that persons may be liable for conspiracy even though it was in fact impossible to commit the intended substantive offence. This abrogates the decision in *DPP* v *Nock* [1978] AC 979 (see the discussion above concerning impossibility in relation to attempts — the same principles should apply at least to statutory conspiracies and, since *R* v *Shivpuri* [1987] AC 1, legal impossibility will not be a defence to such a charge).

Fellow conspirators

Also, remember that certain persons do not qualify as persons with whom anyone may conspire. Section 2(2) of the Criminal Law Act 1977 states that there cannot be a conspiracy:

(a)   If the *only* parties to the agreement are a person and his or her spouse (unless the accused spouse knew of other conspirators (*R* v *Chrastny* [1992] 1 All ER 159 and *R* v *Lovick* [1993] Crim LR 890).

(b)   If the *only other* person is under the age of criminal responsibility (i.e., under 10 years old).

(c)   If the *only other* person is a victim or intended victim of the intended offence (a person is a victim if the complete offence in question exists for the protection of that person).

(d)   If the only purported parties to the agreement are a registered company and a director of that company. It is true that following the decision in *Salomon* v *A. Salomon & Co. Ltd* [1897] AC 22, a company is a separate legal entity distinct from its members and that an individual associated with a company may wear many different hats ranging from acting as the mind of the company to acting as a shareholder or as an employee of the company. But the court held in *R* v *McDonnell* [1966] 1 QB 233 that it would be unrealistic to say there was a conspiracy between the company and its managing director because the director was acting as the mind of the company. If the company was to be liable it was for its own acts not for a conspiracy in that instance. A company can, however, conspire with someone other than a single director of itself and it can even conspire with one of its own directors *and* someone else.

(e)   If the only other party to the purported agreement is someone who is mentally disordered (because s. 1(1) requires an agreement). If the disordered person can form *mens rea* or understand sufficiently to agree then the party who is not mentally ill should be liable for conspiracy.

Jurisdiction

Finally, conspiracy can have an extraterritorial aspect. The House of Lords held that a conspiracy in England against persons abroad was not triable here unless the conspiracy was intended to cause loss to persons here or to cause a public mischief here (*Board of Trade* v *Owen* [1957] 1 All ER 411). But now a conspiracy entered into abroad to commit a crime in England will be indictable here even though no overt act takes place in England

(*Liangsiriprasert* v *US Government* [1990] 2 All ER 866, PC; and *R* v *Sansom* [1991] 2 QB 130; *R* v *Williams* [1991] 2 QB 130; *R* v *Smith* [1991] 2 QB 130; *R* v *Wilkins* [1991] 2 QB 130). Part 1 of the Criminal Justice Act 1993 extends the jurisdiction of courts in England and Wales to try a range of substantive and inchoate 'fraud' offences where there is a significant foreign element in the commission. The general rule is that jurisdiction is determined by where the last act or event took place or was intended to take place, irrespective or whether it was a 'conduct' crime or a 'consequence' crime. For purposes of the 1993 Act all that is required for the full offence is proof that one of the elements of the offence occurred in England and Wales and in the case of a conspiracy or attempt to commit abroad offences prescribed by that Act, it is now triable here (provided certain conditions are met where the offence concerned was to be committed wholly abroad). Incitements, conspiracies, attempts performed in England but which are aimed at the commission abroad of an equivalent substantive crime to those prescribed in the Act can be tried here so that, for example, persons who conspire to defraud victims in Bermuda or Hong Kong will commit an offence contrary to English Law and will now be triable here.

INCITEMENT

Actus Reus

Remember that the third and final inchoate offence occurs if you endeavour to persuade or induce another to participate in a crime or to commit any act or omission which, had that person done it of his or her own volition, would have been a crime. In such a situation it is irrelevant whether or not your incitement is successful.

The *actus reus* is satisfied by proof that your words or deeds were such that they could threaten or pressurise, encourage or exhort another person, group or all persons generally, to commit a crime whether the person incited knows it is a crime or not (*Race Relations Board* v *Applin* [1973] QB 815).

Incitements may be express (e.g., publishing an article in a London newspaper urging foreigners to assassinate their heads of state is an express incitement to murder *R* v *Most* (1881) QBD 224), or (e.g., advertising to the general public the availability of a warning device to detect police speed radar-traps is an express incitement to an offence under the Wireless Telegraphy Act 1949: *Invicta Plastics* v *Clare* [1976] Crim LR 131). Incitements may also be implied.

An incitement must reach (i.e., get through to) the person being incited. Whether or not, after that, the incitement has any effect is irrelevant. The incitement or attempt at incitement is the offence.

Mens Rea

Whether or not you knew it was a crime you will have sufficient *mens rea* if it is proved that you intended to persuade, encourage, goad or exhort another person or other persons into committing a crime. Like the other inchoate offences the incitement must be to the commission of a substantive offence: that must be the inciter's intention therefore it is a specific-intent offence.

Be careful not to confuse the *mens rea* of incitement with the *mens rea* of the offence incited. For example, in the case of incitement to obtain property by deception it is necessary to show that the accused intended another person to act dishonestly and with the intention to permanently deprive, but it is not necessary to show that the accused had any such dishonest intention. Sometimes the courts get this wrong (see *R* v *Shaw* [1994] Crim LR 365). If the Draft Criminal Code (Law Comm. No. 177) was to be implemented then proposed cl. 47 would help clarify the law on this point. It reads:

(1)   a person is guilty of incitement to commit an offence or offences if:

(a)   he incites another to do or cause to be done an act or acts which, if done, will involve the commission of the offence or offences by the other; and

(b)   he intends or believes that the other, if he acts as incited, shall or will do so with the fault required for the offence or offences.

Inciting the Impossible

Incitement is in the main a common law offence unaffected by either the Criminal Attempts Act 1981 or the Criminal Law Act 1977 (as amended by the 1981 Act).

On the issue of inciting the impossible remember that since *R* v *McDonough* (1962) 47 Cr App R 37 incitement has been out of line with attempts and conspiracy. Prior to 1981, it was not an offence to attempt (*Haughton* v *Smith* [1975] AC 476) or conspire (*DPP* v *Nock* [1978] AC 979) to commit a crime if it was physically or legally impossible to commit it. *McDonough*, on the other hand, had held that whether or not the crime *incited* could be committed was irrelevant and the accused could be liable.

The 1981 Act on attempts (which also amended the law of conspiracy contained in the 1977 Act) appeared to bring those two offences into line with *McDonough* at least in so far as saying that physical impossibility is no longer a defence. That unity did not last long because in *R* v *Fitzmaurice* [1983] QB 1083, where inciting a physically impossible crime was directly in issue, the Court of Appeal held that *McDonough* was only correct because the incited crime was physically impossible at that time. In other words if the crime incited was absolutely, physically, impossible at any time then the physical impossibility would provide a defence at common law to a charge of incitement. Whereas now under the Criminal Attempts Act 1981, s. 1(2), and the Criminal Law Act 1977, s. 1(1)(b), you are liable for attempts or conspiracies which are physically impossible whether or not that is a temporary, transient or permanent thing. The *Fitzmaurice* decision may give a person charged with incitement two defences (namely physical impossibility and legal impossibility) that are not available if the charge is attempt or conspiracy. This has been given support by the decision in *R* v *Sirat* (1986) 83 Cr App R 41.

INCHOATE OFFENCES AND PARTICIPATION

Table 7.1 shows, e.g., that there is no liability for thinking thoughts even of incitement, conspiracy, attempts, participation, etc. It then traces potential liability, in relation to each of the inchoate offences, for completing and participating in an inchoate offence and in the full offence intended by the accused. In Table 7.1 'CLA 1967' refers to the Criminal Law Act 1967, 'CLA 1977' refers to the Criminal Law Act 1977 and 'CAA 1981' refers to the Criminal Attempts Act 1981. In relation to answering problem questions it may well be worth remembering the following:

(a) It would appear to be an offence:

(i) to attempt to incite (see *R* v *Banks* (1873) 12 Cox CC 393), or
(ii) to incite another to attempt (see *R* v *Cromack* [1978] Crim LR 217), or
(iii) possibly, to incite another to incite (see *R* v *Cromack*); definitely a full 'incitement offence' can be incited, see (c) below.

(b) It is *not* an offence:

(i) to attempt an attempt (see the Criminal Attempts Act 1981, s. 1(1)) because that would be mere preparation for which there is no liability unless the conduct falls within a special statutory provision such as s. 3 of the Criminal Damage Act 1971, or s. 25 of the Theft Act 1968, or
(ii) to attempt to conspire (Criminal Attempts Act 1981, s. 1(4)), or
(iii) to incite either a statutory or a common law conspiracy (see Criminal Law Act 1977, s. 5(7)).

(c) Where a statute creates a special offence involving incitement such as the Criminal Law Act 1977, s. 54 (the offence of *inciting incestuous sexual intercourse*), that particular incitement thereby becomes a substantive rather than an inchoate offence and consequently persons may be charged with inciting, conspiring at or attempting that 'incitement' offence.

(d)   Where a person's incitement is successful in the sense that an incited person goes and commits the crime incited then the inciter can be charged not only with incitement but also as a party (see chapter 6) to the completed, substantive offence unless the person incited was an innocent agent in which case the inciter would be the principal offender. The Criminal Attempts Act 1981, s. 1(4)(b), states that there is no offence of attempting to participate in (i.e., attempting to aid, abet, counsel or procure) an offence. Logically there does not appear to be any problem with making persons liable for conspiring to participate in a crime.

Note too that by the Criminal Law Act 1977, s. 5(8), if one party to an alleged conspiracy is found guilty then the fact that the only other parties have been acquitted (whether after being tried with the person convicted or separately) shall not be a ground for quashing that person's conviction (unless it is inconsistent with the acquittal of the other party or parties in question).

TABLE 7.1 LIABILITY FOR INCHOATE, COMPLETE AND PARTICIPATION OFFENCES

A person accused of:	May be liable as follows for:						
	Thoughts	Incitement	Conspiracy	Attempt	An offence	Participation	CLA 1967, ss. 4(1) and 5(1)
Thinking	NO	NO	NO	NO	NO	NO	NO
Inciting	POSSIBLY (incitement).	POSSIBLY incitement R v Cromack [1978] Crim LR 217; R v Sirat (1986) 83 Cr App R 41.	NO CLA 1977, s. 5(7).	YES R v Cromack [1978] Crim LR 217 or for inciting the full offence and as a party to attempt.	YES liable for incitement and as a party for full offence.	PROBABLY NO in re counselling and abetting (Bodin) [1979] Crim LR 176 CLA 1977, s. 30(4).	YES for incitement and as a party.
Conspiring	POSSIBLY (conspiracy if an agreement is communicated).	YES (Law Com. No. 76, para. 1.44).	YES i.e., common law conspiracies. No re statutory conspiracies: R v Hollingshead [1985] 1 All ER 550.	NO, but liable for conspiring to commit the full offence and as a party to attempt.	YES liable for conspiracy and as a party for the full offence. See also CLA 1977, s. 5(8).	YES See CLA 1977, s. 5(8).	YES for conspiracy and as a party.
Attempting	NO	YES R v Banks (1873) 12 Cox CC 393.	NO CAA 1981, s. 1(4)(a).	NO CAA 1981, s. 1(1).	YES liable for attempt only.	NO CAA 1981, s. 1(4)(b).	NO CAA 1981, s. 1(4)(c).
Completing	NO	YES (incitement).	YES (conspiracy).	YES (attempt).	YES liable as the principal for full offence.	YES liable as a party for the full offence.	YES either or both of CLA 1967, s. 4 s. 5.
Participating	POSSIBLY for conspiracy if the thoughts are agreed and communicated otherwise NO.	YES (incitement).	YES (conspiracy).	YES (attempt).	YES liable as a party for the full offence.	YES liable as a party for the full offence.	YES liable as a party for a full CLA 1967, s. 4(1) or s. 5(1), offence.

EXAMPLES OF QUESTIONS

The inchoate offences are a source of useful and testing questions of both the problem and the essay variety.

Essay Questions

Conspiracy

(1)   It has been argued that the crime of conspiracy should no longer exist. Explain how far the Criminal Law Act 1977 has limited its scope. Is the result satisfactory?

(2)   Discuss critically the reform of the law of conspiracy by the Criminal Law Act 1977.

(3)   How far have the Legislature and the House of Lords helped to clarify the instances in which the accused will be guilty of conspiracy even though their contemplated action would not be criminal if done by a single individual?

(4)   'The operation of the law of conspiracy is vague. It operates on the premise that an agreement can be socially more menacing than its fulfilment.' Discuss.

Questions (1), (2) and (3) above basically seek a discussion of the same material relating to conspiracy. In each instance the same order is probably best, dealing first with a discussion of the common law prior to the Criminal Law Act 1977, with emphasis being placed on those aspects which you consider unsatisfactory.

This means you must be able (a) to recite the old common law definition of conspiracy as applied in cases like *Mulcahy* v *R* (1868) LR 3 HL 306 and (b) to indicate that criticism revolved around the width of that definition. It was wide open to abuse in that an agreement simply to do an unlawful act (i.e., not necessarily a criminal act) was sufficient. This could and did include agreements to do things which were not crimes. It came to pass that agreements to do certain non-criminal things were held to be criminal because of the width of the net of conspiracy. These things included:

(a)   an agreement to do a tortious act (e.g., trespass) (see *Kamara* v *DPP* [1974] AC 104);
(b)   an agreement to copy or reproduce the contents of films which, because no damage was done to the original and there was neither theft of

the original nor an obtaining of it or its contents by deception, apparently did not amount to a criminal act (see *Scott* v *Metropolitan Police Commissioner* [1975] AC 819 and *R* v *Lloyd and others* [1985] 3 WLR 30); and

(c) even agreements to do acts which were apparently lawful but which through the so-called residual powers of the judiciary suddenly became new criminal offences of conspiracy (see *Shaw* v *DPP* [1962] AC 220 and *Knuller (Publishing, Printing & Promotions) Ltd* v *DPP* [1973] AC 435).

Secondly you must discuss the Criminal Law Act 1977, its contents and consequences. The main features are:

(a) By s. 1(1)(a) the statutory offence of conspiracy is created, i.e., an agreement which 'will necessarily amount to or involve the commission of any offence or offences by one or more of the parties to the agreement'. The accused must be proved to have agreed on conduct which will *undoubtedly* result in the crime they conspired to commit if carried out as they intended. It is a specific-intent offence, i.e., the conspirators must have a substantive criminal offence as their intended object.

(b) The Criminal Attempts Act 1981, s. 5(1), introduced into the 1977 Act s. 1(1)(b), which states it is irrelevant whether or not the commission of the offence or any of the offences conspired is impossible. This was necessary to negate the decision in *DPP* v *Nock* [1978] AC 979 which had held the accused *not* liable for conspiracy to produce a prohibited drug from chemicals which could never produce it. Now those persons *would be* liable even if what they conspired to do was legally rather than physically or factually impossible (see *R* v *Shivpuri* [1987] AC 1).

(c) In relation to offences where knowledge of a fact or circumstance is not essential, such as in some strict liability offences, the accused and one other party must have intent or knowledge as to the requisite facts or circumstances (and arguably the consequences also) at the time they conspired to commit such an offence.

(d) Agreements to commit summary offences are declared by s. 1(3) not to be criminal conspiracies within s. 1(1) if they are made in contemplation or furtherance of a trade dispute.

(e) The word 'offence' as used throughout s. 1 is defined in s. 1(4) to mean an offence triable in England and Wales but includes murder even if it would *not* be so triable if committed as the parties intended.

(f) Certain persons are declared by s. 2 not to qualify as 'another person' for purposes of the law on conspiracy, i.e., a spouse, a child under 10 years, a mentally disordered person or a victim or intended victim of the offence cannot be the *only other* party to an agreement which otherwise would be a conspiracy (as to who is a 'victim' in such instances, see *R* v *Tyrrell* [1894] 1 QB 710). In the case of a registered company there can be no conspiracy if it and a director of it are the only alleged conspirators, see *R* v *McDonnell* [1966] 1 QB 233).

(g) The 1977 Act, by s. 5(1), purported to abolish the offence of conspiracy at common law but by subsections (2) and (3) retained conspiracy to defraud (*Scott* v *Metropolitan Police Commissioner* [1975] AC 819), conspiracy to corrupt public morals (*Shaw* v *DPP* [1962] AC 220) and conspiracy to outrage public decency (*Knuller (Publishing, Printing & Promotions) Ltd* v *DPP* [1973] AC 435) as conspiracies at common law.

Thirdly, you must then express *an opinion* whether or not this legislation is successful, i.e., does it get rid of any anomalies, dangers, conflicts or uncertainties in the law of conspiracy prior to this enactment? Is the Act easily understood? Is it narrower and less of a threat to freedom or liberty? Is the scope for abuse or misuse curtailed? In stating *your* views, however, you could refer to the commentators and mention *R* v *Ayres* [1984] AC 447 and *R* v *Tonner* [1984] Crim LR 618 which created problems by maintaining that if the conspiracy contemplated the commission of a substantive offence it must be charged under s. 1(1) of the Criminal Law Act 1977 and not as one of the three remaining common law conspiracies. You should show you are aware that these decisions have been overruled by s. 12(1)) of the Criminal Justice Act 1987 (at least in so far as conspiracy to defraud is concerned).

Much of the material mentioned above could be usefully presented in answer to question (4) or a question like it *but note* a comprehensive review of the whole of the old and new law is not required. You are asked to emphasise only *those situations where* the contemplated action of those accused *would not be criminal* if done by a single individual. This means a brief coverage of the 1977 Act, especially s. 1, to show how it has cut down the width of the old definition of conspiracy negating the decision in *Kamara* v *DPP* and then a mention of s. 5 leading straight into a discussion of the remaining common law conspiracies.

You must deal in detail with conspiracy to defraud and in doing so you must cite *Scott* v *Metropolitan Police Commissioner* but there are other cases as well (e.g., *R* v *Sinclair* [1968] 3 All ER 241) which illustrate the point and, of course, s. 12(1) of the Criminal Justice Act 1987.

You must deal in detail with both the conspiracy to corrupt public morals (*Shaws*) and the conspiracy to outrage public decency (*Knullers*).

In addition this question permits you to display your knowledge of other situations ruled out by the legislature or the courts as instances where a person will not be held to have conspired, in particular *DPP* v *Bhagwan* [1972] AC 60 where the House of Lords took a different view (to that in *Shaw*) in a non-sexual context and the so-called 'conspiracy to effect a public mischief' which the House of Lords in *DPP* v *Withers* [1975] AC 842 declared not to be a separate and distinct class of criminal conspiracy. The idea that such an offence could be charged arose from the decision in *R* v *Manley* [1933] 1 KB 529, which had wrongly held that the common law recognised an offence of 'public mischief'. This was despite the fact that the description had been applied to a number of cases coming within well-known heads of conspiracy. In effect the House recognised the fact that most of these instances were either agreements to commit substantive crimes or conspiracies to defraud or corrupt morals at common law and that they should be charged as such. See, for example, the possible conspiracy dealt with in the outline answer to question (12)(c) below, taken from *R* v *Bassey* (1931) 22 Cr App R 160. Where two or more persons fabricate false documents to establish an educational qualification it cannot now be charged as a conspiracy to effect a public mischief, it must be charged today as a conspiracy under s. 1(1) of the Criminal Act 1977, e.g., to commit the crime of forgery or else as a common law conspiracy to defraud and in relation to those two there is no choice. According to *R* v *Ayres* [1984] AC 447 (and see *R* v *Tonner* [1984] Crim LR 618) in a situation like that where both charges are possible the prosecution must charge the statutory offence under s. 1(1) of the 1977 Act but if the charge involves fraud then the prosecution is now free to choose whether to charge with the statutory or common law offence according to s. 12(1) of the Criminal Justice Act 1987.

Attempts
(5) 'Neither the definition in s. 1(1) of the Criminal Attempts Act 1981 nor the common law theories do much to elucidate the central problem that makes the definition of an attempt so difficult.'
   Discuss.

(6) What effect has the Criminal Attempts Act 1981 had on the law relating to attempts to commit crimes?

(7) 'In either case, he cannot be convicted of an attempt when he could not be convicted of the full offence if he had succeeded in doing all that he attempted to do. Conduct which is not criminal is not converted into criminal conduct by the accused believing that a state of affairs exists which does not exist.' (Viscount Dilhorne in *Haughton* v *Smith* 1975.)
   Discuss how far this statement accurately represents the present law on the offence of attempt.

Question (5) expects you to confine your answer to the specific problem of defining attempt but it is the sort of question you should be relieved to see in an examination because it permits the display of extensive knowledge in a confined area.

First, if you are not permitted to have the Criminal Attempts Act 1981 with you in the examination room then you *must* know intimately the words of s. 1. Attempt is defined in s. 1(1) as the taking of a step which is more than merely preparatory. By s. 6 attempt at common law was abolished and the definition in s. 1(1) stated to be the law but the words of that or any other section give no guidance as to what conduct or steps taken should fall over the dividing line and be classed as more than merely preparatory and what conduct or steps taken fall short of that. Clearly s. 1(1) is paramount but reference by analogy at least back to the old common law tests is not unacceptable (see *R v Ilyas* (1984) 78 Cr App R 17 and *R v Widdowson* (1985) 82 Cr App R 314) and indeed is endorsed by *R v Boyle* (1987) 84 Cr App R 270 but care should be used and in particular the 'last act' and 'Rubicon tests' should be avoided: *R v Jones* [1990] Crim LR 800; *R v Gullefer* [1990] 3 All ER 882. This still permits you to mention the methods used prior to the passing of the 1981 Act to distinguish between mere preparation and acts of perpetration which were held to be attempts. Those tests are:

(a)   Proximity (*R v Robinson* [1915] 2 KB 342; *R v Button* [1900] 2 QB 597; *Comer v Bloomfield* (1970) 55 Cr App R 305; and *DPP v Stonehouse* [1978] AC 55 but excluding the discredited 'Rubicon test').

(b)   Equivocality (*Davey v Lee* [1968] 1 QB 366 and *Jones v Brooks* (1968) 52 Cr App R 614).

(c)   *Locus paenitentiae* (the principle governing change of mind or repentance) (cf. *Stonehouse* and the 'Rubicon test').

(d)   Impossibility (in recent years prior to the 1981 Act the law was contained in *Haughton v Smith* [1975] AC 476 but this test has been altered by s. 1(2) and (3) of the Act in that both physical and legal impossibility are no longer defences: see *R v Shivpuri* [1987] AC 1).

(e)   Social danger (e.g., see *R v Brown* (1889) 24 QBD 357 as an illustration only of the prospect that a judge's decision whether or not certain conduct is preparation or perpetration could be affected by the social danger perceived in that conduct).

Finally, this question warrants some discussion of whether or not there is a common law offence of preparation (see *R v Gurmit Singh* [1966] 2 QB 53 and the Criminal Attempts Act 1981, s. 6, abolishing any offence at common law of *procuring materials* for crime) and some mention of what are in effect offences of preparation created by statute such as s. 3 of the Criminal Damage Act 1971 and s. 25 of the Theft Act 1968. Both offences protect the integrity of property but it should be noted that no similar statutory offence of preparation exists to protect persons as shown by *R v Geddes* [1996] Crim LR 894. Arguably these two offences would not be necessary if conduct amounting to an attempt could be clearly defined.

Question (6) requires a wider-ranging answer. Much of the material you would have used to answer question (5) can be usefully incorporated into your answer to question (6) but you must go further. Whereas in question (5) the emphasis was on s. 1(1) of the Criminal Attempts Act 1981, question (6) requires you to deal also with subsections (2) and (3) of s. 1 and their effect on attempting the impossible. That would lead also to a discussion of *Anderton v Ryan* [1985] AC 560 and especially *R v Shivpuri* [1987] AC 1. You could mention the effect of s. 6 and also s. 9 (interfering with a motor vehicle).

Finally, remember *to sum up* at the end stating what *you think* the effect of the 1981 Act has been on the law of attempts.

Question (7) is difficult. It is the sort of question which is best avoided unless you can identify with confidence the limited issue it wants discussed. The question definitely does not seek an outpouring of all you know about attempts and it does not even seek a discussion of that sort confined to the *mens rea* of attempt. It is about *mens rea* but the very heart of the point in issue is the effect of s. 1(2) and (3) of the 1981 Act, knowledge of circumstances in relation to attempts and to a minor extent whether or not attempts can be committed recklessly or negligently. First, now, despite s. 1(1), on the issue of legal impossibility it is no longer true that 'conduct which is not criminal is not converted into criminal conduct by the accused believing that a state of affairs exists which does not exist'. If the accused thinks he is stealing someone else's umbrella but in fact it turns out already to belong to the accused then he has committed an attempt even though arguably there is no *actus reus* (see *R v Shivpuri* [1987] AC 1).

But there is another aspect to the question and that is whether or not knowledge of circumstances is essential to obtain a conviction for attempting crimes which have knowledge of circumstances as a necessary part of their definition? The Criminal Attempts Act 1981, s. 1(1), requires proof of intention to bring about an offence together with proof of knowledge of the factual circumstances required for that substantive offence. This is where s. 1(3) becomes significant. (If you are not permitted to have the Act in the examination you must learn the gist of this subsection beforehand.) In effect it imputes the accused's belief at the time of the *actus reus* to him as though he had actual knowledge. For example, if a man believes but does not know for certain that the girl with whom he intends to have sexual intercourse is under age then he will be convicted of attempt to commit an offence contrary to s. 5 or s. 6 of the Sexual Offences Act 1956 in the same way as if he knew the girl was under age. The subsection does not go so far as saying that recklessness as to the girl's age will be deemed to be knowledge. (On this, see Scanlan and Ryan, *An Introduction to Criminal Law*, para. 5.6.7.)

As far as reckless and negligent attempts are concerned you must know *R v Mohan* [1976] QB 1 and *R v Pearman* [1984] Crim LR 675 from which an argument can be built to the effect that neither state of mind will be sufficient *mens rea* for an attempt. You need to be able to explain the decision in *R v Khan* [1990] Crim LR 519.

You could in your summing up conclude that the quotation is inaccurate to the limited extent now provided for by s. 1(3) of the 1981 Act.

The inchoate offences and impossibility
(8) What is the legal position today if a person:

(a)   incites another,
(b)   conspires at, or
(c)   attempts

to do that which it is impossible to do? Explain how the current law of impossibility came about in relation to each inchoate offence.

Be careful. This is not a question which invites, 'Write all you know about inchoate offences'. You *must* confine your answer to the limited but complex issue of inciting, conspiring and attempting the impossible. But because the word 'impossible' is not qualified you must discuss both physical (sometimes called factual) impossibility and in relation to each offence compare and contrast that with legal impossibility.

Inciting is a common law offence. Two cases deal specifically with the issue in point:

(a)   *R v McDonough* (1962) 47 Cr App R 37 (there the accused was convicted of inciting the handling of stolen lamb carcasses even though there were none at that time).

(b)   *R v Fitzmaurice* [1983] QB 1083 which held *McDonough* correctly decided on its facts, because it was not impossible that some time in the future stolen lamb carcasses would be available, but stated that if the thing incited is absolutely, permanently, physically impossible then there can be no conviction for incitement at common law. (This view has been confirmed in *R v Sirat* (1985) 83 Cr App R 41.)

This last proposition would appear to have been the position in relation to attempt and conspiracy at common law under *Haughton v Smith* [1975] AC 476 and *DPP v Nock* [1978] AC 979 respectively. The Criminal Attempts Act 1981, s. 1(2), provided (and, by s. 5(1), amended the Criminal Law Act 1977, s. 1(1), to provide) that in relation to both attempts and conspiracies a person commits an offence even though the facts are such that the commission of the offence (attempted or conspired at) is impossible. Neither Act affects incitement and given that *Fitzmaurice* states the common law position relating to impossibility then absolute, physical impossibility should still be a defence to a charge under any of the three remaining common law heads of conspiracy as well as under incitement.

Note the word 'impossible' in both statutory provisions was not defined or qualified. Academic opinion had gone both ways on whether or not a distinction is to be drawn between physical and legal impossibility. Now the House of Lords has come down in favour of the view that in the statutory provision (at least in relation to attempt but as the wording of the conspiracy provision is analogous, for it as well) 'impossible' means physically and legally impossible (cf. *Anderton v Ryan* [1985] AC 560 and *R v Shivpuri* [1987] AC 1).

This means that both absolute, physical impossibility and legal impossibility are a defence to incitement and possibly the three remaining common law conspiracies but not to attempt or statutory conspiracy.

Problem Questions

One or other of the inchoate offences may be the central issue in a problem but more often than not they are each simply one of the several issues in the problem. Those issues may include more than one inchoate offence.

(9) (a) John, the licensee of a public house, is charged with attempting to sell liquor to a customer who was drunk. John is incensed at the charge as he claims that the public house was crowded at the time, and he had no means of knowing the customer was drunk. Advise John.

(b) Mike agrees to buy a bag of cannabis for £50, and the bag is duly handed over. On the way home, he is questioned by the police and makes a full confession. The police then examine the contents of the bag which turn out to be hedge clippings. Is Mike guilty of the offence of attempting to have a controlled drug in his possession?

(c) Roger is questioned by a policeman who sees him trying door handles on various cars. Roger admits he would have taken anything of value had he opened a door. The policeman is considering charging Roger with attempted theft or attempting to take a conveyance without authority under s. 1 or s. 12 of the Theft Act 1968. Advise him as to Roger's liability.

(10) Comment on the possible criminal liability arising in each of the following situations:

(a) Eric and Bruce make a video film which they intend to show in certain clubs of their nine-year-old children engaging in sexual activity.

(b) Alf and Fred provide children with glue-sniffing kits in exchange for money or anything of value which the children have been told they can supply with 'no questions asked'.

(c)   Derek and a person unknown cause a false examination result to be entered in the public records in order to make it appear that Derek has fulfilled university matriculation requirements.

Problem Outlines

Question 9(a)
You should know from your study of strict liability that in relation to serving alcohol to a man who is drunk, *Cundy* v *Le Cocq* (1884) 13 QBD 207 held that it was no defence for an accused to prove a belief that the customer was sober (whereas in *Sherras* v *De Rutzen* [1895] 1 QB 918 serving drink to a policeman on duty was excusable if the publican could prove that he believed the officer not to be on duty because he was not wearing his armlet). The issue here is whether John, who could be convicted without *mens rea* for the full offence, must be proved to have *mens rea* in order to be convicted of attempt to commit the offence. Having discussed *R* v *Mohan* [1976] QB 1 and dicta in *R* v *Pearman* [1985] RTR 39, *R* v *Whybrow* (1951) 35 Cr App R 141 and *R* v *Easom* [1971] 2 QB 315, you could conclude, paradoxically, that John would not be liable for an attempt even if he was reckless or negligent in attempting to serve the drunk customer. Though had he been charged with the full offence he would have been strictly liable.

Question 9(b)
In 9(b) the central issue is whether M is guilty of the attempted possession of a controlled drug. Though as a full crime it is in effect a strict liability offence (see *Warner* v *Metropolitan Police Commissioner* [1969] 2 AC 256 and *R* v *Marriott* [1971] 1 All ER 595), an attempt is governed by the Criminal Attempts Act 1981. M will need to have intended to possess a controlled drug and believe that he did so because an attempted offence always requires *mens rea*. The Criminal Attempts Act 1981, s. 1(3), would appear to supply M with the *mens rea* required for an attempt. The final matter to consider is the fact that M possesses hedge clippings. That is no defence, nor is the fact that it is impossible for him to commit the intended offence. In the case of physical impossibility M has no defence, he will be held guilty of an attempt, see Criminal Attempts Act 1981, s. 1(1) and (2). If the facts suggest a case of legal impossibility then, following *R* v *Shivpuri* [1987] AC 1, M will likewise have committed the offence of attempted possession of a controlled drug.

Question 9(c)
First, has Roger taken a step that is more than merely preparatory within s. 1(1) of the Criminal Attempts Act 1981 towards (a) theft from within a vehicle or (b) taking a vehicle? Discuss the cases that interpret the section i.e.,

Jones; Gullefer; Campbell; Geddes and *Tosti* and mention the common law tests as endorsed by *R v Boyle* (1987) 84 Cr App R 270 and in particular *Jones v Brooks* (1968) 52 Cr App R 614.

Secondly has he sufficient *mens rea* for a charge of attempting either offence? See *R v Easom* [1971] 2 QB 315; *R v Husseyn* (1978) 67 Cr App R 131; *Attorney-General's Reference (Nos. 1 and 2 of 1979)* [1980] QB 180 and *R v Bayley and Easterbrook* [1980] Crim LR 503, all of which discuss and detail the law relating to conditional intent. Conditional intent, i.e., intent to commit an offence provided certain circumstances are established, has been held insufficient *mens rea* to constitute conduct criminal for the purpose of both a full and an attempted offence (see *R v Easom*). However, cases such as *R v Bayley and Easterbrook* have held that where an individual has e.g., a *general* conditional intent to steal anything he may find (e.g., conditional upon it being of value) or a conditional intent to steal anything within a specified class of objects (e.g., within a room), a conviction for an attempt may be sustained (see *Attorney-General's Reference (Nos. 1 and 2 of 1979)*). Thus if Roger intends to steal anything he may find, he will have sufficient *mens rea* for attempt; if he intends to steal a specified object provided it is of value then the defence recognised in the two earlier cases may be available to him.

Thirdly mention the new offence of interference with a motor vehicle specifically created by s. 9 of the Criminal Attempts Act 1981 to overcome this very problem.

Question (10)
This set of short problems raises issues mainly concerning conspiracy. Is each of these situations a conspiracy to commit a crime under s. 1(1) of the Criminal Law Act 1977? Or is the situation in (a) a conspiracy to corrupt public morals (*Shaw v DPP* [1962] AC 220) or a conspiracy to outrage public decency (*Knuller (Publishing, Printing & Promotions) Ltd v DPP* [1973] AC 435)? In (b), if glue sniffing is not illegal, is this a conspiracy at all? Have Alf and Fred incited children to commit crimes, e.g., theft? In (c) has Derek committed a substantive criminal offence? Is there a conspiracy? The facts are similar to but not the same as those in *R v Bassey* (1931) 22 Cr App R 160 which held (on a charge of conspiracy) that it was a public mischief to procure and use forged certificates of educational qualification in order to obtain admission to a law course. If forgery or obtaining by deception is involved there clearly can be a conspiracy within s. 1(1) of the Criminal Law Act 1977 as each is a crime. If not, could it involve a common law conspiracy to defraud (*Scott v Metropolitan Police Commissioner* [1975] AC 819, *Allsop* [1976] 64 Cr App R 29, *Adams* [1995] 1 WLR 52, *Moses* [1991] Crim LR 617, *Welham* [1961] AC 103 and *Wai Yu-tsang* [1991] 4 All ER 664)? It is not, however, a conspiracy to effect a public mischief because *DPP v Withers* [1975] AC 842 denied the existence of

any such offence. Whether there is an actual offence of public mischief as claimed in R v *Manley* [1933] 1 KB 529 is doubtful.

Be sure in each instance to do what the question asks of you, i.e., having discussed the law, state whether or not you think criminal liability will attach to Eric, Bruce, Alf, Fred and Derek.

CONCLUSION

Issues involving inchoate offences may be easily worked into problem questions dealing with substantive offences against the person or against property. In dealing with *any* problem questions ostensibly on any area of substantive law *check carefully* to ascertain whether or not one or other of the inchoate offences and/or participation offences and/or any of the general defences warrant being discussed.

You must know the following:

(a) *For attempts:*

(i) The difference between mere preparation and criminal perpetration, i.e., something that is more than merely preparatory.

(ii) An example of a statutory offence of preparation such as s. 25 of the Theft Act 1968.

(iii) How to ascertain what is more than merely preparatory.

(iv) How far, if at all, impossibility is a defence to a charge of attempt.

(v) The *mens rea* of attempt.

(b) *For conspiracy:*

(i) The statutory definition of a criminal conspiracy.

(ii) The definitions of the remaining three common law conspiracies and their applicability today.

(iii) The *mens rea* of conspiracy.

(iv) The effect, if any, of impossibility of purpose on the offence of conspiracy.

(v) Those persons with whom by statute it is impossible to conspire.

(c) *For incitement:*

(i) The *actus reus* and *mens rea*.

(ii) Whether or not there is an offence of inciting the impossible.

Finally, you need to know whether or not you can be charged with inciting, attempting or conspiring to incite, attempt or conspire to commit a criminal offence (see Table 7.1).

FURTHER READING

Incitement

Williams, G., 'Inciting the Impossible' [1979] Crim LR 239 (see particularly pp. 384–390).

Conspiracy

Card, R., 'Reform of the Law of Conspiracy' [1973] Crim LR 674.
Dennis, I., 'The Rationale of Criminal Conspiracy' (1977) 93 LQR 785.
Elliot, D. W., '*Mens Rea* in Statutory Conspiracy' [1978] Crim LR 202.
Ferguson, P., 'Intention, Agreement and Statutory Conspiracy' (1986) 102 LQR 26.
Law Commission Working Paper No. 50: Codification of the Criminal Law, General Principles: Inchoate Offences (1973).
Law Commission Working Paper No. 55: Codification of the Criminal Law: General Principles, Defences of General Application (1974).
Law Commission Paper No. 228, Criminal Law: Conspiracy to Defraud (1994)
McFarlane, G., 'Another New Chapter in Conspiracy' (1978) 137 NLJ 7.
Silber, S., 'The Law Commission, Conspiracy to Defraud and the Dishonesty Project' [1995] Crim LR 461.
Spencer (1982) CLJ 222.
Smith, A. T. H., 'Conspiracy to Defraud: The Law Commission's Working Paper No. 104' [1988] Crim LR 508.
Smith, J. C., 'Conspiracy under the CLA 1977' [1977] Crim LR 598 and 638.
Smith, J. C., 'Conspiracy to Defraud: Some Comments on the Law Commission's Report' [1995] Crim LR 209.
Smith, J. C., 'Proving Conspiracy' [1996] Crim LR 386.
Smith, J. C., 'More on Proving Conspiracy' [1997] Crim LR 333.
Williams, G., 'The New Statutory Offence of Conspiracy' (1977) NLJ 1164.

Attempt

Buxton, R., 'Incitement and Attempt' [1973] Crim LR 656.
Dennis, I., 'The Criminal Attempt Act 1981' [1982] Crim LR 5.
Glazebrook, P., 'Should we have a Law of Attempted Crime?' (1969) 85 LQR 28.
Hogan, B., 'Attempting the Impossible and the Principle of Legality' (1985) NLJ 454.
Hogan, B., 'The Criminal Attempts Act and Attempting the Impossible' [1984] Crim LR 584.

Law Commission Report No. 76: Criminal Law: Report on Conspiracy and Criminal Law Reform (HC 176) 1976, pp. 483-704.

Law Commission Working Paper No. 50: Codification of the Criminal Law: General Principles, Inchoate Offences (1973).

Ryan, C. and Scanlan, P., 'Attempted Impossibility — Dead or Alive' 80 *Law Society Gazette* 1902.

Smith, J. C., 'Commentary on *DPP* v *Stonehouse*' [1977] Crim LR 545.

Smith, J. C., 'Commentary on *Walkington*' [1979] Crim LR 526.

Smith, K. J. M., 'Proximity in Attempt: Lord Lane's Midway Course' [1991] Crim LR 576.

Williams, G., 'The Problems of Reckless Attempts' [1983] Crim LR 365.

Williams, G., 'The Government's Proposals on Criminal Attempt' (1981) 131 NLJ 80 at 104 and 128.

Williams, G., 'Attempting the Impossible — the Last Round?' (1985) 135 NLJ 337.

Williams, G., 'The Lords Achieve the Logically Impossible' (1985) 135 NLJ 502.

Williams, G., 'At the Second Attempt' (1986) 136 NLJ 477.

Williams, G., 'The Lords and Impossible Attempts, or *Quis Custodiet Ipsos Custodes*' (1986) 45 CLJ 33.

8 DEFENCES

After a brief mention of a simple 'not guilty' plea this chapter will consider various generally applicable defences. The first is insanity, followed by automatism, intoxication, age, mistake, self-defence and prevention of crime, duress and coercion, superior orders and finally necessity. Remember that various special defences are discussed in other chapters, e.g., in relation to murder, the defences of infanticide, diminished responsibility, provocation and suicide pact are dealt with in chapter 9 and in relation to 'assault'-based offences the defences of consent and reasonable chastisement are also dealt with in chapter 9.

FORMS OF GENERAL DEFENCE

Denial of Basic Elements

The stock, standard defence which is commonplace and therefore taken for granted is for the accused to plead 'not guilty', i.e., to deny that he caused the *actus reus* or to deny that one of the definitional elements of the *actus reus* can be proved and/or to deny that he had the requisite *mens rea*. The burden is on the prosecution to prove all the elements of the *actus reus* and *mens rea* and to disprove any defence that is raised by the accused subject to one or two exceptions. Blaming what has happened as an 'accident' is simply another way of denying *mens rea*. The jurors are being asked to conclude on the facts that the accused was not to blame because he had no *mens rea*. (Note, however, that the term 'accident' does not apply in the context of an act done by a person in such a state of self-induced intoxication that he failed to appreciate the risk of what he was doing (*R* v *Cullen* [1993] Crim LR 936. See also 'Intoxication' below.)

Insanity

Although no longer of practical importance insanity is still a favourite of examiners. Its nature and the circumstances in which it would be available was discussed in *M'Naghten's case* (1843) 10 Cl & F 200.

Insanity is not available in respect of every criminal charge. It is available to an accused in a summary trial (*R* v *Horseferry Road Magistrates, ex parte K* [1997] QB 23). Insanity, however, can only be a defence to a charge in which *mens rea* was in issue. For strict liability offences where no *mens rea* is required the defence of insanity is not available (*DPP* v *H, The Times*, 2 May 1997). It is an unusual defence because everyone is assumed to be sane at the time of an alleged offence and the burden is on the *accused* to establish, on a balance of probabilities (see *Woolmington* v *DPP* [1935] AC 462) that he is insane. This means that:

(a) he was suffering from a 'disease of the mind' and that as a consequence —

(b) he was labouring under a 'defect of reason' and, as a consequence —

(c) he did not appreciate the nature or quality of his actions or, if he did so, he did not know his conduct was wrong. Therefore,

(d) where a person has a delusion induced through insanity his criminal liability should be judged on the basis of the facts as he believed them to be.

Disease of the mind as formulated in *R* v *Sullivan* [1984] AC 156 is to be understood in the ordinary sense of the word, i.e., the mental faculties of reason, memory and understanding. Any condition which impairs these faculties so as to produce a 'defect of reason' (see below) is sufficient. Such conditions may be organic in origin, e.g., epilepsy or arteriosclerosis, see *R* v *Kemp* [1957] 1 QB 399 and diabetes per Lord Lane CJ in *R* v *Hennessy* [1989] 1 WLR 287 and a persistent pattern of conduct while asleep in *R* v *Burgess, The Times*, 28 March 1991, or functional, i.e., a mental illness such as paranoia, but they must arise from an internal physiological or psychological cause. It is *irrelevant* that the impairment is permanent or transient and intermittent, curable or incurable.

'Defect of reason' means either:

(a) the accused did not appreciate the nature (see *R* v *Codere* (1916) 12 Cr App R 21) or quality of his act, i.e., because he was an automaton (without conscious appreciation of his conduct), or

(b)   he was incapable of realising the consequences of his actions and/or the circumstances in which that conduct takes place or,

(c)   he did not know his conduct to be wrong. This has been interpreted as *legally* wrong, i.e., an appreciation that it is contrary to law, an insane, deluded belief in the morality of your conduct is no defence, see *R* v *Windle* [1952] 2 QB 826. You should fully appreciate the very restricted nature of this defence (cf. diminished responsibility, see chapter 9) and its limited application in the modern criminal law.

Problems can arise where the accused's state of mind results from the combined effect of intoxication and disease of the mind. In relation to a specific intent offence the intoxication defence might result in a complete acquittal, while the insanity defence would result in a special verdict. The defence may not wish to raise the latter and the judge should do so only in exceptional circumstances (*R* v *Thomas (Sharon)* [1995] Crim LR 314). A proposal for reform which would resolve issues such as these is contained in the Draft Code (Law Com. No. 177), cl. 36.

Procedural matters
The accused bears the burden of establishing the defence of insanity (see above). He cannot escape the consequences of this rule by claiming insanity by another name, thus suggesting he bears only an evidential burden in relation to the defence as is the case with defences generally (see Murphy, *A Practical Approach to Evidence*). If his claim amounts to a plea of insanity he bears the burden of establishing the defence. This is the explanation of *Bratty* v *Attorney-General for Northern Ireland* [1963] AC 386, an authority which sometimes confuses students because it seems to turn on issues of semantics. The judge may raise the issue of the defence of insanity in rare and exceptional cases of his own volition (*R* v *Dickie* [1984] 1 WLR 1031 and *R* v *Thomas (Sharon)* [1995] Crim LR 314).

By s. 1 of the Criminal Procedure (Insanity) Act 1964 the verdict of a jury if it is satisfied the accused is insane is 'not guilty by reason of insanity', though, by s. 5 of the 1964 Act, following that verdict, the accused is liable to be detained in a hospital by the Home Secretary until he is satisfied that this is no longer necessary for the public's protection.

By the Criminal Appeal Act 1968, s. 12, an accused has a right of appeal from such a verdict if he can establish certain grounds, e.g., a separate defence.

In two situations the prosecution can adduce evidence of an accused's insanity:

(a)   By s. 6 of the 1964 Act, where the accused has adduced evidence of his diminished responsibility.

(b)   Where the accused has raised the issue of his mental capacity, e.g., by claiming he was a non-insane automaton (see below).

In both instances it is thought on general principles of the law of evidence that the prosecution must establish the issue of the accused's insanity beyond reasonable doubt, but as regards (b) see to the contrary per Lord Denning in *Bratty* who suggested that in this particular instance the prosecution bears only the civil standard of proof.

By s. 4 of the 1964 Act and ss. 47, 48 and 51 of the Mental Health Act 1983, an accused found insane before trial may be committed to a mental institution, as he may if on arraignment he is found unfit to plead. This does not apply to individuals who suffer from hysterical amnesia and cannot recall events at the time of the offence, see *R v Podola* [1960] 1 QB 325.

Non-insane Automatism and Involuntary Conduct

An accused bears an evidential burden in establishing that he was the involuntary agent in the commission of an offence. This may arise through (a) spasm, (b) involuntary reflex, (c) the action of external non-human agents (see *Hill v Baxter* [1958] 1 QB 277) or (d) being a non-insane automaton. This form of automatism, unlike cases of insanity, must arise from an external source, e.g., concussion, sleep-walking, diabetic coma produced by taking too much insulin (see *R v Quick and Paddison* [1973] QB 910 and *R v Bailey* [1983] 2 All ER 503) or the effect of drugs or drink (but not when this is the result of voluntarily taking the drugs or drink with the intention of, or reckless indifference to, producing that state of mind). Furthermore, stress, anxiety and depression are not external factors of the kind capable in law of causing or contributing to a state of automatism. The ordinary stresses and disappointments of life which are the common lot of mankind do not constitute an external cause (Martin J in the Canadian case, *Raby* (1980) 54 CCC (2d) 7); likewise for conditions encountered driving on long motorway journeys. They are states of mind prone to recur and lack the features of novelty or accident. Where those states of mind indirectly induce an hyperglycaemic episode (due to high blood sugar levels) the consequential automatic state has an internal cause, i.e., the disease of diabetes. The accused in such a case suffers from insanity and not non-insane automatism, see *R v Hennessey* [1989] 1 WLR 287. Where an accused establishes his automatic state or involuntary conduct is due to external factors he must in general be acquitted. In *Attorney-General's Reference (No. 2 of 1992)* [1994] Crim LR 692 it was made clear that the defence of automatism requires a total destruction of voluntary control. Impaired, reduced or partial control is not enough. Therefore 'driving without awareness' (an alleged trance-like state as to forward awareness only, induced by monotonous motorway driving) is not automatism because some control or awareness is retained.

But in *R v Burgess* [1991] 2 WLR 1206, the accused claimed that the wound inflicted on the victim was caused while the accused was sleepwalking. At the trial, in order to prove automatism, he had shown a pattern or practice of sleepwalking. The evidence, however, led to a finding of not guilty by reason of insanity. The Court of Appeal agreed that such sleepwalking was insane automatism despite the transitory nature of the disorder.

Intoxication

Automatism, alcohol and drugs

An individual who knowingly or recklessly takes drink or drugs may consequently become an automaton (self-induced automatism) or deprive himself of the ability to foresee the consequences of his actions and/or to perceive the circumstances in which his conduct takes place (voluntary intoxication). In both these cases he *may* have a defence to a criminal charge, in the first instance because he is an automaton and in the second because he lacks *mens rea*. Although both mental states are radically different in nature they should be considered identical for the purposes of the following discussion. Whether or not there is a defence depends on the nature of the offence charged. But if these two mental states have been induced involuntarily then they should take effect as defences to any criminal charge (see below).

If either mental state has been induced by the intentional or reckless taking of drink or drugs it will *not* provide a defence in the following cases:

(a) Crimes of negligence. The fact of voluntary intoxication or self-induced automatism supplies the negligent element for such offences, see *Moses v Winder* [1980] Crim LR 232.

(b) Offences of basic intent. This is the consequence of the decisions in *DPP v Majewski* [1977] AC 443 and *R v Bailey* [1983] 2 All ER 503. It has been determined in these cases that in offences of basic intent voluntary intoxication or self-induced automatism are not to be admitted in establishing defences, i.e., non-insane automatism or lack of *mens rea*. This is because offences of basic intent can be committed recklessly and becoming voluntarily intoxicated or a self-induced non-insane automaton actually satisfies this element. A person who is voluntarily intoxicated will be assumed to have been aware of any risk of which he would have been aware if he had been sober.

A *statutory* offence, though one of basic intent, may permit the fact of voluntary intoxication or self-induced non-insane automatism to be admitted as a defence if the terms of the statute so permit. (A good example for you to consider is to be found in the case *Jaggard* v *Dickinson* [1981] QB 527 regarding the defence of 'honest belief' in the presence of a lawful excuse to destroy property as providing a defence to a charge of criminal damage, see Criminal Damage Act 1971, s. 5.) This defence may still persist though it takes the form of an honest but mistaken belief induced through the voluntary taking of drink or drugs.

Since the case of *R* v *O'Grady* [1987] 3 All ER 420 a mistaken belief in the right to use reasonable force in self-defence will not provide a defence to any 'assault' offence if that belief has been induced as a consequence of voluntary intoxication. This authority would appear to apply also to offences of specific intent (see below) as well as offences of basic intent to which the defence of self-defence may apply. Note, however, that *O'Grady* has been severely criticised on the basis that a person should not, e.g., be convicted of murder if he thought for whatever reason that he was acting to save his life and would have been acting reasonably had he been right. Also it is said to be illogical to declare that drunkenness is irrelevant to the issue of whether he intended to act in self-defence but is relevant to the issue of whether he intended to kill or cause grievous bodily harm. Nevertheless, the Court of Appeal was inclined to follow *O'Grady* on this point in *R* v *O'Connor* [1991] Crim LR 135. See also *R* v *Fotheringham* (1989) 88 Cr App R 206 where the Court of Appeal determined that self-induced intoxication is no defence to a charge of rape, whether the issue be intention, consent or mistaken identity.

A general common law exception to *DPP* v *Majewski* is provided by *R* v *Hardie* [1984] 3 All ER 848. Voluntary intoxication or self-induced automatism is a possible defence even in offences of basic intent where such states of mind have followed the taking of a soporific or sedative drug (with or without prescription), as opposed to 'recreational' drugs which are dangerous or alcohol, but *not* where the taking of the soporific or prescribed drug is, in the circumstances of the case, itself a reckless act.

There is no principle that an accused exceptionally may be acquitted where, although an act was intentional, the intent arose out of circumstances for which the accused was not to blame. Likewise, even if the accused was not to blame or fault was absent it does not necessarily mean that *mens rea* is also absent. For example, an intent induced by a secretly administered drug is nevertheless an intent. Secretly administered alcohol or drugs which affect the accused but do not render him insensible will not annul his criminal liability if he does something criminal as a result (*R* v *Kingston* [1994] 3 WLR 519).

Insanity induced through drugs or intoxicants
You must be prepared to consider the relationship between alcohol abuse and the resulting mental impairment. If an accused, through the use of intoxicants or drugs, renders himself insane, he may have the defence

of insanity available to him. However, this is not the case if the use of such substances induces a temporary insanity in persons who are mentally unstable but not normally insane (see *Attorney-General for Northern Ireland* v *Gallagher* [1963] AC 349).

Where voluntary intoxication or self-induced automatism may provide defences.
Offences of specific/ulterior intent
Offences of specific/ulterior intent are those in which one or more of the external elements of the offence (i.e., the *actus reus*) can *only* be committed with an intention on the part of the accused to bring such an element or elements about (e.g., murder: *R* v *Moloney* [1985] AC 905). In certain offences, such as s. 9(1)(a) of the Theft Act 1968 (see chapter 10), the accused must have an intent to bring about certain consequences ulterior to the actual *actus reus* of the offence. Such specific-intent offences are sometimes also called offences of ulterior intent (*DPP* v *Majewski* [1977] AC 443 and *DPP* v *Morgan* [1976] AC 182, see below). In specific/ulterior-intent offences, voluntary intoxication or self-induced automatism *may* prevent an individual from forming the required intent. Unless he has that intent the accused cannot be held criminally liable for such an offence. It is irrelevant that an accused has been reckless (e.g., in becoming intoxicated) as this is insufficient to render an accused liable for the external elements of an offence which requires a specific/ulterior intent on his part. Whether an accused is incapable of forming the specified intent with regard to a specific/ulterior intent offence because of the fact of voluntary intoxication or self-induced automatism is a matter of fact (see *Majewski* and *R* v *Bailey* [1983] 2 All ER 503).

Dutch courage
Even with regard to an offence of specific/ulterior intent an accused who lacks the required specific/ulterior intent at the time of the commission of the *actus reus* through voluntary intoxication or self-induced automatism may still be held criminally responsible for such an offence. This may happen if he had earlier formed the prescribed intent to execute the offence and, e.g., got drunk to give himself 'Dutch courage' to carry out the crime, see *Attorney-General for Northern Ireland* v *Gallagher* [1963] AC 349. You could perhaps make reference to the strong policy element which underpins what we would suggest is an example of rather strained legal reasoning.

Involuntary intoxication or automatism
Students frequently fall into the trap of seeing all examination questions which involve drink and drugs as being cases of self-induced automatism or voluntary intoxication. Read such a question carefully to see whether it is actually a case of involuntarily induced automatism or intoxication. This is

important for the following reason. An accused who is involuntarily rendered drunk and incapable of forming the *mens rea* of an offence, e.g., by 'spiked' drinks, or who is an *involuntary* automaton may generally have a defence even to an offence of *basic* intent (see *DPP* v *Majewski* [1977] AC 443). However, where a person though involuntarily intoxicated is capable of forming the required *mens rea* with regard to an offence and the fact of his intoxication merely weakens his ability and will to control his conduct then he is guilty of any such offence he may commit (see *R* v *Bailey* [1983] 2 All ER 503). Involuntary intoxication is clearly not a defence where the accused has been proved to have the necessary *mens rea* when he committed the offence (*R* v *Kingston* [1994] 2 WLR 519). The fact of his intoxication is then relevant to sentence only. Furthermore, where an accused knows that he is drinking alcohol, such drinking does not become involuntary for the reason only that he may not know the precise nature or strength of the alcohol that he is consuming (*R* v *Allen* [1988] Crim LR 698).

Minority

A child below the age of 10 is *incapable* of committing a criminal offence. This is achieved through the medium of an *irrebuttable* presumption of law to this effect (see Children and Young Persons Act 1933, s. 50 as amended, and Murphy, *A Practical Approach to Evidence*). In addition there has been a rebuttable presumption of law that a child between the ages of 10 and 14 is also incapable of committing a criminal offence. This presumption could be rebutted, however, if the prosecution established the commission by such a minor of an *actus reus* with full *mens rea* and knowledge that the act was wrong. This meant either morally or legally wrong (see *R* v *Gorrie* (1918) 83 JP 136 and *McC* v *Runeckles* [1984] Crim LR 499). The fact that an offence is of such a nature that any normal child of the defendant's age would know it was seriously wrong was not in itself sufficient to rebut the presumption unless the prosecution could establish that the child was of a normal mental capacity (*IPH* v *Chief Constable of South Wales* [1987] Crim LR 42). See also *T* v *DPP* [1989] Crim LR 498 the effect of which seems to be that the *doli incapax* rule has no part to play in offences of dishonesty. The Queen's Bench division recently considered the rebuttable presumption of youth incapacity and declared that it was objectionable and no longer formed part of the Law of England (*C (A Minor)* v *DPP sub nom; Curry* v *DPP, The Times,* 30 March 1994). The House of Lords subsequently overruled that decision and ruled that the rebuttable presumption of *doli incapax* in children between the ages of 10 and 14 is still an effective doctrine of the criminal law: *C (a minor)* v *DPP* [1995] 2 All ER 43. Lord Lowry said that guilty knowledge cannot be presumed from the mere commission of the act. Circumstances in which it was committed must be considered. The older the accused is and the more obviously wrong or the more sophisticated in character the act, the easier it will generally be to prove guilty knowledge, e.g., 12-year-old boys taking a distressed, protesting 11-year-old girl to a remote, concealed place, forcibly indecently assaulting her and running away at the sound of an adult approaching (*A* v *DPP* [1997] 1 Cr App R 27). For several other illustrations of the presumption being rebutted, see *T, L, H and others* v *DPP* [1997] Crim LR 127 and *W (a Minor)* v *DPP* [1996] Crim LR 320 and the commentaries of Professor J. C. Smith which accompany both reports. See also *CC (a minor)* v *DPP* [1996] 1 Cr App R 375 which requires the prosecution to prove that the accused is mentally normal.

There was also a general rule (an *irrebuttable* presumption of law) that a boy between the ages of 10 and 14 was incapable of committing, as a *principal offender*, any offence involving the act of sexual intercourse (see *R* v *Waite* [1892] 2 QB 600). The Sexual Offences Act 1993, s. 1 abolished this presumption that a boy under 14 being incapable of sexual intercourse was therefore incapable of rape or attempted rape.

Mistake

This defence is one which causes students considerable problems. It has undergone constant judicial development in the past decade or so and the following is an attempt to explain its basic outline. Where a person commits the *actus reus* of an offence but at that time he mistakenly believes in the existence of facts which he believes renders his conduct lawful then he may lack the prescribed *mens rea* for such an offence. This is because the mistaken belief may negate the intention or recklessness which the accused must possess with regard to the consequences of the offence or nullify knowledge of or recklessness as to the circumstances that constitute an element or elements in the crime. The central issue is whether such a mistaken belief needs only to be honestly held, or whether such a belief needs, in addition, to be based on reasonable grounds. There is an important distinction between the situations where the defence of mistake is based on the nullification of an element in the *actus reus* or *mens rea* of the offence charged and where it is claimed that the mistaken belief provides a defence or justification independent of the central, constituent elements of that offence.

Mistaken beliefs which need to be only honestly held
Such is the case in respect of any mistaken belief which negates or relates to a constituent element in an offence (usually an element in the *mens rea* as discussed above). This was established by the House of Lords in *DPP* v *Morgan* [1976] AC 182. It was once thought that the element of 'unlawfulness' when prescribed in offences involving the application of violence did *not* form an element in the *actus reus* of an offence (see Hodgson J in the Divisional Court in *Albert* v *Lavin* [1981] 1 All ER 628 and chapter 3). On this basis, and

in respect of such crimes, in order to provide a defence, a mistaken belief with regard to the lawfulness of one's conduct was not governed by the principles in *Morgan* but had in addition to be based on reasonable grounds. Since the case of *R* v *Gladstone Williams* (1984) 78 Cr App R 276, it has been determined that the element of 'unlawfulness' does form an element of the *actus reus* in offences involving the application of violence. On this basis a mistaken belief held by an accused which may negate the intention or recklessness to act 'unlawfully' (i.e., the *mens rea* that must accompany the element of 'unlawfulness' in such offences) so as to afford a defence needs now only to be honestly held by him (see *R* v *Kimber* [1983] 3 All ER 316 and *Beckford* v *R* [1987] 3 All ER 425) as per *DPP* v *Morgan* which now seems to determine the general rule as to the form a mistaken belief may take in order to constitute a defence in so far as such a mistaken belief may negate a constituent element of an offence. See also *Blackburn* v *Bowering* [1995] Crim LR 38.

Situations where the mistaken belief needs to be honestly held and based on reasonable grounds
The simple picture discussed above is complicated by certain situations where, in order to constitute a defence, a mistaken belief must not only be honestly held by an accused but in addition it must be based on reasonable grounds. You should be aware of these situations and appreciate the different 'nature' of such mistaken beliefs from those discussed above. The factor of reasonableness is required in the following cases.

(a)   Crimes of (gross) negligence. A mistaken belief, in such cases, if not based on reasonable grounds, is itself negligent.
(b)   Defences of justification. Where an accused commits the *actus reus* of an offence with the prescribed *mens rea* but claims that he did so under the mistaken belief that his conduct was nevertheless justified, it would appear that the mistaken belief, in order to afford a defence, needs to be based upon reasonable grounds. In *R* v *Tolson* (1889) 23 QBD 168 the accused was charged with the offence of bigamy contrary to the Offences against the Person Act 1861, s. 57. Her defence, that she honestly and *reasonably* believed her first husband to be dead, was accepted, though it was a plea of justification independent of the constituent elements of the offence for she had committed the offence with the prescribed *mens rea*. It appears to have been accepted in *Tolson* and in *R* v *Gould* [1968] 2 QB 65 that the accused's mistaken belief in the death of her spouse coupled with the latter's absence for a period of seven years would also have provided a defence. This mistaken belief, it seems, in order to afford a defence would only have to have been honestly held. This is because it would have satisfied a particular statutory defence contained in s. 57 which states that it is a defence for an accused charged with bigamy if he or she can show a seven-year absence of the first 'spouse' and further that

he or she does not know that that 'spouse' is alive. Though this defence does not *require* a positive belief in the first 'spouse's' death, logic and *R* v *Gould* determine that such a belief will satisfy this defence. Such a belief would not, in the circumstances, require an element of reasonableness. Thus whether a mistaken belief needs to be based on reasonable grounds to constitute it a defence or not may be dependent not only upon the fact that it relates to the establishing of a defence which is independent of the constituent elements of an offence but also upon the terms of the statute creating a given offence. It is a matter in such cases of statutory construction (see *R* v *Smith* [1974] QB 354 and *Westminster City Council* v *Croyalgrange Ltd* [1986] 2 All ER 353). Many of these statutory offences have aspects of strict liability or are 'quasi-criminal' or 'regulatory' offences. You should also consider the following examples:

(i)   Sexual Offences Act 1976, s. 1(2), concerning the offence of rape. This subsection determines that a jury should consider the presence or absence of reasonable grounds in assessing whether a mistaken belief as to a woman's consent to sexual intercourse is genuinely held by an accused, a belief relating to the *mens rea* of the offence.

(ii)   Criminal Damage Act 1971, s. 5, which determines that an accused's belief (mistaken or not) in the right to destroy property need only be honestly held to provide an accused with the defence of 'lawful excuse' (see s.1). However, s. 5 determines that the accused's resultant conduct must be reasonable in all the circumstances. This should be determined objectively, see *R* v *Hill* (1989) 89 Cr App R 74 and *R* v *Ashford and Smith* [1988] Crim LR 682.

Conclusion
Remember that, to constitute a defence, a mistaken belief, irrespective of the form it may take, must relate to the constituent elements of the offence or a recognised substantive defence (i.e., a justification). It must also generally be a mistake of fact, a mistake of law usually being no defence, see *R* v *Esop* (1836) 7 C & P 456 and, e.g., *R* v *Jones* [1995] QB 235. However, a mistaken belief of law may provide a defence if it relates, e.g., to a belief in a proprietary right to goods. In such instances it may *negate mens rea* in offences such as theft and criminal damage, see *R* v *Smith* [1974] QB 354. Such a belief needs only to be honestly held in order to afford a defence.

Self-defence and the Prevention of Crime

The defences to be discussed, though technical, have at the least the merit of a certain uniformity of structure and share certain common elements.

An individual may have a defence to his use of reasonable force against another in the following circumstances:

(a)   At common law:

(i)   if its use is in self-defence, or in
(ii)   the defence of others.

(b)   By virtue of the Criminal Law Act 1967, s. 3(1):

(i)   in the prevention of crime, or
(ii)   in effecting or assisting in the lawful arrest of offenders or of persons unlawfully at large.

Both the common law and statutory defences noted above may overlap, for example the use of reasonable force in self-defence from a murderous assault is also preventing a crime, see *R v Cousins* [1982] QB 526. There are situations, however, where only the common law defences may be available, namely, where there is no crime committed because the person who otherwise may have been held responsible for the commission of a criminal offence has a defence such as automatism.

Reasonable force defined
You must be able to show a full understanding of the concept of reasonable force. It is the factor which unites all the defences discussed in this section. The common law once determined by the use of rules, and as a matter of law, whether the use of force was reasonable in the circumstances of a given case for each common law defence. It was once the law that an accused needed first to retreat from the scene of potential violence in order to justify his subsequent use of force where he claimed he had acted in self-defence. In the case of the situations within s. 3(1) this common law concept of reasonable force was abrogated by s. 3(2) of the 1967 Act. Within the statutory defences, whether or not the use of force by an accused against another is reasonable is a matter of fact dependent upon all the circumstances of the case. Thus the old common law rules (which applied to the common law defences) and which determined as a matter of law whether the use of force was reasonable within such situations are, within the situations envisaged in s. 3(1), now merely factors to be taken into account in determining whether, within the context of the statutory defences, the force used was reasonable. However, it appears to be the law that this approach to the concept of reasonable force is now also applicable to the common law defences (see *Attorney-General for Northern Ireland's Reference (No. 1 of 1975)* [1977] AC 105).

The factors which may be taken into account in determining what is reasonable force in both the context of the common law and statutory defences are as follows:

(a)   The nature and degree of the force used.
(b)   The gravity of the crime or evil to be prevented.
(c)   Whether it was possible to prevent the crime or evil by other means (see *Allen* v *Metropolitan Police Commissioner* [1980] Crim LR 441).
(d)   The relative strength of the parties concerned and the number of persons involved.
(e)   An unwillingness to use violence (*R* v *McInnes* [1971] 3 All ER 295 and *R* v *Bird* [1985] 1 WLR 816).

Although a matter of fact, the concept of *reasonable* force, by definition, requires an element of objectivity, i.e., in order to reject it as a defence, the jury must be satisfied that *no* reasonable man put in the position of an accused and with the time for reflection available to him in the actual case would consider the violence used by the accused to be justifiable (see *Farrell* v *Secretary of State for Defence* [1980] 1 All ER 166). Nevertheless this objectivity must be tempered with the personal situation of an actual accused. The test is whether or not it was the use of reasonable force by the accused in the agony of the situation and not whether the force used would be considered reasonable by the accused or a reasonable man viewing the situation in cool isolation (see *Palmer* v *R* [1971] AC 814, *R* v *Shannon* (1980) 71 Cr App R 192 and *R* v *Whyte* [1987] 3 All ER 416). The 'subjective element' is important, i.e., did the accused go beyond what was reasonable in light of the circumstances as they appeared to him? If he has only done what he honestly and instinctively thought was necessary that is strong evidence that the force was reasonable in the circumstances. In *R* v *Scarlett* [1993] 4 All ER 629 a publican forcibly ejected a drunken person who fell, as a result, down some stairs and died. The Court of Appeal took the view that the publican was justified in the circumstances in using some force and could only be guilty of an assault if the force was excessive. Even if he acted intentionally or recklessly he should only have been convicted if the jury were satisfied that the degree of force was excessive in the circumstances as he perceived them. Provided he believed the circumstances called for the degree of force used, he was not to be convicted even if his belief was unreasonable. The Court of Appeal in *R* v *Owino* [1996] 2 Cr App R 128 has now said that does not mean a person is entitled to use any degree of force he believed to be reasonable, however ill-founded the belief. He may use such force as is (objectively) reasonable in the circumstances as he (subjectively) believes them to be.

In *Attorney-General's Reference (No. 2 of 1983)* [1984] AC 456 it was accepted that a person may in appropriate circumstances strike first but his conduct may still be regarded as the use of reasonable force.

Excessive force
Where an accused has used excessive and therefore unreasonable force, neither the common law defences nor those contained in the Criminal Law Act 1967, s. 3(1), will be available to him. His criminal liability will be determined by his *mens rea* and the harm he has inflicted by his use of such force (see *R* v *McInnes* [1971] 3 All ER 295, *Palmer* v *R* [1971] AC 814 and *Zecevic* v *DPP* (Victoria) [1987] 162 CLR 645). If the accused used more force in self-defence than was necessary in the circumstances and causes death he is guilty of murder; there is no distinction between the use of excessive force in self-defence and the use of excessive force in the prevention of crime or in arresting an offender and it makes no difference that the person using it is a soldier or policeman acting in the course of his duty (*R* v *Clegg* [1995] 2 WLR 80, HL — this is the controversial case of the soldier on duty patrol in Northern Ireland who shot at an approaching car and then again, allegedly, after it had passed, killing a passenger in it). The excess of force does not simply reduce the offence to one of manslaughter.

Evidential matters
An accused seeking to claim that the common law defences or those contained within the Criminal Law Act 1967, s. 3(1), are applicable to his case bears an evidential burden in establishing them (see *R* v *Lobell* [1957] 1 QB 547). If the accused's account of the facts which if accepted could raise a prima facie case of self-defence, that issue should be left to the jury even where the accused has not relied on self-defence (*DPP (for Jamaica)* v *Bailey* [1995] Crim LR 313).

The effect of mistaken belief
This has already been considered above as has the effect of intoxication on the accused's belief in the right to use reasonable force (see *R* v *O'Grady* [1987] 3 All ER 420 and *R* v *Fotheringham* (1989) 88 Cr App R 206). With regard to the issue of mistaken belief, in addition to the authorities cited above, see also *R* v *Jackson* [1985] RTR 257; *R* v *Asbury* [1986] Crim LR 258 and *R* v *Fisher* [1987] Crim LR 334.

The common law defences
You must show you are aware of the ambit of the various common law defences discussed above. The concept of self-defence needs no explanation. Remember, however, that reasonable force may also be used in the defence of relatives (*R* v *Rose* (1884) 15 Cox CC 540) or in the case of any person who needs assistance or protection from a breach of the peace or from a violent act (see *R* v *Duffy* [1967] 1 QB 63 and *Albert* v *Lavin* [1982] AC 546). Furthermore an individual may use reasonable force in the protection of his home (*R* v

Hussey (1924) 18 Cr App R 160) but it is doubtful that this principle extends to permit killing in order to protect property, however valuable.

Criminal Law Act 1967, s. 3(1)
The prevention of crime needs no explanation: it covers any criminal offence, from murder to a breach of the peace.

Effecting, or assisting in, the lawful arrest of offenders or suspected offenders is also straightforward. Whether or not the suspect has *actually* committed an offence is immaterial: the defence applies if he is suspected of having committed an offence for which there is a power of arrest (see Emmins, *A Practical Approach to Criminal Procedure*).

Duress

This defence is comparatively straightforward. It negates neither *mens rea* nor *actus reus* (see *R* v *Howe* [1987] 1 All ER 771). It is a defence which is recognised as a matter of policy, a recognition of the weakness of human nature (see *DPP for Northern Ireland* v *Lynch* [1975] AC 653) when the mind of the accused is so overpowered by a threat of death or really serious injury that he cannot reasonably act otherwise. It does not extend to a case where the accused believed that the act was immediately necessary to avoid serious psychological injury (*R* v *Baker and Williams* [1997] Crim LR 497). It is a defence where the accused bears only an evidential burden in order to establish it. Its nature is as follows:

(a)   The individual commits the *actus reus* of an offence with full *mens rea* but he is overborne by the threats of another to the extent that he cannot be said to be a free agent, i.e., he would not have committed the offence but for the threat (see *R* v *Valderrama-Vega* [1985] Crim LR 220).

(b)   The threat (express or implied) must be of violence encompassing the accused's death or serious bodily harm (see *R* v *Hudson and Taylor* [1971] 2 QB 202) though such threats need not be the sole threats. Authority on the sufficiency of the threat of lesser injuries for the purposes of the defence (see *R* v *Steane* [1947] KB 997) must be viewed with suspicion in view of the House of Lords' decision in *DPP for Northern Ireland* v *Lynch* [1975] AC 653 (although this decision has been overruled on other points, see below). That decision reaffirmed the necessity for death or serious bodily harm to be the subject-matter of the threat against an accused. It is uncertain whether the defence is available when such threats are made in relation to an accused's relations, or to a third party, but there appears to be nothing in principle to prevent such threats being the subject-matter of a defence of duress (see *R* v *Shepherd* (1988) 86 Cr App R 47). However, threats to family pets and even genuine fear for personal safety because of a past history of violence, but where no specific threat has been made, will not entitle anyone to rely on the defence of duress (*DPP* v *Milroy* [1993] COD 200).

(c)   The accused, in order to invoke the defence of duress, must show that he has possessed the steadfastness of an ordinary citizen in his situation in resisting or at least in attempting to resist the threat to his bodily integrity (see *R* v *Graham* [1982] 1 All ER 801 and *R* v *Howe* [1987] 1 All ER 771). He must by evidence raise the issue and ultimately it must be established that he was compelled to act as he did as a consequence of the threat *and* that an ordinary reasonable man with *his* characteristics and in *his* situation would have acted in the same way. It is difficult to say what are relevant characteristics for the purposes of the objective test for duress but being a drug addict is not a relevant characteristic because that condition does not affect that person's ability to resist threats (*R* v *Flatt* [1996] Crim LR 576). Also, being more pliable, vulnerable, timid or susceptible to threats than a normal person are not relevant characteristics. However, being in a category of persons possibly less able to resist pressure is a relevant characteristic. Such categories would include: age, sex, serious physical disability or a recognised mental illness or psychiatric condition (*R* v *Bowen* [1997] 1 WLR 372).

(d)   The accused's belief in the circumstances of duress must be based on reasonable grounds. This requirement distinguishes duress from self-defence where the presence or absence of reasonable grounds for an alleged belief is only evidence of whether or not that belief was actually held (see *Beckford* v *R* [1987] 3 All ER 425).

(e)   The threat must be operative at the time of the commission of the offence. In addition, there must be no 'avenue of escape' available to the accused, e.g., by informing the police (see *R* v *Hudson and Taylor* and *R* v *Shepherd* (1988) 86 Cr App R 47).

Failure to take a *reasonable* opportunity of an 'avenue of escape' negates the defence of duress. The 'avenue of escape' must in all the circumstances of the case (and having regard to the characteristics of the accused) be a *reasonable* course of action for him to take (see *R* v *Hudson and Taylor* and *R* v *Graham*).

(f)   The threat, though it must be an immediate one (i.e., operating on the mind of an accused), need not be capable of being *executed* instantly (see *R* v *Hudson and Taylor*). The more remote the possibility of execution of the threat, however, the less likely can the threat be said to operate on the mind of an accused, rendering the defence by degrees ultimately unavailable to an accused.

If in considering this defence in an examination question you remember the five points just discussed in the order set out above, you should be able to determine whether the defence is available to an accused in any given case, or give a structured logical account of its nature.

Availability of the defence

The defence of duress is available in respect of all offences but one (namely the offence of murder, see below) although the balance of authority recognises its applicability even to cases of treason (see *Oldcastle's case* (1419) 1 Hale PC 50).

The defence is unavailable to an accused in the following circumstances:

(a) It is unavailable to persons who commit a crime as a consequence of threats from members of a terrorist or criminal organisation which they have voluntarily joined (see *R* v *Calderwood and Moore* [1983] 10 NIJB and *R* v *Sharp* [1987] 86 Cr App R 47). However, in the case of *Shepherd* it was suggested that an accused, though a voluntary participant in a criminal organisation, may be able to claim the defence of duress if at the time he joined the criminal enterprise, he failed to appreciate the risk of violence. If the accused knew of a propensity for violence in those with whom he was working, then he cannot rely on duress if they threaten him with violence to do what they want (*R* v *Ali* [1995] Cr App R 16).

(b) It is unavailable to a *principal* offender or a secondary party to the crime of murder (*R* v *Howe* [1987] 1 All ER 771) or in the case of attempted murder (*R* v *Gotts* [1991] Crim LR 366).

However, it may be available to a party to a conspiracy or incitement to murder because of the greater remoteness of these from the completed offence (see *Gotts*).

The defences now to be discussed have been mentioned for completeness but generally they do not figure prominently in examination papers. Remember, however, the peculiarity of your criminal law course which might (at least as regards necessity, see below) give an undue prominence to them with obvious potential consequences.

Coercion

This defence, now governed by the Criminal Justice Act 1925, s. 47, is similar to duress (in that it involves threats). Its differences are:

(a) It is available only to a *wife* who commits the offence *'in the presence of her husband'*.

(b) It is unavailable in the case of certain offences, principally treason as well as murder.

(c) The threats may involve not only death or serious bodily harm but encompass any physical harm or even moral pressure (see *R* v *Richman* [1982] Crim LR 507).

The defence is of little practical importance, its ambit is uncertain and clearly it is overshadowed by duress. An accused must show she is married; a reasonable belief that she is married is not sufficient to enable her to claim the defence (see *R* v *Ditta* [1988] Crim LR 42).

Superior Orders
The actual existence of this defence is uncertain. Its possible characteristics are:

(a) The accused is compelled to act because of the orders of a superior.

(b) He must not know his conduct is wrong, and must act in good faith (see *R* v *James* (1837) 3 C & P 131).

The authorities which appear to recognise the defence could be explained on other grounds, e.g., that the accused lacks *mens rea*. The defence, if it exists, may be limited only to military situations (see *Lewis* v *Dickson* [1976] RTR 431, but see *McKee* v *Chief Constable for Northern Ireland* [1984] 1 WLR 1358 which may suggest the contrary).

The accused's belief that he has the authority of God, no matter how strongly or sincerely held, does not amount to a defence under English Law (*Blake* v *DPP* [1993] Crim LR 586).

Necessity

The characteristic of this defence is that an accused may have the defence of necessity available to him where he commits the *actus reus* of an offence with *mens rea*, but from the motive of avoiding a greater evil. Its existence is uncertain though it is recognised as a defence in certain statutory offences, e.g., the Road Traffic Regulation Act 1984, s. 87, permitting, *inter alia*, fire engines to exceed speed limits where necessary to ensure they can carry out their emergency functions. Authorities such as *Southwark London Borough Council* v *Williams* [1971] 2 All ER 175 appear to recognise the defence as being generally available (see also *R* v *Willer* (1986) 83 Cr App R 225 and contrast *R* v *Denton* [1987] RTR 129 with *R* v *Conway* [1989] Crim LR 74 which held that if from an objective standpoint the accused's actions (i.e., reckless driving in that instance) were taken to avoid a threat of death or serious injury then a defence is available. Whether such 'duress of circumstances' is called 'duress' or 'necessity' does not matter although the concept and language of duress is inappropriate in some of these instances (a police car colliding while crossing a red light in pursuit of potential robbers (*DPP* v *Harris* [1995] 1 Cr App R 170)). What is important is that, whatever it is called, it is subject to the same limitations as to the 'do this or else' species of duress). Cases such as *Buckoke* v *Greater London Council* [1971] 2 All ER 254, however, deny its existence. The defence does exist under legislation, e.g., the Traffic Signs Regulations and General Direction 1981, reg. 34(1)(b) permits police and emergency service vehicles to drive through red lights, and at common law, though it may exist, is never available in cases of murder (*R* v *Dudley and Stephens* (1884) 14 QBD 273) or attempted murder and some forms of treason (*R* v *Fitzroy Derek Pommell* [1995] 2 Cr App R 607). That case made it clear that where the defence is available the accused must desist from committing the crime in question (there the possession of a loaded machine gun) as soon as he reasonably can.

In the case of *R* v *Martin* [1989] 1 All ER 652 the Court of Appeal recognised a defence of necessity (duress of circumstances) which arises from wrongful threats of violence to another or from 'objective dangers'. These threats or dangers must affect the accused or others.

The defence is only available however, where the accused can be said (objectively) to be acting reasonably and proportionately to avoid the threat of death or serious injury. It is for the tribunal of fact to determine whether the accused reasonably believed he had good cause to fear death or serious injury, and, if so whether a person of reasonable firmness having the accused's characteristics would have acted as the accused did.

Objective Test in Defences

In relation to the availability of either the defence of duress by threats and duress by circumstances (see under 'Necessity' above) the test is not purely subjective; it requires an objective criterion to be satisfied. It is a matter for the jury. The jury has to consider whether a sober person of reasonable firmness 'showing the characteristics of the accused' would have responded to the situation confronting him (the accused) by acting as he did. The jury may take into account the age, sex and physical health of the accused, but as the test predicated a sober person of reasonable firmness there is no scope for attributing to that hypothetical person as one of the characteristics of the accused a personality disorder or pre-existing mental condition such as emotional instability or being in a highly neurotic state (*R* v *Hegarty* [1994] Crim LR 353). See also the comments on 'Duress' (para. (c) above) dealing with the guidance given in *R* v *Flatt* [1996] Crim LR 576 and *R* v *Bowen* [1997] 1 WLR 372.

While the law continues to require an objective test the judge has the difficult job of explaining to the jury which of the accused's characteristics may be taken into account in deciding whether or not he should have resisted the threat. To take into account all his characteristics would be to apply a subjective test and that is not the current law (although there are proposals to change to a subjective test: Law Comm. No. 218, 1993, Cmnd. 2370 and draft Criminal Law Bill, cl. 25(2)). Note for comparative purposes the similar objective test applied in relation to the defence of provocation. There, the characteristic to be viewed objectively is self-restraint. In duress it is firmness of purpose, i.e., the ability to resist threats of physical harm.

PLANNING YOUR REVISION

The average criminal law course nearly always concentrates on the following defences in some detail:

(a) Insanity (although more for historical reasons, than practical considerations).
(b) Non-insane automatism (this is not a large topic).
(c) Voluntary intoxication and self-induced automatism.
(d) Mistake.
(e) The defences relating to the lawful application of reasonable force.
(f) Duress.
(g) Necessity.

The other defences discussed earlier in the text which have not been listed bove were mentioned for the sake of completeness.

Generally defences are mixed in with problem questions involving the commission of substantive offences. However, the defences themselves, when contained within questions, tend to be grouped in 'families'. Thus non-insane automatism is frequently combined with the issue of self-induced automatism. This latter matter may itself be combined with voluntary intoxication and the defence of mistake, and these issues themselves are frequently combined with the various defences which may be subsumed under the heading of the lawful application of reasonable force, e.g., self-defence. It is suggested as a tactic that you should be familiar with all these defences and be prepared to consider them in various combinations within examination questions.

Necessity, duress and insanity are usually the exclusive subject-matter of half and occasionally full questions. The questions are nearly always essay questions. If you must drop the detailed revision of one or two important defences, as an emergency tactic, these perhaps are the ones which you might consider for that purpose. Should you choose to do that then unless you are desperately unlucky you will generally only be unable to answer one half or one full question on the examination paper.

EXAMPLES OF QUESTIONS

Essay Questions

(1) 'The concept of insanity is both outdated and unnecessary.'

How far is this true?

(2) How have the courts interpreted the phrase 'defect of reason from disease of the mind' in the context of the M'Naghten rules?

(3) 'The survival of the M'Naghten rules is a clear illustration of the conservative nature of the criminal law. They are neither sensible nor useful.'
Discuss.

Outline Answers

Question (1)
This question requires a full discussion of the constituents of the defence of insanity as provided for in the M'Naghten rules. However, this alone is obviously insufficient fully to answer this question. The two concepts which dominate the issue of insanity are 'disease of the mind' and 'defect of reason'. You may well consider that the defence of insanity is outdated because of the anachronistic interpretation given by the courts to the term 'defect of reason'. This is restricted in several respects. Remember that an accused, because of a 'defect of reason', must principally:

(a) be unable to appreciate the nature or quality of his act, or
(b) though he may appreciate the nature or quality of his act he must not know his conduct is wrong.

You should fully discuss the implications of the courts' formulation of 'defect of reason'. This limited concept takes no cognisance of the modern advances in the understanding of the human psyche. You should contrast this concept with the more modern statutory defence of diminished responsibility (see chapter 9). You should also consider whether the defence is unnecessary. You may well come to the conclusion that, though it is little used and rarely to be found even in cases of murder, the defence of insanity still has its uses. You should consider that ironically it still may be used by the prosecution in situations where they seek to have an individual put into protective custody.

Question (2)
This question merely requires a descriptive analysis of the two elements of 'disease of the mind' and 'defect of reason'. A full understanding of the nature of the defence of insanity should enable you to score heavily.

Question (3)
This question is a slant on the first one. Again, it needs a discussion of the defence of insanity. However, it requires a critical approach or angle. A

general consideration of the criminal law, whether it is conservative in nature, can be examined and tested by a detailed review of the history of the defence of insanity to the present day and its place in modern criminal procedure. It is a matter of opinion for you to express whether the M'Naghten rules remain useful or are sensible.

Problem Question

(4) Eric surreptitiously pours a large quantity of vodka into a glass of lemonade which is being drunk at the Christmas office party by Albert, a young, genial man of 25 who is a total abstainer from alcohol. Being affected by the drink Albert goes into the photocopying room and has sexual intercourse with Rita the office cleaner. She did not consent to the act. Albert later claims he was not aware that Rita was not consenting. Albert arrives home and has a bath to clear his head (he is aware that he is not thinking clearly); he slips and falls and strikes his head and is rendered unconscious. He awakes but is in a state of concussion and while in this state he kills his flatmate Eric who has just returned from the office party.

Discuss Albert's criminal responsibility.

Would the situation differ if the vodka merely inflamed Albert's passion and weakened his ability to control his actions?

What would be Albert's criminal responsibility if he had known of the vodka in his drink and decided it would be fun to get 'tipsy' for once?

Outline Answer (4)

In this type of question you should take yourself through the incidents as they arise, first dealing with the question as originally posed, and then considering the whole of the question anew in each of the alternative situations set out at the end of the question. Your answer in outline may take into account the following matters.

The two offences with which Albert could be charged are the rape of Rita and the murder of Eric. Do not fall into the trap of discussing the question initially from the viewpoint of basic and specific/ulterior-intent offences, and DPP v Majewski [1977] AC 443. This is not (as the question initially stands) a case of voluntary intoxication but *involuntary* intoxication. In respect of the rape the fact is that Albert may be incapable of forming the intent to have sexual intercourse, knowing or being reckless as to the fact of Rita's lack of consent. He thus may lack *mens rea* and because the question is initially a case of involuntary intoxication he is not precluded from admitting the fact of his intoxication in establishing his lack of *mens rea*.

As to the fact of his concussion, this can be said to be a case of non-insane automatism since Albert cannot be said to have self-induced this state. In accordance with the principle of law in *Hill v Baxter* [1958] 1 QB 277 he should have a defence to the charge of the murder of Eric.

You should now turn to the second situation posed in the question where the alcohol, though taken involuntarily, only deprives Albert of the ability to control his will-power. Since he can be said to have in such cases an intent to act, albeit a drunken intent, he can be convicted of the rape of Rita (see *R v Davies* [1983] Crim LR 741 and *DPP v Majewski*).

However, this fact does not affect the situation involving the autonomic state which it can be argued has been caused through the accidental blow to Albert's head in the bath. Thus he still may use the fact of his autonomic state as a defence to the charge of murder.

The final situation to consider is when Albert intentionally takes the alcohol knowing, or at least being reckless as to, what its effects are likely to be upon him. This is a case of voluntary intoxication. You should thus discuss *DPP v Majewski* and consider that, because rape is a basic-intent offence (i.e., one that may be committed recklessly), the law does not permit the fact of voluntarily induced intoxication to be adduced as a defence or as an explanation for an absence of *mens rea*. The law actually regards such voluntary conduct as satisfying the element of recklessness which can constitute the prescribed *mens rea* in offences of basic intent (see also *R v Fotheringham*).

Apart from the fact that it may be argued that the autonomic state can be said to have resulted from a cause independent of the intoxication, the murder of Eric is a specific-intent offence (see *R v Moloney* [1985] AC 905). An autonomic state, whether self-induced or not, will constitute a defence to the charge of Eric's murder (see *DPP v Majewski* and *R v Bailey* [1983] 2 All ER 503).

Another Problem Question

Another question may deal with the issues of the lawful application of reasonable force combined perhaps with the defence of mistake, for example:

(5) Cecil is queuing at a football ground. He has had a lot to drink and is noisy and boisterous. A scruffily dressed man tells him to leave the queue just as he is approaching the turnstile. Cecil tells him to get lost. The man says quietly, 'I am a police officer', and when Cecil does not move he starts to push him away. Hubert, who is with Cecil, has not heard what was said and thinks Cecil is being attacked. He strikes the man who is a police officer a severe blow to the face.

Advise Hubert.

Outline Answer (5)

This question requires a consideration of several issues but only from Hubert's point of view. Since the House of Lords' decision in *Albert v Lavin*

[1982] AC 546 any individual has a right, and it has been suggested possibly a duty, to take action to prevent a breach of the peace. According to that same authority and *R v Duffy* [1967] 1 QB 63 an individual can use reasonable force in the protection and defence of others.

It is a difficult and intricate area of the law which determines whether the police officer is acting lawfully at the time he is assaulted by Hubert. He may (because it is suggested from the question that Cecil is no longer breaching the peace and is unlikely to do so in the future) be acting unlawfully himself, and 'assaulting' Cecil. In such a case Hubert would be justified in using reasonable force (see below) to protect Cecil from any 'assault' by the police officer. It is a trite point whether Hubert would need to be aware of the possible unlawful nature of the conduct of the police officer before he could claim the right to use reasonable force on this basis per *R v Dadson* (1850) 4 Cox CC 358 (see chapter 3).

If we assume that the officer was acting lawfully the only defence open to Hubert is to claim that he believed (though mistakenly) that Cecil was the victim of an assault and that he was, when he used force against the police officer, merely acting in the defence of another, i.e., Cecil. Hubert should be charged with assaulting the police officer within the terms of one of the statutory 'assaults' contained in the Offences against the Person Act 1861. These offences require the 'assault' to be 'unlawful'. This element has been determined, since *R v Gladstone Williams* (1984) 78 Cr App R 276 and *R v Kimber* [1983] 3 All ER 316, as being part of the *actus reus* of the offence which must be accompanied by a corresponding *mens rea*. The mistaken belief of Hubert that he is acting to protect Cecil deprives him of the *mens rea* necessary to constitute his conduct an 'unlawful' assault within the meaning discussed above. The only issue remaining on this point for you to consider is whether this mistaken belief needs only to be honestly held or based in addition upon reasonable grounds to be operative as a defence. It is clear since *R v Gladstone Williams*, *R v Kimber* and *Beckford v R* [1987] 3 All ER 425 that the mistaken belief, in this case, since it relates to and negates the *mens rea* that must accompany the element of unlawfulness, needs only to be honestly held, since it is governed by the principles enunciated in *DPP v Morgan* [1976] AC 182. You must finally consider whether the force used by Hubert was reasonable. Since *Attorney-General for Northern Ireland's Reference (No. 1 of 1975)* [1977] AC 105 it has been settled law that, whether one relies upon the common law defences or those within s. 3(1) of the Criminal Law Act 1967, the determination of whether the force used was reasonable in a given case is a matter of fact. However, various factors such as the nature and degree of the force used, the gravity of the evil to be avoided, the possibility of preventing the evil by other means, the relative strength and number of the parties involved and the unwillingness to use violence, are matters to be taken into account in considering whether the force used in a given case was reasonable.

You must come to a conclusion whether Hubert's striking of the officer on the facts as disclosed by the question was justified and whether the degree of force used was reasonable in that instance. Remember also that this latter requirement has an element of objectivity. A jury might consider that no reasonable man in this situation having had the time for reflection, which Hubert had, could call the conduct on Hubert's part reasonable force in the circumstances (see *Farrell* v *Secretary of State for Defence* [1980] 1 All ER 166). Note, however, that this objective test is tinged with subjectivity. The jury must consider what is reasonable force using the above test but also have regard to the actual situation of the accused in the agony of the situation (see *Palmer* v *R* [1971] AC 814, *R* v *Shannon* (1980) 71 Cr App R 192, *R* v *Whyte* [1987] 3 All ER 416, *R* v *Scarlett* [1993] 4 All ER 629, *R* v *Owino* [1996] 2 Cr App R 128 and *R* v *Clegg* [1995] 2 WLR 80).

We have not included a question involving the defence of duress or the other defences such as coercion, necessity and superior orders. Nevertheless they may feature in an examination question in either essay or problem form.

Of the defences just discussed duress is the most important and likely to merit a half or full question devoted to its incidents. As in the case of all defences duress could be part of a composite question requiring consideration of several defences, though it is frequently combined, if at all, with issues of necessity or superior orders.

A question involving duress will notwithstanding its format generally seek to test your knowledge of the nature of duress and its applicability to various individuals in relation to certain offences. Remember that it is unavailable to a person charged as a party to the offence of murder (see *R* v *Howe* [1987] 1 All ER 771).

CONCLUSION

The defences discussed in this chapter display two consistent themes:

(a) They may deprive an individual of the ability to possess the prescribed *mens rea* or some more fundamental mental element of an offence. Such are the defences of insanity, automatism, and intoxication. The defence relating to the incapacity of minors *presumes* such an individual to lack certain mental states irrespective of the actual facts.

(b) Other defences, namely those relating to the lawful application of force, coercion, superior orders and necessity seem united by the principle of public policy.

It is only when you consider the defence of mistake in its various forms that you may see a defence which, depending upon the nature of the mistake, may be justified on either of the grounds considered above.

FURTHER READING

General Defences

Ashworth, A., 'Reason, Logic and Criminal Liability' (1975) 91 LQR 102.
Ashworth, A., 'Self-Defence nd the Right to Life' (1975) 34 CLJ 282.
Law Commission Report No. 218: Legislation the Criminal Code (1993).
Leigh, L., 'Self-Defence against a Constable' (1967) 30 MLR 340.
Smith, J. C., 'Justification and Excuse in the Criminal Law', The Hamlyn Lecture Series (London: Sweet & Maxwell, 1989).

Necessity

Glazebrook, P., 'The Necessity Plea' (1972) 30 CLJ 87.
Huxley, P. H., 'Proposals and Counter Proposals on the Defence of Necessity' [1978] Crim LR 141.
Law Commission Working Paper No. 55: Codification of the Criminal Law: General Principles, Defences of General Application (1974).
Simpson, A. W. B., Cannibalism and the Common Law (Chicago: University of Chicago Press, 1984).
Williams, G., 'Defences of General Application, Necessity' [1978] Crim LR 128.

Mistake

Ashworth, A., 'Excusable Mistake of Law' [1974] Crim LR 652.
Crowley, D., 'The Retreat from Morgan' [1982] Crim LR 198.

Duress

Edwards, J., 'Compulsion, Coercion and Criminal Responsibility' (1951) 14 MLR 297.
Gardner, S., 'Duress in the House of Lords' (1992) 108 LQR 349.
Gardner, S., 'Duress in Attempted Murder' (1991) 107 LQR 389.
Gearty, C., 'Duress — Members of Criminal Organisations and Gangs' (1987) 46 CLJ 379.
Horder, J., 'Occupying the Moral High-Ground. The Law Commission on Duress' [1994] Crim LR 334.
Law Commission Working Paper No. 55 (1974).
Smith, A. T. H., 'Defences of General Application: Duress' [1978] Crim LR 122.
Wasik, M., 'Duress and Criminal Responsibility' [1977] Crim LR 453.

Intoxication

Clarkson, C., 'Drunkenness, Constructive Manslaughter and Specific Intent' (1978) 41 MLR 478.

Dashwood, A., 'Logic and The Lords in *Majewski*' [1977] Crim LR 532 and 591.
Glazebrook, P., 'The Involuntary Intoxicated Diabetic' (1984) 43 CLJ 5.
Law Commission Consultation Paper No. 127: Intoxication and Criminal Liability (1993).
Lynch, A., 'The Scope of Intoxication' [1982] Crim LR 139.
Milgate, H., 'Intoxication, Mistake and Public Interest' (1987) 46 CLJ 380.
MacKay, R. D., 'Intoxication as a Factor in Automatism' [1982] Crim LR 146.
Sellers, J., '*Mens Rea* and the Judicial Approach to "Bad Excuse"' (1978) 41 MLR 245.
Smith, J. C., 'Commentary on *Majewski*' [1976] Crim LR 375.
Smith, J. C., 'Commentary on *Majewski*' [1975] Crim LR 572.
Sullivan, G. R., 'Involuntary Intoxication and Beyond' [1994] Crim LR 272.
Sullivan, G. R., 'Intoxicants and Diminished Responsibility' [1994] Crim LR 156.
Virgo, G., 'The Law Commission Consultation Paper on Intoxication and Criminal Law: Reconciling Principle and Policy' [1993] Crim LR 415.

Insanity

Ashworth, A., 'The Butler Committee and Criminal Responsibility' [1975] Crim LR 687.
Butler Report, The [1975] Crim LR 673.
Clements, L., 'Epilepsy, Insanity and Automatism' (1983) 133 NLJ 949.
Glazebrook, P., 'The Involuntary Intoxicated Diabetic' (1984) 43 CLJ 5.
Munday, R., 'Insanity, The Epileptic Offender and the House of Lords' (1983) 42 CLJ 192.
Report on the Butler Committee on Mentally Abnormal Offenders (Cmnd 6244), chapters 10, 13, 14, 18 and 19.

Self-defences

Ashworth, A., 'Self-Defence and the Right to Life' (1975) 34 CLJ 282.
Harlow, C., 'Self-defence: Public Right or Private Privilege' [1974] Crim LR 528.
Howard, C., 'Two Problems of Excessive Defence' (1968) 84 LQR 343.
Smith, P., 'Excessive Defence — a Rejection of Australian Initiative?' [1972] Crim LR 524.

Superior Orders

Brownlee, I., 'Superior Orders — Time for a new Realism' [1989] Crim LR 396.

9   OFFENCES AGAINST THE PERSON

The law protects us all by prohibiting threats to injure, actual infliction of injury and the causing of death.

(a)   Threats to injure are dealt with by the common law of assault.

(b)   Actual non-fatal infliction of injury can be put in one of two categories:

(i)   non-sexually motivated offences, examples of which are:

(1)   common law battery,

(2)   statutory 'assaults' such as causing grievous bodily harm (Offences against the Person Act 1861, s. 18), and

(ii)   sexually motivated offences such as rape.

(c)   Causing death can fall into one or other of several categories depending on the factors and circumstances accompanying the death. These categories include murder and manslaughter. To obtain a much more comprehensive picture of the range and type of offences against the person, see Figure 9.1 (p. 219).

NON-SEXUAL, NON-FATAL OFFENCES

In answer to any examination question concerning offences against the person you must show you understand the terminology. At common law, assault is the putting of someone in fear of injury. If you actually hit someone, that, at common law, is not assault but battery. In relation, however, to statutory offences against persons the Legislature has chosen to use the word 'assault' (as we do in everyday language) as synonymous with common law battery. Assault and battery are treated as one. But remember the distinction between them still remains at common law. Today, battery is almost never charged because of the number of statutory 'assault' offences that can be used instead. All of these offences are really battery rather than assault-based because the *actus reus* of each involves actual physical contact or violence and not just the threat of it.

Battery

Common law battery is simply any unlawful physical contact with another. Whether or not the 'victim' is aware of the contact or the blows being struck and whether or not harm results are immaterial. Furthermore the *actus reus* of battery may be produced indirectly by the doing of something which results in the 'victim' being struck or suffering a physical injury, e.g., through falling or slipping.

Assault

Common law assault is simply causing another person to believe that unlawful physical contact is imminent, i.e., putting another in fear of immediate injury is the *actus reus*. The *mens rea* is simply your intentionally or recklessly producing that belief. It is a basic-intent offence (*R v Venna* [1976] QB 421; *Fagan v Metropolitan Police Commissioner* [1969] 1 QB 439). The recklessness referred to is the *Cunningham* type (i.e., conscious risk-taking). *Caldwell*-type recklessness (failure to consider an obvious risk) does not apply because assault is akin to old statutory offences defined in terms of 'maliciousness' rather than recklessness and any offence defined in terms of maliciousness requires proof of intention *or Cunningham*-type recklessness only (see *W v Dolbey* [1983] Crim LR 681 and *R v Grimshaw* [1984] Crim LR 109; and, in particular, *R v Morrison, The Times,* 12 November 1988) which confirm the view that *Caldwell* recklessness is not relevant to offences expressed in terms of 'maliciousness'. Moreover in *R v Spratt* [1990] 1 WLR 1073, CA, it was held that in every offence against the person recklessness was to be given the *Cunningham* meaning. Although this point was not specifically addressed by the House of Lords in *Savage and Parmenter* [1991] 4 All ER 698, dicta indicates their lordships' agreement on this issue.).

Two cases, *Mead's and Belt's case* (1823) 1 Lew CC 184 and *R v Wilson* [1955] 1 All ER 744, support the proposition that words alone cannot be a common assault. There seems, however, to be no logical reason why this should be so. Provided they create a fear that violence is immediate or imminent, that should be enough. Words alone may prevent threatening conduct from becoming an assault, so why shouldn't they alone be capable of being an assault? Surely if you threaten to strike a blind man or make that sort of threat to anyone in pitch darkness, the words and tone alone will give rise to immediate fear. That is an assault even if the speaker in fact is incapable of carrying out his threat (*R v St George* (1840) 9 C & P 483), where the pointing of an unloaded gun was held to be an assault). Difficult though it may be to envisage, both common assault and battery may be committed by omission. For example, the deliberate decision not to say something which would reassure a person threatened by your conduct or a decision not to end a battery which you had not previously been aware of, could be sufficient *mens rea* (see *Fagan* v *Metropolitan Police Commissioner* [1969] 1 QB 439; this case involved parking on a policeman's foot and then refusing to remove the car when made aware of the officer's predicament).

Special Defences to 'Assault' and Battery Offences

Persons charged with common law assault or battery or any of those statutory 'assault'-based offences (the so-called aggravated assaults which incorporate the basic elements of the two common law offences) have available to them the general defences (see chapter 8) and in addition three special defences may be available in the appropriate instances. These are:

(a) Lawful and reasonable chastisement of a child by its parent or schoolteacher.
(b) Consent.
(c) Inevitable accident.

Of these three, the most limited in its application is the first. The common law permits reasonable chastisement of a child by parent or schoolteacher with the authority of the pupil's parent (see *Cleary* v *Booth* [1893] 1 QB 465). The jury must decide whether or not the chastisement was carried out in a reasonable, moderate and controlled way. Provided it is not unreasonable and the accused did not know, or ought not reasonably to have been expected to know, that death or grievous bodily harm was likely to result, then he or she will not be liable even for the death of the child. Death from unreasonable chastisement would warrant a charge of manslaughter (see *R* v *Hopley* (1869) 2 F & F 202). Death caused deliberately or resulting from deliberately inflicted grievous bodily harm would warrant a charge of murder (see *R* v *Moloney* [1985] AC 905).

The European Court of Human Rights has ruled in effect in *Campbell and Cosans* v *United Kingdom* (1982) 4 EHRR 293 that corporal punishment in schools contrary to the wishes of parents infringes Article 2 of Protocol No. 1

to the European Convention on Human Rights and it is the duty of the British government as a signatory to the Convention to respect parental convictions and abolish corporal punishment in all its schools. Now the Education (No. 2) Act 1986, s. 47(10), states that a member of school staff has no right, without the authority of the pupil's parent, to administer corporal punishment. The common law still applies, perhaps, to schools outside the ambit of this Act and to teachers who do have parental permission to chastise school children.

Inevitable Accident

Purely accidental, physical contact (or the likelihood of it) in ordinary daily life, even where negligent, does not amount to battery or assault and in fact modern city life would be impossible if a certain amount of intentional and reckless contact with others ('pushing and shoving') was not permissible. The legal system would collapse under the weight of criminal and civil actions if it were not considered that such 'contacts' are too trivial (*de minimis non curat lex*) and that we all have impliedly consented to a certain amount of physical contact irrespective of the other person's state of mind. But although not stated it seems the object or circumstances of the contact are relevant, e.g., to touch and rub the hem of a womans dress while she is wearing it would be a battery (*R v Thomas* (1985) 81 Cr App R 331), whereas to be squeezed or to push against her in a rush hour crush would not.

Consent

The third special defence is significant because it provides a defence to battery and some 'assault'-based statutory offences, in particular rape. Remember, consent, to be a defence, must have been freely given. Consent is ineffective if it is obtained by fear, force or threat of force or even if it is obtained by other types of threats, if founded on a known mistake or if given by a person under 16 years of age who lacks sufficient understanding to give consent, or if obtained by fraud. However, in relation to fraud that is so only if it causes a mistake:

    (a)   as to the nature of the act itself or
    (b)   as to the identity of the person who does the act; see *R v Clarence* (1888) 22 QBD 23 which explains what does and does not come within these two categories. It shows that these categories, especially the latter, are limited and that the law in this area aims to prevent physical 'assaults' rather than punish morally bad conduct.

Even if consent is freely given, however, it cannot excuse physical contact which is inherently unlawful (e.g., 'assault' in the course of a prize-fight or duel (*R* v *Coney* (1882) 8 QBD 534) or assault likely to occasion bodily harm or even more serious harm (*R* v *Donovan* (1934) 25 Cr App R 1) or is sado-masochistic (*R* v *Brown* [1993] 2 All ER 75)). If, on the other hand, the injury is caused during the course of a lawful game played according to the rules (see *R* v *Billinghurst* [1978] Crim LR 553) or during the rough and tumble of schoolboy play (see *R* v *Jones* [1987] Crim LR 123 or during 'horseplay' at any age (see *R* v *Muir* (1986) 83 Cr App R 375, CA) or if it consists of tattooing, or branding of a wife by her husband without aggressive intent or sexual gratification (*R* v *Wilson* [1996] Crim LR 573), then the consent of the 'players' will be a defence to contact *and* injury. See Law Commission Consultation Paper No. 134, 'Consent and Offences against the Person', London: HMSO, 1994, which suggests that personal freedom of choice in relation to our bodies can be over-ridden by the law where another person is inflicting an injury on the basis that participation in consensual injuries is harmful to society generally and may encourage the inflicter to inflict injuries on non-consenting parties. It recommends, however, that the general rule should be that a person can consent to any non-serious injury (for the proposed distinction between 'non-serious' and 'serious', or between 'injury' and 'serious injury' see Law Comm. Paper No. 218, 'Legislating the Criminal Code'). If this rule was introduced there would be no need to make exceptions for such things as tattooing, ear-piercing or religious flagellation or circumcision, because there is no risk of serious injury in such practices. 'Horseplay' (pranks) and some physical contact sports do involve a risk of serious injury and would still need exceptions to be made, but not so as to extend to serious injuries caused intentionally or with subjective recklessness.

In *Donovan* such an exception, together with others, was recognised to the general rule that there can be no consent to any unlawful act, i.e., one likely to result in death or serious bodily harm. The exceptions recognised there for lawful sports, 'horseplay' and surgical operations are worth remembering because there is no satisfactory explanation why they should be exceptions. Why should caning for sexual pleasure be non-consentable whereas injury caused in manly sports or in idle horseplay is? Likewise query the views of Denning LJ in *Bravery* v *Bravery* [1954] 3 All ER 59 concerning the lawfulness of certain 'unnecessary' surgical operations whether consented to or not. The conclusion borne out by these cases and especially by *Attorney-General's Reference (No. 6 of 1980)* [1981] QB 715 (concerning a fist-fight in a public street) is that where public interest requires it an exception may be made, but it is not in the public interest for persons to try to cause, or to cause, each other actual bodily harm for no good reason in public or in private. And yet it was held not to be s. 47 assault for a husband to deliberately use a hot knife to brand his initials onto his wife's buttocks: *R* v *Wilson* [1996] Crim LR 573. What is in the public interest is a matter of policy and prevailing social morals both of which change with time. In *R* v *Brown* [1993] 2 All ER 75 in a 3:2

majority the House of Lords decided that it was not in the public interest for adult men to indulge in consensual acts of sado-masochism in private, albeit that the resulting injuries did not require medical treatment. Lord Templeman said 'public policy required that society be protected by criminal sanction against (this) cult of violence'. (This simply means the law is uncertain and at the whim of the judiciary.) In *R v Simon Slingsby* [1995] Crim LR 570 the victim's death was caused by vigorous sexual activity to which she had consented. There was no deliberate infliction of injury and no consent to injury because that was not contemplated by either participant. The injuries were an accidental consequence. The judge held that it would be contrary to principle to treat as criminal what otherwise would not amount to assault merely because in the course of the activity an injury occurred. See also *R v Boyea* [1992] Crim LR 574.

Note that the three men convicted of sado-masochistic practices in *Brown* took their case to the European Court of Human Rights claiming their prosecution was an interference in their private lives contrary to Article 8 of the European Convention. The European Court held that there had been no violation of Article 8. The State was entitled to consider the interference 'necessary in a democratic society' for the protection of health or morals. It was not a matter for private morality alone because there was a significant degree of injury or wounding involved and the State is entitled to consider not only the actual harm but also the potential for more serious injury inherent in the activities (*Laskey, Jaggard and Brown v United Kingdom* (case 109/1995/615/703–705), *The Times*, 20 February 1997).

Statutory 'Assaults'

Parliament by statute has created numerous 'assault' and battery-based offences in order to specify appropriate levels of punishment for the various degrees of aggravation involved. As shown in Figure 9.1 (p. 210) these are largely contained in the Offences against the Person Act 1861. (In *R v Mandair* [1994] 2 WLR 700, Lord Mustill stated that: 'this unsatisfactory statute is long overdue for repeal and replacement by legislation which is soundly based in logic and expressed in language which everyone can understand'. The Law Commission has such a draft, Law Comm. No. 218, ready and waiting for enactment.) The 1861 Act contains numerous substantive offences, approximately 12 of which are apparently crimes of specific intent generally described in terms of unlawfully and maliciously (i.e., intentionally or recklessly) doing something (the *actus reus*) with a *specified intent* beyond the simple doing of the prohibited *actus reus* itself. There are also approximately 18 basic-intent offences, at least five of which involve assaults on particular persons such as clergymen, magistrates, officers and authorised persons in relation to a wreck, and any female or any boy under 14 years of age. One of the 'assault on a particular person' offences (i.e., s. 40, assault on a seaman) is a specific-intent offence. One offence in the Act (i.e., s. 56, taking a child out of the custody of its parent, but see now Child Abduction Act 1984, s. 2) appears to be a specific-intent offence but has been interpreted to be a strict liability offence as to some aspects (see *R* v *Prince* (1875) LR 2 CCR 154). Finally, s. 51 of the Police Act 1964 appears to create a basic-intent offence of 'assault on any constable or any person assisting him in the execution of his duty'.

Of all these offences it generally will be sufficient for you to be conversant with a few. If you are not permitted to have the statute with you in the examination you *must* know the gist (if not the actual wording) of the following:

(a)   Section 18: wounding with intent to cause grievous bodily harm. This is an indictable, *specific-intent* offence as befits the most serious of the aggravated 'assaults' in English law. Maximum penalty, life imprisonment.

(b)   Section 20: unlawful wounding. An indictable *basic-intent* offence. Open to the jury as an alternative where a s. 18 charge is not proved. Maximum penalty, five years' imprisonment.

(c)   Section 47: occasioning actual bodily harm. An indictable, *basic-intent* offence. The penalty is not specified in s. 47 but sentencing generally reflects the view that the offence is less serious than s. 20 but more serious than an indictment for a common law battery or assault (which, by s. 47, carries a maximum penalty of one year's imprisonment).

Check your course syllabus and your lecture notes to see whether or not your examiner has placed emphasis on any of the other statutory assaults. If so, know what it states.

Remember that what was said above in relation to s. 20 as an alternative to s. 18 applies equally to any of the statutory 'assaults' because their bases and origin are the same: it is only the degree of aggravation that varies. Consequently the jury may return a verdict on any *lesser* 'assault' offence even though that has not been charged (*R* v *Carpenter* (1983) 76 Cr App R 320 and *Commissioner of Police for the Metropolis* v *Wilson; R* v *Jenkins* [1984] AC 242), in which case an indictment for inflicting grievous bodily harm contrary to s. 20 was held to include an allegation of assault occasioning actual bodily harm contrary to s. 47. Therefore, 'causing' may be done by 'inflicting' and 'inflicting' may be done by 'assaulting'. However, this practice has been criticised (see Professor Glanville Williams (1984) 43 CLJ 290). *R* v *Mearns* [1990] Crim LR 708 held that on an indictment alleging actual bodily harm the jury could not convict of common assault in the absence of a specific count, but this case may well be overruled in effect by the *Wilson/Jenkins* principle which has recent House of Lords' support in *R* v *Mandair* [1994] 2 WLR 700.

Mens Rea

The distinction between s. 18 and s. 20 of the Offences against the Person Act 1861 illustrates the fundamental distinction between all specific- and basic-intent offences (see chapter 4). Both open with the same words and require that the accused 'unlawfully and maliciously' injure another person, but s. 18 in addition requires further proof that the accused *intended* to cause a serious injury, i.e., grievous bodily harm. That is a specific intention which can *only* be satisfied by proof of intention to cause grievous bodily harm.

In relation to *both* s. 18 and s. 20 the *mens rea* relating to unlawfully and maliciously injuring another may be satisfied by proof of intention *or* recklessness but in s. 18 (and in other specific-intent offences) that additional 'with intent' element requires proof of intention and only intention (*R* v *Mowatt* [1968] 1 QB 421). The House of Lords in *Savage* and *Parmenter* [1992] 1 AC 699, affirming Lord Diplock in *Mowatt* [1968] 1 QB 421, said for a defendant to be convicted of a s. 20 offence it was sufficient that the defendant intended/foresaw that his act might cause some physical harm (albeit of a minor character) to some other person. This was most recently confirmed by the Court of Appeal in *R* v *Beeson* 1994 Crim LR 191.

All statutory 'assaults', of which s. 20 is an example, which do not contain the words 'with intent' are basic-intent offences and that means the *mens rea* required can be satisfied by proof of either intention or recklessness.

In relation to basic-intent statutory 'assaults', the recklessness to be proved arguably is confined to *Cunningham*-type (conscious risk-taking) recklessness because that is precisely what the facts in *Cunningham* dealt with (i.e., s. 23, 'unlawfully and maliciously administering ... any poison or other noxious thing', which is otherwise similar to s. 20). Arguably so far no case has extended or applied *Caldwell*-type (failure to consider an obvious risk) recklessness to the basic-intent statutory assaults. The fact that it does not apply has been confirmed by *R* v *Morrison*, *The Times*, 12 November 1988, *R* v *Farrell* [1989] Crim LR 376 and more particularly by *R* v *Spratt*, *The Times*, 14 May 1990 and *R* v *Parmenter* [1991] Crim LR 41. 'Maliciously' includes a requirement that the accused foresaw. It is a subjective test. These cases hold that *Cunningham* recklessness alone is sufficient for the *mens rea* of assault and for assault occasioning actual bodily harm in relation to s. 47. In effect *R* v *Savage* [1990] Crim LR 709 and *DPP* v *Khan* [1990] Crim LR 321 are overruled on this point. It means that only *Cunningham* recklessness is relevant in proving the *mens rea* for common law assault, battery, s. 47 and s. 20.

Actus Reus

Both s. 18 and s. 20 of the Offences against the Person Act 1861 require injury in the form of a 'wound' or, in s. 18, proof that the accused *caused* grievous bodily harm' and in s. 20 that he or she *'inflicted* grievous bodily harm'.

In *R* v *Wood* (1830) 1 Mood CC 278 it was held that a broken collar-bone, bruises, burns and possibly even scratches are not necessarily wounds. There must be a breach or breaking of the victim's skin. (This was confirmed in *C (a minor)* v *Eisenhower* (1984) 78 Cr App R 48). Alternatively, in relation to s. 18 the prosecution may prove *causing* and in s.20 *inflicting* grievous bodily harm even though in either case such activities may not amount to a 'wound' in the above sense.

Those words 'grievous bodily harm' mean any really serious bodily harm (Viscount Kilmuir LC in *DPP* v *Smith* [1961] AC 290) and in *R* v *Saunders* [1985] Crim LR 230 the Court of Appeal held there is no difference between *'really serious injury'* and 'serious injury', either will be correct when directing a jury.

In relation to s. 47 the words 'bodily harm' were interpreted expansively in *R* v *Miller* [1954] 2 QB 282 to include a hurt or injury calculated to interfere with a person's health or comfort, including causing an hysterical or nervous condition. The Court of Appeal in *R* v *Dawson* (1985) 81 Cr App R 150, however, held that an unlawful act might (in the context of manslaughter) constitute 'harm' only if it so shocked the victim as to cause physical injury and that emotional disturbances produced by terror did not amount to such 'harm'. Arguably as a statement of a general rule these remarks are *obiter dicta* and the case should be seen as depending on its special facts. The Court of Appeal, however, has now ruled that the phrase 'actual bodily harm' can include psychiatric injury where proved by medical evidence but it does not include 'emotions' or 'states of mind' (whatever they may be!) (*R* v *Chan Fook* [1994] 1 WLR 689) and serious psychiatric injury can be grievous bodily harm for the purposes of s. 20 (and possibly s. 18) (*R* v *Burstow* [1997] 1 Cr App R 144). The *mens rea*, i.e., intention or foresight of psychiatric injury may be very difficult to prove. In *Burstow, R* v *Ireland* [1997] 4 All ER 225 and *R* v *Constanza* [1997] Crim LR 576 alleged psychological damage was suffered by the victims of repeated silent telephone calls or constant mail or visits. The accused's convictions for s. 47 or s. 20 offences were upheld. Bodily harm includes psychiatric illness and could be occasioned, inflicted or caused where no physical violence was applied directly to the body of the victim. There is also an assault if the accused induces a fear of violence at some time not excluding the immediate future. To be afraid the victim does not need to see the potential assailant and it is now established that an assault can be committed by words alone.

However, where on a charge of assault occasioning actual bodily harm, the alleged harm stems from a non-physical assault (such as stalking or silent phone calls) then the case should not go to the jury without psychiatric evidence (*R* v *Morris (Clarence Barrington), The Times,* 13 November 1997).

In relation to the *actus reus* of each offence, (a) the word 'cause' in s. 18 and (b) the word 'occasion' in s. 47 have given rise to little difficulty in interpretation but (c) the word 'inflict' in s. 20 has. The House of Lords has ruled that 'causing' grievous bodily harm is wide enough to include 'inflicting' grievous bodily harm; consequently, it is open for a jury trying a count of causing grievous bodily harm to convict of the lesser s. 20 count irrespective of whether or not that is referred to by the judge as 'causing' instead of 'inflicting' when he directed the jury (*R* v *Mandair* [1994] 2 WLR 700). In *R* v *Clarence* (1888) 22 QBD 23, it was stated that 'inflict' requires proof of an injurious assault of some sort and later cases show it need not be brought about directly (see *R* v *Halliday* (1889) 61 LT 701 and in particular *R* v *Martin* (1881) 8 QBD 54 where the practical joker who produced panic in a theatre was held liable under s. 20 for 'inflicting'). Strangely, in *R* v *Wilson* [1984] AC 242, the House of Lords held that 'inflict' does not require or involve an assault but maintained that a direct application of force must be proved, which (a) seems to amount to the same thing and (b) is clearly in conflict with long-established authorities such as *R* v *Halliday* and *R* v *Martin* in which the force was indirect. However, as a result of the decisions in *Burstow* and *Ireland* 'cause' and 'inflict' now have the same meaning. This means that *Clarence* must have been wrongly decided and should now be disregarded.

SEXUAL/INDECENT, NON-FATAL ASSAULTS

The cases in this area appear to have interpreted 'assault' to mean the doing of something to another so that words alone, no matter how lewd or threatening or both, will be insufficient without more. In *DPP* v *Rogers* [1953] 2 All ER 644 it was held that an invitation to touch was not an assault. (The Indecency with Children Act 1960 then made it an offence to commit an act of gross indecency with *or towards* a child under 14 years of age *or to incite* such a child to do such an act with the accused or another person.)

In *R* v *Sutton* [1977] 3 All ER 476 an accused who photographed partially clothed boys with their consent was held not liable of indecent assault (even although s. 15(2) of the Sexual Offences Act 1956 stated that boys under 16 years of age could not consent to such activities) because there was no 'assault' (indecent or otherwise) in that there was no threat or hostile gesture or actual battery. Earlier in *R* v *Mason* (1968) 53 Cr App R 12 this view had been taken and in addition it was said even if there was an assault it would be an indecent assault only if there was indecency in the contact or some compulsion, threat, duress or show of reluctance. However, it is generally accepted that the assault must be accompanied by circumstances of indecency on the part of the accused (*Beal* v *Kelley* [1951] 2 All ER 763). This raises the issue whether an assault can be converted into an indecent assault simply by the accused's indecent motive. Without evidence of circumstances of indecency, the accused's secret indecent intention will not convert his assault into an indecent assault. There should be some indecent act to the person of the victim (*R v Thomas* (1985) 81 Cr App R 331). (Cf. *Coward* v *Baddeley* (1859) 28 LJ Ex 260; *Fairclough* v *Whipp* [1951] 2 All ER 834 and *DPP* v *Rogers* [1953] 2 All ER 644 which seem to confuse motive and *mens rea* by suggesting that 'hostility' was significant in deciding the matter whereas it should depend on proof of *mens rea* (i.e., intention or recklessness).) The cases were not clear but it seemed that only an intentional or reckless indecent touching would constitute indecent assault (see *R v Pratt* [1984] Crim LR 41). However, in *R v Court* [1987] QB 156, in which the accused spanked a 12-year-old girl's bottom, the Court of Appeal overruled *R v Pratt* and held that although the accused must be proved to know of, or to be reckless as to, the circumstances of indecency it does not have to be proved that he had an indecent motive or purpose. Whether or not the circumstances known to him are indecent is an objective question of fact for the jury and what was in his or the victim's mind is irrelevant. What is relevant is whether an assault (or the circumstances accompanying it) could be considered indecent by right-minded persons. Circumstances of indecency do not necessarily require either an indecent touch or the threat of such (*R v Sargent* [1997] Crim LR 50). Accordingly, any evidence explaining the accused's conduct was admissible to establish whether or not the assault was indecent. An admission was therefore admissible either to support or negative the contention that the assault was indecent. If the charge is one of taking an indecent photograph of a child contrary to s. 1(1)(a) of the Protection of Children Act 1978 then the circumstances in which the photograph was taken and the motives of the photographer are not relevant to the question whether or not the photograph was, in fact, indecent (*R v Graham-Kerr, The Times,* 12 July 1988).

Other Sexual Assaults

The Sexual Offences Act 1956, s. 15, states it is an offence for a person to make an indecent assault on a man or boy. By s. 13 it is an offence for a man to commit an act of gross indecency with another male or to be a party to or to procure such an act. By s. 16 it is an offence to assault another person (not confined to males) with intent to commit buggery. Note, however, that the law now permits homosexual acts in private between consenting males over the age of 18 (s. 143 of the Criminal Justice and Public Order Act 1994). Note that the issue of consent, discussed above, is relevant here as it is in relation to the next topic.

Rape

Actus reus

The definition of rape for the purposes of the Sexual Offences Act 1956 and the Sexual Offences (Amendment) Act 1976 (as amended by s. 142 of the Criminal Justice and Public Order Act 1994) now states that:

(a) it is an offence for a man to rape a woman or another man;
(b) a man commits rape if he has:

(i) sexual intercourse (vaginal or anal),
(ii) with a woman or another man,
(iii) who does not consent, and
(iv) he knows or he is reckless as to whether or not the other person (the victim) consents.

Sexual intercourse as defined in s. 44 of the 1956 Act means in effect that the slightest degree of penetration by the male sexual organ of the female sexual organ will be sufficient, without more, to be intercourse. In both the Privy Council decision in *Kaitamaki v R* [1985] AC 147 and *R v Cooper and Schaub* [1994] Crim LR 531, it was held that if a man continues intercourse once a woman has withdrawn her consent after penetration by him has occurred, he will be liable for rape if he refuses to withdraw knowing or being reckless as to the fact that the woman is no longer consenting to the act of sexual intercourse.

These same principles should now apply for non-consensual anal intercourse of a woman or another man since the new definition of rape under s. 1 as introduced by s. 142 of the Criminal Justice and Public Order Act 1994 makes it clear that this sort of violent sex attack on the unconsenting female or male will be rape.

Whereas males over the age of 18 acting in private may consent to anal intercourse (see s. 143 of the 1994 Act), females cannot. In the case of non-consensual male intercourse the range of chargeable offences in the Sexual Offences Act 1956 now available include s. 1 (rape) and ss. 12, 13 or 15 (buggery, gross indecency or indecent assault on a man) or an attempt at one of those offences. In a case of attempted rape it has been held that it is not necessary for the prosecution to prove a physical attempt at penetration (e.g., where the accused had pushed a girl behind a bush, pushed up her skirt and had dropped his own trousers when apprehended, he was convicted of attempted rape: *Attorney-General's Reference (No. 1 of 1992)* [1993] 1 WLR 168). Since the 1994 Act the same principle should now apply whether the victim is female or male.

With regard to (iii) and (iv) above lack of consent on the female's part and knowledge or reckless indifference as to this fact is absolutely vital, without it the accused has a complete defence. In *R* v *Olugboja* [1982] QB 320 it was made clear that under the Sexual Offences (Amendment) Act 1976 the main issue is whether or not in reality the female genuinely consented. Where the victim is asleep and remembers nothing of what happened, the intercourse may be rape because of the absence of consent (*R* v *Larter and Castleton* [1995] Crim LR 75). There the court reiterated that 'every consent involves submission but it did not follow that a mere submission involves consent'. It is immaterial whether lack of genuine consent was produced by force, fear or fraud or some other consideration such as blackmail, moral or economic leverage or other sorts of 'threats' short of death or violence. Whether, in sexual acts between adults, reluctant acquiescence can amount to consent or submission is a matter for the good sense of the jury to decide (*R* v *McAllister* [1997] Crim LR 233). (The issue is whether or not she genuinely consented, motivating factors are not important.) Likewise whether or not the female was walking alone at night or scantily dressed or intoxicated are immaterial to whether or not sexual intercourse was forced on her without her genuine consent. Notions of contributory negligence are totally irrelevant and inapplicable to the issue of rape.

Note s. 1(2) of the 1956 Act: it is rape to induce a woman to have sexual intercourse by impersonating her husband and according to *R* v *Elbekkay* [1995] Crim LR 163, the same applies at common law whether it is a husband, cohabitee or lover who is impersonated. Likewise the common law holds it is rape to induce sexual intercourse by misrepresenting the nature of the act being performed (see *R* v *Flattery* (1877) 2 QBD 410 and *R* v *Williams* [1923] 1 KB 340) but be prepared to show the limits of this principle. This is best illustrated by a knowledge of the Australian case *Papadimitropoulos* v *R* (1957) 98 CLR 249 where a woman who could not speak the local language was misled into believing she was married and therefore consented to intercourse when in fact she was not married (and therefore would not have so consented) but because she consented to intercourse knowing what it was, the man was held not liable for rape even though she had been tricked. In *R* v *Linekar* [1995] Crim LR 320, the Court of Appeal held (where a prostitute had agreed to intercourse with the appellant for £25 and after intercourse he had left without paying) that it is the absence of consent and not the existence of fraud which makes conduct rape as shown by the so-called 'medical' impersonator cases and by the husband impersonating cases. It is the non-consent to sexual intercourse or to intercourse with the man who penetrates the victim rather than the fraud of the 'doctor' or 'impersonator' which makes the conduct rape. The prostitute had consented to sex with a particular person (the appellant). The reality of the consent was not destroyed by being induced by the appellant's false pretence that he intended to pay the agreed price of £25. In this instance the accused might more properly have been charged with procuring a woman by false pretences or representations to have sexual intercourse (Sexual Offences Act 1956, s. 3).

Note also that the Sexual Offences Act 1993, s. 1 has abolished the former presumption that a boy under 14 years of age was incapable of sexual intercourse and therefore was incapable of rape. No such presumption now exists.

Mens rea

Rape is a basic-intent offence. The Sexual Offences (Amendment) Act 1976 states in effect that the man must be proved either (a) to know that the woman does not consent (i.e., he intends to have sex even though she does not consent) or (b) to have been reckless as to whether she consents. The definition in s. 1 embodies the House of Lords' decision in *DPP* v *Morgan* [1976] AC 182. It had been asked whether or not an accused can be properly convicted of rape, even though he believed the woman had consented, if that belief was unreasonable? The House replied that he could not be properly convicted in such circumstances. The controversy following this decision was offset by s. 1(2) of the 1976 Act to the effect that in deciding what the accused believed the jury may consider the presence or absence of reasonable grounds together with any other relevant matters. As with s. 8 of the Criminal Justice Act 1967 (which deals with proof of intention), s. 1(2) entitles the jury to deduce what the accused actually knew or foresaw from what an ordinary reasonable person would have known or foreseen in those circumstances. The accused's reasonable belief in consent must be judged against other relevant matters (in this case, abduction with an apparent gun: *R* v *McFall* [1994] Crim LR 226). In ascertaining whether there were reasonable grounds for believing that the accused was having consensual sex with his wife (and not their babysitter) self-induced intoxication is to be disregarded. It is not relevant to the issue of consent (*R* v *Woods* (1982) 74 Cr App R 312), likewise where recklessness was sufficient to constitute *mens rea* (*Majewski* [1977] AC 443) a mistake induced by self-induced intoxication is not generally a defence (*R* v *O'Grady* [1987] 3 WLR 321) and this principle applies equally to mistaken identity in a rape case. See *R* v *Fotheringham* (1989) 88 Cr App R 206.

Recklessness in rape

By the use of the word 'reckless' in s. 1 of the Sexual Offences Act it is clear rape is a basic-intent offence. Proof of either intent or recklessness will constitute *mens rea*. The recklessness referred to, however, is only the *Cunningham* (conscious risk-taking) type of recklessness. For a period it was thought that the new *Caldwell* (failure to consider an obvious risk) type of recklessness would also suffice (see *R* v *Pigg* [1982] 2 All ER 591, chapter 4). In *R* v *Mohammed Bashir* (1983) 77 Cr App R 59 the Court of Appeal had ruled in a rape case that the test was whether the accused acted recklessly, *not* whether a reasonable man would have acted in the same way. This ruling was a rebuff to the *Caldwell* concept of recklessness (as objectively ascertained) having any application to rape. The reiteration in *Bashir* of the subjective approach was confirmed as correct in so far as reckless rape is concerned by the Court of Appeal in *R v Satnam S and Kewal S* (1984) 78 Cr App R 149 to the effect that ordinary observers or hypothetical reasonable men (and therefore *Caldwell*-type recklessness) have no part to play in ascertaining recklessness under s. 1 of the 1976 Act. (Note that no mention, however, was made of the House of Lords' judgment in *R v Seymour* [1983] 2 AC 493 to the effect that *Caldwell*-type recklessness is of general application to basic-intent offences). *R v Gardiner* [1994] Crim LR 455 is another example of the Court of Appeal *per curiam* affirming the state of mind of the actual defendant on the occasion in question is relevant, not that of some hypothetical reasonable person, in spite of the reference to 'reasonable man' grounds in the Sexual Offences (Amendment) Act 1976.

For a discussion of the mental state required for attempted rape and the case of *R v Khan* [1990] 2 All ER 783, see chapter 5.

Today, a rapist is a male over the age of 10:

(a)   who intends to have and does have sexual intercourse (whether vaginal or anal) without the victim's consent (the victim being either a female or a male: Criminal Justice and Public Order Act 1994, s. 142), and

(b)   who knows that the victim does not consent to the intercourse or is reckless as to whether the victim consents (i.e., who knows there is a risk that the victim does not consent but who nevertheless takes that risk), or

(c)   who, having received consent and being engaged in intercourse, refuses to stop and withdraw once consent is withdrawn and he knows or is recklessly indifferent to this fact (*Kaitamaki's* case and *Cooper v Schaub* [1994] Crim LR 531), or

(d)   who is not interested in the victim's feelings at all (i.e., who does not care about it one way or the other), in other words, who could not care less (*R v Kimber* (1983) 77 Cr App R 225). Those who could not care less cannot be said to have an honest belief that the victim was consenting. To proceed is to be reckless (in the *Cunningham* sense). This was reiterated by the Court of Appeal in *R v Breckenridge* (1984) 79 Cr App R 244,

(e)   who induces a married woman to have sexual intercourse with him by impersonating her husband.

Note, however, that irrespective of the new definition of rape in s. 143 of the Criminal Justice and Public Order Act 1994, the Court of Appeal has rightly concluded in *R v Elbekkay* [1995] Crim LR 163 that obtaining consent to sexual intercourse by impersonation of the victim's boyfriend is rape because, in the court's view, there is no distinction between impersonating a husband and others (common law husband, fiancé, partner, boyfriend, etc.).

Rape of a Wife

Once it was thought that a husband could not rape his wife (*R v Clarke* (1949) 33 Cr App R 216), because according to the great seventeenth century jurist, Hale, the common law maintained that by consenting to the marriage contract she had consented to sexual intercourse. But after the breakdown of the marriage and at times before a divorce is finalised he could be held liable, e.g., if there was (a) judicial separation, (b) an agreement to separate, (c) a matrimonial (court) order including a non-cohabitation clause, (d) a formal non-cohabitation agreement or (e) a decree *nisi*. In these situations the 'husband' had either consented to give up his matrimonial rights or given his 'wife' grounds to end the marriage. (A petition for divorce was not sufficient: *R v Miller* [1954] 2 QB 282.) Those exceptions aside, the fact that husbands could not be liable for rape of their wives did not mean they were exempt from assault, battery and the statutory 'assault' offences and other offences. Now, however, the House of Lords in *R v R (a Husband)* [1991] 3 WLR 767, has ruled that a husband can be convicted of raping his wife. In the courts' view a rapist remains a rapist subject to the criminal law irrespective of his relationship with the victim. The decision has now been confirmed by Parliament by s. 142 of the Criminal Justice and Public Order Act 1994. The affect of that section is to remove the word 'unlawful' from the statutory definition of rape and to define sexual intercourse to include anal intercourse. Rape within marriage and 'male rape' are new offences.

A man may also be guilty as a secondary party to the rape of his wife (*R v Lord Audley* (1631) 3 St Tr 402) and even though the principal is found innocent of the offence (*R v Cogan and Leak* [1976] QB 217).

HOMICIDE

Homicide is the killing of a human being by another human being. Not all homicide is criminal. See Figure 9.1 for a simple schematic representation of the various types of homicide.

Remember that in any permitted instance of lawful or justified homicide, no offence is committed even though death is caused deliberately or intentionally (or recklessly or negligently), because there is deemed to be no *actus reus* (no *unlawful* killing). Unlawful killings range from the most serious offence of murder through child destruction, infanticide and manslaughter to causing death by reckless driving. By providing a number of offences of unlawful killing the law takes account of the different possible states of mind (*mens rea*) of the persons responsible and does not simply treat the fact of causing death as sufficient to give rise to liability.

The House of Lords publicly regretted in *R v Clegg* [1995] 2 WLR 80 that under existing law there is no provision for degrees of murder as opposed to degrees of homicide. Trial judges currently have no flexibility available to them. In that case it was held that if a plea of self-defence to a charge of murder fails because of the use of excessive force, a verdict of manslaughter is not open to the court even though the force had been used in the prevention of a crime or arresting an offender and the accused was a soldier acting in the course of his duty. The point is really whether the offence in such a case should, because of the strong mitigating circumstances, be regarded as manslaughter rather than murder. It is for the legislature, and not the House of Lords in its judicial capacity, to do something about this situation.

Figure 9.1 **Main offences against the person**

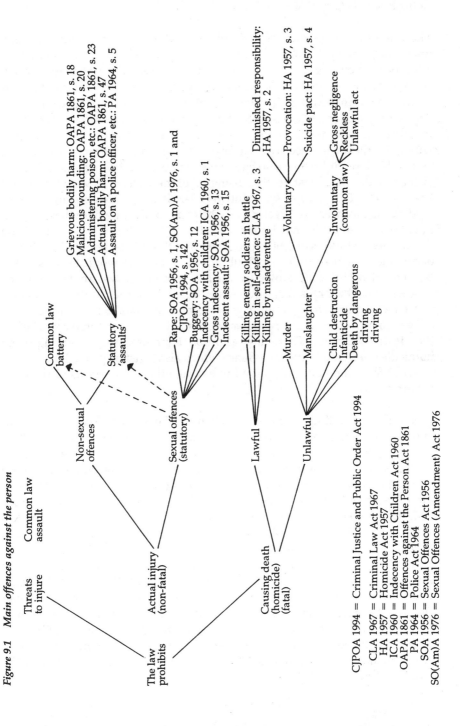

CJPOA 1994 = Criminal Justice and Public Order Act 1994

CLA 1967 = Criminal Law Act 1967
HA 1957 = Homicide Act 1957
ICA 1960 = Indecency with Children Act 1960
OAPA 1861 = Offences against the Person Act 1861
PA 1964 = Police Act 1964
SOA 1956 = Sexual Offences Act 1956
SO(Am)A 1976 = Sexual Offences (Amendment) Act 1976

Actus Reus of Homicide

The core of the *actus reus* for each offence is the same, i.e., voluntarily and unlawfully causing the death of another human being by an act or omission. In addition (depending on the particular offence charged) there may be other conditions or circumstances which are part of the particular *actus reus* (although it is in the main differences in *mens rea* that account for the number and variety of homicide offences). Remember, however, in relation to *actus reus* that, unless a statute states otherwise, the death must have been caused within the 'Queen's peace', i.e., within the jurisdiction of the courts of England and Wales. Up until 1996 it also had to be proved that the victim died within a year and a day of the last death-causing act of the accused (*R v Dyson* [1908] 2 KB 454. The *Dyson* rule was controversial. It arose presumably because medical science was not precise as to the cause of death where there was an interval between criminal injury and death. The Criminal Law Revision Committee, 14th Report (1980) proposed that the rule be retained so that no one would be left indefinitely in doubt as to whether they would be prosecuted on a charge of murder!). However, the *Dyson* principle was abolished by the Law Reform (Year and a Day Rule) Act 1996, s. 1. Now the Attorney-General's consent is required to commence proceedings for a fatal offence if the injury alleged to have caused the death was sustained more than three years before the death occurred. There are additional circumstances varying from homicide offence to homicide offence which also must be proved.

Apart from the issues of unlawfulness the other two aspects of the *actus reus* are:

(a)   That the killing is of a 'human being'. The law is not certain when an individual becomes and ceases to be a human being (see *R v Reeves* (1839) 9 C & P 25, which holds that a child must be completely expelled from its mother's body before it can be the victim of a murder (although reference should be made now to the Infant Life (Preservation) Act 1929, s. 1(2) and *Attorney-General's Reference (No. 3 of 1994)* [1996] 2 All ER 10, CA and [1997] Crim LR 829, HL (see chapter 4, under 'transferred malice')). Also see *R v Malcherek and Steel* [1981] 2 All ER 422 concerning when death can be said to have occurred and *Airedale NHS Trust v Bland* [1993] 1 All ER 821.

(b)   That the killing takes place within the 'Queen's peace'. If the Queen is at war the killing of her enemies is lawful (*R v Page* [1954] 1 QB 170). Wartime aside those words also mean 'within the jurisdiction'. It encompasses killing by anyone (irrespective of their nationality) within England or Wales, their territorial waters or on a British ship or aircraft and further the Offences against the Person Act 1861 states that murder or manslaughter committed by a British citizen anywhere in the world are within the jurisdiction of the courts of England and Wales.

Murder

Actus reus: unlawful homicide as defined above (including the rule in *Dyson*).
Mens rea: This is defined at common law as 'malice aforethought'. The traditional full definition of murder being 'unlawful homicide with malice aforethought' of another human being within the Queen's peace, death occurring within a year and a day.
What do the two words 'malice aforethought' mean?

(a) The Homicide Act 1957, s. 1, abolished the old, dangerous notion of 'constructive malice', which had previously attributed an intention to kill in certain situations where death was caused (namely, while in the commission of some other serious crime or while resisting arrest or effecting or assisting an escape or rescue from legal custody). In those situations the prospect of death occurring may never have entered the accused's head and certainly may not have been intended by him. Soon after the passing of the Homicide Act, however, the Court of Appeal in *R v Vickers* [1957] 2 QB 664 reintroduced a limited doctrine of constructive malice in holding that an accused who had caused death while intending to cause grievous bodily harm was to be guilty of murder despite the Homicide Act and despite the fact that there exists within the law a specific intent offence of causing grievous bodily harm (Offences against the Person Act 1861, s. 18). That *Vickers* is now the law is irrefutable, see *R v Cunningham* [1982] AC 566 and *R v Moloney* [1985] AC 905, both of which are House of Lords' decisions.

(b) The House of Lords in *R v Moloney* [1985] AC 905 has reiterated that murder is a specific-intent offence. This means that only proof of either an intention to kill or an intention to cause grievous bodily harm will be sufficient *mens rea*. Intention in this context means direct intention (i.e., proof that the accused had death or grievous bodily harm as his aim, goal or purpose). In some rare cases, however, foresight of inevitable consequences might, as a matter of evidence, lead a jury to conclude that the accused intended such consequences.

Since *Moloney's* case if the prosecution prove foresight even of a high probability of death or grievous bodily harm they are not entitled to a conviction unless the judge considers it an appropriate case to leave that to the jury as evidence from which intention (to kill or cause grievous bodily harm) might properly be inferred in the circumstances and he should direct them that they may do so only if they think the accused foresaw death or grievous bodily harm as 'virtually certain' or 'overwhelmingly probable'.

Note this important decision in effect negates the apparent, previous law contained in *Hyam v DPP* [1975] AC 55. That case had arguably created two states of mind (beyond intent to kill or intent to cause grievous bodily harm) which would be sufficient *mens rea* for murder. These were (a) foresight that death was a highly probable consequence and (b) foresight that grievous bodily harm was a highly probable consequence. The calling of these additional states of mind 'malice aforethought' meant that murder strictly was no longer a specific-intent offence (at least not in the way that other offences like s. 18 of the Offences against the Person Act 1861 were and still are) because *Hyam* permitted proof of other less blameworthy states of mind than intention to constitute *mens rea* for the offences of murder. Following *Hyam*, however, murder continued to be treated as a specific-intent offence for certain purposes (e.g., the availability of the defence of voluntary intoxication).

Foresight of consequences as a test was objected to because it involves slippery questions of degree. Even the judges in the House of Lords in *Hyam* disagreed on what degree of foresight of death or grievous bodily harm should make an accused liable for murder (certainty, high probability, probability, possibility, a risk, remote probability etc.). Note too that the use of synonyms, such as 'likely', makes no difference to the basic issue which is a matter of degree. Moreover foresight, even that grievous bodily harm is highly probable (or likely), as a test meant that an accused could be convicted of murder when he had not foreseen and indeed no reasonable man would have foreseen, that death was even a remote probability. These flexible concepts involving foresight appear to have been devices to make a reckless accused liable for murder, the most serious offence of all; an offence which by tradition had required proof of nothing short of intention. *Moloney's* case has reassuringly reinstated the traditional view of malice aforethought.

No discussion would be really complete without some mention of the notorious House of Lords' decision in *DPP* v *Smith* [1961] AC 290, which, although it has never been formally overruled has been severely criticised (for introducing the idea of an objective test of liability for murder) by Lords Diplock, Bridge of Harwich and Scarman in *Hyam*, *Moloney* and *R* v *Hancock* [1986] AC 455 respectively and has been declared by the Privy Council in *Frankland* v *R* [1987] AC 576 to state the law of England and Wales incorrectly. In *DPP* v *Smith*, the accused was driving away with stolen goods; a police officer threw himself on to the car to make the accused stop but he only drove faster and in a more erratic fashion calculated to dislodge the police officer. The accused's efforts were successful and the police officer was struck by another vehicle and killed. The conviction for murder was reduced to manslaughter by the Court of Appeal and reinstated by the House of Lords. It was held that intention was to be implied to the accused on the basis of an objective (rather than the traditional subjective) test as to the accused's state of mind.

In effect the House was saying that a man is presumed to intend the natural and probable consequence of his acts and that therefore it is not necessary to prove that the actual accused intended death or grievous bodily harm. In short if a hypothetical reasonable person would have concluded that the outcome of the conduct undertaken would be death or grievous bodily harm then *a fortiori* the accused intended that outcome.

'*Actus non facit reum, nisi mens sit rea*' traditionally imports into the law that it is the accused's actual state of mind that must be proved: in the case of murder that he actually intended to kill or cause grievous bodily harm. What someone else might have thought or foreseen or intended in the circumstances should not be good enough.

Parliament responded to the criticism of this decision by passing the Criminal Justice Act 1967, s. 8 of which states in effect that in relation to an offence which requires proof of intention then the court or jury is not bound in law to infer that he intended or foresaw a result of his actions by reason only of its being a natural and probable consequence of those actions but should consider all the evidence drawing such inferences as appear proper in the circumstances.

It means the jury is permitted to draw the inference propounded in *Smith* if it thinks it proper but it precludes the judge mandatorily directing that as the only conclusion they can reach. A direction to the jury generally in a murder trial should make no mention of objective tests or 'ordinary' or 'reasonable' men (*R v Wallett* [1968] 2 QB 367); the jury must apply a subjective test. Trial judges must make it absolutely clear that foresight is no more than an evidential guide (*R v Scalley* [1995] Crim LR 504).

You must make a point of reading *R v Hancock* [1986] AC 455 and *R v Nedrick* [1986] 1 WLR 1025 which explain and endorse the decision in *Moloney*. *Hancock* concerns the unfortunate death of a taxi driver killed when striking miners dropped a concrete block onto his cab as it passed beneath a motorway bridge. The miners were convicted of murder after the trial judge's direction to the jury purportedly in the terms set by Lord Bridge in *Moloney*. This was one of those rare instances where the jury, properly directed, might consider the accuseds' foresight to ascertain whether or not as a matter of fact those accused intended to kill or cause grievous bodily harm. The Court of Appeal reduced the conviction to manslaughter on the basis that Lord Bridge's formula used by the trial judge referred to foresight of natural consequences as being sufficient for the jury to infer intent, should they choose to do so. The Court of Appeal thought that would be too wide in that there was a risk that a jury might take this to mean 'direct consequences', which was not what was intended by Lord Bridge, and that only if the accuseds were shown to have foresight that death or grievous bodily harm was highly probable, might the jury be entitled to infer intention. That view is not at variance with the basic tenet of both *Moloney* and s. 8 of the Criminal Justice Act 1967 that foresight of whatever degree is only something from which the jury *might* infer intention. The House of Lords suggested that the foresight, awareness or knowledge of death or grievous bodily harm should be an 'overwhelming probability'. The Court of Appeal in *R* v *Nedrick* confirmed this view, stating that the jury should infer that the accused intended death or grievous bodily harm only if either consequence was *virtually certain* and that they believed that he knew that either was *virtually certain* to occur. See also *R* v *Walker* (1990) Cr App R 261. (In reality, the instances in which the jury might be called upon to consider intention from an accused's foresight should be few and far between; see the discussion of intention in chapter 4.)

An illustration of the fact that counsel and trial judges still get it wrong is provided by *R* v *Ward* [1987] Crim LR 338 and *R* v *Donnelly* [1989] Crim LR 739, where the trial judge wrongly told the jury that they could infer intention if the accused foresaw that the result would 'probably' follow. Even the Court of Appeal can confuse itself and others (see *R* v *Woollin* [1997] 1 Cr App R 97). Attempted murder is a specific-intent offence, but the application of the *Moloney/Nedrick* direction to it is not easy (see *R* v *Fallon* [1994] Crim LR 519 and *R* v *Walker and Hayles* (1990) 90 Cr App R 226). Such a direction is only necessary if the accused claims, or there is evidence, that he intended something other than what he is alleged to have attempted.

Manslaughter

Actus reus: unlawful homicide *without* malice aforethought (as defined in *R* v *Moloney* [1985] AC 905). There are two categories of manslaughter, (a) voluntary and (b) involuntary, each of which can be subdivided into various constituents (see also Figure 9.1, p. 219).

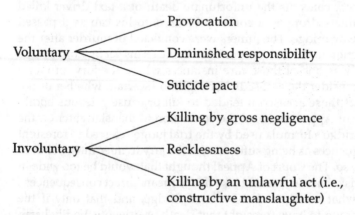

Voluntary
- Provocation
- Diminished responsibility
- Suicide pact

Involuntary
- Killing by gross negligence
- Recklessness
- Killing by an unlawful act (i.e., constructive manslaughter)

Voluntary Manslaughter

In relation to voluntary manslaughter, remember that a person who would *otherwise* be convicted of murder may be convicted of manslaughter instead if one of those three mitigating factors is present. They will simply reduce murder to manslaughter, they do *not* lead to the accused's acquittal. A conviction for murder carries a fixed penalty, i.e., life imprisonment, so that mitigating factors cannot affect the sentence imposed, unlike other offences. Therefore Parliament has provided that proof of provocation, diminished responsibility or suicide pact may reduce the killing to manslaughter, the penalty for which is then at the court's discretion.

You need to have a good knowledge of both provocation and diminished responsibility. A passing acquaintance with suicide pact generally is sufficient. While all these are categorised as voluntary manslaughter they can be viewed as defences to a charge of murder, so look out for key facts in problems which have murder as the main descriptive feature for the opportunity to bring in these 'defences'.

Provocation

The Homicide Act 1957, s. 3, provides that on a charge of murder if the jury finds:

(a)   that the accused was provoked to lose his self-control,

(b)   by things done or said or by both together then

(c)   whether the provocation was enough to make a reasonable man lose self-control shall be for the jury to decide, and in doing so

(d)   they shall consider everything done and said (now, words alone may constitute provocation) according to the effect which, in their opinion, it would have on a reasonable man (see *R* v *Doughty* (1986) 83 Cr App R 319).

The words 'consider everything' require the jury to consider the whole course of the accused's conduct even though some factors may have occurred after the killing such as the electrocution of the victim following her strangulation in *R* v *Clarke*. Provided the conduct causing death was part of a continuing assault then in deciding whether a reasonable man would do as he did the jury were not limited only to considering things the accused did in causing the death of the deceased. Although some subsequent conduct might be too remote, such as disposing of the body (*R* v *Clarke* [1991] Crim LR 383). Provocation can be directed at third parties (see *R* v *Pearson* [1992] Crim LR 192 where the Court of Appeal held that a defendant could rely on the defence of provocation where he had acted in response to the violence and abuse which his father had inflicted on the accused's brother).

The loss of self-control referred to is, in the words of Devlin J in *R* v *Duffy* [1949] 1 All ER 932, 'a sudden and temporary loss of self-control rendering the accused so subject to passion as to make him for the moment not master of his mind'. This was approved in *R* v *Thornton* [1992] 1 All ER 306, CA, and in *R* v *Richens* (1994) 98 Cr App R where the Court of Appeal added that proof of a sudden and temporary loss of self-control did not require evidence that the accused had completely lost control and did not know what he was doing. Therefore despite the deceased's appalling and otherwise 'provocative' behaviour such conduct will not be thought to have caused a loss of self-control if, e.g., a plan to attack the deceased was in existence (*R* v *Ibrams and Gregory* (1981) 74 Cr App R 154) or the rantings and ravings of an incurable wife who wanted to be killed produced behaviour (her asphyxiation and death) which was the opposite of provocation, i.e., an acceding to what she wished to happen, a giving way to her entreaties (*R* v *Cocker* [1989] Crim LR 740). There must be some evidence suggesting that the accused might have lost his self-control due to provocation (of the deceased) for it to be properly considered by the jury. Inferences or suggestions in cross examination are not enough (*R* v *Acott* [1997] 1 All ER 706). However, mention should be made of the so-called 'cumulative provocation' cases involving a long history of domestic violence, also known as slow-burn reactor cases, such as *R* v *Thornton* [1992] 1 All ER 306 and *R* v *Ahluwalia* [1992] 4 All ER 889. In both these cases the plea of provocation was rejected. (Ahluwalia's appeal was allowed, however, on the grounds of fresh evidence of diminished responsibility). There was some evidence of premeditation, and while their lordships would not change the *Duffy* test, in the *Ahluwalia* judgment there was consideration of slow-burn reaction cases or those where there is a delayed reaction to provocative conduct, and it was stated that:

the defence of provocation would not as a matter of law be negatived simply because of the delayed reaction in such cases provided that there was at the time of the killing 'a sudden and temporary loss of self-control' caused by the alleged provocation. However, the longer the delay and the stronger the evidence of deliberation on the part of the defendant, the more likely it will be that the prosecution will negative provocation.

In *R* v *Thornton* [1996] 2 All ER 1023 the court said that battered woman syndrome was relevant in that:

a jury might more readily find a sudden loss of control triggered by even a minor incident on the 'last straw' basis ... and ... depending on the medical evidence, the syndrome might have affected the (accused's) personality so as to constitute a significant characteristic relevant to provocation.

The mention in s. 3 of the 'reasonable man' indicates Parliament's intention in this instance that an objective test be applied. The apparent reason for this is to ensure a test which is applicable to everyone disregarding an individual's peculiar susceptibility to provocation caused, for example, by mental abnormality, subnormal intelligence, want of maturity or excitable disposition.

In the past courts have held that the reasonable man is not:

(a) excitable (see *R v Lesbini* [1914] 3 KB 116), or

(b) drunk (see *R v McCarthy* [1954] 2 QB 105), or

(c) impotent (see *Bedder v DPP* [1954] 2 All ER 801), or

(d) addicted to glue sniffing (see *R v Morhall* [1993] 4 All ER 888) unless, according to the House of Lords, the provocation was directed at his addiction (*R v Morhall* [1995] 3 All ER 659), or

(e) brain damage or mental infirmity (see *Luc v R* [1997] AC 131) unless the provocation was directed at that condition (but see below).

In *Bedder* it was not the effect of things done (or said) on an impotent, or even a reasonable impotent, man *but* on a reasonable man. Note that today, however, s. 3 of the 1957 Act permits the jury to consider all the circumstances (even the accused's impotency). The judge cannot now withdraw this defence from the jury except on grounds of lack of evidence (*R v Gilbert* (1977) 66 Cr App R 237) and should reiterate any peculiarities of the accused which may be material or relevant (see *R v Burke* [1987] Crim LR 336).

This is confirmed by the leading post s. 3 case, *DPP v Camplin* [1978] AC 705, in which the House of Lords held that *Bedder v DPP* had been overruled by s. 3 so that now the particular characteristics of the accused may be taken into account. Age is one of those characteristics but if the court cannot see that a jury on the facts of the case would see any difference between a reasonable man of the accused's age and a reasonable man of any other age then the judge need not focus the jury's attention on the reaction of a reasonable person of the accused's age (*R v Ali* [1989] Crim LR 736). You should know Lord Diplock's description in *DPP v Camplin* of the 'reasonable man' today. Its effect is that juries are placed in a difficult position. They have to consider the accused's attributes or characteristics (age, mental abnormality, etc.) and then assess the effect of the 'provocation' on such a person (e.g., *R v Raven* [1982] Crim LR 51 where the accused, a squatter, had a physical age of 22 years but a mental age of a 9-year-old: the reasonable man will have lived that sort of life for 22 years but have his mental retardation). In *R v Morhall* [1993] 4 All ER 888, it was held that self-induced addiction to glue sniffing (resulting from a voluntary and persistent abuse of solvents) was not a characteristic to be taken into account for the purposes of the defence of provocation, since self-induced addiction to glue-sniffing was wholly inconsistent with the concept of a reasonable man in s. 3 of the Homicide Act 1957. In *R v Ahluwalia* it was left open as to whether battered woman syndrome or post traumatic stress disorder is a relevant characteristic when considering provocation. But in R v *Thornton* [1996] 2 All ER 1023 the Court of Appeal thought that it could. In R v *Dryden* [1995] 4 All ER 987 the Court of Appeal held that the accused's 'eccentric and obsessional personality traits' were mental characteristics which ought to have been left to the jury for the purposes of the objective test in provocation. This was followed by the Court of Appeal in R v *Parker* [1997] Crim LR 760.

In R v *Humphries* [1995] 4 All ER 1008 the Court of Appeal said that the trial judge should have left it to the jury as to whether the accused's 'immaturity and attention-seeking' were characteristics of the reasonable person for the purposes of the defence of provocation. There is a blurring of the subjective and the objective. Arguably, the Privy Council decision in *Luc* v R [1997] AC 131 is the correct objective test in which case *Raven, Dryden, Parker, Thornton* and *Humphries* (above) are incorrect. Ultimately, the House of Lords must settle this issue. Also the *Camplin* test may mean that the reasonable man could be a criminal, e.g., a blackmailer (see *Edwards* v R [1973] AC 648) who claims that the victim responded in such a way as to provoke the accused into killing him, i.e., provocation may be self-induced (R v *Johnson* [1989] Crim LR 738). The jury needs to consider everything said and done whether or not it is a predictable result of the accused's own unlawful conduct. Also, where there is evidence of provocation, it is the judge's duty to leave the question to the jury even where it has not been raised specifically as a defence (R v *Cascoe* (1970) 54 Cr App R 401; R v *Camplin* [1978] AC 705 and R v *Hopper* [1915] 2 KB 431).

Even since s. 3, and although no longer rules of law, it will be imperative to the credibility of the accused that:

(a)   the killing was in the heat of the moment,

(b)   there was a reasonable correlation between provocation and retaliation, and

(c)   the provocation came from the deceased.

(See *Mancini* v DPP [1942] AC 1; R v *Brown* [1972] 2 QB 229; R v *Davies* [1975] QB 691.)

Although the thing said or done does not have to be illegal or wrongful (R v *Doughty* (1986) 83 Cr App R 319), nevertheless it is unlikely that a lawful act (except in rare cases such as the baby crying in *Doughty*) will be held to have provoked a reasonable person to lose self-control. See also R v *Rickens* [1993] Crim LR 385.

In a murder trial the judge is obliged to leave the jury the issue of provocation if he thinks there is evidence on which the jury could find that the accused might have been provoked to lose his self-control, even if this was not raised in the trial or was contrary to the defence, and even if he himself believed the circumstances to be such that no reasonable man would have so acted (*R* v *Cambridge* [1994] 1 WLR 971, *R* v *Stewart* [1995] Crim LR 66, *R* v *Burgess and McLean* [1995] Crim LR 425, *R* v *Dhillon* [1997] 2 Cr App R 104 and *R* v *Acott* [1997] 1 All ER 706).

There must be such evidence as might leave a reasonable jury in doubt, and if they are left in doubt they must acquit of murder. Russell LJ said in *R* v *Rossiter* [1994] 2 All ER 752: 'wherever there is material which is capable of amounting to provocation, however tenuous it may be, the jury must be given the privilege of ruling upon it'. The decision in *R* v *Baille* [1995] 2 Cr App R 31 reinforces that view. Even though the judge envisages difficulties in the defence succeeding, the matter is one for the jury and the defence has been accepted in cases like *Baille* where there was clearly a desire for revenge, a similar lapse of time, and degree of planning (getting the gun from the attic) and control (successfully driving some distance before killing the alleged provoker) to justify leaving it to the jury.

Diminished Responsibility

An accused may be charged with manslaughter on the basis of his killing with diminished responsibility or the accused may be charged with murder and plead diminished responsibility as a defence (Homicide Act 1957, s. 2(1), (2) and (3)).

When it is raised as a defence the accused (as with insanity), must prove (on a balance of probabilities) that he was suffering from mental abnormality in which case the accused will be convicted of manslaughter unless the prosecution prove (beyond reasonable doubt) that he or she is in fact insane. Even if that does not happen the judge has a discretion in a manslaughter verdict to consider the accused's abnormality of mind in passing sentence.

The Homicide Act 1957, s. 2(1), states that where a person kills or is a party to a killing he shall not be convicted of murder if he was suffering from such abnormality of mind (whether arising from a condition of arrested or retarded development of mind, or any inherent causes or induced by disease or injury) as substantially impaired his mental responsibility for his acts and omissions in doing, or being a party to, the killing. Note:

(a)   The accused must suffer from an abnormality or disease of the mind but unlike insanity it is immaterial whether or not he appreciates what he is doing and that it is wrong.

(b)   The abnormal state of mind must have arisen from arrested or retarded development, some inherent defect or injury or by way of disease. 'Injury' could not apply to the effects of the drug Halcion which as taken by the accused was rapidly absorbed by and eliminated from the body within six hours (*R* v *O'Connell* [1997] Crim LR 683). But battered woman syndrome can now cause diminished responsibility (*R* v *Hobson* [1997] Crim LR 759).

(c)   That abnormality must have substantially impaired the accused's mental responsibility in killing or being a party to the killing.

(d)   Substantial impairment is a matter for the jury, but see *R* v *Lloyd* [1967] 1 QB 175, which stated that the impairment must be more than trivial but need not be total. 'Substantial impairment' means making an appreciable difference to a person's ability to control himself, but does not amount to 'total impairment' (*R* v *Egan* (1992) 95 Cr App R 278). Furthermore, the elements of the defence do not always have to be considered in the order in which they are set out in the section (*R* v *Mitchell* [1995] Crim LR 506).

In *R* v *Sanderson* [1993] Crim LR 857 it was held that the phrase 'induced by disease or injury' did not necessarily refer to an organic or physical injury or disease of the body including the brain.

According to *R* v *Gittens* [1984] QB 698 the effect of alcohol or drugs should be ignored by the jury in deciding what the substantial cause of the accused's conduct was because any effect produced by those substances is *not* due to inherent causes within s. 2(1) of the 1957 Act. (A history of prolonged alcohol or drug abuse, however, may become an inherent cause of mental abnormality: *R* v *Tandy* (1989) Cr App R 45, but clearly a drunken or alcoholic state induced by voluntary drinking does not amount to diminished responsibility.)

(e)   Finally, diminished responsibility may be constituted by a degree of mental abnormality, according to *R* v *Seers* (1984) 79 Cr App R 261, which is less than what in popular language 'can be described as ... partially insane or on the borderline of insanity'.

Note that diminished responsibility as a defence only applies where death is caused by the accused. Consequently it is not available as a defence to a charge of attempted murder (*R* v *Campbell* [1997] 1 Cr App R 190).

Suicide Pact

The Homicide Act 1957, s. 4, states it shall be manslaughter (not murder) for a person acting in pursuance of a suicide pact to kill the other party to the pact or be a party to that other being killed by a third person. The onus is placed on the defence by s. 4(2) to prove that the accused was acting in pursuance of a suicide pact with the victim.

'Suicide pact' is defined in s. 4(3) as a common agreement between two or more persons having for its object the death of all of them, whether or not each is to take his own life. Note that nothing done by a party to a suicide pact will be treated as done in pursuance of the pact unless it is done while he has the settled intention of dying in pursuance of the pact.

To sum up, s. 4 provides a defence to murder provided the accused can prove on a balance of probabilities that the killing was pursuant to an agreement whereby he was to have killed both the victim and then himself. He must have intended also to die at the time of the killing.

Note that by the Suicide Act 1961, s. 2, it is a serious offence to aid, abet, counsel or procure another to take his own life so where there is a suicide pact and one party takes his own life the other (or others) could be liable under this provision.

INVOLUNTARY MANSLAUGHTER

The instances of involuntary manslaughter (i.e., killing by gross negligence, by recklessness and killing by an unlawful act) arise where the accused has unjustifiably killed another person but does not have sufficient *mens rea* (blameworthiness) to be convicted of murder. Murder, remember, according to *R v Moloney* [1985] AC 905, requires proof of intention which is proof of a conscious, deliberate aim to kill or cause grievous bodily harm. That state of mind might also be inferred from the fact that either consequence was foreseen by the accused as inevitable.

Gross Negligent Killing

Manslaughter (killing) arising from gross negligence was outlined in chapter 4.

Remember that negligence is basically a failure to exercise that degree of care which a reasonable, prudent person would have exercised in the circumstances and to that must be added the words of Lord Hewart in *R v Bateman* (1925) 19 Cr App R 8 to the effect that the want of care must be so reprehensible in the circumstances as to warrant the imposition of a criminal sanction. In effect, for gross-negligence manslaughter the prosecution must prove that in the circumstances a reasonable man would have foreseen that somebody would almost probably be killed. The foreseeability or likelihood of that fact obviously must be greater than in instances of simple negligence. Note that generally this concept of gross negligence will encompass killings which are caused by an omission or failure to act (see chapter 3). Those instances require proof of a failure to perform a duty (arising under contract, relationship, office or by way of statute or conduct).

Reckless Killing

Reckless killing will amount to manslaughter. Recklessness of the *Cunningham* type (i.e., conscious risk-taking) which causes death will be manslaughter as will that of the *Caldwell* type (i.e., where death or grievous bodily harm would have been obvious to a reasonable man).

Causing death by recklessly omitting to act (whether *Cunningham* or *Caldwell*-type recklessness) will amount to manslaughter (*R* v *Stone and Dobinson* [1977] QB 354). Furthermore even if the harm foreseen (by the accused or a reasonable man) was something less than grievous harm to the victim, the accused's killing of the victim could nevertheless amount to manslaughter (*R* v *Pike* [1961] Crim LR 547). See also *R* v *Lamb* [1967] 2 QB 981 where there was no recklessness in either sense but it was said that it was open to the jury to find Lamb guilty of manslaughter for accidentally shooting his friend while they were fooling about with a revolver if they 'consider [that] his view as to there being no danger was formed in a criminally negligent way'.

Finally, remember that in *R* v *Seymour* [1983] 2 AC 493 the House of Lords in effect purported to equate *Caldwell*-type recklessness with gross negligence at least for the purposes of manslaughter by use of a motor vehicle and probably for all purposes. This view was clearly endorsed by the Privy Council in *Kong Cheuk Kwan* v *The Queen* (1985) 82 Cr App R 18, which went so far as to deny that a gross negligence test existed separate from the *Caldwell-Lawrence* test.

Distinguishing Those Two types

The so-called abolition of the *Bateman* test, however, was premature. An analysis of involuntary manslaughter was conducted by the Court of Appeal in: *R* v *Sulman*; *R* v *Prentice*; *R* v *Adomako* and *R* v *Holloway* [1993] 3 WLR 927. The first two cases involved doctors under supervision injecting a lethal drug into the spine rather than the arm of leukaemia patients. *Adomako* concerned a locum anaesthetist who did not notice that the patient being operated on had become disconnected from the oxygen supply for about five minutes. *Holloway* concerned an electrician whose faulty wiring of a heating programmer resulted in the victim's death. In all the cases, except *Adomako*, the convictions for manslaughter were quashed. In *Adomako*, expert evidence was given that a competent anaesthetist would have been aware of the disconnection within seconds. *Adomako's* conduct in the circumstances was considered grossly negligent.

Lord Taylor reiterated that gross negligence as a type of manslaughter still existed. Leaving motor manslaughter aside, the proper test in manslaughter cases based on breach of duty was the gross negligence test established in *Bateman* (1925) 133 LT 730, *Andrews* [1937] AC 576 and *Stone* [1977] 2 WLR 169. Their lordships say nothing new. They confirm what many had thought to be the position, i.e., that the *mens rea* for gross negligent manslaughter could be established by proof of either:

(a)   *Caldwell* objective inadvertent recklessness, or
(b)   *Cunningham* subjective, advertent recklessness, or

(c) *Shimmin*-type recklessness, appreciation of risk and an intention to avoid it, but accompanied by a high degree of negligence in the attempted avoidance, or

(d) *Bateman*-type 'traditional' gross negligence, i.e., a breach of duty through inattention or failure to be aware of a serious risk which goes beyond mere inadvertence in respect of an obvious and important matter.

Manslaughter by Unlawful Act

Sometimes called 'constructive manslaughter' this is the most significant and the most difficult category with which you must deal. Constructive murder used to apply where the killing occurred during the course of a felony (today a serious indictable offence) and there was at that time also a doctrine of constructive manslaughter which applied if the killing occurred in the course of an unlawful act even if that happened to be only a civil wrong (a tort) and not a criminal offence. Constructive murder was in theory abolished by the Homicide Act 1957 although the subsequent decision in *R v Vickers* [1957] 2 QB 664 reintroduced the doctrine to a limited extent by allowing proof of intention to cause grievous bodily harm to be sufficient to produce a conviction for murder (see chapter 6). Constructive manslaughter has continued to be part of our law although its ambit is uncertain.

Actus Reus and Mens Rea

Constructive manslaughter today seems to be limited to death resulting from a criminal offence which was likely to cause some harm. It does, however, require proof that there was an unlawful act: that that act involved an obvious risk of bodily harm to someone as a result of the act; and that death resulted from the act (*R v Jennings* [1990] Crim LR 588). In that case going outside the house carrying an unsheathed knife did not amount to carrying an offensive weapon in itself and that therefore the accused's intentions whether to use it to inflict injury was relevant and should have been left to the jury to consider whether or not in the circumstances he was carrying the knife (which killed his intervening brother) to frighten (in which case it would be unlawful) or whether he was simply or absentmindedly carrying a knife of that sort which would not be unlawful. Unlawful in this context requires *mens rea* in relation to the alleged unlawful acts, which must be identified and criminal. In *R v Larkin* [1943] 1 All ER 217 it was said that where a person does an unlawful act 'then, if at the same time it is a dangerous act, that is, an act which is likely to injure another person, and quite inadvertently he causes the death of that other person by the act, then he is guilty of manslaughter'. Anything that amounts even to a common law assault together with resulting, accidental death will be sufficient for manslaughter (*R v Hall* (1961) 45 Cr App R 366; but cf. *R* v *Dawson* (1985) 81 Cr App R 150 and *R* v *Mackie* (1973) 57 Cr App R 453 where a person was accidentally killed while fleeing from the accused's common law assault). In *R* v *Church* (1965) 49 Cr App R 206 it was stated that: 'The unlawful act must be such as all sober and reasonable people would inevitably recognise must subject the other person to, at least, the risk of some harm resulting therefrom, albeit not serious harm'. In *R* v *Arobieke* [1988] Crim LR 314 the Court of Appeal quashed the accused's conviction of manslaughter on the basis that his merely looking at or into a train without knowing that the deceased (who, in fleeing, was electrocuted) was on it, could not amount to an unlawful act. Likewise self-generated fear or terror in the presence of someone is not enough. That person must do something criminal, e.g., he must threaten.

It is sufficient if a reasonable man would have recognised or foreseen the danger. The accused need not appreciate the fact or even that his conduct was unlawful. *But* take care, this does not mean that the test for constructive (unlawful-act) manslaughter is purely objective. This offence is a crime of basic intent. The accused must be proved to have intended to do the things which constitute the unlawful acts or else be proved to have been reckless (in either the *Cunningham* or the *Caldwell* sense) as to whether or not the unlawful act occurred. If either *mens rea* is proved then whether or not he realised the act was unlawful or dangerous and whether or not he foresaw the consequential harm or injury is irrelevant; it is enough if a reasonable man would have foreseen it (see *DPP* v *Newbury and Jones* [1977] AC 500 where youths who pushed stones on to a passing train killing the guard were held properly convicted of manslaughter even if they had not foreseen that their acts might cause harm to another person). In *R* v *Simon Slingsby* [1995] Crim LR 570 the court said it would be wrong to 'treat as criminal activity which would not otherwise amount to assault merely because in the course of the activity an injury occurred'.

You need to be able to elaborate this aspect of the law by some discussion of three recent cases: *R* v *Dalby* [1982] 1 All ER 916, *R* v *Pagett* (1983) 76 Cr App R 279 and *R* v *Mitchell* [1983] QB 741. In *Dalby* it was said that the unlawful act must be directed at the victim *and* likely to cause *immediate* injury (i.e., it introduced a subjective element — an act can be 'directed at' only if there is an intention to so direct it). The significance of those notions has, however, been denigrated (wrongly) in *R* v *Goodfellow* (1986) 83 Cr App R 23, but irrespective of that decision their significance has been reduced for most cases by the decisions in *Pagett* and *Mitchell*. In *Pagett* no mention was made of any need for the unlawful act of the accused to be directed at the victim. (There the victim was shot and killed by a police officer while being used as a shield by the accused who fired shots at the police.) In *Mitchell* the court rejected the *Dalby* argument and held that the doctrine of transferred malice applied to constructive (unlawful-act) manslaughter and further that the identity of the victim was irrelevant. (There the accused had pushed in a queue causing an old woman to fall and later die.) In *Pagett* and *Mitchell*, neither accused's conduct was directed at the victim.

Those candidates confused about the relationship between unlawful act manslaughter and reckless and gross negligent manslaughter should see *R v Ball* [1989] Crim LR 730. In relation to unlawful manslaughter questions of gross or criminal negligence are not material. In many cases a judge might have to give a direction on the question of lawful act and gross negligence because the jury might not accept that an accused deliberately did an unlawful act.

On the issue of *mens rea* in unlawful act manslaughter, the accused's state of mind is relevant only to establish (a) that the act was committed intentionally and (b) that it was an unlawful act. Once (a) and (b) are established, the question whether or not the act was dangerous is to be judged not by the accused's appreciation but by that of the sober and reasonable man. At this point his intention, foresight or knowledge are irrelevant (*R v Jennings*). (There the possession of a weapon, not offensive *per se*, was not an unlawful and dangerous act unless accompanied by the requisite intention to use it to inflict injury.) See also *R v Watson* [1989] Crim LR 733.

You will appreciate that all three branches of involuntary manslaughter are complex, difficult and uncertain. It should be no surprise to you that some people are calling for their abolition and the substitution of a new statutory offence of recklessly causing death. An examiner may be interested in your arguments for or against such a proposal. However, the prospect of that change seems remote now in light of the decisions in *R v Sulman, R v Prentice; R v Adomako; R v Holloway* [1993] 3 WLR 927.

Other Homicide Offences

See Figure 9.1 (p. 219).

Infanticide

Under the Infanticide Act 1938, s. 1, infanticide can be charged *only* against a mother who has killed a child who has been born but not reached the age of 12 months. Alternatively a woman charged with murder in such an instance may plead infanticide as a defence. In either case if convicted or if the defence is accepted in relation to the charge of murder, she will be guilty of manslaughter. But *note* that the mother must adduce evidence that the balance of her mind was disturbed by, and not yet recovered from, childbirth or from lactation consequent on the birth of the child.

Child destruction

By the Infant Life (Preservation) Act 1929 the offence of child destruction came into existence. Until then the deliberate killing of an unborn child was neither murder nor infanticide. Then and now to constitute murder or infanticide the child must first be born before it dies (its whole body brought out of the body of its mother (*R* v *Poulton* (1832) 5 C & P 329)). It is possible that an act may constitute murder if it causes a child to be born early so that its chances of survival are reduced and it does die soon after its premature birth.

Unlike infanticide, child destruction under s. 1 of the 1929 Act can be charged against any person who, *with intent* to destroy the life of a child capable of being born alive, by any wilful act causes it to die before it has an existence independent of its mother. In *C* v *S* [1988] QB 135 medical opinion was divided on whether or not a foetus between 18 and 21 weeks after conception was 'capable of being born alive'. The Court of Appeal held that on the evidence it would not be capable of breathing and therefore was not capable of being born alive. The section adds that it will be prima facie proof that a woman was at the time pregnant with a child capable of being born alive if there is evidence that she has been pregnant for 28 weeks or more. The section, however, contains the proviso that if the death of the child is caused in good faith for the purpose only of preserving the life of the mother then no offence is committed. (*R* v *Bourne* [1939] 1 KB 687 held preserving the life of the mother to encompass the mother's physical and/or mental health although these sentiments were *obiter dicta* in a case brought under s. 58 of the Offences against the Person Act 1861.)

Today the Infant Life (Preservation) Act 1929 overlaps with the Offences against the Person Act 1861 (administering drugs or instruments with intent to procure an abortion) and the Abortion Act 1967 which legalises abortion in the manner and form specified in that Act as significantly amended by s. 37 of the Human Fertilisation and Embryology Act 1990 (although these changes will only take effect from a date to be announced). The offence of child destruction means that a foetus 28 weeks or more old may not be aborted. A less than 28 week old foetus even though viable may be destroyed (aborted) contrary to s. 58 of the Offences against the Person Act 1861 if the conditions of the 1967 Act are complied with. Those conditions, as amended by the Human Fertilisation and Embryology Act 1990, include that two registered medical practitioners in good faith certify that the pregnancy has not exceeded 24 weeks and continuance would involve greater risk of physical or mental injury to the woman or any existing children of her family or grave, permanent mental or physical injury to the woman or greater risk to the life of the woman or a substantial risk that the child if born will be seriously handicapped. If those conditions are not complied with then, irrespective of the viability of the foetus, an offence is likely to have been committed under s. 58 of the Offences against the Person Act 1861 unless, arguably, the operation is performed in good faith for the purpose of preserving the life of the woman (see *R* v *Bourne* [1939] 1 KB 687). Compliance with the Abortion

Act 1967 (as amended) will provide those responsible for the termination of a pregnancy with a defence to a charge under s. 58 of the Offences against the Person Act 1861 or under s. 59 of the same Act (procuring or supplying drugs or instruments to cause an abortion). In addition the newly amended s. 5(1) of the Abortion Act states that no offence under the Infant Life (Preservation) Act 1929 shall be committed by a registered medical practitioner who terminates a pregnancy in accordance with the provisions (as amended) of the Abortion Act.

One final, significant, statutory offence involving homicide which is worth remembering is s. 1 of the Road Traffic Act 1991: the offence of causing death by the dangerous driving of a motor vehicle. The definition of dangerous driving is complex and set out at length in s. 2A of that Act. (Remember that since *R* v *Seymour* [1983] 2 AC 493 the prosecution may choose to charge common law manslaughter — sometimes referred to as 'motor-man-slaughter' — in such a situation (see *R* v *Governor of Holloway Prison (ex parte Jennings)* [1983] 1 AC 624).)

EXAMPLES OF QUESTIONS

Essay Questions

(1) What consequences does the decision in *R* v *Moloney* [1985] AC 905 and subsequent cases have on:

(a) the *mens rea* of murder; and
(b) the concept of intention in the criminal law?

(2) 'The difficulties of definition of the *mens rea* required to establish murder were increased rather than lessened by the Homicide Act 1957.' How far have subsequent developments in the law added to, or decreased, the difficulties?

(3) 'Manslaughter is based mainly, though not exclusively, on the absence of intention to kill but with the presence of an element of "unlawfulness" which is the elusive factor.'
How far has this statement stood the test of time?

(4) '[B]ut it appears to the court that the passage of years has achieved a transformation in this branch of the law and, even in relation to man-slaughter, a degree of *mens rea* has become recognised as essential. To define it is a difficult task.' (*R* v *Church* (1966) per Edmund-Davies J.)
How has that task been approached by the courts in relation to involuntary manslaughter?

(5)   'In the light of the law laid down in *Morgan's* case, there can be no such thing as a reckless rape, at least it cannot be reckless in the sense envisaged by the decisions in *Caldwell's* and *Lawrence's* cases.'

Discuss the *mens rea* of rape in the light of this statement and any effect that mistake of fact might have on any relevant state of mind.

(6)   Distinguish between the offences of infanticide, child destruction and abortion.

Outline Answers

Questions (1) and (2)
Note that basically questions (1) and (2) require a discussion of substantially the same material relating to the *mens rea* of murder as it has been altered over the years. In answering question (1) you are invited to work back from the present day whereas in answering question (2) you are invited to work forward from 1957, but the starting-point is immaterial.

In order to answer either question well you must know:

(a)   the doctrine of constructive murder prior to 1957,
(b)   the relevant content and effect of the Homicide Act 1957,
(c)   the effect of the Court of Appeal's decision in *R v Vickers* [1957] 2 QB 664,
(d)   the effect of the House of Lords' approval of Ackner J's direction to the jury in *Hyam v DPP* [1975] AC 55, and
(e)   the effect of the House of Lords' decisions in *R v Moloney* [1985] AC 905 and *R v Hancock* [1986] AC 455 and the Court of Appeal's view of those decisions as expressed by Lord Lane CJ in *R v Nedrick* [1986] 1 WLR 1025.

Those are the core points for discussion in both questions (1) and (2). Where the two questions differ are:

(a)   The second issue in question (1) requires some comment from you on the consequences for the whole concept of intention in the criminal law (and not just the *mens rea* of murder) of the decision in *Moloney* together with some comment on the elaboration of it expressed in the House of Lords in *Hancock* and by the Court of Appeal in *Nedrick*. In relation to this some comment might well be made that *Moloney* affirms the idea that intention consists of:

(i)   direct intent (i.e., the deliberate aim, goal or want of the accused; sometimes called the *Steane* type), and
(ii)   those rare situations where the accused's foresight of the consequences was that they were virtually certain or inevitable and therefore the

jury may infer from that degree of foresight that the accused really intended those consequences to occur.

At this point in time any lesser degree of foresight will *not*, as a matter of law, constitute intention. Such a state of mind must be recklessness and that being so it will not be sufficient to convict any person of a crime of specific intent. Remember that the *mens rea* for crimes of specific/ulterior intent will be satisfied by proof of intention alone.

Although not essential, it would do no harm briefly to mention, in so far as intention is concerned, that the judges in *Moloney* considered that there is no rule of law that proof of foresight is proof of intention but only a rule of evidence which permits it to be considered along with everything else by the jury in deciding whether or not the accused did intend his conduct and the consequences of it. This reiterates the view expressed in s. 8 of the Criminal Justice Act 1967. Now foresight of overwhelming probability or virtual certainty *may* be considered by a jury in trying to ascertain the intention of the accused (see *Hancock* and *Nedrick*).

(b) In question (2), in addition to the core point mentioned above, you are required to comment on whether or not the developments subsequent to 1957 have added to or decreased the difficulties in defining the *mens rea* of murder. That is something on which each examination candidate can hold a view in light of the discussion presented to the examiner about the core material. In addition to that material this question warrants a specific mention of what was said in the House of Lords in *R v Cunningham* [1982] AC 566 (and earlier in *Hyam v DPP* [1975] AC 55) about *R v Vickers*.

Questions (3) and (4)
Likewise any answer to either question (3) or (4) would contain the same core of material in relation to the *mens rea* of involuntary manslaughter.

The quotation in question (3) comes from Lord Atkin in *Andrews v DPP* [1937] AC 576 at 581, a more full quotation being:

[O]f all crimes manslaughter appears to afford most difficulties of definition, for it concerns homicide in so many and so varying conditions.... [T]he law ... recognises murder on the one hand, based mainly, though not exclusively, on an intention to kill, and manslaughter on the other hand, based mainly, though not exclusively, on the absence of intention to kill but with the presence of an element of 'unlawfulness' which is the elusive factor.

That elusive factor is *mens rea* in the following forms:

(a) An intention to do an unlawful and dangerous act or unlawfully and dangerously to omit to act, being grossly negligent whether or not any personal injury, however slight, may be caused. Whether or not the accused knew it was an unlawful and dangerous act is immaterial but the act must be both in fact.

(b) An intention to do any act, or to omit to act where there is a duty to do so, being grossly negligent whether death or at least grievous bodily harm be caused.

(c) An intention to do any act, or to omit to act where there is a duty to do so, being reckless whether death or any personal injury be caused.

In relation to point (a) above an examiner would expect to see a mention of authority to support the proposition. This may be best done by tracing through the case developments:

(a) *R* v *Larkin* [1943] 1 All ER 217 showed that death caused by an unlawful and dangerous act was manslaughter.

(b) *R* v *Church* [1966] 1 QB 59 made it clear that not every unlawful act which causes death will constitute manslaughter, only those unlawful acts which are dangerous in the sense that all sober and reasonable people would inevitably recognise that they must subject the other person to, at least, the risk of some harm resulting therefrom, albeit not serious harm.

(c) *DPP* v *Newbury* [1977] AC 500 held that an unlawful act which is not obviously dangerous to the accused may be sufficient if, by chance, it causes death because there need only be an intention to do an act which is in fact unlawful and dangerous according to the view of all sober and reasonable people. Also mention *R* v *Ball* [1989] Crim LR 730 and *R* v *Watson* [1989] Crim LR 733.

(d) *R* v *Dalby* [1982] 1 All ER 916; *R* v *Pagett* (1983) 76 Cr App R 279; *R* v *Mitchell* [1983] QB 741 and *R* v *Goodfellow* (1986) 83 Cr App R 23 are relevant to the issue of whether or not the act or omission must be directed at the victim or anyone at all.

In relation to either question (3) or (4) you must draw an appropriate conclusion from your discussion of the cases whether or not the statement in (3) has stood the test of time and how in relation to question (4) the courts have approached the process of defining *mens rea* for involuntary manslaughter.

Question (5)
In question (5) the examiner is looking not simply for a knowledge of the basic law relating to rape but an ability to discuss in detail the *mens rea* of that

offence and the concept of recklessness as an aspect of *mens rea* in the criminal law. You must be prepared to show you know the following:

(a)   The definition of rape and rape offences set out in the Sexual Offences Act 1956, the Sexual Offences (Amendment) Act 1976, as amended by the Criminal Justice and Public Order Act 1994.

(b)   The reasoning of the decision of the House of Lords in *DPP v Morgan* [1976] AC 192 and the public reaction which led to the legislation contained in the Sexual Offences (Amendment) Act 1976.

(c)   The first limb of recklessness as defined in *R v Cunningham* [1957] 2 QB 396 and the second limb as defined in *Metropolitan Police Commissioner v Caldwell* [1982] AC 341.

(d)   The decision in *R v Pigg* [1982] 2 All ER 591.

(e)   The decision in *R v Mohammed Bashir* (1983) 77 Cr App R 59.

(f)   The decision in *R v Satnam S and Kewal S* (1984) 78 Cr App R 149.

(g)   The decision in *R v Breckenridge* (1984) 79 Cr App R 244.

Remember that *Morgan* had reiterated that rape is a crime of basic intent and therefore that *Cunningham*-type recklessness at least would be sufficient *mens rea* but it also held that an honest belief that the victim was consenting would provide the accused with a good defence. The Sexual Offences (Amendment) Act 1976 reiterated the correctness of that view but made it clear that the jury could consider the reasonableness of the accused's belief in deciding whether or not he honestly held that purported belief. In *Pigg*, which came after the creation of the second limb of recklessness in *Caldwell*, the court suggested that a person would be found guilty of rape if he was reckless in the sense of having failed to consider whether or not the victim was consenting in circumstances where it would have been obvious to a reasonable man. The logical difficulty with this notion is that a man accused of rape cannot claim he did not think about whether or not the victim was consenting and at the same time claim he believed that the victim was consenting. Once an accused admits that he did not believe that the victim was consenting then he is liable to be convicted of rape. *Pigg*, however, raises the query how, especially in relation to recklessness, the state of mind of the accused is to be ascertained. *Mohammed Bashir* maintained that *Pigg* was wrong in suggesting that *Caldwell*-type recklessness could apply to rape, and reiterated that the traditional subjective approach was correct and that the *Caldwell* objective criteria had no application to rape. This view was confirmed in *R v Satnam S and Kewal S* which contains the current law in relation to rape including the notion, adopted from *R v Kimber* (1983) 77 Cr App R 225, that if a jury came to the conclusion that the accused 'could not care less whether [the victim] wanted to [have sexual intercourse] or not, but pressed on regardless, then he would have been reckless and could not have believed that the victim wanted to, and they would find him guilty of reckless rape'.

Question (6)
Question (6) is a simple test of knowledge. No application of intellect or mental dexterity is called for. Either you know the law or you do not. In setting out your answer you must make the following points clear at least:

(a)   For infanticide (Infanticide Act 1938, s. 1):

(i)   The child must be born alive (it is a true form of homicide because a life in being is killed).
(ii)   An omission may be sufficient.
(iii)   Its death within 12 months of its birth would constitute murder by the mother but for the mother's mental disturbance.
(iv)   The latter being due to that child's birth or lactation consequent upon that birth.
(v)   The person protected is the child.
(vi)   Maximum of life imprisonment.

(b)   For child destruction (Infant Life (Preservation) Act 1929, s. 1):

(i)   The child must be killed *before* it has an existence independent of its mother (therefore it is not a true form of homicide).
(ii)   An omission is *not* sufficient because there is no duty of care owed to unborn children.
(iii)   The person protected is the child (capable of being born). What is 'capable of being born alive' is a matter of evidence but see the 28-week presumption and *C v S* [1988] QB 135. Also note that for a permissible abortion under s. 1 of the Abortion Act 1967, the medical practitioners must now be of the opinion that the pregnancy has not exceeded 24 weeks.
(iv)   There is a special defence which means that the prosecution must prove that the act was not done in good faith for the purpose only of preserving the mother's life.
(v)   'Mother's life' as interpreted in *R v Bourne* [1939] 1 KB 687.
(vi)   Proof of 28 weeks' pregnancy is prima facie proof that the child is capable of being born alive. For permissible abortion purposes that period has been reduced to a definite 24 weeks.
(vii)   Maximum of life imprisonment.

(c)   For abortion (Offences against the Person Act 1861, s. 58):

(i)   Procuring of a miscarriage.

(ii)   There must be a specific act.

(iii)   It can be committed in the first 24 or 28 weeks (or any time thereafter up until the child has been born).

(iv)   The person protected is the mother.

(v)   Any person may be liable (including the pregnant woman herself) but note that the woman must in fact be pregnant if she herself is to be liable whereas any other person so acting with intent to procure a woman's miscarriage may be liable whether or not that woman was in fact pregnant.

(vi)   It requires the unlawful administering of poison or noxious things or the use of any instrument with intent to procure a miscarriage.

(vii)   There are special defences provided under the Abortion Act 1967 as amended by s. 37 of the Human Fertilisation and Embryology Act 1990 (see above).

(viii) Maximum of life imprisonment.

Mention might also be made of the relevant provisions of the Abortion Act 1967 and also of s. 59 of the Offences against the Person Act 1861 (the offence of procuring drugs, instruments, etc., knowing they are intended to be unlawfully employed with intent to procure a miscarriage whether or not the woman is with child) and the effect of the Criminal Attempts Act 1981, s. 1(2) — the administering of harmless things may now be an attempt at a s. 58 offence.

Problem Questions

(7) Discuss the criminal liability of Doris in the following circumstances:

(a) Doris, intending to cause Andrew's death, renders the brakes on Andrew's car inoperative by cutting the brake lines and cables. She then seeks out Andrew with a view to persuading him to drive his car. Before she finds him, an unauthorised person takes the car. The brakes fail but the driver is unhurt and the car undamaged.

Would your answer be any different:

(i)   if the driver was injured or killed;

(ii)   or the car damaged?

(b) Doris, who is pregnant, is advised that she has certain deficiencies in her blood and, unless she regularly takes certain prescribed drugs, there is a grave danger to her unborn child. She fails to take the drugs and, because of this, the child, although born alive, dies within a week of its birth.

Discussion of the following would be expected in answer to question (7).

In part (a) there are three situations requiring attention. First, where Doris's handiwork fails to cause death, injury or damage (apart from the direct damage resulting from the cutting of the brake cables), secondly, where her handiwork causes the injury or death of the unsuspecting stranger and thirdly, where her handiwork causes Andrew's car to be damaged although the unsuspecting stranger who was driving it is unhurt. Be sure you deal with all three situations.

(a)   The first of them requires you to apply s. 1(1) of the Criminal Attempts Act 1981 to the facts. Since no one has been killed or injured and nothing damaged, Doris can only be liable for attempting to do one or other of those things.

Remember the *mens rea* necessary for an attempted crime is specific intent and that probably is only satisfiable by proof of direct intention (*R v Mohan* [1976] QB 1, see chapter 7). The *actus reus* requires the taking of a step that is more than merely preparatory. In the light of *R v Moloney* [1985] AC 905 (defining the *mens rea* of murder) and s. 8 of the Criminal Justice Act 1967 (establishing how intention may be ascertained by the jury) the likelihood is that Doris may be held liable for attempted murder provided you consider she has taken a step that is more than merely preparatory — *R v Boyle* (1987) 84 Cr App R 270 permits you to discuss some of the older cases which distinguish acts of mere preparation (for which there is probably no liability) from acts of perpetration (which will make the accused liable for attempt). On this you should refresh your memory by reviewing chapter 7 and the discussion there of the common law tests of proximity, equivocality, social danger, etc.

Alternatively:

(b)   Doris could be charged with and convicted of criminal damage under s. 1(1) and (2) of the Criminal Damage Act 1971 (see also chapter 10). The first of these is the lesser charge of intentionally or recklessly destroying or damaging the property of another, the second subsection contains the more serious charge of intentionally or recklessly destroying or damaging property with intent to endanger life or being reckless as to whether life would be endangered. Because of the use of the word 'reckless' in both subsections, clearly subsection (1) and probably subsection (2) are basic-intent offences: see *R v Orpin* [1980] 1 WLR 1050 and especially *Metropolitan Police Commissioner v Caldwell* [1982] AC 341; *R v Lawrence* [1982] AC 510 and *R v Sangha* [1988] 1 WLR 519. Remember that *Caldwell* and *Lawrence* establish the new limb of recklessness which consists of a failure to give thought to whether or not there was a risk in circumstances where, if any thought had been given, the risk would have been obvious (see chapter 4). But on the facts in question Doris either has foreseen the risk and consciously taken it or in fact she has actually consciously, deliberately intended to cut the brake cables knowing and intending both the immediate direct damage to the car as well as the contemplated death or serious injury to Andrew. Proof of any of those states of mind will produce a conviction for either charge under s. 1(1) or (2) of the Criminal Damage Act 1971.

(c) In the situation where the stranger who has taken Andrew's car is killed because of Doris's tampering with it her potential liability for murder turns on proof that the facts satisfy the definition at common law of murder as enunciated in *R v Vickers* [1957] 2 QB 664 and especially *R v Moloney* [1985] AC 905. You should display sufficient knowledge of the definition and the principles set out in those cases to satisfy the examiner that you have more than a passing acquaintance with them. You should mention s. 8 of the Criminal Justice Act 1967 which states how the jury may ascertain intention. If you consider that on the facts her intention is equivocal then you may consider that her foresight needs to be discussed. This may warrant a mention of *Hyam v DPP* [1975] AC 55 and in particular the effect of *R v Moloney* and of the interpretation of Lord Bridge's views in that case by Lord Lane CJ and the House of Lords in *R v Hancock* [1986] AC 455 and by the Court of Appeal in *R v Nedrick* [1986] 1 WLR 1025 on the part that foresight of consequences may play in a charge of murder. Clearly too you would need to make some mention of the doctrine of transferred malice given that Doris's 'malice' was intended for Andrew and not the unfortunate stranger. (You could speculate briefly on the question whether or not it would make any difference if the person who was driving Andrew's car had in fact stolen it.)

(d) In the situation where the driver has been injured, if he does not die then Doris could be liable for attempted murder, criminal damage with intent to endanger life (s. 1(2) of the 1971 Act), battery or one or other of the statutory 'assault' offences, either the most serious (i.e., s. 18 of the Offences against the Person Act 1861, which requires proof of specific intent to cause grievous bodily harm), or the somewhat lesser s. 20, unlawful wounding offence or the s. 47 offence of occasioning actual bodily harm. Both the latter are basic-intent offences as is common law battery. Transferred malice warrants a mention.

(e) In the situation where the car crashes and is further damaged and the driver injured (in addition to the damage directly caused to the brake cables), Doris could still be charged with attempted murder and more particularly with either or both criminal damage charges under s. 1(1) and (2) of the Criminal Damage Act 1971, discussed above.

In answer to question (7) part (b): Doris, in principle, could be charged with murder. The law only requires that the child be born before it dies (*R v Reeves* (1839) 9 C & P 25). Also birth need not precede the injury which causes the child's death. Therefore an act (or as in this instance an omission on Doris's part) which causes the child to be born earlier than it would in the normal course of events or injures it while still inside its mother, so that it is less able to survive when it is born or (in this instance) it dies soon after, may amount to murder. Whether or not Doris is convicted of murder will depend on proof of the requisite *mens rea* for murder (i.e., an intention to kill or to cause grievous bodily harm. You would do well to comment that this may be one of those rare situations envisaged in *Moloney* where it might be appropriate for the judge to direct the jury on the matter of Doris's foresight). He might direct them that her foresight (since the House of Lords' decision in *R v Hancock* and the Court of Appeal's decision in *R v Nedrick*) that death or grievous bodily harm was either *virtually certain* or *overwhelmingly probable* would be something from which they *might* properly infer that she intended to kill or seriously harm her baby. In such cases, their lordships equate Lord Bridge's foresight of natural consequences with foresight that they were virtually certain. (In passing it would not be inappropriate to mention briefly why Doris could not be charged with infanticide contrary to the Infanticide Act 1938 or with child destruction contrary to the Infant Life (Preservation) Act 1929 or with 'abortion' contrary to s. 58 of the Offences against the Person Act 1861: see the outline answer to essay question (6) above.)

Alternatively, Doris might be charged with involuntary manslaughter either because of (i) her subjective *Cunningham* conscious risk-taking type of recklessness, or (ii) her objective *Caldwell* failure to consider a risk which is obvious to reasonable persons type of recklessness, or (iii) her gross negligence in the *Bateman* (1925) sense. The difficulty with gross negligence (and possibly the *Caldwell*-type recklessness since *R v Seymour* [1983] 2 AC 493) is that negligence requires proof of a breach of a duty of care. The law (criminal and civil) has not, as a general rule, envisaged such a duty being owed to an unborn child. Some discussion of *Attorney-General's Reference (No. 3 of 1994)* [1996] 2 All ER 10 would be required.

Remember, however, that the doctrine of constructive manslaughter permits a conviction where the accused has done an unlawful act (or omission?) which involves some harm (trivial or serious) to another. Doris's wilful act (or omission) in failing to take the prescribed medication should be discussed in the light of the facts and decisions in *R v Church* [1966] 1 QB 59; *R v Lamb* [1967] 2 QB 981; *DPP v Newbury and Jones* [1977] AC 500; *R v Dalby* [1982] 1 All ER 916; *R v Pagett* (1983) 76 Cr App R 279; *R v Mitchell* [1983] QB 741; *R v Goodfellow* (1986) 83 Cr App R 23; *R v Ball* [1989] Crim LR 730 and *R v Watson* [1989] Crim LR 733. *Attorney-General's Reference (No. 3 of 1994)* [1996] 2 All ER 10 must be discussed.

Question (8)

At a party where everybody has had a lot to drink Geoffrey and Robert agree to play a form of Russian roulette. This involves Geoffrey putting a bullet in a revolver belonging to Robert and pointing it at Robert, who thinks that there is no great danger because the revolver's firing mechanism is defective. Geoffrey pulls the trigger twice without any effect, but the third time he does so, the gun fires. The bullet misses Robert, but kills Brian who is standing nearby, but who had refused to have anything to do with the game on the grounds that it is folly.

Discuss the criminal liability of Geoffrey and Robert.

Because it involves homicide the best starting-point is to state the *actus reus* for most homicides (i.e., the unlawful killing of a human being under the Queen's peace, death occurring within a year and a day of the injury). Homicide generally may be murder or manslaughter depending on the accused's *mens rea*. If there is no 'malice aforethought' (see *R v Moloney* [1985] AC 905 and *R v Vickers* [1957] 2 QB 664), and there does not seem to be on these facts, then any further protracted discussion of murder would be irrelevant. You should rather address yourself to the central issue, which is involuntary manslaughter. This may occur where death has been caused without 'malice aforethought' but with, according to Lord Atkins in *Andrews v DPP* [1937] AC 576, 'the presence of an element of unlawfulness which is the elusive factor'.

The facts set out in the question bear a marked similarity to those of *R v Lamb* [1967] 2 QB 981. Needless to say a familiarity with that case would be not simply useful but virtually essential. You will need to discuss and apply to the facts the law relating to constructive manslaughter, manslaughter by recklessness and manslaughter by gross negligence. *Lamb* shows that there may be a difference between manslaughter by recklessness and manslaughter by gross negligence. (Lamb and a friend were foolishly playing with a loaded revolver. Lamb ascertained that neither of the two bullets was in the chamber opposite the barrel and he assumed it was safe to point the gun at his friend and pull the trigger. Unbeknown to either of them when the trigger is pulled the chambers of any revolver rotate and bring the next chamber into the firing position. Lamb made a mistake, he was not reckless; if anything he was grossly negligent.)

You should pose the following questions and apply them to the facts set out in the problem:

(a) Was there an intention to do any unlawful and dangerous act, or unlawfully and dangerously to omit to act, being grossly negligent whether or not any personal injury, however slight, might be caused?

If you consider the facts to be on all fours with *R v Lamb* then the answer must be in the negative because Lamb did not intend to alarm his companion and in fact did not alarm him so that there was no assault. It could be argued therefore that there was a misdirection to the effect that the jury was told his conduct constituted an unlawful and dangerous act.

(b)   Was there intention to do any act or to omit to act, where there is a duty, being grossly negligent whether death (or at least grievous bodily harm) is caused? In *Lamb* the Court of Appeal said that the accused could be liable in terms of *R v Bateman* (i.e., that the jury thought the negligence 'went beyond a mere matter of compensation and showed such disregard for life and safety of others as to amount to a crime against the state and conduct deserving of punishment').

(c)   Was there intention to do any act being reckless whether any personal injury was caused? Such a state of mind was considered sufficient *mens rea* in *R v Pike* [1961] Crim LR 547 (a much-criticised case in which the accused was held guilty of manslaughter where his girl-friend died having taken an anaesthetic so that the accused might gratify his perverse sexual desires).

Finally, if you conclude that Geoffrey and Robert may be liable for manslaughter you must make some mention of the doctrine of 'transferred malice', in particular whether or not the doctrine has any application or even needs to be applied in cases of manslaughter. In *R v Mitchell* [1983] QB 741 it was stated that it may be manslaughter if any act directed at a person causes the death of another person, though in *R v Dalby* [1982] 1 All ER 916 the view had been expressed that the act had to be directed at the victim. *R v Pagett* (1983) 76 Cr App R 279 and *R v Goodfellow* (1986) 83 Cr App R 23 should also be discussed in relation to this point. You also might consider whether or not Robert is a joint principal or a party to any offence committed by Geoffrey.

This particular problem question is both taxing and typical in the sense that it requires you to deal with difficult and uncertain aspects of the law. Note that while the facts are similar to *R v Lamb* there are marked differences which may be so material as to alter the potential outcome. An examiner will be looking for some ability to discuss the facts and the significance of the differences to those in *Lamb*. Whether your conclusion is right or wrong is not so important but how you argue your case and your use of the authorities will be vital.

Question (9)

Bruce spends the night with Jane who knows that her husband, Sam, is extremely jealous of her, and wishes to get her own back on him for refusing to buy her some jewellery. The next morning Jane persuades Bruce to take her to her husband's office where Bruce tells Sam of his conquest. Sam picks up a paperweight and threatens to kill Jane who urges Bruce to 'do for Sam'. Bruce wrests the paperweight from Sam and, in a towering rage, throws the paperweight out of the window, and hurls Sam to the floor and kicks him several times before he is restrained. It transpires Bruce has had several spells in a mental hospital to try to help him cope with his uncontrollable temper.

Consider the possible defence of Bruce and Jane to a charge of murder if Sam dies, or attempted murder if he lives.

The points that you need to discuss in answer to this question are:

(a) *Murder.* This is defined as the unlawful killing of a human being under the Queen's peace with malice aforethought, the death occurring within a year and a day of the injury (mention appropriate case authorities in support, e.g., *R* v *Dyson* [1908] 2 KB 454).

(b) *Malice aforethought.* This is the intention to kill or to cause grievous bodily harm (*R* v *Vickers* [1957] 2 QB 664 and especially *R* v *Moloney* [1985] AC 905).

Thus Bruce is liable for murder unless a defence is available (and Jane is liable as a joint principal or party and/or for incitement to murder or possibly incitement to attempt).

(c) *Homicide* is *lawful* if it results from using such force as is reasonable in the circumstances in the prevention of crime, or in effecting or assisting in the lawful arrest of offenders, or suspected offenders or persons unlawfully at large (Criminal Law Act 1967, s. 3) Prevention of crime includes prevention of crime upon oneself.

(d) There is no question of a defence under s. 3 because the force used is much more than is reasonable. (Mention the Australian case *R* v *McKay* [1957] VR 560, which suggested that such excess would lead to a conviction only for manslaughter. This notion was rejected in England by the Court of Appeal in *R* v *McInnes* [1971] 3 All ER 295.)

(e) *Provocation.* See Homicide Act 1957. In relation to murder, if the jury can find the accused was provoked (whether by things done or by things said or by both together) to lose his self-control, then whether it was enough to make a reasonable man do as he did shall be left to the jury which shall take into account everything done and said according to the effect which in their opinion it would have on a *reasonable man* (*DPP* v *Camplin* [1978] AC 705, *Luc* v *R* [1997] AC 131, *R* v *Morhall* [1995] 3 All ER 659 and *R* v *Dryden* [1995] 4 All ER 987).

It is irrelevant that the accused has had several spells in hospital to help him cope with his uncontrollable temper. In *Edwards* v *R* [1973] AC 648 the Privy Council said the accused cannot rely on predictable results of his own conduct but if the hostile reaction of his victim (Sam) went to extreme lengths it might constitute sufficient provocation, even, as in *Edwards*, for a blackmailer or, in this case, Bruce, who was himself provocative.

(f) If Sam does not die Bruce has no defence of provocation to a charge of attempted murder (*R* v *Bruzas* [1972] Crim LR 367 and *R* v *Campbell* [1997] 1 Cr App R 190).

(g)   If Bruce is convicted of murder Jane can be convicted of aiding, abetting, counselling or procuring that offence. She encouraged the offence and had the necessary *mens rea* of intending to encourage.

If Bruce is only convicted of manslaughter this does not preclude Jane being convicted of the offence of being a secondary party to Sam's murder. Her liability is dependent upon her *mens rea* (see *DPP* v *Merriman* [1973] AC 584).

(h)   *Insanity.* Discuss whether or not it could provide a defence (see chapter 8).

(i)   *Diminished responsibility.* Discuss whether or not it could provide a defence (see chapter 8).

CONCLUSION

Offences against the person cover a multitude of crimes ranging from the mere threat of injury (common assault) to the most serious offence known in our society of murder (intentional homicide). In between these two extremes are various aggravated assaults (largely contained in the Offences against the Person Act 1861), indecent/sexual assaults (largely contained in the Sexual Offences Acts) and both unintentional killing (involuntary manslaughter) and intentional killing in mitigating circumstances (voluntary man-slaughter).

There is no doubt that examiners of a standard criminal law course are likely to question you on some of the following in either an essay or a problem form:

(a)   Murder and especially the *mens rea* relevant to that offence: in addition, the general defences may be combined with that topic (see chapter 8) and either some or all of the special defences (the voluntary manslaughter provisions of the Homicide Act 1957 dealt with in this chaper, especially provocation and diminished responsibility).

(b)   Involuntary manslaughter and the *mens rea* necessary for each of its incidents, i.e., causing death by dangerous conduct, by reckless conduct or by grossly negligent conduct.

(c)   Aggravated assaults. You must be able to show an appreciation of the distinction between specific-intent offences such as s. 18 of the 1861 Act and basic-intent offences such as ss. 20 and 47 of the 1861 Act, common law battery and assault. This whole topic is generally examined in a problem form and often combined with issues of general defences, especially self-defence and intoxication and sometimes duress, insanity or automatism.

(d)   Rape. Unless your lecturer emphasises other sexual/indecent assault offences you can virtually leave aside all the other offences except rape. Rape is often used by examiners:

(i)   to ascertain that you know its definition and incidents, but also

(ii)   to see that you understand the defences of consent and mistake and

(iii)   to test you on the issue of *mens rea* and more importantly how it is to be ascertained (by an objective or a subjective criterion) especially in so far as reckless rape is concerned,

(iv)   to test you on the applicability of other general defences in addition to mistake, such as intoxication or possibly duress.

(e)   Common law battery and assault. This area is a good vehicle to test you on the special defences — consent, lawful chastisement and inevitable accident together with some of the general defences.

(f)   The causing of the death of the unborn and newly born child provides examiners with scope to test your knowledge of murder, manslaughter, abortion, infanticide, child destruction, inchoate offences and the provisos and special defences to the various statutory assault and homicide offences and general defences both to the above mentioned offences and to the common law offences.

(g)   Remember that in relation to all the offences against the person the issue of participation may be raised and often there is the possibility of discussing inchoate offences or aspects of these general principles of criminal liability.

(h)   Finally, depending on whether or not it was emphasised in your particular course you may have to answer a theoretical essay-type question orientated towards ascertaining your views on the role of the law and the need for reform. Abortion is a topic that is not uncommonly used for this purpose seeking your views of the legitimacy of intervention by the law, the rights of the State, the female, the male and the foetus. Apart from discussing the statutory provisions mentioned above there are at least three cases tailor-made for discussion: *R v Bourne* [1939] 1 KB 687; *Paton v United Kingdom* (1981) 3 EHRR 408 and *Royal College of Nursing of the United Kingdom* v *Department of Health and Social Security* [1981] AC 800 as well as (by analogy) cases such as *Bravery v Bravery* [1954] 3 All ER 59 which deal with the legitimacy of surgical operations, maiming, etc.

FURTHER READING

Homicide

Ashworth, A., 'Reforming the Law of Murder' [1990] Crim LR 75.
Beyon, H., 'Doctors as Murderers' [1982] Crim LR 17.
Brownlee, I. D., and Seneviratne, M., 'Killing With Cars After *Adomako*: Time for Some Alternatives' [1995] Crim LR 389.

Criminal Law Revision Committee, 14th Report, Offences Against the Person (1980), Part III B–I.

Farrier, M. D., 'The Distinction between Murder and Manslaughter in its Procedural Context' (1976) 39 MLR 414.

Finnis, J. M., 'Bland: Crossing the Rubicon?' (1993) 109 LQR 329.

Gardner, S., 'Manslaughter by Gross Negligence' (1995) 111 LQR 22.

Goff, Lord, 'The Mental Element in the Crime of Murder' (1988) 104 LQR 30.

Hogan, B., 'The Killing Ground' [1974] Crim LR 387.

Keating, H., 'The Law Commission Report on Involuntary Manslaughter: (1)' [1996] Crim LR 535.

Keown, J., 'Doctors and Patients: Hard Case, Bad Law, "New" Ethics' (1993) 52 CLJ 209.

Keown, J., 'Homicide, Foetuses and Appendages' (1996) 55 CLJ 207.

Law Commission Consultation Paper No. 135: Involuntary Manslaughter (1994).

Leigh, L., 'Liability for Inadvertence' (1995) 58 MLR 457.

Leng, R., 'Death and the Criminal Law' (1982) 45 MLR 206.

McColgam, A., 'The Law Commission Consultation Document on Involuntary Manslaughter — Heralding Corporate Liability' [1994] Crim LR 547.

Report of the Select Committee on Murder and Life Imprisonment (1988–89).

Smith, K. J., 'Causation in Homicide' (1976) 92 LQR 30.

Virgo, G., 'Reconstructing Manslaughter on Defective Foundations' (1995) 54 CLJ 14.

Wells, C., 'The Law Commission Report on Involuntary Manslaughter: (2) The Corporate Manslaughter Proposals' [1996] Crim LR 545.

Williams, G., 'The Mens Rea for Murder: Leave it Alone' (1989) 105 LQR 387.

Assault

Ashworth, A., and Campbell, K., 'Non-Fatal Offences: mend and make do?' (1992) 108 LQR 187.

Bamforth, N., 'Sado-Masochism and Consent' [1994] Crim LR 661.

Consultation Paper No. 134: Offences against the Person (1994).

Cooper, R. J., 'Grievous Bodily Harm By Telephone' [1995] JCL 401.

Editorial, 'The Revisiting of Consent' [1996] Crim LR 73.

Gardner, S., 'The Law and the Sports Field' [1994] Crim LR 513.

Grayson, E., Sport and the Law, 2nd ed. (London: Butterworths, 1994).

Grayson, E., 'Boxing Clever' (1992) 142 NLJ 48.

Hall, J., 'Can Children Consent to Indecent Assault?' [1996] Crim LR 184.

Kell, D., 'Psychiatric Injury and the Bodily Harm Criterion' (1995) 111 LQR 27.

Khan, A. N., 'Grievous Bodily Harm' (1984) 81 Law Society Gazette 671.

Leng, R., 'Consent and Offences Against the Person: Law Commission Consultation Paper No. 134' [1994] Crim LR 480.

Ormerod, D., 'Consent and Offences against the Person: Law Commission Consultation Paper No. 134' (1994) 57 MLR 928.
Ormerod, D., and Gunn, M., 'Consent — a Second Bash' [1996] Crim LR 694.
Roberts, P., 'Consent to Injury: How Far Can You Go?' (1997) 113 LQR 27.
Seabrooke, M., 'Going to Hell in your own way' (1992) 142 NLJ 438.
Shute, S., 'The Second Law Commission Consultation Paper on Consent (1): Three Aspects of the Project' [1996] Crim LR 684.
Williams, 'Assault and Words' [1957] Crim LR 216.
Williams, 'Consent and Public Policy' [1962] Crim LR 74.

Rape

Alder, Z., 'Rape — The Intention of Parliament and the Practice of the Courts' (1982) 45 MLR 664.
Barton, J. L., 'The Story of Marital Rape' (1992) 108 LQR 260.
Cowley, D., 'The retreat from *Morgan*' [1982] Crim LR 198.
Criminal Law Revision Committee 15th Report: Sexual Offences (1984).
Elliot, D. W., 'Rape Complainants' Sexual Experience with Third Parties' [1984] Crim LR 4.
Gardner, S., 'Appreciating *Olugbuja*' (1996) 16 Legal Studies 275.
Power, H., 'Consensual Sex, Disease and the Criminal Law' [1996] Crim LR 412.
Samuels, A., 'Consent — Rape' (1983) 127 SJ 742 and 'Defending a rape' (1983) 127 SJ 314.
Temkin, J., 'The Limits of Reckless Rape' [1983] Crim LR 5.
Temkin, J., *Rape and the Criminal Justice System* (Aldershot: Dartmouth Publishing Co., 1995); reviewed at [1996] Crim LR 455.
Williams, G., 'Rape is rape' (1992) 142 NLJ 11.

Provocation

Ashworth, A., 'Self-Induced and the Homicide Act' [1973] Crim LR 483.
Brett, 'The Physiology of Provocation' [1971] Crim LR 634.
Brigg, A., 'Provocation Reassessed' (1996) 112 LQR 403.
English, P., 'What did s. 3 do to the law of provocation?' [1970] Crim LR 249.
Herring, J., 'Provocation and Ethnicity' [1996] Crim LR 490.
Horder, J., 'Provocation and the Loss of Self-Control' (1992) 108 LQR 191.
Horder, J., 'Provocation's "Reasonable Man" Reassessed' (1996) 112 LQR 35.
Nicolson, D. and Sanghvi, R., 'Battered Women and Provocation' [1993] Crim LR 728.
Padfield, N., 'Why Does Provocation Diminish Culpability?' (1996) 55 CLJ 420.
Wasik, M., 'Cumulative Provocation in Domestic Killing' [1982] Crim LR 29.

Diminished Responsibility

Dell, S., 'Diminished Responsibility Reconsidered' [1982] Crim LR 809.

Doran 'Alternative Defences: the Invisible Burden on the Trial Judge' [1991] Crim LR 878.

Fingarette, H., 'Diminished Mental Capacity as a Criminal Law Defence' (1974) 37 MLR 264.

Goodliffe, J., 'R v Tandy and the Concept of Alcoholism as a Disease', (1990) 53 MLR 809.

Leng, R., 'Mercy Killing and the CLRC' (1982) 132 NLJ 76.

Wootton, B., 'Diminished Responsibility: A Layman's View' (1960) 76 LQR 224.

10 OFFENCES AGAINST PROPERTY — THE THEFT ACTS

This area of the substantive law causes considerable difficulties for a student. This type of book cannot attempt a full discussion of the various offences within the Theft Acts (see Smith, *The Law of Theft*, for a full consideration of this area of the law). Nevertheless this chapter outlines various offences within the Theft Acts as illustrations of this topic. The offences were chosen with a view to the kinds of questions that are most often used in assessments and exams to test a student's knowledge of this area of law.

THEFT

The first offence to consider is theft contrary to s. 1 of the Theft Act 1968 which provides:

> A person is guilty of theft if he dishonestly appropriates property belonging to another with the intention of permanently depriving the other of it.

The offence consists of the following elements. The subject-matter of theft is *property* — you should be aware of the definition of this term which *includes* (see s. 4(1)) money, real property (generally interests in land), personal property, things in action, e.g., cheques, and patents. This wide definition is limited and qualified by case law and by the other provisions of s. 4.

Thus a corpse may not be stolen as the law does not regard a cadaver as property (*Handyside's case* (1746) 2 East PC 652), although parts of the human body prepared as medical specimens or body fluids may be (see *R* v *Welsh* [1974] RTR 478 where the accused poured away the contents of the bottle of his bodily fluid in relation to a drink driving offence). Other cases have determined that neither electricity nor confidential information are property within the Theft Acts (see *Lowe* v *Blease* [1975] Crim LR 513 and *Oxford* v *Moss* [1976] Crim LR 119).

Statutory Definition of Property

By s. 4(2) of the Theft Act 1968 it is determined that land cannot be stolen. The law deems buildings, trees, cultivated plants and shrubs and fixtures to be land but such appendages to the physical earth may be stolen by persons not in possession of the 'land' who sever such things from the physical earth (see s. 4(2)(b)).

A tenant occupying land may steal fixtures let for use with the land but cannot steal any other interest in land. Fixtures are defined as things attached to the physical earth or a building which are intended to be permanent and to be an improvement to the land. Note that theft of a fixture by a tenant may take place without it being severed from the 'land' (see s. 4(2)(c)). An individual may steal land including the physical earth but *only* where he holds the land for the benefit of another while in a position of trust — this includes holding land as a trustee or personal representative or being a person authorised to sell another's land by power of attorney or as the liquidator of a company.

Wild Foliage

Wild foliage, including mushrooms (fungi) and flowers, fruit and foliage from a plant (including a shrub or tree), may not generally be stolen, though cultivated foliage may be stolen. Wild foliage may be stolen, however, if a person not in possession of the land upon which such foliage grows, takes it for reward or commercial purposes as opposed to personal use or consumption (see Theft Act 1968, s. 4(3)).

Wild Animals

Wild animals may not be stolen but domesticated animals can be stolen as can animals ordinarily kept in captivity.

Where wild animals are reduced into possession on a person's land, i.e., killed or captured, they become property capable of being stolen by anyone *other* than the person who actually reduced them into possession (i.e., killed or captured them). The latter individual may thus be convicted of poaching but not theft of the carcass or the wild animal itself. The situation may be different if the poacher left the land and abandoned the animal or carcass but returned some time later and subsequently took the animal or carcass away. For reasons which will be explained later the theft of a wild animal or a carcass may even be theft from a poacher (see Theft Act 1968, s. 4(4)).

Property Belonging to Another

An individual may generally only steal property which belongs to another. By the Theft Act 1968, s. 5(1), property belongs to another if that other has a proprietary right or interest in it.

This includes full ownership in such property or a qualified interest such as being a trustee, or conversely being the beneficiary of property which is subject to a trust (this latter right being known as an equitable interest). See *R v Hallam and Blackburn* [1995] Crim LR 323 and J. C. Smith's commentary to it. Other interests include a lien, i.e., a right to retain possession of property until payment has been made for work executed upon it. It has been held that the 'profits' made by an employee while using his employer's property may be property in which the employer has a proprietary right or interest. (But see *Attorney-General's Reference (No. 1 of 1985)* [1986] QB 491 below.) Though the law recognises that a person may have an equitable interest in land following the execution of a contract of sale for such land with the vendor, s. 5(1) determines that that particular equitable interest does not constitute a proprietary right or interest for the purposes of theft.

Note also that when someone dishonestly inserts an identically shaped but lower value coin, a piece of wire, an iced lolly stick or any other unauthorised object into a gaming or vending machine, the ownership in the coins, tokens or items dispensed does not pass but remains the property of the owner of the machine. The taking of such items would be theft (*R v Goodwin* [1996] Crim LR 262). (In *Goodwin* having and using foreign coins in a machine also constituted 'going equipped' under the Theft Act 1968, s. 25.)

Possession and Control

By the Theft Act 1968, s. 5(1), property also belongs to another for the purposes of theft if another has possession or control of that property. A person has 'possession' of property e.g., when he is entrusted with it under a contract of bailment. Whatever the purpose of the bailment, hire, lease or hire-purchase contract, the person in *possession* of the goods (known as the bailee) does not have ownership — this right is reserved to the person, e.g., hiring the goods to the bailee (i.e., the bailor).

A person who owns goods generally, of course, also possesses them. He does not cease to possess them because he is not exercising actual physical dominion over them, e.g., because they are at his home while he is at work. But possession in goods may be lost by abandoning those goods. In such instances the rights of possession may be exercised by the finder of that property or by the person on whose land such property remains (see *Hibbert* v *McKiernan* [1948] 2 KB 142).

'Control' is the right in property someone has when goods are in his hands, e.g., shoppers examining wares. This is the merest right or interest in property which an individual may have and it may be exercised by someone when it is uncertain who enjoys possession or a greater interest in such property (see *R* v *Woodman* [1974] QB 754). These interests which collectively constitute full ownership in property can be split between more than one individual with regard to the same piece of property. The law recognises a strict hierarchy with regard to these proprietary incidents which may be exercised in respect of property. A proprietary right or interest in a piece of property, such as a lien, is thus a greater interest than enjoying the right of possession and that in turn is a greater interest than control.

Summary

A difficulty for a student is the realisation that the various rights or interests in property discussed above may be vested in different people in respect of the same piece of property. The taking of a piece of property by another from one individual who has a limited right in that property is theft from him and from *all* the other individuals who enjoy the balance of the rights in that piece of property which collectively (and if vested in one person) would amount to full ownership.

It is clear that a person with a limited right in a piece of property may steal *that* property from another who enjoys a *greater* right or interest in it. This principle is readily understandable to a student. Once accepted and combined with the realisation of the ways in which the incidents of full ownership in property can be split between various individuals, it follows that an individual who enjoys a greater interest in a possession may steal that property from an individual who enjoys a *lesser* interest in it. This, it is suggested, is clear from *R* v *Turner (No. 2)* [1971] 2 All ER 441. A case said to conflict with *Turner* is that of *R* v *Meredith* [1973] Crim LR 253. This latter case can, however, be explained on grounds which do not relate to the issues discussed above.

Special Forms of Proprietary Right

Areas of acute difficulty for a student are the provisions in the Theft Act 1968 which deal with the special circumstances where, for the purposes of the offence of theft, an individual is to be regarded as having a proprietary right or interest in property.

By s. 5(2), where a property is subject to a trust which has no beneficiaries, e.g., a charitable trust, a person having a right to compel the trustees to perform the terms of the trust (generally the Attorney-General) shall be regarded as being a person to whom the beneficial interest in the trust belongs for the purposes of theft by the trustees.

Section 5(3) provides that property handed to an individual (usually money) which he is to account for and is legally obliged to deal with in a particular way will, if misused by the recipient, be regarded for the purposes of theft as belonging to the person who parted with the money, see *Davidge* v *Bunnett* [1984] Crim LR 297. This provision is necessary because the presumption where there is a handing over of property by an individual to a recipient (especially in cases of money) is that an obligation is imposed upon the recipient only to provide goods or services or subsequently to return money or goods of equivalent value to that individual or to a third party (see *Lewis* v *Lethbridge* [1987] Crim LR 59 and *DPP* v *Huskinson, The Times*, 24 May 1988). Failure to carry out such obligations may be a breach of the civil law (e.g., breach of trust or contract), but since the *ownership* of the property has generally passed to the recipient the property belongs to him, see *R* v *Hall* [1973] QB 126, and he cannot commit the offence of theft in respect of that property. Section 5(3) notionally regards property as belonging to another (the original owner) for the purposes of the offence of theft when he parts with property, but only where the recipient *must* use *that* property for a *particular* purpose *only*, e.g., money given by a client to a solicitor in relation to a house purchase (cf. *Attorney-General's Reference (No 1 of 1985)* [1986] QB 491 which determines that where an employee makes a secret profit by selling his own goods at his employer's shop the employee does not steal the resultant profits he makes at the expense of his employer). This provision is also applicable to any proceeds of the original property which are retained by the recipient of the original property after exchange, sale or the undertaking of a commercial activity by him. It does not matter if the recipient of property with an obligation to retain and deal with it in a certain way, was the 'true owner' if by agreement he has recognised an obligation to deal with it in the interests of the transferor and in breach of the agreement has misappropriated it to his own use (*R* v *Arnold* [1997] Crim LR 833).

In *R* v *Hallam and Blackburn* [1995] Crim LR 323 investment products were sold by the accused (financial advisers) through a company. In some cases the investors' cheques were paid into the company account and accounts of the accused which were never invested for the clients. The Court of Appeal held them rightly convicted of theft. Their advisory service was not equatable to that of a travel agent. The accused were entrusted with funds to invest; the clients retained an equitable interest in any cheque they drew or any cheque for investment proceeds drawn by their insurers. That interest attaches not only to the cheques but to their proceeds and to any balance in accounts operated by the accused or their company to which the payments could be traced. It is immaterial whether the property belongs to the clients under s. 5(1), (2) or (3). The property or its proceeds belongs to them and the accused's intention to deprive them of their interest in the property or proceeds was an intent to deprive them of their property.

Section 5(4) creates acute problems for students and academics alike. This subsection provides for the situation where a person receives property from another because of the latter's mistaken belief as to the former's entitlement to that property. To the extent that the recipient is regarded by the law as being under an obligation to return that property (or its proceeds) to another under the civil law, i.e., the law of restitution, that property will be regarded, for the purposes of the offence of theft, as belonging to the person who parted with it under the mistaken belief. This provision need only apply where *ownership* in that property passed to the recipient. The obligation to make restitution must be a *legal* one for s. 5(4) to apply, see *R v Gilks* [1972] 3 All ER 280. Furthermore where the property has passed out of the hands of the recipient *without him realising* that he has the obligation to make restitution and there are no proceeds in his hands any potential liability under s. 5(4) ceases, see *Attorney-General's Reference (No. 1 of 1983)* [1985] QB 182 and by way of contrast *R v Davis* (1989) 88 Cr App R 347.

There is no need to rely upon this subsection where the mistaken belief has the effect of preventing the transfer of ownership in the property concerned. In such instances the person parting with the property still retains a proprietary right and interest in it within the terms of s. 5(1). Such mistakes include:

(a) Mistake as to the *identity* of the recipient of the property.
(b) Mistake as to the *nature* of the goods transferred.
(c) Possibly, mistake as to the quantity or value of goods transferred.

Where the owner of property transfers it to another under a contract of sale which has been induced by fraud the recipient of the property nevertheless generally obtains ownership. However, there is no need to rely upon s. 5(4) if the original owner renders void the contract on discovery of the fraud. In that case the ownership in the property reverts to the original owner and belongs to him for the purposes of theft under s. 5(1) (see *R* v *Hamid, The Times,* 23 February 1988 and *R* v *Shadrock-Cigari* [1988] Crim LR 465, which determine that a bank retains an equitable interest in drafts it issues as a result of a mistake).

The Conduct Element of Theft

A thief must appropriate the property the subject-matter of the theft. This is constituted by an 'assumption of the rights of an owner' (see Theft Act 1968, s. 3(1)). An assumption of *any* of the rights noted above will suffice (see *Anderton* v *Burnside* [1984] AC 320). The act of appropriation requires not an act expressly or impliedly authorised by the owner, but an act by way of adverse interference with or usurpation of those rights (i.e., the rights of ownership).

This apparently simple requirement has proved difficult to analyse and raises problems for the student. It would appear to need:

(a) Conduct in respect of a piece of property which usurps or interferes with the rights of others in that property, though this does not have to be overtly demonstrable, i.e., objectively established to be adverse to the interests of owners.

(b) The conduct of a thief must be accompanied by a mental resolve to treat the property as his own (see chapter 3 for a discussion of why this element forms no part of the *mens rea*).

(c) The thief's conduct must be without the express or implied authority of the owner to deal with his property.

This latter element was capable of being interpreted in two ways following the House of Lords' decision in *Anderton* v *Burnside* [1984] AC 320. Lord Roskill, in approving prior decisions on the meaning of 'appropriate' (i.e., *Eddy* v *Niman* (1981) 73 Cr App R 237; *R* v *Skipp* [1975] Crim LR 114 and *R* v *Meech* [1974] QB 549), appeared to have given authority to the view that only when a thief had been seen to have acted outside the express or implied authority given to him by the owner of property to deal with his goods could appropriation take place, e.g., by taking the goods from a supermarket shelf and placing them in one's own bag (see *R* v *Fritschy* [1985] Crim LR 745 as an illustration).

However, an alternative view of the nature of appropriation from a differing interpretation of the speech of Lord Roskill, was that a mental resolve on the part of a potential thief to treat property as his own together with conduct which amounted to an assumption of the rights of an owner, e.g., physical seizure, would constitute conduct which was outside the authority given by the owner to deal with such property. There was no need for the conduct to be objectively established as being outside the authority of the owner by reference to external criteria, as required in the earlier interpretation discussed above. On this basis, the putting of wares from a supermarket shelf into a wire basket provided by the shop accompanied by a resolution to steal would be outside the express or implied authority of the store owner to deal with the goods. This opinion as to the nature of appropriation is based on Lord Roskill's approval of *R v McPherson* [1973] Crim LR 191 and the opinion of Viscount Dilhorne in *Lawrence v Metropolitan Police Commissioner* [1972] AC 626. In two cases *R v Philippou* [1989] Crim LR 585 and the civil case of *Dobson v General Accident* [1989] 3 WLR 1066, the judiciary appear to have endorsed this latter interpretation of the nature of appropriation. That has been confirmed in *R v Gomez* [1993] 1 All ER 1, where the meaning of 'appropriates' in s. 1(1) of the Theft Act 1968 was revisited by the House of Lords.

The appellant was the assistant manager of an electrical retail store. He was approached by a customer and asked to supply that person with goods on the strength of stolen building society cheques. The appellant, knowing the cheques to be stolen, asked the manager whether the 'customer' could purchase goods with the cheques and the manager told him to find out from the bank whether they would accept the cheques. The appellant pretended to have contacted the bank and to have been assured that the cheques were as good as cash. The manager then consented to the transaction and the 'customer' was presented with £16,000 worth of goods in exchange for the cheques, which were dishonoured on presentation. The appellant claimed that there had been no appropriation within s. 1(1) because of the manager's authorisation of the transaction.

The two previous key authorities were considered, namely: *Lawrence v Commissioner of Police for the Metropolis* [1971] 2 All ER 1253 in which Lord Dilhorne said: 'appropriation' may occur even if the owner has permitted or consented to the goods being taken; and *R v Morris* [1983] 3 All ER 288 where Lord Roskill said: 'appropriation' involves '*not* an act expressly or impliedly authorised by the owner but an act by way of adverse interference with or usurpation of those rights'.

The House of Lords has now emphatically decided that Lord Roskill got it wrong. No 'adverse interference' with the rights of the owner is necessary. Now an act done with the authority or consent of the owner may amount to an appropriation of goods for the purpose of the Theft Act where such authority has been obtained by deception. See *Dobson v General Accident Fire and Life Assurance Corp plc* [1989] 3 All ER 927. A person may appropriate property even where the owner transfers ownership to him under the terms of a contract negotiated between them.

Remember that appropriation is not limited to physical seizure of goods but also includes conduct such as purporting to sell property to another which does not belong to the thief, see *R v Pitham and Hehl* (1976) 65 Cr App R 45 and *Chan Man-Sin v R* [1988] 1 WLR 196 in relation to the appropriation of the rights of a company as owner of a credit balance in a bank account by drawing, presenting and negotiating a forged cheque on that account. See also *R v Wille* (1988) 86 Cr App R 296. Appropriation can take place through an innocent agent e.g., where a person in authority signs a false invoice intending innocent people to take steps that result in money being debited from a bank account (*R v Stringer and Banks, The Daily Telegraph,* 11 April 1991). Whether purported gifts, i.e., the *inter vivos* transfer of property, money or valuables particularly by elderly employers or patients can result in theft convictions for the alleged donees has arisen recently. In *R v Mazo* [1996] Crim LR 456 the court stated that the circumstances of the transfers needed to be considered, as did the state of mind of the donor and the donee. A 'transaction' might be theft notwithstanding it was done with the owner's consent if induced by fraud, deception or a false representation. However, where the recipient or party to a transaction receives an absolute, indefeasible title to the property transferred to him, then the transaction cannot be a theft of that property by him. Both *Mazo* and *R v Hopkins* [1997] Crim LR 359 turned on the mental competence of the alleged donor/victim. Where that person is incompetent then the recipient of the gift is liable to be guilty of theft.

Problems of jurisdiction can arise depending on where appropriation occurs. In *R v Atakpu* [1993] 4 All ER 215 the accused was involved in conspiracy to obtain hire cars on the continent which were then brought to the UK to be sold. He was charged with conspiracy to steal. However, in order to establish jurisdiction, the prosecution had to prove that the conspiracy would result in an offence being committed in the UK. The Court of Appeal purporting to apply *Gomez* held that because the consent of the owner is irrelevant to appropriation the cars were appropriated in France, when they were obtained by deception in France. Property cannot be appropriated twice. Once stolen, goods cannot be stolen again by the same thief exercising the same or other rights of ownership over that property. Therefore, there was no offence committed in UK, and the charge must fail on the ground of lack of jurisdiction. Remember, once property has been stolen, later dealing with it does not constitute appropriation. The conspiracy conviction was quashed. (Note, however, the significance of the Criminal Justice Act 1993, discussed in chapter 7, under 'Conspiracy'.)

Special Instances of Appropriation

Although a person has possession or control of property he may nevertheless appropriate it (see Theft Act 1968, s. 3(1)). By s. 3(1), an individual who has come by property, innocently or not, who (though he has possession or control of such property) later assumes the rights of an owner by keeping or dealing with the property as owner, may be deemed to have appropriated the property (see also *R v Hircock* (1978) 67 Cr App R 278).

Section 3(2) states that a person who comes by property innocently which is in fact stolen and who subsequently maintains a right of ownership on discovering the truth as against the true owner is thereby provided with a defence against a charge of theft (*R v Adams* [1993] Crim LR 72).

Theft is a continuing offence: the continuous use of a stolen object by the thief constitutes a single offence of theft (see *R v Devell* [1984] Crim LR 428).

The Mens Rea of Theft

The *mens rea* required for a theft is that the thief must act dishonestly and *intend* permanently to deprive the true owner of his property. Both these elements have been subject to considerable statutory and judicial definition and must be examined in turn.

Dishonesty

The Theft Act 1968 partially defines what may constitute dishonesty in s. 2, which determines as matters of *law* that certain situations may *not* be regarded as dishonest. These include:

(a)   Where an accused believes he has a right in law to deprive another of property either for himself or for a third party.

Such a belief need not be reasonable, and is not negated because an accused uses force (see *R v Robinson* [1977] Crim LR 173). It must be a belief in a *legal* right not a moral one.

(b)   Where an accused appropriates another's property believing the latter would have consented to this fact knowing of the circumstances.

(c)   Where a person appropriates property believing the owner cannot be found. This situation is inapplicable to a person who holds such property as trustee or personal representative.

By s. 2(2) the appropriation of property is still dishonest notwithstanding an individual's willingness to pay for the property. However, the requirement that an accused charged with theft be dishonest is a matter still to be left to the jury. Apart from the presence of the above situations the judge should direct the jury that it is for them to determine the question of dishonesty. It has been determined in *R v Ghosh* [1982] QB 1053 that a judge should not leave this issue to the jury without explanation but that he should give them the following guidelines:

(a)   An accused may be dishonest if he regards himself as dishonest by reference to his own standards of honesty and such standards of honesty are shared by the general community; or

(b)   he has acted dishonestly by reference to the standards of ordinary men and he is aware of this standard of normal mores.

In either instance he can be regarded as dishonest. It is a misdirection to inform a jury that an unreasonable belief that property has been abandoned cannot be an honest belief (*R v Small* [1988] RTR 32).

In *R v Mazo* [1996] Crim LR 456 and *R v Hopkins* [1997] Crim LR 359 the issue of whether or not accepting purported *inter vivos* gifts could be theft was held to turn on the honesty or otherwise of the recipient. If the donor lacked the capacity (through fraud, undue influence etc.) and the recipient knew this he is dishonest and his acceptance is appropriation and if he intends to keep it then he should rightly be convicted of theft.

Intention permanently to deprive
This means that an intention to borrow is insufficient to constitute what would otherwise amount to the offence of theft. Such an intention permanently to deprive may be inferred from the surrounding circumstances, e.g., the nature of the property appropriated, i.e., its life span. Whether an accused has such an intention is primarily a matter of fact (*R v Lloyd and others* [1985] QB 829).

By s. 6 of the Theft Act 1968, an individual will be *regarded* as having an intention permanently to deprive an owner of property where:

(a)   he intends to treat the thing, i.e., property, as his own to dispose of regardless of the other's rights, or

(b)   he borrows or lends the property for a period and in circumstances rendering it equivalent to an outright taking. See *DPP v Lavender* [1994] Crim LR 297 and *R v Cahill* [1993] Crim LR 141 (on the meaning of the phrase 'dispose of').

The above situations are clear. Furthermore, by s. 6(2), if a person parts with property belonging to another under a condition as to its return which he may not be able to perform and this is done for that person's private purposes and without the owner's authority, this will be regarded as establishing an intent permanently to deprive the owner of that property. This deals with situations such as the bailee of goods passing them to a third party in order to raise money for his own purposes. The fact that he may not be able to redeem the property determines that he is to be regarded as having intended permanently to deprive the true owner of that property.

Conditional intent

An individual who intends to appropriate or permanently to deprive another of a *particular* piece or pieces of property conditional upon certain factors, e.g., upon the property being established as valuable, commits no offence of theft or attempted theft since he lacks *mens rea* or, in the case of conditional appropriation, a constituent element in the *actus reus* (see *R* v *Easom* [1971] 2 QB 315 and *R* v *Husseyn* (1978) 67 Cr App R 131).

It has been determined, however, that where an individual has a *general* conditional intent to steal anything he may find, or a conditional intent to steal any number of objects within a specified group of objects, e.g., within a handbag, room etc., then he may nevertheless in such circumstances be convicted of *attempted* theft (see *Attorney-General's References (Nos. 1 and 2 of 1979)* [1980] QB 180 and *R* v *Bayley and Easterbrook* [1980] Crim LR 503) provided he is not charged with attempting to steal specific items but with 'attempting to steal from a room' (handbag or whatever). The fact that the handbag or room is empty is irrelevant (Criminal Attempts Act 1981, s. 1(2)).

BURGLARY

There are several distinct ways in which the offence of burglary may be committed. All the forms of burglary have common elements which should be understood by you. They are as follows:

Entry of a Building or Part of a Building

A building is partially defined by the Theft Act 1968, s. 9(3), as including 'any inhabited vehicle or vessel, and shall apply to any such vehicle or vessel at times when the person having habitation in it is not there as well as at times when he is'.

Apart from this, 'building' bears its ordinary meaning, and thus includes any structure on a permanent site which is used as a building (see *B and S* v *Leathly* [1979] Crim LR 314 and *Norfolk Constabulary* v *Seekings* [1986] Crim LR 167).

A building may be divided into parts, e.g., flats or parts of a shop split between areas where the public may go and where they may not (see *R* v *Walkington* [1979] 2 All ER 716). A person may commit burglary in one part of a building though not in another because he may enter the former part of the building as a trespasser but enter the other part lawfully. Entry of a building or part of a building as a trespasser is a necessary element in the offence of burglary.

Trespasser

An individual is a trespasser to a building or part thereof:

(a)   when he enters therein and there is no right in law to do so, or
(b)   he enters without the permission (express or implied) of the owner and/or occupier of the premises.

Remember *entry* of the premises or part of the premises must be as a trespasser, see *R* v *Collins* [1973] QB 100. A person does not become a burglar if *after* entering a building *or* part thereof he *becomes* a trespasser (although it is true that once inside a building or part thereof a person may become a trespasser for the purposes of the offence of burglary by *entering* as a trespasser other parts which he had no right or permission to enter). In the case of *R* v *Jones and Smith* [1976] 3 All ER 54 it was accepted that where an individual enters a building or part thereof with the permission of the owner and/or occupier, but he has a secret plan which he intends to carry out in that building or part thereof and the owner and/or occupier would not have consented to the individual entering the premises had he known the latter's intentions, the individual enters as a trespasser. The actual entry of a building must be a 'substantial or effective entry' by an individual, see *R* v *Collins*. Although not entirely clear, it would seem that not all of the body need cross the threshold for effective entry, see *R* v *Brown* [1985] Crim LR 212. It is unclear whether the intrusion of an instrument to effect a crime, e.g., a fishing-line to hook out a trinket, is an entry, though it is clear that using an instrument, e.g., a jemmy, to *effect* an entry is not an *entry* for the purposes of burglary.

Brown has been re-endorsed by *R* v *Ryan* [1996] Crim LR 320 where the fact that the accused was trapped half-way through a window was held to be clearly entry for the purposes of burglary and it was irrelevant whether or not he was capable of stealing anything (because he was trapped by the window). The 'substantial or effective' entry in *Collins* is no longer essential.

Mens Rea of Burglary

An individual must enter a building or part thereof knowing or being reckless as to the fact that he is trespassing. However, in addition he must have either (a) upon entry the specific/ulterior intent to commit one or more of the offences in s. 9(1)(a), or (b) after having entered as a trespasser the prescribed *mens rea* for any offence actually committed under s. 9(1)(b).

Conditional intent will suffice (*Attorney-General's Reference (Nos 1 and 2 of 1979)* [1980] QB 180 and see above).

Also, because one of the ulterior intents for s. 9(1)(a) is the intent to rape the decision in *R v Khan* [1990] 2 All ER 783 that attempted rape (a specific intent offence) may be committed where the accused is reckless as to the victim's consent must equally apply to burglary (also a specific intent offence).

The Various Forms of Burglary

The various forms of burglary are set out in Table 10.1.

Where there is an overlap between the two forms of burglary it is usual to charge an accused under Theft Act 1968, s. 9(1)(b), see *R v Taylor* [1979] Crim LR 649. However, since *R v Whiting* (1987) 85 Cr App R 78, a trial judge may allow the jury to give an alternative verdict of burglary under s. 9(1)(a) as opposed to s. 9(1)(b) when the latter form of the offence has been charged.

Aggravated Burglary

This offence involves committing either form of burglary as noted in Table 10.1 but with the aggravating factor that at the time of the commission of the burglary the accused has with him or her:

(a)   A firearm or imitation, see Theft Act 1968, s. 10(1)(a).

(b)   A weapon of offence, i.e., 'any article made or adapted for use for causing injury to or incapacitating a person, or intended by the person having it with him for such use, see s. 10(1)(b).

(c)   An explosive, see s. 10(1)(c).

The accused must be aware of the fact of the presence of such objects and they must be in his physical possession ready for use at the time he commits either form of burglary (see *R v Russell* [1985] Crim LR 231). The prosecution need not show, however, that the accused intended to use such objects in the course of the burglary (see *R v Stones* [1989] 1 WLR 156). The relevant time for consideration of the accused's intent to use the weapon is at the time of the actual theft. Use at that point shows the necessary intent (i.e., the intent to injure if the need arose) (*R v Kelly* (1993) 97 Cr App R 245).

TABLE 10.1   ELEMENTS COMMON TO BURGLARY UNDER s. 9

(a)   Entry
(b)   of a building or part thereof

(c)   as a trespasser

(d)   knowing or being reckless as to the fact of trespass.

Burglary under s. 9(1)(a)

On entry of a building or part thereof an accused must specifically *intend* to commit one or more of the following offences:

(a) To steal anything in the building or part thereof.

(b) To inflict grievous bodily harm upon any person in the building or any part thereof.

(c) To rape any person* in the building or part thereof.

(d) To do any unlawful damage to the building or part thereof or to anything contained therein.

Conditional intent is applicable to this form of burglary.

An accused must be aware of or reckless to the fact that he is a trespasser before entry of a building or part thereof.

Burglary under s. 9(1)(b)

Having *entered* the building or part thereof an accused *actually commits* one or more of the following offences:

(a) The offence of theft or attempted theft.

(b) The infliction or attempted infliction of grievous bodily harm upon a person within the building or part thereof.

Conditional intent is applicable to the situation where the accused has *attempted* one of the above-mentioned substantive offences.

An accused must know or be reckless as to the fact he is a trespasser before he commits or attempts one of the above-mentioned substantive offences.

*Schedule 10, para. 26, of the Criminal Justice and Public Order Act 1994 amends the Theft Act 1968, so that an offence intended by a trespasser which will constitute burglary now includes 'raping any person' rather than 'raping any woman'. This is to take account of the new offence of 'male rape'.

DISHONESTY OFFENCES OTHER THAN THEFT

Theft Act 1968, s. 15 — obtaining property by deception

'A person who by any deception dishonestly obtains property belonging to another, with the intention of permanently depriving the other of it' commits an offence.

Elements common with theft

(a) *Actus reus:*

(i)   *Property.* This has generally the same meaning as in theft but note by Theft Act 1968, s. 34(1), only s. 4(1) of the Act applies to s. 15(1). This means all property may be the subject of an offence under s. 15(1) *including* land.

(ii)   *Belonging to another.* By s. 34(1), s. 5(1) of the Act and only that subsection applies to offences under s. 15(1).

(b) *Mens rea:*

(i)   *Dishonesty.* Section 2(1) of the Theft Act 1968 is inapplicable as regards s. 15(1) but the common law test of dishonesty formulated in *R v Ghosh* [1982] QB 1053 is applicable (see *R v Woolven* (1983) 77 Cr App R 23).

(ii)   *Intention permanently to deprive.* This has the same meaning as in theft. Furthermore, s. 6 is applicable to s. 15(1) but is suitably adapted to the offence by s. 15(3) (see *R v Coffey* [1987] Crim LR 498 and *R v Atwal* [1989] Crim LR 293).

An accused must make the deception knowing or intending it to be false or being reckless as to that fact. This always has meant, and still means, *Cunningham'* subjective-style recklessness (see *R v Staines* (1974) 60 Cr App R 160 and also *R v Forsyth* [1997] Crim LR 589).

The constituents of the offence
An accused must obtain a proprietary right or other interest in property belonging to another by virtue of a deception of another.

A deception is defined as 'any deception (whether deliberate or reckless) by words or conduct as to fact or as to law, including a deception as to the present intentions of the person using the deception or any other person', see s. 15(4) (see *R v Silverman* (1987) Crim LR 574).

Its elements require: that a person is deceived (see *DPP v Ray* [1974] AC 370). A deception may be:

(a) *By conduct,* e.g., impersonating a person of a particular status in order to obtain credit otherwise unobtainable, see *R v Barnard* (1837) 7 C & P 784.

(b) *Implied from conduct* — see *Metropolitan Police Commissioner v Charles* [1977] AC 177 and *R v Bevan* (1986) 84 Cr App R 143 in which it was held that drawing a cheque (conduct) is an implied representation that the cheque will be met on presentation. In cases where a cheque is backed by a cheque card the representation is that the drawer of the cheque has the authority of the bank to enter into a contract on its behalf with the payee that the bank will honour the cheque in accordance with the terms contained on the cheque card (see *Metropolitan Police Commissioner* v *Charles*, see also *R* v *Lambie* [1982] AC 449 concerning credit cards). If either implied representations are false, due to inadequate funds or withdrawal by the bank of the authority to use a cheque card, a deception has occurred.

(c) *By omission* — generally an individual may not deceive by omission. However, if an individual induces another to believe facts which are initially true but the facts are rendered false by later events and this is known to the individual then failure to inform that other of the changed circumstances may amount to a deception by omission (see *DPP* v *Ray* [1974] AC 370).

A deception may be

(a) As to fact, see *Metropolitan Police Commissioner* v *Charles*.
(b) As to law (though this will generally involve a deception as to fact).
(c) As to an accused's present or future intentions, see *DPP* v *Ray*.

An individual must be deceived
This has rather a technical meaning as regards the Theft Act 1968, s. 15(1). It appears to require:

(a) That the individual concerned was not aware of the truth.
(b) That he had acted in reliance upon the deception.
(c) That he would not have acted in such a way had he known the truth (see *Metropolitan Police Commissioner* v *Charles* [1977] AC 177).

The deception must be the cause of the obtaining of the property
An individual who obtains property after using a falsehood, though another has not been deceived thereby, does not commit a full offence under the Theft Act 1968, s. 15(1), although he may be charged with attempt (see *R* v *Hensler* (1870) 22 LT 691). The situation is the same where the deception has not been a causal link in obtaining the property because the deception did not influence a person when parting with the property (see *R* v *Laverty* [1970] 3 All ER 432), or the deception took place after the property had been obtained (see *R* v *Collis-Smith* [1971] Crim LR 716, *R* v *King* [1987] QB 547 and *R* v *Coady* [1996] Crim LR 518).

It is not a necessary requirement of the offence that the property is obtained from the person actually deceived, it is only necessary that the deception is one of the causative factors in the accused obtaining a proprietary right or interest in the property, i.e., ownership, possession or control (see *Metropolitan Police Commissioner* v *Charles* [1977] AC 177 and s. 15(2)). By s. 15(2) the offence is also committed where an accused obtains property for a third party or enables another to obtain or retain property, through a deception.

The relationship between theft and obtaining by deception
This is an area of the law which causes considerable problems to a student. It is a favourite source of examination questions. It may be rendered comprehensible by remembering the following general rules:

(a)   Where there is no deception by an accused and he obtains property belonging to another he may only be charged with theft.

(b)   Where an accused by a deception obtains the full proprietary right or interest in property, i.e., ownership, but he has not at the time of, or prior to, obtaining ownership appropriated the property, he may only be convicted of an offence of obtaining property by deception. Likewise, where the property in question is incapable of being stolen but can be obtained by deception — namely, land.

(c)   It is only in cases where the accused, though obtaining property by deception, has not at the time he appropriates the property obtained full ownership that the two offences may be charged. If another thus retains some interest in the property at the moment the accused appropriates it then the accused will commit the offence of theft as well as an offence under the Theft Act 1968, s. 15(1). This will be the case in the following situations:

(i)   Where an accused by a deception obtains only possession or control of goods, e.g., by representing that he wishes only to borrow or hire the property.

(ii)   Where at the moment of appropriation of property by an accused consequent upon a deception the owner retains possession or control of that property. This, it is suggested, is the rationale of the House of Lords' decision in *Lawrence* v *Metropolitan Police Commissioner* [1972] AC 626, which is discussed in textbooks to a far greater extent than perhaps it deserves.

(iii)   Where the deception induces the owner of property to part with it to the accused (or even to a third party) under a mistaken belief, but the nature of that mistake is such that it may have the effect of negating the transfer of ownership. These forms of mistake have been considered above (in the area of text relating to the Theft Act 1968, s. 5(4)). Since in such cases the owner retains a proprietary right or interest in the property within the terms of s. 5(1), an appropriation of that property by the accused or a third party will generally amount to theft (assuming the prescribed *mens rea*). Do not forget the possible effect of s. 5(4); although this subsection is inapplicable to cases of obtaining property by deception, it must be considered by you where the accused (or possibly a third party) having obtained the property undertakes a course of conduct which might amount to theft.

Deception and Money Transfers

The obtaining of cheques, telegraphic transfers and credit transfers of money by CHAPS (clearing automated payment system) has given rise to some very complex and difficult cases (e.g., *R v Preddy* [1996] AC 815 and *R v Hopkins* [1997] Crim LR 359), a Law Commission Report, *Offences of Dishonesty: Money Transfers*, Law Com. No. 243 and new legislation (the Theft (Amendment) Act 1996).

In *Preddy* a large amount of mortgage money was obtained by false representations. These advances were paid by cheque, telegraphic or automated payment (CHAPS). The House of Lords held that no property belonging to another was obtained and no identifiable property passed from payer to payee. Instead, a chose-in-action (the credit) in the payer's account was extinguished or reduced and a new chose-in-action (for credit) created in the payee's bank account. In the case of payment by cheque the chose-in-action represented by the cheque (like the credit in the payee's bank account) belonged to the payee. Therefore there was no obtaining of property belonging to another contrary to s. 15(1). At that time Preddy could not have been charged with obtaining services by deception contrary to s. 1 of the 1978 Act because the Court of Appeal decision in *R v Halai* [1983] Crim LR 624 had ruled that mortgage advances were not to be regarded as a service. That has now been changed both by the courts in *R v Graham* [1997] 1 Cr App R 302 and *R v Cooke* [1997] Crim LR 436 and by Parliament in the Theft (Amendment) Act 1996, s. 4(1) which inserts a new subsection into s. 1 of the Theft Act 1978 so that the provision of loans is now a service within that section. But see *R v Naviede* [1997] Crim LR 662 for obtaining services by deception situations that occurred before the 1996 amendment came into effect (also *R v Hilton* [1997] Crim LR 761).

The 1996 legislation also creates a new offence of dishonestly obtaining a money transfer for himself or another by deception contrary to the Theft Act 1968, s. 15A. Section 15A defines a money transfer as a situation where:

(a) a debit is made to one account,
(b) a credit is made to another, and
(c) the credit results from the debit or the debit results from the credit.

This offence will catch the types of transfers made in the *Preddy* and *Graham* cases and the only *mens rea* for this new offence is dishonesty. Intent to retain the credit transferred is irrelevant.

That offence aside, it may be possible to charge the obtaining of most advances referred to in *Preddy* as procuring the execution of a valuable security contrary to the Theft Act 1968, s. 20(2) (see *R v Graham* [1997] 1 Cr App R 302).

Other Offences Involving Deception

You must be aware of other offences within the Theft Acts which involve deception. They are similar in all respects to s. 15(1) except for what is obtained by the act of deception.

By s. 16(1) it is an offence for an individual to obtain a pecuniary advantage by deception. This includes borrowing by way of overdraft, taking out an insurance policy or annuity contract (or obtaining an improvement of the terms on which he is allowed to do so) (see s. 16(2)(b) and *Metropolitan Police Commissioner* v *Charles* [1977] AC 177). By s. 16(2)(c) an offence is committed where a person by a deception obtains an opportunity to earn remuneration or greater remuneration in an office or employment, or to win money by betting.

You must be fully conversant with the peculiar incidents of these offences.

The Theft Act 1978

There used to be an offence of obtaining a pecuniary advantage by deception provided for in s. 16(2)(a) of the Theft Act 1968 but it has been repealed and replaced by a set of offences contained in the Theft Act 1978.

These offences are as follows:

(a) Section 1: obtaining services by deception — e.g., a meal in a restaurant or a taxi ride or, now, the provision of loans (Theft (Amendment) Act 1996).

(b) Section 2: it is an offence if an accused (subject to s. 2(2) of the Act) by a deception:

(i) Dishonestly secures the remission of the whole or part of any existing liability to make a payment whether his own liability or another's.

(ii) With intent to make permanent default in whole or in part on any existing liability to make a payment, or with intent to let another do so, dishonestly induces the creditor or any person claiming payment on behalf of the creditor to wait for payment (whether or not the due date for payment is deferred) or to forgo payment. The liability referred to in this subsection is a liability of the person seeking to evade it, and not a liability of someone else: *R* v *Attewell-Hughes* [1991] 1 WLR 955).

(iii) Dishonestly obtains any exemption from or abatement of liability to make a payment.

These complicated offences cover the multifarious and devious ways in which debtors may seek by deception to escape their liabilities for their debts, or the debts of others, either in whole or in part or with regard to instalments that may become payable in respect of a debt. This includes not only full evasion but improperly obtained extensions of credit with a view to eventual evasion. These offences should be fully understood by you.

(c) Section 3. Deception does not form a requirement of this offence. However, deception is frequently used in this offence by an accused as an instrument of execution. By s. 3(1) a person who, knowing that payment on the spot for any goods supplied or service done is required or expected from him, dishonestly makes off without having paid as required or expected and with intent to avoid payment of the amount due is guilty of an offence.

This offence under the Theft Act 1978 will be given further consideration below when we consider the types of question that may occur in your criminal law examination.

Handling

This is a crucial offence. It is as important in practice as in theory. It merits your special consideration in examinations.

By the Theft Act 1968, s. 22(1), an accused handles stolen goods if '(otherwise than in the course of the stealing) knowing or believing them to be stolen goods he dishonestly receives the goods, or dishonestly undertakes or assists in their retention, removal, disposal or realisation by or for the benefit of another person, or if he arranges to do so'.

The words in parentheses in s. 22(1) determine that a thief, during the course of appropriation, cannot be a handler, though a handler may be a thief (see *R* v *Sainthouse* [1980] Crim LR 506). However, an individual may not be convicted of both offences in respect of the same circumstances (*R* v *Shelton* (1986) 83 Cr App R 379). Though the prosecution are relieved from the burden of proving the handler is not the original thief, or that the handling is otherwise than in the course of stealing, the jury must make these inferences for an accused to be convicted (see *R* v *Cash* [1985] 1 QB 801).

The actus reus of handling: conduct

An accused may commit one or more of the following acts with regard to stolen property:

(a) *Receiving stolen goods*, i.e., taking physical possession or control of them. This may be done personally or through an agent or employee authorised to take receipt. The latter individuals also commit the act of receiving.

(b) *Arranging to receive stolen goods*, i.e., agreeing to undertake the activity noted above. These forms of conduct cause little consternation to students. However, the forms of activity noted below (and their relationship *inter se*) cause considerable problems. It is suggested that you give the following matters your utmost attention as they are the key to understanding this area of the law.

(c) *Retention of stolen goods* — this requires the 'keeping possession of, not losing or continuing to have stolen goods' (see *R* v *Pitchley* (1972) 57 Cr App R 30). Note that retaining stolen goods bought in good faith after discovering their true nature is not handling (see *Broom* v *Crowther* (1984) 148 JP 592).

(d) *Removal of stolen goods*, i.e., taking them from one place to another.

(e) *Disposal of stolen goods* — this includes changing their form, e.g., breaking up a stolen car with a blowtorch.

(f) *Realisation of stolen goods*, i.e., the sale of such goods to a third party or their exchange for other articles.

(g) *Arranging* to commit any of the above four forms of activity.

Taking the four principal forms of activity noted above (i.e., (c) to (f)), you must show awareness of the fact that the Theft Act 1968, s. 22, requires an accused to undertake or assist (or to arrange to undertake or assist) in any such forms of conduct by or for the benefit of another. This has been interpreted as follows by the House of Lords in *R* v *Bloxham* [1983] 1 AC 109 (see Table 10.2). Since *R* v *Park* (1988) 87 Cr App R 164 it has been determined that an accused can only be guilty of arranging to handle stolen goods, if he makes his arrangements to do so *after* the goods have been stolen. This authority does not preclude an accused from being charged with an offence of attempting to handle stolen goods in such circumstances.

TABLE 10.2

(1) Undertaking the retention of stolen goods.	(2) Undertaking the removal of stolen goods.	(3) Undertaking the disposal of stolen goods.	(4) Undertaking the realisation of stolen goods.
(5) Arranging to undertake the retention of stolen goods.	(6) Arranging to undertake the removal of stolen goods.	(7) Arranging to undertake the disposal of stolen goods.	(8) Arranging to undertake the realisation of stolen goods.

Whenever an accused undertakes or arranges to undertake any of the above forms of activity it must be *for* the benefit of another, see Lord Bridge of Harwich in *R* v *Bloxham* [1983] 1 AC 109.

(9) Assisting in the retention of stolen goods.	(10) Assisting in the removal of stolen goods.	(11) Assisting in the disposal of stolen goods.	(12) Assisting in the realisation of stolen goods.
(13) Arranging to assist in the retention of stolen goods.	(14) Arranging to assist in the removal of stolen goods.	(15) Arranging to assist in the disposal of stolen goods.	(16) Arranging to assist in the realisation of stolen goods.

Where an accused assists or arranges to assist (for the meaning of assist, see *R* v *Kanwar* [1982] 2 All ER 528 and *R* v *Coleman* [1986] Crim LR 56) in any of the above forms of activity, such conduct must be principally carried out *by* another, see Lord Bridge of Harwich in *R* v *Bloxham*.

If one adds the acts of receiving and arranging to receive you can see that there are 18 forms of handling.

Handling by omission

It would appear that where an individual has assisted in the retention of stolen goods, he may do so by an omission to act, e.g., by doing nothing once stolen goods are left on his premises (see R v *Pitchley* (1972) 57 Cr App R 30 and R v *Brown* [1970] 1 QB 105).

Procedural elements

Lord Bridge of Harwich in R v *Bloxham* [1983] 1 AC 109 suggested that receiving and arranging to receive stolen goods constituted distinct forms of handling, different from the other forms noted in Table 10.2. This view has consequences for criminal procedure, regarding the issue of charging the wrong form of handling or duplicity (see Emmins, *A Practical Approach to Criminal Procedure*). However, the balance of authority is against this view (see R v *Nicklin* [1977] 2 All ER 444); it is thus suggested that all forms of handling are but variants of one offence.

Circumstances of the offence

Goods. This includes money and every other description of property but excluding land (except things severed therefrom) see Theft Act 1968, s. 34(2)(b).

Stolen. This means goods obtained as a result of theft, by deception or by blackmail (see Theft Act 1968, s. 21). See s. 24(4). Goods stolen abroad if stolen by the law of that country are also stolen for the purpose of the offence of handling, see s. 24(1). If goods cease to be stolen before an act of handling occurs there can be no full offence, though there may well be an offence of attempting to handle stolen goods (see R v *Shivpuri* [1987] AC 1).

Goods cease to be stolen:

(a) If they are restored to the person from whom they were stolen.

(b) If they are restored to other lawful possession or custody. This latter element appears to be satisfied where goods are reduced into the possession of individuals such as police officers. Whether goods are reduced into an individual's possession is dependent upon that person's mental resolve with regard to those goods (see *Attorney-General's Reference (No. 1 of 1974)* [1974] QB 744).

(c) If the person from whom goods have been stolen and any other person claiming through him have otherwise ceased, as regards those goods, to have any right to restitution in respect of the theft (s. 24(3)).

Stolen goods in whole or in part in the hands of a thief or handler remain stolen goods. If exchanged by either such person the goods or money for which they are exchanged also become stolen for they represent the direct or indirect proceeds of the original stolen goods, see s. 24(2)(a) and (b) (read these provisions carefully and be aware of their constituents). When these direct or indirect proceeds of the original stolen goods are themselves exchanged for further goods or money these latter items of property also become stolen goods. When such direct or indirect proceeds of the original stolen goods are acquired by an individual in good faith, i.e., he is not a handler, then though they remain stolen goods, any goods or money which he later acquires in exchange for those goods are *not* themselves to be regarded as stolen.

Note too that the Theft (Amendment) Act 1996 creates a new offence of dishonestly retaining a wrongful credit and broadens the definition of 'stolen goods' to bring within the law of handling dishonest withdrawals from accounts to which 'wrongful credits' have been made (see the new s. 24A of the 1968 Act). It is 'wrongful' if it derives from theft, a s. 15A offence, blackmail or stolen goods. This new offence is wider than handling. If a wrongful credit is made to your account (or one in which you have any right or interest) and you know or believe the credit to be wrongful and you dishonestly fail to take reasonable steps to get the credit cancelled, you are guilty of the offence and liable to up to ten years' imprisonment on indictment. See *R* v *Forsyth* [1997] Crim LR 581.

Mens rea

An accused must act dishonestly — see the common law formulation in *R* v *Ghosh* [1982] QB 1053 and *R* v *Roberts* [1986] Crim LR 122.

He must know or believe the goods are stolen. A person is guilty of handling only if he believes the goods to be stolen at the time he received them: supervening belief or dishonesty after receipt was not enough (*R* v *Brook* [1994] Crim LR 455). Knowledge is to be assessed subjectively (see *Atwal* v *Massey* [1971] 3 All ER 881). Belief as to the fact that goods are stolen is an ambiguous concept. In most cases it is not necessary for a judge to define its meaning (*R* v *Harris* (1987) 84 Cr App R 75). It is assessed subjectively, but objective criteria may help to assess that subjective state of mind (see *R* v *Moys* [1984] Crim LR 495). It is best for a judge in directing a jury not to define belief and certainly never to equate it with mere suspicion or wilful blindness, or suspicion as to the fact that goods are probably stolen (see *R* v *Reader* (1977) 66 Cr App R 33; *R* v *Grainge* [1984] Crim LR 493 and *R* v *Toor* (1987) 85 Cr App R 116). Belief seems to be satisfied only by a positive belief that goods are stolen. This seems to equate belief with knowledge and renders the former term otiose (see also *R* v *Hall* (1985) 81 Cr App R 260). The court in that case accepted that a belief that goods were stolen could be constituted where a person could say to himself, 'I cannot say I know for certain that the goods are stolen, but there can be no other reasonable conclusion in the light of all the circumstances I have heard and seen'. This does appear to have objective overtones from which a jury may make the relevant evidential inference. See also *R* v *Williams* [1995] Crim LR 934.

Other Offences Within the Theft Acts

Robbery

The offences considered in detail in this chapter have been selected for their representative nature. They frequently form the basis of a standard under-graduate lecture course. There are many other offences which will only be referred to in this book, though if they form an integral part of your course doubtless they will be given suitable exposure and prominence by your lecturer. However, you should be aware of the offence of *robbery* contrary to the Theft Act 1968, s. 8(1). This is principally aggravated theft, with the use of force or threat of its use before or at the time of the theft and in order to carry out the theft. A robber is also a thief. Anyone charged with robbery and found not guilty of it may be found guilty of theft (*R v Guy* (1991) 93 Cr App R 108). Thus the defences to a charge of theft will also be applicable to robbery (see *R v Skivington* [1968] 1 QB 166). In *R v Lockley* [1995] Crim LR 656 the accused was convicted of robbery. He had taken cans of beer from an off-licence and when approached by the shop-keeper used violence. On appeal he argued that the theft was completed when he used violence but the court upheld the conviction stating that *R v Hale* (1979) 68 Cr App R 415 was still the law, i.e., that appropriation was a continuing act.

Note also the special offence of 'assault' with intent to rob provided for by Theft Act 1968, s. 8(2).

There are the various offences involving aspects of temporary depriva-tion designed to deal with situations which, though antisocial, cannot be brought within the ambit of the offence of theft. They include removal of articles from a place open to the public, see s. 11 of the Theft Act 1968, and s. 12 which deals with the offences of taking a conveyance without the consent of the owner, and driving or allowing oneself to be carried in such vehicles.

Blackmail

You may consider the offence of blackmail contained in s. 21 of the Theft Act 1968, which involves making unwarranted demands with menaces for the purpose of and with a view to gain for oneself or another or with intent to cause loss to another. The individual has a defence to the fact of an unwarranted demand if he honestly believes he has reasonable grounds for the demand and that the menaces are a proper means of reinforcing the demand.

Offences Regarding Property Outside the Theft Acts

Criminal damage

The two principal examples of such offences that may form an element in your course are criminal damage and forgery.

The offence of criminal damage is contained in the Criminal Damage Act 1971. The mental element required in the various forms of offence of criminal damage has been extensively discussed in chapter 4 (see *R* v *Miller* [1983] 2 AC 161 and *Metropolitan Police Commissioner* v *Caldwell* [1982] AC 341; also *Elliott* v *C* [1983] 1 WLR 939 and *R* v *Sangha* [1988] 2 All ER 385 (see chapter 4 above)). Section 1(1) of the Act provides that a person who, without lawful excuse, destroys or damages any property belonging to another, intending to destroy or damage such property or being reckless as to whether any such property would be destroyed or damaged, is guilty of an offence. By s. 1(3) if the destruction or damage is by fire the offence is known as arson.

By s. 1(2) there is an aggravated form of the above offence, which also involves damage to property but with the intent to endanger life thereby or being reckless whether life would be endangered (see *R* v *Asquith, Webster and Seamans* [1995] 1 Cr App R 492 and *R* v *Parker* [1993] Crim LR 856). Note that:

(a)   property must be destroyed or damaged, the actual property may in fact be different and the degree of damage different to that envisaged by the accused and in such cases it is the destruction or damage which he envisaged that must be considered in deciding whether he was intending by the destruction or damage to endanger the life of another or being reckless as to whether such a life would be endangered, i.e., it is the accused's state of mind at the time he did the act which may lead to destruction or damage of property (*R* v *Dudley* [1989] Crim LR 57);

(b)   'without lawful excuse' is a common factor in the definition of these offences and is itself partially defined in s. 5(2) of the Act.

The subjective and objective elements of the defence of lawful excuse are usefully discussed in *R* v *Hill* and *R* v *Hall* [1989] Crim LR 136 (where the accused had intended to use hacksaw blades to breach a fence around a United States nuclear naval base) and the earlier authorities of *R* v *Hunt* (1978) 66 Cr App R 105 and *R* v *Ashford and Smith*, are explained there. See also *Johnson* v *DPP* [1994] Crim LR 673. Note also the definition of 'property' as provided for by s. 10(1) which is similar to s. 4 of the Theft Act 1968 though it includes land but excludes intangible property from its ambit. The other subsections of s. 10 deal with the concept of 'belonging to another', which is generally similar to the equivalent provisions of s. 5 of the Theft Act 1968. Note, however, the differences in terminology.

Forgery
This is only mentioned to point out that there are a number of offences contained in the Forgery and Counterfeiting Act 1981. These should only be noted if they form a significant part of your course. Otherwise they can with relative safety be relegated from your revision programme.

PLANNING YOUR REVISION

You must concentrate upon a limited selection of offences against property. Any course worth its salt will consider only a selected number of topics in some detail, the kernel of these being theft and deception offences. These at least must be mastered with perhaps one other offence, e.g., burglary and handling. The basic problem for a student is that theft (and related offences) are concerned with concepts of property and that these offences are concerned with the protection through penal sanction of an individual's rights and interest in *property*, an area of the law which is not usually studied by you until after the completion of your criminal law course.

Nevertheless if the following matters are kept clearly in your mind the mysteries of theft may be rendered a little less cloudy.

It is in the *actus reus* of the offence that the greatest problems are caused for the student.

Understand fully the implications of the recent case law on the concept of appropriation and in particular the cases of *Anderton* v *Burnside* [1984] AC 320, *R* v *Philippou* [1989] Crim LR 585 and *Dobson* v *General Accident* [1989] 3 WLR 1066 and, of course, *R* v *Gomez* [1992] 3 WLR 1067. You should be fully conversant with the two conflicting lines of cases on the issue of when an owner's authority to deal with his property may be exceeded by another and thus lay the foundation stone for an act of appropriation. Be prepared to consider the issue that in relation to the offence of theft the act of a potential thief towards an owner's property does not need to be without the latter's consent before it can amount to appropriation (see *Lawrence* v *Metropolitan Police Commissioner* [1972] AC 626, and especially *R* v *Gomez* [1993] 1 All ER 1). There are two further issues to understand, first the concept of the types of property that may form the subject-matter of the offence of theft (which may differ from offence to offence, see s. 4 of the Theft Act 1968) and secondly the fact that the property appropriated must belong to another. If this latter concept is clearly understood by you, you should have little difficulty in dealing with any problem questions which deal with theft.

EXAMPLES OF QUESTIONS

Theft: essays and problems

You may be confronted with a set of essay questions of the following kinds. A half question may read:

(1) 'The attempt in s. 5 of the Theft Act 1968 to define property "belonging to another" still lacks clarity and leaves unresolved difficulties.'
Discuss.

This is a straightforward question if the incidents of s. 5 are clearly understood by you. The question obviously requires a detailed discussion of the various subsections of s. 5. In particular, it is suggested, a full discussion of what constitutes 'a proprietary right or other interest', together with the concepts of possession and control within s. 5(1), will be useful. This should be contrasted with the 'special instances' within the other subsections, especially subsections (3) and (4). It may well be argued by you that the reason why these subsections neither clarify the concept of 'belonging to another' nor resolve difficulties is the fact that they are built upon the civil law which defines the rights in property which a person may enjoy. Thus for example you may discuss s. 5(4), which determines under what circumstances property transferred to another under a mistake may nevertheless still be regarded for the purposes of the offence of theft as belonging to the original owner. The application of this subsection is dependent upon the original owner's right to have the relevant property returned to him under the law of restitution, itself an ambiguous complicated area of the civil law. This is but a particular example of the problem that permeates the whole of s. 5: it is built upon civil law concepts that are themselves unclear and fraught with difficulties (see *Attorney-General's Reference (No. 1 of 1985)* [1986] QB 491). You may well come to the conclusion that the nature of theft is such that this problem is incapable of solution by reference to any penal statutory provisions which concern the offence of theft but requires a reform of the law of property. Your views are important in a question of the above kind; the issues considered above are matters you should perhaps consider in coming to your opinions and thus answering the question.

A half problem question may be in the following form:

(2)   Arthur, a youth of 17, is asked by an elderly next-door neighbour to go on an errand for her to buy provisions from the local greengrocer. He borrows the old lady's bicycle and is given a £10 note. He buys and then delivers the provisions he has purchased but he retains £1.00 change which he uses to buy a magazine. He lends the bicycle to a friend who promises to return it within couple of days. It is now missing.

Discuss Arthur's criminal liability.

The two principal issues in this question to consider are: Has Arthur committed theft in relation to the £1 and the bicycle? After considering the elements of theft as contained in s. 1 of the Theft Act 1968 you must consider the following matters:

(a)   *Actus reus* in relation to the £1:

(i)   Is it property? See s. 4(1).

(ii) Does it belong to another? This element could be established either on the basis that the elderly neighbour retained a proprietary right or interest in the £10 or more realistically, since we are concerned with the £1 change and not the original £10 note, because she handed the £10 over on the understanding that Arthur was under a legal obligation to deal with that money or *its proceeds* (i.e., the provisions and the £1 change) in a particular way and for a particular purpose (see s. 5(3)). That is to say, Arthur should spend that money to purchase the provisions and should account to his neighbour for the proceeds, i.e., the provisions and the £1 change.

(iii) Has he appropriated the £1? Clearly he has (see *Anderton* v *Burnside* [1984] AC 320, *R* v *Fritschy* [1985] Crim LR 745, *R* v *Gomez* [1993] 1 All ER 1 and s. 3(1) of the Theft Act 1968).

(b) *Mens rea* in relation to the £1:

(i) Is he dishonest? See the test in *R* v *Ghosh* [1982] QB 1053.
(ii) Did he intend permanently to deprive? Clearly he did.

(c) *Actus reus* in relation to the bicycle:

(i) It is property within the terms of the Theft Act 1968, s. 4.
(ii) Does it clearly belong to the neighbour by reference to s. 5(1)? Since she only lent it to Arthur she retains a proprietary right in it.
(iii) Arthur has undoubtedly appropriated the property.

(d) *Mens rea* in relation to the bicycle:

(i) He may well be dishonest within the test propounded in *R* v *Ghosh*.
(ii) The principal difficulty in order to convict him is to establish his intention permanently to deprive the neighbour of her bicycle. However, this may be established possibly by reference to s. 6(2) which determines that such an *intention* may be presumed where a person like Arthur, who is borrowing another's property, parts with it for his own purposes (and without the owner's authority) under conditions as to its return that he may not be able to perform and thus runs the risk of losing the property. This provision is more applicable to cases where, e.g., a person pawns another's property, rather than merely lending another's property to a third party.

It may well be argued therefore that there is no need to rely on s. 6(2) (which may be inappropriate to the facts of the case). The intention permanently to deprive may nevertheless be presumed more clearly by reliance upon s. 6(1) of the Act, which provides, *inter alia*, that the required *intention* will also be presumed where the accused's 'intention is to treat the thing [which belongs to another] as his own to dispose of regardless of the other's rights'. Lending the bicycle to his friend is such conduct. He may thus be charged with theft of the bicycle.

A final short essay question upon the offence of theft may seek from you a close analysis of a particular leading case, e.g., *R v Ghosh* on dishonesty or *R v Gomez* on appropriation. These questions cannot be easily disguised and giving examples would serve little purpose. These questions should be avoided unless the particular authority is one with which you are fully conversant and when required by the question unless you are also aware of the earlier and subsequent case law and the criticism attached to them.

Burglary

A particular substantive offence within the Theft Acts may arise in the following form.

(3)　'The offence of burglary has a number of ingredients and in reality comprises two separate concepts co-existing under the same umbrella for the simplest reasons of policy and expediency.'

Discuss.

Question (3)

This is a comparatively easy question. You should seek, rather as in Table 10.1, to differentiate between the two forms of burglary contained in s. 9(1)(a) and s. 9(1)(b). The first form, as contained in s. 9(1)(a), is concerned with an accused's *intent* on entering a building or part thereof as a trespasser, s. 9(1)(b) with the conduct of an accused after he has entered a building or a part thereof as a trespasser.

You must consider whether the two forms of the offence (which have a number of common elements) are the products of policy and expediency, and whether their existence within a common framework and offence is justified by their common constituent elements.

Ultimately this is a matter for you to consider. Nevertheless it may be argued that the underlying rationale of the two forms of burglary is the protection of households, offices, warehouses etc. and their contents from the conduct of thieves, vandals and arsonists. However, an offence such as burglary should also seek to protect the occupants of those buildings from assault and injury. These matters would seem to justify the creation of a comprehensive offence capable of being committed in a number of ways. Once these principles are accepted it can be seen that policy and expediency do play a part in formulating the present offence of burglary. Furthermore the protection of occupants and buildings and property would be served little if it was not provided that an accused commits the offence of burglary if he *intends* to commit a number of offences on entering a building as well as when he *actually* commits certain offences once inside a building. Both the common elements of the offence of burglary to be found within s. 9(1)(a) and (b) are necessitated by the fundamental nature, ambit and purpose of the offence of burglary and the differences between the various forms by the need to ensure the effectiveness of the offence. Policy and expediency may well be said to play a crucial part in the formulation of s. 9 of the Theft Act 1968.

We have avoided discussing a problem based on the rather salacious facts of *R* v *Collins* [1973] QB 100. Such questions are popular with examiners and may be combined with other issues, e.g., conditional intent. However, a problem question which involves entry of an ardent nocturnal lover (such as Collins) into a young lady's bedroom cannot fail to be spotted by you, and dependent upon you being alert as to any other matters it raises it should not prove difficult to answer if you have read the case of *R* v *Collins* amongst the well-thumbed law reports. Be prepared for a question which considers the fact that a building may be divided into parts, with the possible consequences that an individual may be a trespasser in relation to part of a building only (*R* v *Walkington* [1979] 2 All ER 716).

Deception and Other Offences

(4)   Max has three GCSEs and wishes to take an HND course which requires five. He borrows a certificate showing six GCSEs from a friend who has the same name but an additional initial. He uses the certificate to gain entry to the course, pays his fees and has passed the first-year examination before the true facts are discovered. It appears that the admissions officer had failed to notice the discrepancy. During his first year Max has done some paid practical work with a private firm as part of the course.

You are asked to advise the police.

(5)   David asks a garage attendant to put eight gallons of petrol into his (David's) car. The attendant fills the tank and David drives off without paying for it.

Discuss David's criminal liability.

Question (4)
Max has falsely represented his academic qualifications by using another's examination certificates. It is certain that what he has done is a deception though it cannot amount to forgery. The admissions officer has been deceived and it matters not that he could possibly have discovered the truth by a thorough investigation into the certificate's authenticity and its owner. Max has not committed an offence within the terms of the Theft Act 1968, s. 15, merely by obtaining a place on a course. The central issue of this question is whether the fact that Max has obtained money (i.e., property) as a result of

paid practical work has nevertheless been obtained by the original deception. It has been determined that in general the obtaining of the money in such cases cannot be an offence under the Theft Act 1968, s. 15, since the obtaining of the money is generally too remote from the deception: it is obtained as a consequence of working (see *R* v *Martin* (1867) LR 1 CCR 56 and *R* v *Moreton* (1913) 8 Cr App R 214 and cf. *R* v *King* [1987] QB 547). However, by s. 16(2)(c) of the Theft Act 1968 it is provided that an individual commits an offence if by a deception he is given, *inter alia*, 'the opportunity to earn remuneration or greater remuneration in an office or employment'.

The issues to consider are the fact that Max has gained the *opportunity to earn* remuneration, which is established in the facts of the case. However, has he done so as a result of holding an office or under a contract of employment? The meaning of this provision is unclear, though you may express an opinion on the balance of authority and by the plain meaning of the term that the work carried out by Max is an employment, see *Treacy* v *DPP* [1971] AC 537 at p. 565. On this basis Max has committed an offence under s. 16(2)(c).

Question (5)

The simple facts disclosed by question (5) give rise to many legal problems. David cannot commit the offence of theft because according to the law of property (viz. Sale of Goods Act 1979, s. 18) the petrol becomes David's own property when it is put into the tank. Thus at the moment of appropriation (i.e., when he drives off without paying) the petrol belongs to him.

The issue as to the offence of obtaining the petrol by deception contrary to Theft Act 1968, s. 15, is also fraught with difficulty. The petrol-pump attendant must be deceived into filling David's tank and David must, as a result of that deception, obtain the petrol. David's conduct may in itself be deceptive or it may bring about a deception by implication, in the sense that he leads the attendant to believe that he intends to pay for the petrol and therefore obtains it. Apart from evidential problems in establishing this fact there are two legal difficulties in most cases of this kind. The first is that frequently the deception will not operate upon the mind of anyone, e.g., because such stations are self-service stations; thus an element of the offence is missing, i.e., that an *individual* be deceived. In other instances the deception only takes place after the petrol has been put into the petrol tank and the property in the petrol has passed to the car driver, and is thus not a causal link in the obtaining of the petrol (see *R* v *Collis-Smith* [1971] Crim LR 716 and *R* v *Coady* [1996] Crim LR 518). These issues, as regards the facts in the question, do not seem to be relevant. It may therefore be possible to hold David liable for an offence under s. 15.

The law has, however, provided a particular offence to deal with individuals who obtain services or goods and who then seek to avoid payment. By s. 3 of the Theft Act 1978, a person who, knowing that on-the-spot payment should be made for goods or services supplied and where it is *required* or *expected* that he should pay, *dishonestly makes off without making payment with the intent to* avoid payment commits an offence. This seems to cover David's situation exactly, and would appear to be the most appropriate charge (see *R* v *Allen* [1985] 3 WLR 107).

One favourite type of question posed by examiners is to test a student's understanding of the relationship between the offence of theft and deception offences. A clear allusion to this issue may be made by a question in the following vein:

(6) 'The distinction(s) between theft and obtaining property by deception are clear.'
Discuss in the light of principle and authority.

Remember this question requires only a consideration and comparison between the offences contained in s. 1 and s. 15 of the Theft Act 1968. You should be able carefully to review the House of Lords' decision in *Lawrence* v *Metropolitan Police Commissioner* [1972] AC 626 and explain that this decision accepted that theft and obtaining by deception are not mutually exclusive offences. Also mention *R* v *Gomez* [1993] 1 All ER 1. Thus there is an overlap between the two offences but you may suggest the situations where this overlap occurs are clear and cause few difficulties, or you may suggest the alternative. In any event if you can fully explain the areas of overlap (see above) together with the situations where either offence alone can be charged you have answered the question.

You should be prepared to consider in a deception question the intricate body of law concerning the fraudulent use of credit cards and cheque books (in the case of the latter usually in conjunction with cheque cards) in order to obtain property (see *R* v *Lambie* [1982] AC 449 and in particular *Metropolitan Police Commissioner* v *Charles* [1977] AC 177). Identify whether the credit card or cheque book (and cheque card) is used not by the person so entitled but by a rogue, in which case you should consider offences under s. 15 of the Theft Act relating to any property obtained, and possibly offences under s. 16 in relation to any loss that may be caused to a credit company or a bank by the rogue's fraudulent use of another's credit card or cheque book and cheque card. Remember that the fraudulent use of a credit card or cheque book (and cheque card) by the person who is entitled to use these facilities to a given credit limit, where the authority to use such facilities has been withdrawn, does not result in the commission of an offence under s. 15 in relation to any property obtained. Nevertheless in such circumstances an offence under s. 16 is committed in relation to the unauthorised credit facility obtained from the bank or credit company.

Finally consider the nature of the deception where a person draws a cheque on his account where there are insufficient funds to meet it and when, in addition, he uses a cheque card when his bank has withdrawn his authority to use it.

You might also discuss the complex case law dealing with obtaining a credit transfer by deception (*R v Preddy, R v Halai, R v Graham, R v Hopkins* and *R v Cooke*) and the consequential Theft (Amendment) Act 1996.

Handling

Questions upon this offence are generally problem questions and tend also to be combined with an offence of theft or deception. This is an obvious ploy for examiners since it supplies the question with a necessary requirement, i.e., stolen goods. A typical question will look something like the following:

(7) George owes Alfred £100. After many applications for repayment, all of which have been refused, Alfred takes £100 from George's wallet which George carelessly left lying about. With this money he repays a loan due from himself to Brian of £50. Brian knows the circumstances in which the money has been taken. Brian buys goods for £50 with the money received. Meanwhile Alfred has employed Claud to service Alfred's motor car and has paid Claud with the other £50 which he took from George. Claud does not know how Alfred acquired the money. Claud buys goods with the £50.

Who is guilty of what offences, if any? What if anything represents stolen goods in this question?

The first thing to consider is whether there are any stolen goods which can form the subject-matter of the offence of handling. Remember goods may only be stolen for the purposes of s. 22 of the Theft Act 1968 when they have been the subject-matter of an offence of theft, deception or blackmail, see s. 24. Although undoubtedly Alfred has appropriated property belonging to another with the intention permanently to deprive the owner, it is uncertain whether he can be said to be dishonest within the test propounded in *R v Ghosh* [1982] QB 1053. This is a matter of fact and is thus unclear. You should therefore deal with the situation on the either/or basis. If Alfred is not to be regarded as dishonest there is no offence of theft, no stolen goods and thus no possibility of there being an offence of handling though the question of whether there is an offence of attempted handling remains open (see *R v Shivpuri* [1987] AC 1). Nevertheless, the possibility of Alfred being regarded as a thief is strong and you should deal with the rest of the question on this basis.

If the £100 is stolen goods then, although Alfred may not be charged with handling (see *R v Sainthouse* [1980] Crim LR 506), there is a possibility of other parties in the question being so charged.

Taking the case of Brian first. He would appear to be a potential handler of the £50 he receives (being part of the original stolen goods). Assuming the original £100 to be stolen goods and assuming that Brian is found to be dishonest, he has committed the *actus reus* of handling; he knows or believes the money to be stolen goods and has received the same. (Be prepared to discuss the other forms of handling where appropriate in questions of this sort.)

Claud cannot be a handler since he is neither dishonest, nor does he know or believe the money he has received is stolen. The importance of the distinction between the positions of Brian and Claud becomes of importance when we consider s. 24(2) of the Theft Act 1968 and the special meaning attributed to the term 'stolen goods'. This subsection and its two paragraphs (a) and (b) have already been discussed earlier. They provide that the direct or indirect *proceeds* of the original stolen goods, be they in whole or in part, or be they in the hands of the original thief or a handler, and which represent or have represented the stolen goods in the hands of the original thief or a handler are also to be regarded as stolen goods. Thus we must consider whether the goods purchased by Brian and Claud are themselves to be regarded as stolen goods for the purposes of the offence of handling.

Taking Brian's case first, the £50 he receives is part of the original stolen goods and will always remain stolen goods. Since he is a handler (or may be assumed to be such) the goods he purchased are the *direct* proceeds of part of the original stolen goods in his possession. The goods thus purchased themselves become stolen goods, capable of being the subject-matter of a separate offence of handling. If these goods were further exchanged by Brian for other goods these latter goods would indirectly represent the original stolen goods and would themselves be regarded as stolen by virtue of s. 24(2)(b).

You should now turn to consider whether the goods received by Claud which he bought with the £50 he received should themselves be regarded as stolen within the terms of s. 24(2)(b). The simple answer to this question is no. The reason for this is that Claud, lacking *mens rea*, is not a handler, thus the goods he receives in exchange for the £50 (which does remain stolen goods) do not represent in his hand either the direct or indirect proceeds of the realisation or disposal of stolen goods handled by him.

The rule is simple to remember, stolen goods remain stolen goods (unless they cease to be stolen within the terms of s. 24(3)); goods regarded as stolen by virtue of s. 24(2)(a) or (b) also remain stolen goods.

Thus stolen goods, whether original or regarded as stolen by virtue of s. 24(2)(a) or (b), in the hands of a person who lacks *mens rea* and who is not a handler remain stolen but if those stolen goods are in such circumstances subsequently exchanged in whole or in part for other goods these latter goods do not themselves become stolen goods within the terms of s. 24(2)(b).

CONCLUSION

The above questions are of course not intended to be comprehensive in their coverage of potential topics. Beware of composite questions which may involve more than one offence relating to property and remember that in such questions the amount of detailed knowledge required for the discussion of each offence is correspondingly reduced. You should not study the offences relating to property in isolation but consider them within an interlocking framework.

To sum up, because of the general nature of examination questions on offences against property you should seek to integrate a number of them in your mind, and be prepared to consider their interrelationship. Whether or not it is possible to revise all the topics which have formed the subject-matter of your course is a matter for you. Nevertheless you should consider a minimum revision programme. Very few courses go beyond a consideration of theft, deception offences, burglary and handling as the central core of their studies. Concentrate on them. As a subsidiary area of study there may be a broad, outline review of criminal damage, robbery, blackmail and the temporary deprivation offences, e.g., s. 12 of the Theft Act 1968.

You should modify these suggestions to suit your course structure and having regard to the emphasis that is placed upon the topics by your lecturer. Remember (subject to what has been said in chapter 2) that study of past examination papers may prove fruitful.

FURTHER READING

Property Offences

Andrews, J.A., 'The Theft Bill — Robbery' [1966] Crim LR 524.

Criminal Law Revision Committee 8th Report — Theft and Related Offences' Cmnd. 2977.

Elliott, D. W., 'Criminal Damage' [1988] Crim LR 403.

Glazebrook, P., 'Thief or Swindler: who cares?' (1991) 50 CLJ 389 and 'Revising the Theft Acts' (1993) 52 CLJ 191.

Griew, E., 'Dishonesty: The Objections to Feely and Ghosh' [1985] Crim LR 341.

Halpin, A., 'The Test for Dishonesty' [1996] Crim LR 283.

Heaton, R., 'Belonging to Another' [1973] Crim LR 736.

Shute, S., and Horder, J., 'Thieving and Deceiving: What is the Difference?' (1993) 56 MLR 548.

Silber, S., 'The Law Commission, Conspiracy to Defraud and the Dishonesty Project' [1995] Crim LR 461.

Smith, A. T. H., 'The Idea of Criminal Deception' [1982] Crim LR 721.

Smith, A. T. H., 'Stealing the Body and its Parts' [1976] Crim LR 395.

Smith, A. T. H., 'Constructive Trust in the Law of Theft' [1977] Crim LR 395.

Smith, A. T. H., 'Theft and/or Handling' [1977] Crim LR 517.

Smith, J. C., *Law of Theft*, 7th ed. (London: Butterworths, 1993).

Smith, J. C., 'Obtaining Cheques by Deception or Theft' [1997] Crim LR 396.

Spencer, J. R., 'Dishonesty: What the Jury thinks the Defendant Thought' (1982) 41 CLJ 222.

Spencer, J. R., 'The Theft Act 1978' [1979] Crim LR 24.

Sullivan C. R. and Warbrick, C., 'Territoriality, Theft and *Atakpu*' [1994] Crim LR 650.

Williams, G., 'Temporary Appropriation should be Theft' [1981] Crim LR 129.

Williams, G., 'The Theft Act 1978' (1979) 38 CLJ 4.

Williams, G., 'Theft, Consent and Illegality' [1977] Crim LR 127 at 205 and 327.

BIBLIOGRAPHY

A. Ashworth, *Principles of Criminal Law* (Oxford: Oxford University Press).

J. F. Archbold, *Pleading, Evidence and Practice in Criminal Cases* by S. Mitchell (London: Sweet & Maxwell).

Blackstone's Criminal Practice, annual (London: Blackstone Press).

C. M. V. Clarkson and H. M. Keating, *Criminal Law: Text and Materials*, (London: Sweet & Maxwell).

Sir Rupert Cross and P. A. Jones, *Introduction to Criminal Law* by R. Card (London: Butterworths).

J. Dine, *Cases and Materials on the Theft Acts* (London: Blackstone Press, 1985).

J. Dine and J. Gobert, *Cases and Materials on Criminal Law* (London: Blackstone Press, 1993).

R. A. Duff, *Criminal Attempts* (Oxford: Clarendon Press, 1996).

D. W. Elliott and J. C. Wood, *Elliott and Wood's Casebook on Criminal Law* by D. W. Elliott and C. Wells (London: Sweet & Maxwell).

Emmins on Criminal Procedure by John Sprack (London: Blackstone Press).

P. R. Glazebrook, *Blackstone's Statutes on Criminal Law* (London: Blackstone Press, Annual).

S. Lees, *Carnal Knowledge — Rape on Trial* (London: Penguin, 1997).

S. W. Mayson, D. French and C. Ryan, *Mayson, French and Ryan on Company Law* (London: Blackstone Press, annual).

Murphy on Evidence (London: Blackstone Press).

G. Scanlan and C. Ryan, *An Introduction to Criminal Law* (London: Blackstone Press, 1985).

P. Seago, *Criminal Law* (London: Sweet & Maxwell).

A. T. H. Smith, *Property Offences* (London: Sweet & Maxwell, 1994).

J. C. Smith, *The Law of Theft* (London: Butterworths).

J. C. Smith and B. Hogan, *Criminal Law* (London: Butterworths).

J. C. Smith and B. Hogan, *Criminal Law: Cases and Materials* (London: Butterworths).

P. Smith (ed.), *Criminal Law — Essays in Honour of J. C. Smith* (London: Butterworths, 1987).

G. Williams, *Textbook of Criminal Law* (London: Sweet & Maxwell).

INDEX

TITLES IN THE SERIES